Prehistory of
North America

Cover: *Engraved marine shell gorget showing two bird-men, Late Mississippian period, A.D. 1300–1500. Jesse D. Jennings recovered this 11.5 cm ornament from the Hixon site, Hamilton County, Tennessee during excavations in the Tennessee Valley Authority's Chickamauga Reservoir in 1936. This specimen is on display at the McClung Museum, University of Tennessee, Knoxville, Tennessee.*

THIRD EDITION

Prehistory of North America

Jesse D. Jennings

University of Oregon

Mayfield Publishing Company
Mountain View, California

Library of Congress Cataloging-in-Publication Data

Jennings, Jesse David, 1909–
Prehistory of North America.

Bibliography: p.
Includes index.
1. Indians of North America—Antiquities.
2. North America—Antiquities. I. Title.
E77.9.J4 1989 970.01'1 88-13308
IBSN 0-87484-865-2

Manufactured in the United States of America

10 9 8 7 6 5 4 3 2

Mayfield Publishing Company
1240 Villa Street
Mountain View, California 94041

Sponsoring editor, Janet M. Beatty; production editor, Linda Toy; manuscript editor, Loralee Windsor; text and cover designer, Adriane Bosworth; cover photograph, Dirk Bakker, cover specimen, Frank H. McClung Museum, The University of Tennessee, Knoxville; illustrator, Rulon Nielson. The text was set in 10/12 Palatino by Carlisle Communications and printed on 50 # Finch Opaque by Ringier America, Inc.

Illustration credits appear on a continuation of the copyright page, p. 349.

Preface

The problems of writing a general introduction to North American archaeology mount with time. The problem is that as data accumulate from on-going research, the outlines of old knowledge blur and the landscape of archaeological fact changes; old landmarks disappear. Another problem lies in the question: Should a text be encyclopedic, or do selected data and examples serve best? I have opted against the encyclopedia. An archaeological text, it seems to me, should be a reliable guided tour through the bewildering body of detail rather than an aimless scrabbling in the mountains of fact or wandering down every path (some of which dead-end). Wallowing in detail will more likely confuse than instruct. Therefore, not every piece of competently executed and reported fieldwork I know about is described or even mentioned. I have provided, however, an adequate sample of important sites for each culture and period.

The book reflects my position that culture history comprises the traditional goal of archaeological study, as well as its indestructible core, because it is an account of prehistoric lifeways. In following that history one discovers the threads of continuity in human behavior from the earliest cultures to the very latest. The evolution of prehistoric cultures can be perceived in subsistence patterns, trade in rare raw materials, artifact forms, and even the elusive hints at prehistoric social systems through time. Although continuity can often be recognized, change is also always evident. Many innovations in technology appear (stone polishing, basketry, textiles, ceramics, and agriculture, for example). The origin of the new technologies is not always clear; they may be developed or invented locally, but often they have clearly diffused or been introduced from other areas. But there is more to be considered in North American archaeology today than culture sequence, continuity, and changes through time.

Today many new theoretical perspectives are used in analyses of archaeological data. These theories have, in some cases, led to advances in interpretation. Those advances cannot be ignored in a book that is intended to help the beginning student learn the content and state of North American archaeology. So while this book will narrate generally accepted outlines of North American prehistory, the narration will also occasionally touch on appropriate theory.

In my previous efforts to summarize American prehistory north of the Mexican border I have neither emphasized nor denied the continuity-evolutionary relationship that can be detected in the successive cultures in every major culture area of North America for the past 10,000 years. I merely took that evolution for granted. Instead of evolution, change and the origins of change took precedence in my presentations; in short, I stressed differences instead of likenesses. I suppose I assumed that the continuity would be as obvious to readers as it was to me. In this edition, however, both continuity and change in culture will be dealt with where they appear in the archaeological record.

With the help of more than a dozen conscientious, candid, and insightful reviewers I have been able to create a better balanced and more accurate introduction to North American archaeology in this edition. Aside from extensive revision and greater use of theory, this volume differs from others I have done in at least one other aspect. Following advice, and with some qualms, I have deleted the extensive citation and documentation and lengthy bibliographies of my earlier books. Annotated bibliographic lists at the ends of chapters offer a few titles that support occasional points in the text.

Acknowledgments

I am indebted to many people who have helped me bring this book to its final form. Among them I wish to thank the following individuals by name.

For manuscript assistance: My wife, Jane C. Jennings, for half a century of support and (usually) patient tolerance and her phenomenal skill with copyediting and proofreading. Patricia A. Dean, herself an anthropologist, for her unselfish and uncomplaining help as research assistant while this version took shape. Ursula Hanly, research typist and long-time friend at the Department of Anthropology, University of Utah, who typed and constructively criticized early versions of some chapters during my periodic visits to that department.

For illustrations: Rulon (Jay) Nielson, Chief Preparator, Utah Museum of Natural History, Salt Lake City, who has done most of the art work other than photographs in this book and all previous editions.

For constructive criticism: My enormous debt to the reviewers of this edition is gratefully acknowledged: C. Melvin Aikens, University of Oregon; Russell J. Barber, California State University at San Bernardino; David L. Browman, Washington University at St. Louis; James Brown, Northwestern University; James B. Stoltman, University of Wisconsin at Madison; Vincas P. Steponaitis, University of North Carolina at Chapel Hill; Nancy-Marie White, University of South Florida at Tampa. Several of the reviewers discussed and amplified their comments upon my request, and I appreciate the extra time that took.

For help at every stage of moving the book from manuscript to published form at Mayfield Publishing Company: Janet M. Beatty, Linda Toy, and freelance copyeditor Loralee Windsor.

To all those I have mentioned above, to those listed on page 349, and to any I should have cited but have overlooked, my sincere thanks.

Contents

Prehistory of North America

Definitions, Distinctions, and Background

The human past, or almost any ancient thing, always seems to interest the human mind. There are many ways to study the past—through ancient history, art forms, legends and myths, and even oral history. But archaeology is different in that it examines the history of the world through the tangible remains of past lifeways, both simple and complex. Of course, some intangible aspects of a vanished lifeway can be inferred from those tangible remains and their relationship to each other in the ground.

Archaeology presents many fascinating faces. But the novice is rarely ready to deal with all the exciting subtleties of archaeological data or the burgeoning theoretical manipulations of the factual material that underpin modern archaeology. In the main this book will describe the prehistoric cultures of North America, their sequences through time, the regional cultural variation in the widely diverse environments of the continent, the changes in those cultures, and, perhaps, some reasons for the changes. Continuity from one stage to another will be noted as well.

Culture history has traditionally been the goal—some would say the only goal—of archaeology. But the raw data—the material evidence of human activity that archaeologists recover—offer far more than mere chronology or history. As culture history becomes more accurate through continuing research, *why* questions naturally emerge, and theories, concepts, and assumptions are developed to search for answers to those questions. For example, from roughly 200 B.C. to A.D. 200 in the Middle West and later in much of the

1

Southeast the dominant culture was the Hopewellian. Particularly in Ohio, elaborate tombs covered by earthern mounds contained beautiful and distinctive **artifacts** of copper, shell, **obsidian,** and ceramic. The occurrence, distribution, and exotic materials of the beautiful objects suggested that they had some special value for the original owners. Why? And how did obsidian from Yellowstone and conch shells from the Gulf of Mexico come together in the Scioto Valley of Ohio in the tombs of the Hopewell culture? One explanation is that a vast, organized exchange/trade network in exotic materials existed to supply rare goods that had some great religious, mortuary, or ritual value. Such a network is said to imply a measure of social control over a large area; possibly there was also control over at least the sources of the desired raw materials. Moreover, in theory the network operated for the benefit of an elite social class.

Or consider the matter of the locations of prehistoric sites in a given area. They appear to cluster nonrandomly. Why should they be clustered? What cultural significance can be ascribed to that nonrandom patterning? Are special use sites, such as hunting stands and quarries, clustered or diffuse? Are they near the living sites? These questions move from mere site locations and inventories to attempts to understand the reasons—natural and cultural—for settlement patterning.

The same sites can be studied with a concentration on environmental rather than social constraints. If one assumes that habitation sites are located at places where as many basic resources (food, plants, animals, water, shelter, fuel, etc.) as possible can be exploited effectively from one spot, possibly the clustering can be understood. To be useful, that theory requires another that assumes the archaeologist can reconstruct the environment that was being exploited in the past. Doing this requires data (e.g., soils, geologic processes, pollen, and charred seeds or hulls) not often

collected in archaeological work until recent years. The examination of a single kind of archaeological data—in this case, the distribution of sites—clearly provides finer interpretations of the human behavior represented by the raw archaeological data.

Another question often asked is "Why did agriculture develop and what were the results?" One frequent answer is that population was increasing to a point that exceeded the carrying capacity of natural plant food resources. Another is that agriculture was an accidental or coincidental set of genetic and cultural events that led to increased food availability and population growth. The answers are contradictory and form hypotheses; the archaeologists expect that they can test those hypotheses with firm knowledge of paleoenvironment, paleoresources, and the archaeological evidence itself, along with whatever inferences can be supported by the data. One hypothesis or the other, or perhaps neither, will gain support in the testing.

Another example of new lines of thought is the study of Mississippian burial patterns that seem to demonstrate that a stratified social system was basic to the Mississippian lifeway. That leads to the inference that there were "royal" lineages and that high status was ascribed at birth, not achieved. The system is often described as a chieftainship.

Invoking self-conscious theory in archaeological interpretation is more characteristic of the 1960s, 1970s, and 1980s than of earlier years. While culture history is a legitimate concern of archaeologists, the history of the past is much enriched and enlivened by the questions raised, and occasionally answered, by the theoreticians. Of course there are scores of theoretical questions other than those dealing with trade or settlement patterns; the many ways in which theory has influenced today's archaeological reconstructions will be exemplified, where appropriate, throughout the text. Archaeology has other facets, but in an introductory text something must be left out.

Therefore, this book is largely confined to culture history.

In preparing this book I have made a few assumptions that should be mentioned. The first assumption is that most human behavior is adaptive; adaptation to a specific social and natural environment is the price of cultural survival. In archaeology few elements of the social environment survive in tangible form, but evidence of the technology, the subsistence strategies, even land use—all of which are essentially materialistic data—are recovered. The second assumption is that adaptation must be treated as a set of culturally controlled human interactions with the natural environment, in a two-way relationship that is called ecology. Thus the concept of adaptation quickly leads to an ecological perspective. Not all scholars agree with this adaptation/ecological stance.

My third assumption is that what we call culture can be understood as a dynamic open system. The cultural system includes the many social and natural subsystems that interact in many ways, almost none of which are understood. But the effects of some interactions can be detected. For example, a long-term climatic change could force changes in the food species collected; there would be consequent changes in procurement-harvesting schedules and technology. Changes in land use would follow protracted changes in the procurement subsystem. Usually, however, the immediate effect of changes in the cultural system cannot be perceived through archaeological findings. On the other hand, long-term changes in the subsistence, technological, settlement pattern, mortuary, and religious subsystems can be observed or inferred as new cultures are seen to evolve from older ones.

In sum, while archaeology has many other facets as interesting as culture history and archaeological theory, this book attempts only to (1) develop the culture history of North America and (2) enliven that account with such insights as theory has provided.

Culture history is descriptive and is presented here, as it usually is in American archaeological writing, in what is called a normative way. That concept implies that most human behavior is guided by a series of culturally established concepts or precepts of what are correct, proper, and acceptably patterned activities in a given cultural entity, whether extant or extinct. What is usually described has been built up synthetically as excavation or research data accumulate and some uniformity in architecture, minor arts, weaponry, subsistence technology, and so on is seen to characterize a particular extinct culture. The uniformity of behavior is true of a bounded region over a known or estimated time span. The leveling effects of a normative approach may be misleading or even falsify the state of things. It cannot be denied that a generalizing description is a kind of averaging of observed phenomena and thereby obscures or cancels out the anomalies. Such averaging might obscure or erase any local diversity that today's fine-grained research might see as evidence for incipient culture change or a new adaptational stance. Normative thought may thus obstruct the search for explanations of a locally divergent behavior that is observed archaeologically. There simply isn't enough space here to take account of all anomalies in the archaeological record, important as they are. Therefore this is a normative or generalizing account. It will, however, review some of the interesting diversities and what scholars think are their causes.

With the goals and biases of this account enumerated, the remainder of this chapter will consider briefly a number of ideas, concepts, techniques, and terms that provide some of the background information essential for anyone who wishes to work with or evaluate archaeological material.

Like everything else, American archaeology has its own history. It began in Europe but shifted to America nearly two centuries ago, although events in Europe continued to influence American thought. The formal history probably began with Thomas Jefferson's investigation of a burial mound on his estate in Virginia. The next century of study was hampered by a series of romantic myths or misconceptions. One was the belief that the thousands of mounds in the East and their rich burial goods were the relics of a Golden Age when a now-vanished race dominated the continent. It was generally conceded that American Indians, today more commonly called Native Americans, were incapable of the artistry and craftsmanship needed to create the beautiful objects of metal, stone, and clay found in the earthen burial mounds, which were also deemed to be beyond the skills of the aboriginal population. Those myths were laid to rest only by the careful work of archaeologists from the Smithsonian Institution in the 1880s.

Most of the culture history we take for granted has been learned in the twentieth century. Although the history of any discipline is important, we need not dwell on it here because there is a good book that deals with both the chronological facts and the prevailing and changing intellectual forces influencing the scholars of the day. Every student who reads this book should also read *A History of American Archaeology* by Gordon Willey and Jeremy Sabloff. Of particular interest is their recognition of developmental phases or periods during which the aims, or at least the accomplishments, of archaeologists changed. From 1492 to 1840 is called the Speculative Period, and most of what was done seems to have led up blind alleys to false conclusions and the birth of many hardy myths. From 1840 to 1914 was the Classificatory-Descriptive Period when some of the myths were weakened or destroyed. The Classificatory-Historical Period from 1914 to 1940 was devoted to chronology, with the 1940–1960 era devoted to context and function. Since 1960, the Explanatory Period has witnessed many excursions into theory, as archaeologists be-

gan the quest for answers why. The thrust of each historical period is evident in its name. The Willey-Sabloff book illustrates how scholars are products of their times, tied to the ideas and information available at these times. Although the statement that scholars in every field stand on the shoulders of their elders is a cliché, in American archaeology its truth is abundantly evident.

Archaeology Defined

One well-known definition of archaeology is that it "reconstructs the past"; another is that it "makes the past live again." Like all slogans, these say either too much or too little, although the implications of both are quite appropriate.

Archaeological research has continuously contributed to the larger field of anthropology, of which it is a branch. Both European and North American archaeological findings have proved fundamental in the growth and content of anthropological knowledge and theory. Anthropology is generally divided into two fields: physical (or biological) and cultural. Physical anthropology defines *Homo sapiens* as a mammalian species subject to genetic and biological study like any other species. Cultural anthropology is concerned with human behavior in groups and includes the subfields of linguistics, archaeology, and ethnology.

For present purposes, archaeology can be defined as dealing with material objects, structures, and other remnants of extinct lifeways. Context and relationships of the tangible objects to each other are as important as the objects, possibly even more important. The behavior, histories, and development of vanished cultural groups and their relationships to contemporary cultures are some of the things that archaeology seeks to learn. Archaeology can further be defined as an incomplete extension of history into prehistoric time. There is almost no recorded history of most of the Americas prior to 1492, and the full history, such as it is, must be written through interpretations of archaeological findings. This, of course, provides a continuity and deep chronological perspective for such modern ethnological studies as can firmly be connected with archaeological collections of earlier origin. Archaeology always has a chronological or historical bias, regardless of any other defined aims. An important contribution made by archaeology is that its findings provide data for artists, architects, or chroniclers. But archaeology itself uses all those data as *documents* in the larger task of learning and explaining culture history. In sum, archaeology aims ultimately to learn about and explain human behavior, but it is largely limited to material objects and their context or association, any evidence of past environments and resources, and whatever inferences these can support.

A word about two terms that frequently appear in this book—*archaeologist* and *prehistorian*—is necessary. I hold that *archaeology* is the proper word for the techniques and methods used in collecting and studying the objects (and relationships) residual from human behavior. It is "analytic." Prehistory on the other hand is "synthetic," which implies a holistic overview that results from using archaeological, ethnographical, ecological, geological, linguistic, and any other relevant data in an explanation or more precise statement about the human past in general or about a specific local culture under study. Unfortunately one cannot always be certain whether authors believe they are doing archaeology or prehistory. Actually, most archaeologists do both alternately. In any case, the terms are used almost as synonyms in this book.

Diversity of Aboriginal Cultures in America

Yet another matter to be dealt with is the incredible cultural diversity of historic Native American cultures. Since Columbus's day, Native Americans have been speculated about, misunderstood, and misrepresented. They have been ill-treated and exploited, either protected from or forced into civilization, loved one day and cast off the next, and given charity while being robbed of their lands and heritage. From four centuries of such history comes an enormous literature. Despite the overall interest and glamor of the cultures discovered in the Western world, even serious lay students fail to realize the extent to which modern Americans and even Europeans are cultural heirs of the Native American. The diversities have engaged more attention than the similarities. The historic Native American did not possess a uniform culture, and this diversity may indeed be the key to our ever-fresh interest. Seven major language stocks are recognized in North America alone. The total of separate, mutually unintelligible languages exceeds 200. How different these languages were from each other can be exemplified by saying that an English-speaking person could understand a Rumanian as readily as a Hopi farmer in Arizona could have talked with a Creek warrior from Georgia. Linguistic diversity is but one of the elusive aspects of Native American history. Today the Native Americans themselves are showing great interest in their own past history and in the preservation of that history and of sacred tribal locations.

Diversity in other cultural achievements can be noted in material things. The rich possessions of the military Aztec—large cities; a powerful army; corn, amaranth, beans, and squash as basic foods; a rich ceramic technology; gems and golden ornaments—are in overwhelming contrast to the scanty possessions of the Paiute of Nevada. Yet the Aztec and the Paiute speak dialects of the same great Uto-Aztecan linguistic stock.

The diversity of Native American cultures has never been fully appreciated; many non-anthropologists, scholars untrained in the observation and analysis of human behavior, have erred in assuming that notions about Native American culture derived from one tribe were valid for other tribes. Nothing could be further from the truth. Language is but one facet of diversity. There is also a vast range of sociopolitical organizations. The stratified, self-destroying theocracy of the Natchez, for example, is poles apart from the simple, invisible controls of the Eskimo cultures. The mythology and religion, art motifs, and technologies of Native American tribes also range over a long and complex set of scales.

Tribal diversity was nonetheless patterned to some degree, as ethnologists long ago showed in their division of the continent into culture areas. A culture area is a geographical area within which the cultures show considerable similarity to each other and relative lack of similarity to cultures in adjacent areas. There is a strong correlation between culture area and subsistence resources. The culture areas—such as the Plains, the Arctic, or the Eastern Woodland—do provide a coarse, broad system of classification of the historically observed and reported tribes, a classification based largely on subsistence and material culture. The concept is a static one, with no great concern for the dimension of time.

Despite the static nature of the concept of the culture area as normally used, and despite the tendency of archaeologists to recognize (but rarely talk about) the validity of certain culture areas through certain time periods, there is no conflict between the culture area idea and the concept of diversity being expressed here. Within each culture area there were many local environments, and each local culture (group) would perforce adapt its sub-

sistence and social behavior to a very local set of resources, while generally conforming to an ecological pattern characteristic of the culture area because of a gross similarity of climate and resources. For example, in the Fremont culture area of Utah there are five subareal variants (though some students recognize only two). In their adaptation they share many attributes, including pit houses, gray pottery, limited horticulture, and numerous specific artifacts. But in the Salt Lake variant, the major meat source was bison, while 300 miles away in Parowan Valley at the Summit site it was the mule deer, and there was no bison at all. In the same subarea (Parowan), at the Garrison site 100 miles away, the major meat source was antelope. Thus we can assume two, if not three, different hunting techniques, a different size task force, and even a different social grouping appropriate for the terrain and the nature of the game being hunted in those two subareas of the Fremont culture. Countless examples could be cited for other culture areas.

A more important kind of diversity known to the archaeologist is seen in culture change through time. The Plains area provides an example. Here, in the years just following the beginning of the retreat of the glacial ice, there were scattered hunters of now-extinct big game, first the mammoth and then the long-horned bison. The mammoth were apparently taken as singles at watering places, but the bison were stampeded in herds over steep bluffs or into cul-de-sacs and there slaughtered. This new hunting technique developed for bison was suited to the numbers, behavior, and limited intelligence of an important meat source.

Probably a different size task force and a new mechanism of social control were both involved in the shift to bison hunting as the mammoth disappeared. Still later the more complex technology of both the Eastern and Western Archaic penetrated the Plains resulting in other exploitive-adaptive measures recognizably Archaic in style but adapted to the immediate resources of the Plains. After the time of Christ, horticulture, permanent housing, and villages became established over much of the Plains area, necessitating yet another exploitive pattern with a different ecological balance and selective use of the different resources of any local area.

The point is that the concepts of broad regional stages, culture areas, and diversity are compatible, being different uses of the same historical data. Perhaps the simplest way to sum up is to say that the idea of diversity is useful because it helps the student realize that every culture (group) has its own history as a result of its immediate environment. The environment includes the climate, all the resources used by humans, the culture of the group, and its neighbors and enemies. Diversity is thus linked with an ecological explanation of adaptation and culture change. So there are simultaneously a broad North American culture history and hundreds of local histories.

Contribution to Modern Civilization

Acknowledgment should be made of the all-pervasive contributions of Native Americans to modern civilization and the American way of life. That heritage enriches our twentieth-century American culture, providing much of its individual flavor; world culture and economy are equally indebted to the Native Americans. The "discovery" of America and its until then unknown populations, was one of the greatest events in European history; it engendered an immediate worldwide interest that has never waned. In the development of modern culture Native Americans contributed (not always willingly) in every sphere of modern life, even while

they and their lifeways were faced with extinction. In medicine the contributions include, for better or worse, the enema tube and such important plant-derived drugs as curare, cocaine, and quinine. To industry and agriculture the Native Americans gave rubber, corn, and tobacco, which have worldwide importance. In the American vocabulary, words such as *chocolate, succotash, hominy, potato,* and *tomato* reflect the origins of common items of modern diet. And thousands of place names from Tallahassee to Walla Walla proclaim our retention of the musical syllables of many tongues. The sports world owes hockey and lacrosse to the Native Americans of the Eastern United States, and the inspiration behind the Boy Scouts must be credited to the same tribes.

Some historians have said that the democratic representational form of government that sustained the Iroquois League was familiar to some of the men who framed the United States Constitution and influenced the final form of that document. Thomas Jefferson was certainly familiar with and admired the Eastern tribes.

For its first three centuries American history is little more than an account of the cooperation and competition of Native Americans with the Europeans of many nations; the progress of westward expansion until the 1880s continued to involve various tribes. It seems somehow fitting that such men as Black Hawk, Tecumseh, Cochise, Geronimo, and Sitting Bull are far better known for their heroic exploits than the men who finally defeated them and that Sacajawea and Squanto are equally well-known for their heroic pro-European behavior. Even the natural resources of the continent—the prairies and plains of the Midwest or the pine stands of the South—memorialize the fires built for a hundred centuries in a deliberate attempt to engineer and preserve a terrain fitted to the cultural patterns of the Native Americans. Native trails have become our highways; modern towns rest on the ashes of ancient settlements. The inspiration of Indian models in painting, sculpture, and music has been widespread. In short, Americans are far more aboriginal in thought, politics, language, diet, and action than is normally realized.

Another important point to be made here is that there is strong evidence that in aboriginal America continuous and long-lived communication and cultural exchange existed between the tribes despite language differences and a few physiographic barriers. Opinions differ about the nature of this contact. Some students see the contact as very limited, involving trade in luxury items such as copper, seashells (from both oceans), turquoise, **catlinite** pipes, and the like over long distances from tribe to tribe. But the dispersal of precious goods may have been the work of professional traders like some who still function in Central America and the Southwest. Another view, one sustained by a host of recorded observations by earlier travelers, is that the Native American was both roving and gregarious. There was much long-distance visitation by entire bands or family groups with other tribes.

A great awareness of cultural diversity as well as considerable cultural exchange existed all over the continent. There is also overwhelming evidence of intermittent hostility—raids or, rarely, pitched battles—between tribes. These hostilities were neither continuous nor universal. Raids conducted for gain in women, horses, scalps, or slaves were common; such raids were most frequently initiated by young leaders who could gather and direct other young hotbloods toward a specific objective. Many historically recorded raids were motivated as much for excitement and prestige or sport as for booty. On the other hand there is the well-documented practice of long winter visitation by Plains tribes or bands with the Pueblos of Pecos, Taos, and Galisteo. Open enemies for much of the year, they declared a kind of cold-weather truce during which trading and social intercourse of benefit to both groups took place; it was a

standard annual event. Some tribes achieved cultural exchange through the common practice of child or woman stealing, followed by adoption into the family of the kidnapper. Sometimes the captives were sold to even more distant tribes.

The view that there has always been much contact between tribes through face-to-face trade, possibly friendly visitation, and hostilities is sustained by archaeological discovery. The continued existence, then, of quite different lifeways and of the several culture areas of the continent must be accepted and evaluated as the result of strong factors other than isolation or ignorance of other ideas.

Culture

Inevitably many passages in this book will comment on the nature of culture as this seems justified by the factual material. There is no intent, however, to weave a new theoretical web or to review theories about Native Americans or any other culture. Nevertheless it seems necessary to take some position about the nature of culture at the very outset. Kroeber's concept of the superorganic nature of culture and White's view that culture is uniquely human are easy for the archaeologist to work with. When one deals with cultural debris—the frozen or materialized expressions of vanished technological, artistic, or religious values—with no social action and no population to obscure the view, one finds it exceedingly easy to accept *Homo sapiens* as a given entity, with culture or the totality of observable behavior as the one matter of importance. The once-living but anonymous individuals who possessed these objects and lived according to the vanished behavior patterns are all too readily and easily ignored; the focus of study is on the inferable customary behavior that determined the situation in which individual lives were lived.

The archaeologist's observations and conclusions are made without distraction by the original people, their behavior, or day-to-day events.

The above remarks are not very helpful or useful when one begins to examine an archaeological collection or read technical archaeological monographs. For the prehistorian and other anthropologists, the word *culture* has had so many uses on so many levels of abstraction that it has almost lost its value. It has already been used in this book in the most general way to signify a lifeway and all that implies in technology, philosophy, language, religious custom, social organization, values, world view, law, and so forth. Obviously the archaeologist can't directly learn all these things from a **midden** heap. Therefore, that meaning of *culture* won't serve. Nor is the nonanthropological use of the term, meaning the finer things of a civilized existence, in any way appropriate. Just what does *culture* mean to an archaeologist? Childe says, in essence, that a culture is a recurrent assemblage of artifact types. Willey and Phillips are content at one level of discourse to limit it thus: "the term 'culture' usually refers to single technologies or 'assemblages' reflecting a similar economic adjustment shared by a large number of social groups."

Generally the practice in these pages will be to refer to the specimens from a site or a level within a site as a *complex, collection, assemblage, congeries,* or some other term that implies a cluster of associated physical objects and their relationships. The word *culture* will be used to express the idea of the unity, or similarity, of a series of site collections that seem to imply or prove the existence of a single widespread lifeway that involves the same level of technology and a shared exploitive or ecologic base. An example of this usage would be the Archaic cultures.

Stage is an indispensable term used to raise to an even higher abstraction the notion of a unity of culture focus from complex to complex. In *stage* there is an additional connotation of sequence and ranking of cultures by level of complexity toward some terminal or final level. Divorcing the term *stage* from both temporal and spatial connotations is necessary if the term is to be useful. Inventing new terms or adding crippling restrictions or overtones to already useful words is one solution to the problem of terminology, but in this account the effort has been toward a consistent use of *stage, culture,* and *complex,* as described above. Although such usage is admittedly imprecise, it approaches that normally employed in the archaeological literature that readers may later consult.

Stage and *culture* are seen to be related, but not synonymous terms. *Culture* concerns a group of specific, named units about whose temporal and spatial existence positive data (and/or beliefs) exist. Ideally, however, *stage* lacks any temporal and spatial connotations except in a local or regional sequence.

Archaeology and History

In view of its concern with chronology it is clear that archaeology, also called prehistory, can be considered a kind of history. Archaeology differs from history in that it often has no available written documents, and it probably benefits from that fact. There were no written languages other than the Mexican codices and Mayan hieroglyphs in the Americas. Thus prehistory is usually fleshed out without the aid of written records. As just implied, the North American archaeologist knows of no leaders or prominent individuals, and there are rare chronicles of individual achievements. No detailed day-to-day records of striving against famine, good crop years, hard winters, important battles or successful raids, or of the introduction of technological innovations or other such records are available here as they are to the archaeologist in some areas of the world. Diaries, religious records, accounts of travel—all are lacking. Since these are the stuff from which history is derived, the archaeologist can't be a proper historian.

Nonetheless, the archaeologist does "write" history and has certain advantages in doing it. Denied written documents, restricted to objects and their relationships, the archaeologist notes technological, religious, and other changes in the overall culture as they occur through time. As site after site is dug and reported, the available information increases. If, let us suppose, only one site of a given culture were dug and reported, it would dangle in time and space without connections; it would exist in a vacuum. If this supposed first site were a cemetery yielding data on burial practices, we might gain information on religion and some idea (through grave goods) of technology, but the full history of the group would be scant indeed. If an adjacent site were studied and found to be the associated village, the data on technology would no doubt be fuller; architecture, village plan, and subsistence base could perhaps be added to the description. If yet another sample of the culture came to light in a stratified reoccupied site under or over an altogether different complex of artifacts, the beginnings of knowledge about the relative chronological position of both complexes would emerge. Thus, as the culture is sampled over and over at site after site—each site having certain unique attributes—a local, then an areal, and even a regional history can be built with increasing confidence. Relationships to other contemporary cultures elsewhere can be inferred from trade objects or other evidence of exchange of ideas.

If culture change through time is regarded as valid history, then prehistory qualifies as history. The lack of documents, the lack of measured, specific points in time when important events occurred, the lack of named personages and their exploits may be an advantage, leaving archaeologists to gather information impartially about all classes of the populace and their lives. The validity and usefulness of this information lie in extending our understanding of human behavior, as well as of human and cultural evolution, deeper into time.

Chronometry and Chronometric Techniques

The prehistorian's interest in the passage of time has been mentioned. Since time is crucial to archaeological interpretation, the devices for telling time deserve attention. Most chronometric methods yield only relative chronologies. Relative time can be defined as establishing an event or culture as being earlier than, coeval with, or later than, some other event or sequence of events lacking a definite age or date in terms of elapsed years or other absolute units of measurement. In short, the event or culture can be placed somewhere in a sequence.

The stratigraphic principle that layers in the earth are laid down slowly through time, with the earliest being the deepest and each successive layer relatively younger, is crucially important here and forms the basic evidence for most archaeological chronology. At any site there may be one or more occupation layers, possibly with alternating bands of sterile fill; in such cases, the stratigraphic sequence is directly observed through physical phenomena.

The relative sequence of the layers of soil and debris is readily established at each archaeological site. But each such sequence from a single site is a unique circumstance revealing only the history of events at that individual location. In order to understand the history of a region, the discrete relative sequences must somehow be fused into a master sequence. Such a sequence can be called synthetic or inferred stratigraphy and involves the principle of typology.

As digging continues through a long-occupied region, it is soon evident that differing artifact assemblages are collected from site to site. Rarely are all the assemblages represented at each location. With different assemblages (or cultures) identified artifactually and giving evidence of several discrete non-identical lifeways, the data can be combined to establish a widely applicable relative chronology for the region. It becomes possible, through a typological comparison of the inventories of objects and traits from each level, to equate or link culture levels across several sites. It is then possible, as shown in Figure 1.1, to build a chronology for increasingly large spatial zones. The cultures represented by letters in Figure 1.1 are the observed sequential occurrences at several sites. They are to be understood as comprising similar components, that is, units so similar in terms of the material and nonmaterial traits collected, observed, or inferred that they are believed to represent the same lifeway of the same people

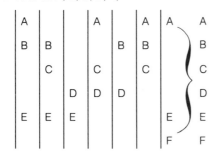

When matched by culture likeness and level, these sites yield the sequence of cultures A, B, C, D, E, F.

Figure 1.1 Developing a synthetic regional chronology from a series of stratified sites.

and are, therefore, of the same age. This system of building a chronology from scattered and disparate sites is called seriation and will be discussed later in the chapter.

Thus typology sometimes carries implications of time as well as of culture. Moreover, cultures A through F may be evolutionary stages of one cultural tradition or may represent quite different traditions over a vast span of time, with varied adaptations to different environmental circumstances. The sequence is clearly a relative one. Culture A is merely the youngest and F the oldest. However, if A represents the debris from a culture identified with a historically known culture or tribe, the sequence is safely anchored at one end in calendrical time. For example, in the vicinity of Natchez, Mississippi, an aboriginal archaeological complex containing a few artifacts of French manufacture can be dated as no earlier than 1699 A.D. (when St. Catherine's Concession was established north of the central town of the Natchez tribe). Given this starting point, the archaeologist can make reasonable guesses about the age of the earlier, entirely aboriginal complexes underlying the 1699 layer. This method of anchoring a sequence in the modern year count or calendar, a well-developed procedure in American archaeology called the direct historical approach, has been widely used.

It must be emphasized that to date no archaeological procedure yields *absolute* or precise dates. As will become apparent, some techniques are far more accurate than others, but all North American archaeologically derived dates are, in the strictest sense, *relative*. Of all the techniques the one already invoked above—stratigraphy—is the oldest and has been the archaeologists' standby for more than a century. It is also the most reliable, although rare cases of *inverted* or *reversed* stratigraphy (due to redeposition of the layers of earth and cultural fill) have been observed.

Two books that have much more detailed treatment of chronometry and many facets of archaeology are by Fagan (1982) and Michels

(1973). These are recommended for students who are interested in those technical aspects of archaeology.

Geological Techniques

Other than stratigraphy, geology provides some useful techniques. These include paleontology and geomorphology. If a cultural deposit—artifacts, charcoal from fires, or food bone scraps—occurs with remains of mammals now extinct, and the date of extinction of the species is known, a minimum age is established for the associated cultural remains. If horse bone is encountered, the age exceeds 6000 years; if mammoth, the age is greater than 10,000 years. In Europe the age of extinction of the cave bear or woolly rhinoceros is set at 80,000 or 90,000 years ago. Even closer dating can be achieved by means of certain microfauna, such as voles, mice, gophers, rats, or even snails, all of which are sensitive to environmental changes.

Also important in some situations is geomorphological data. If an archaeological deposit is in or under an extensive natural stratum—such as flood sediments or volcanic ash—and that deposit has been or can be dated, a minimum date is established for the cultural stratum. But it is merely a "no younger than" age ascription. It can't be more precise and hence is relative. The reverse situation also occurs. The age of the cataclysmic volcanic eruption that left behind Crater Lake in the southern Oregon Cascades was first suggested by radiocarbon dating of sandals found in an Oregon cave beneath the ashes from the eruption. The date of the Crater Lake/Mt. Mazama eruption has since been verified many times over at about 7000 years Before Present (B.P. hereafter).

Relative dating based on superposition does not fully satisfy the archaeologist. Merely knowing that something is old, or older than something else, is not enough. If areal or even local studies of cultural change or succession are to be successful, it is necessary to know more precisely how old the cultures are. There is a constant search for techniques with which to determine more and more exactly the age of any site or object.

Dendrochronology

Precision can be claimed only for dendrochronology, or tree ring dating. Dean (1978) has provided the most lucid of the scores of explanations available, as well as a concise history of the method. Reduced to the simplest terms, tree ring calendars are based on the belief that each tree ring represents one year's growth (Figure 1.2). Any specimen can be dated by matching its ring pattern against a master calendar of rings, the master being a sequence built up from many tree specimens whose rings are matched backward from living trees known to have been cut in certain years. The ring pattern is the sequence of broad and narrow rings that result from favorable (wide rings) and unfavorable (thin rings) growing years. *Favorable* implies more rainfall and also involves amount of sunlight, density of cloud cover, and other factors. These sequences of alternating clusters of broad and narrow rings are shared by all trees over an area, and all of them "keep" and record the same "time" throughout their life span; the record is not only of each year but also of the climate in that year. A tree of unknown antiquity, and unknown cutting or dying date, can therefore be fixed in time by matching its sequence of rings and their pattern with the master chart of wide and thin rings of known date.

But nothing is that simple. Many species do not lay down a ring each year. Others may put on growth on one side of the trunk but not on the other. Still others grow only where there is a constant supply of water and lay down uniform or "complacent" rings, so no pattern develops. Certain pines, possibly red cedar, juniper, sagebrush, and a few other North American species, yield reliable ring counts. Of these the western yellow pine is the best timekeeper. It responds very sharply

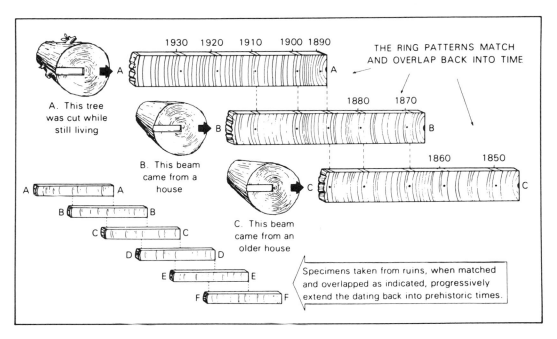

1930 1920 1910 1900 1890

THE RING PATTERNS MATCH
AND OVERLAP BACK INTO TIME

A. This tree
was cut while
still living

1880   1870

B. This beam
came from a
house

1860   1850

C. This beam
came from an
older house

Specimens taken from ruins, when matched
and overlapped as indicated, progressively
extend the dating back into prehistoric times.

Figure 1.2   Deriving dates by means of tree rings.

to nuances of rainfall and climate, especially when it is growing in a location with no constant supply of groundwater and depends on annual precipitation, often scanty in the West. The notoriously variable western climate contributes to the accuracy of the calendar. The alternating good and poor growth years provide sharp, readily identified, wide and narrow ring patterns.

The study of tree rings as calendars was initiated in 1914 for the study of sun spots by the astronomer A. E. Douglass. When the technique was recognized as useful to Southwest archaeologists, many students worked with Douglass to learn the system and apply it. Today dendrochronological studies are in progress over the entire world, and some other sensitive species have been discovered. At present, the longest master chart of use to archaeologists is the one for the American Southwest, which is based on thousands of modern and prehistoric specimens and goes back to 2053 B.P. The specimens on which it is based are among the tens of thousands

housed at the Laboratory of Tree-ring Research at the University of Arizona. Figure 1.2 illuminates the system and illustrates the building of a master chart. When the southwestern United States is reviewed (Chapter Six), the crucial usefulness of this chronological system will be better appreciated. Tree ring studies conducted in Illinois, Georgia, and the Plains and Arctic culture areas have also been very useful. The bristlecone pine sequence from the White Mountains of California goes back about 8200 years. It has had little archaeological application to date but has been of crucial importance in connection with radiocarbon dating. Great progress in dendrochronology is also being made in Europe and Asia.

Radiocarbon Dating

Of greatest general usefulness in developing chronologies is radiocarbon dating, a technique developed after 1945. Based on the disintegration of an isotope of carbon, ^{14}C, the datings derived are generally regarded as accurate within the limits of a small calculated standard deviation. Therefore the technique is regarded as accurate, if not absolute.

The principle itself is very simple. During an early study of the isotopes of carbon, the half-life (or rate of decay) of ^{14}C was determined to lie at about 5570 years. Much later the half-life was established at 5730 plus or minus 40 years. Most calculations continue to be based on the 5570 figure. The radioactive ^{14}C is created in the upper atmosphere as cosmic rays bombard nitrogen atoms. The radioactive carbon eventually diffuses evenly throughout the entire biosphere (except at the Poles where there is more) and is taken up directly along with ^{12}C and ^{13}C, both non-radioactive or stable, by plants making carbohydrates and marine species manufacturing calcium carbonates for their shells. As the life cycle continues, plants contribute carbon, some of it radioactive, to the animals that feed on them, so all living organic matter contains some radioactive carbon. Upon death, carbon intake ceases, but the radioactive ^{14}C continues to decay at the same rate. Although the decay of ^{14}C continues until the atoms are inert (twenty or more half-lives), the current detection limit of most counting devices is ten or twelve half-lives, so deriving radiocarbon dates of 50,000 or 60,000 or more years is possible. Establishing the age of a specimen then becomes a fairly simple technical procedure. Dead organic matter can be tested for radioactivity; by means of refined counters the random emanations per minute can be recorded over a long period (twenty-four to seventy-two hours is common). The rate of decay, that is, the frequency of the emanations, is then transformed by formula into a statement about how many years ago the organism died and what the small plus or minus range of error is.

In order to put this notion to the test in the late 1940s, the chemist Libby ran tests on ancient wooden objects of known age from ar-chaeological collections and other sources. The results were computed and showed ages compatibly close to their known or reliably estimated absolute age. The experiment thus sustained the theory on a limited basis. First released informally in 1948, the results aroused far more excitement in archaeological circles than in the field of chemistry, and a new chronological "industry" emerged.

Since the first few radiocarbon dates were derived, many technical refinements have been made in the technique. In the 1970s eighty laboratories were doing research with radioactive carbon and providing hundreds of age determinations on archaeological and geological specimens. Many of these projects have been discontinued, but there are now commercial installations doing reliable work for a reasonable fee. *Radiocarbon*, an annual publication established in 1959, is devoted to printing lists of derived dates, thousands of which have now been run. Radiocarbon counters are now sensitive and accurate enough to measure the carbon content of specimens representing a time span from ca. 1500 A.D. back to about 40,000 or 50,000 B.P. Thus prehistorians have a calendar covering all of *Homo sapiens's* time on earth!

The best materials for testing (listed in their order of reliability) appear to be charcoal, uncharred wood, bone, shell, and horn. Any organic material can be tested—usually the test involves changing carbon to carbon dioxide after many steps calculated to remove contamination. The carbon dioxide can be used directly by the counter, but many laboratories use methane, acetylene, or other gases for counting. Analysts have most confidence in the results they get from charred plant remains because charcoal is nearly pure carbon, which is chemically quite inert, and because the plant absorbs radiocarbon directly from the atmosphere where it is created.

Dates are often released by the laboratory as Years Ago with a plus or minus factor: for example, 8950 ± 260. The archaeologist either uses the Years Ago figure, usually writing it

Before Present, or B.P., or makes an adjustment to the Christian calendar. It should be noted that the year 1950 A.D. is the baseline date establishing the "present." The plus or minus part of the figure is a statistical statement of uncertainty of one standard deviation based on the nature of counting random events (which the emanations are). Whether the sample was counted twenty-four, forty-eight, or seventy-two hours or longer is also involved in calculating the plus or minus figure. All we need to know here is that the figure says that there are two chances in three that the correct reading of the age of the specimen falls within the plus or minus range. The range for 8950 ±260 is 8690 to 9210. Most archaeologists assume the first figure to be accurate and proceed with their interpretations as if no plus or minus computations were involved, a practice that will be followed in this book. In some cited cases the apparent stratigraphical discrepancies disappear in the plus or minus ranges.

The theoretical or practical limitations of, and questions about, the method are legion but are given relatively little attention by the archaeologists using the data. The most important of these limitations is that the cosmic ray bombardment has not been uniform for the past 50,000 years. Empirical findings for the first millennium show rather sharp fluctuations with radiocarbon assays giving ages both more recent than, and older than, the true age of specimens over the past 1000 years. As in Figure 1.3, the ^{14}C variations fluctuate on both sides of the true age until 1 A.D.; before that there is a consistent lag—the ^{14}C ages being younger than the actual years ago. Figure 1.3 also shows an increasing lag in ^{14}C age for the 3000 to 7000 B.P. span of the known tree ring chronology. These lags and fluctuations in ^{14}C abundance are evidently detected

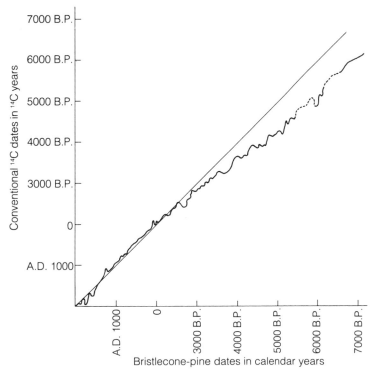

Figure 1.3 Radiocarbon lag behind calendrical time.

worldwide, wherever testable dated materials exist. So the radiocarbon age ascriptions, whether reading younger or older than the actual age of the sample, still bear the same relationship to other radiocarbon dates.

One problem with radiocarbon dating is that relatively large samples of the organic—once living—materials are necessary for testing. There must be enough mass for the random beta ray emissions to be numerous enough to count, even though today's counting devices are much more sophisticated than the ones used in the 1950s. But a new technology has been developed. It can date samples weighing only a few milligrams, in a tandem particle accelerator. The accelerator functions as a mass spectrometer, so the process is called tandem accelerator mass spectrometry (TAMS). It requires only a few hours to measure the individual ^{14}C atoms themselves and derive the radiocarbon age of the sample, but the physics of the process and its instrumentation are complex.

The velocity of the atoms in the accelerator varies with the atomic weight. The ^{14}C atoms are separated from others in the sample by first giving a negative charge to the sample, which prevents acceleration of the nitrogen atoms; partway through the acceleration process a positive charge is given, which eliminates carbon-hydrogen compounds, while the ^{14}C goes on to the counter. The accuracy of the method is about the same as for beta ray emanation counting. The advantages are that a tiny sample, even one milligram in weight, is sufficient for the assay, and the run requires only an hour or two. Thus a charred thread, a few charred seeds, even residual carbon in the paste of a potsherd, or the ^{14}C in cast iron can now be analyzed and dated. The possibilities are limitless. To date, however, only two or three TAMS facilities have been built specifically for assays of ^{14}C and other light particles.

It is very interesting to note that this exciting breakthrough in ^{14}C analysis uses a technology developed for an entirely different purpose—the search for quarks. So this technique is serendipitous to a degree, as was the original research on ^{14}C. Libby, who invented the ^{14}C technique, was interested in cosmic rays not chronology or archaeology!

Archaeomagnetism

Another method for achieving relative dates is archaeomagnetism. Its operation is based on the location of the variation in the earth's magnetic field and the fact that clays contain any of the oxides of iron (not all clays contain iron, although most do) and will acquire the current magnetic declination (from true north) and inclination (dip from the horizonal) when heated to high temperatures, as in a pottery kiln or clay hearth. Heating destroys or cancels the remanent magnetism of the oxide particles, and they realign themselves with the current field. Upon cooling the particles retain the alignment achieved during heating and preserve a record of the magnetic field at the time of heating. All burned clay—bricks, pottery, tile, and so on—preserves the record, but it is meaningful only if the heated clay has never moved from its precise spot of firing.

To determine the archaeomagnetic attributes of burned clay several samples are taken from undisturbed burned clay, with a careful record of its exact orientation to true North; the declination and inclination of the sample are read in the laboratory with sensitive magnetometers. Because reliable records of magnetic variation have been built up for various parts of the world, it is possible to match the several sample variations with earlier variations and arrive at an age or date for the sample.

In recent years, archaeomagnetism has proved very useful as an adjunct to radiocarbon dates, or alone, for dating sites in the western and southwestern United States, where central clay fire basins in prehistoric dwellings have been used as the source of samples. A chart of the magnetic variation in the Southwest has been built up back to about 300 B.C., but all the data have not been made available, so the reliability of the track is questioned. Other researchers have tested the chart, however. It was verified as reasonably accurate by limited research done in southern New Mexico and Arizona for the period 900–1300 A.D. In the Dolores Valley of southwest Colorado, however, the same researchers found fairly wide divergence from the original plotting at some points during the period 700–900 A.D. (Figure 1.4). Although applications of the method are rare, a few archaeometric dates have been developed for several Fremont villages in Utah. They agree with radiocarbon dates from the same houses and appear to be more precise. The time differences noted were consistent with the stratigraphy of the houses sampled. The method seems to hold great promise, and its use will no doubt increase as control data are expanded and improved.

Less Commonly Used Chronometric Procedures

THERMOLUMINESCENCE A chemicophysical dating technique called thermoluminescence has been known for many years, but its use is not common. Thermoluminescence is the release of stored energy in the form of light. The method is based on the fact that there are radioactive trace minerals (e.g., uranium and thorium) in pottery clays and the gritty particles used as grog or temper. As the radioactivity decays, the emissions knock off electrons from other molecules. Some electrons escape; weaker ones are trapped in the crystalline mass. When energized by heat, the trapped electrons escape, releasing a photon (light) as they do so. The photons are collected and enhanced to yield light that can be measured. The intensity of the luminescence is transformed by formula to the number of years since the clay was fired. It is a tedious,

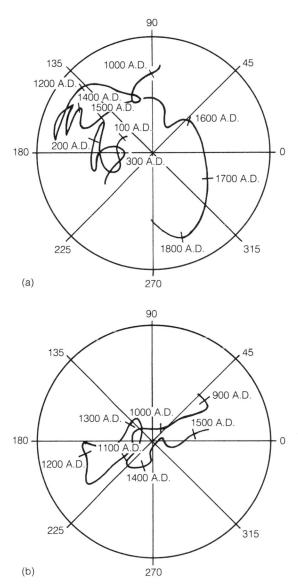

Figure 1.4 Polar views of the magnetic variation charted for (a) England A.D. 100–1800; (b) the Southwestern United States A.D. 900–1500. Determining age is more difficult where the lines of magnetic variation cross each other.

time-consuming method, but it yields reasonably precise results. Use of the thermoluminescence method is increasing because it works with **flint** and **chert** as well as with pottery.

Another very important chemicophysical system, useful only with rocks of volcanic origin, requires detection of the potassium isotope ^{40}K and its daughter product $^{40}Argon$. The K:Ar ratio can be turned into a years ago reading; the higher the ^{40}Ar reading, the older the rocks. This method reaches back almost infinitely into the past. It provided the means for dating the stone strata associated with the Olduvai Gorge, Kenya homonid fossils, and the even older Lucy, found in Ethiopia. The method has not been extensively used in the Americas, but its capabilities range from a few thousand to millions of years. It is a very expensive test requiring many chemical purifying procedures, extraction of the bases in a vacuum after the crushed sample is brought to a very high heat, and a series of traps where various heated metals absorb all the elements except the potassium and argon gases, after which the two are introduced into an accelerator and measured by spectrometers. The skilled personnel, extreme care, and sophisticated apparatus required and the range of the standard deviation may explain why it is not commonly used in American archaeological applications.

FLUORINE DATING   Fluorine dating is an old but recently revived technique. Most groundwater contains fluorine. Buried bone takes up fluorine; the longer the interment, the greater the fluorine accumulation. However, no chronometric value can be derived from the fluorine content of bone because the fluorine content of water is so variable from place to place. A difference in the concentration in bone from shallow levels to deeper levels at one site can sometimes be used in interpretation, and significant differences in fluorine content in bones from the same level suggest disturbance, mixing of specimens after digging, or some other confusion. The most important application of fluorine dating may be in revealing deliberately falsified associations. The famous Piltdown Man hoax in England was exposed in the 1950s by the fluorine test. The most famous use of fluorine dating in North America was in helping establish the contemporaneity of Midland Man, in Texas, with some now-extinct animals.

Amino Acid Racemization

Among various chemical dating techniques that have been developed is amino acid racemization. The technique attracted considerable interest, which later diminished as will be shown. Amino acid racemization is based on the fact that the protein in bones undergoes changes after death. Some twenty amino acids comprise that protein, aspartic acid being one commonly used in testing. The change consists of a reversal of the polarity of the molecule chain. During life there is an L or left twist; after death there is a reversal to a D or right twist. The extent of D twist increases through time, so age can be calculated from the D/L ratio. Many factors affect the rate of change, including temperature, humidity, and possibly soil leaching. Six or eight human burials from southern California were tested for aspartic acid racemization, and ages of 20,000 to 70,000 years were calculated; the ages were regarded as much too old by most archaeologists. Two of the tested burials, Del Mar and Sunnyvale, were dated at 48,000 and 70,000, respectively, based on a temperature control established elsewhere in the state.

The same two skeletons were later tested by means of a somewhat complicated procedure using two uranium series. The bones were tested in two separate tests, for the ratios of ^{238}U to ^{230}Th, and of ^{235}U to ^{231}Pa; the accuracy of the tests were controlled by running identical tests on bone from the La Brea tar pits and a camel from an exposure near San Francisco, both of which were already securely dated by several ^{14}C assays. Both the U:Th and U:Pa test results coincided with the ascribed ^{14}C ages. The uranium series tests showed the Del Mar skeleton to be 11,000 years old, with the Sunnyvale one younger—8300 to 9000 years old. These results were much more acceptable to archaeologists than the aspartic acid assays. However, a later assay by TAMS gave a radiocarbon date of 3500 to 5000 years for the age of the Sunnyvale specimen. In fact the ages of many human skeletons from California tested by the aspartic acid technique have proved to be only 2000 to 6000 years old upon retesting by TAMS.

The problems encountered in controlling the many variables in the aspartic racemization analyses and the wide discrepancy between the findings for the Del Mar and Sunnyvale specimens cited above enforce the conclusion that the aspartic tests are not yet reliable or useful. Probably there will be further efforts to achieve better control over the variables.

OBSIDIAN HYDRATION Quite different in complexity and precision is a dating method called obsidian hydration. It is simple to do and even simpler to understand. Because of an imbalance in its own water content, obsidian (volcanic glass) continuously takes up moisture from the atmosphere or soil where it is stored. Depending more on temperature than humidity, it develops a rind that increases in thickness with time. Thus, a chipped obsidian artifact or scrap of chipping waste begins to adsorb moisture on any newly exposed surface; the thickness of the rind measures time since the artifact was manufactured (chipped). The rind, which does not change the luster of the surface, is analyzed by cutting thin sections perpendicular to the surface and measuring their thickness under polarized light at about 100X. In theory, the age could be read directly from the width of the rind.

Unfortunately the method failed to live up to extravagant early claims. Apparently the rind does develop at a uniform rate, but the rate is different everywhere; presumably the rate per unit of time is very much a function of local storage temperature. The colder the storage, the slower the hydration process. There is an even greater variation in the hydration rate of the obsidian from different flows. Therefore, each local hydration series must be calibrated to some local series of radiocarbon assays. There is no universal adsorption rate.

Several reliable intrasite or restricted regional "rate per hundred years" rates have evidently been established, and suggestive regional chronologies have been achieved. But if obsidian hydration requires a ^{14}C calendar for calibration, and can supply chronological nuances only within a very restricted area, its value is greatly diminished. It does have the advantage of simplicity, low cost, and speed. And no great skill or technical training is required for running the tests. The importance of this approach appears to be restricted, however.

Cultural Chronometry

Typology and Cross-Dating

Another constantly employed chronologic device is cross-dating, which is an entirely cultural approach rooted in typology. The concept of typology used here is related to the biological concept of species but is laden with additional overtones. Discussed, debated, and defined endlessly, typology is an important tool for anyone handling large quantities of objects that must be ordered or "classified" according to some useful scheme. Classification usually implies sorting and grouping like objects together. Such groups are usually called types. A *type* can be defined as a class of objects that share a consistent constellation or combination of similar or identical attributes. The type is therefore an abstraction. It must also be recognized as a construct created by archaeologists for their own purposes. The raw data of archaeology lend themselves to this treatment. Pottery, whether whole or as sherds, stone tools of all sorts, beads and other ornaments, and fabricated bone objects can all be ordered as types. The different classes can be sorted grossly, for example, from a Southwest site, corrugated pottery in one pile and black-on-white painted in another. Or sorting can be done on so fine a scale that the corrugated pottery is separated into several heaps, using corrugation width and details of coiling, pinching, and so forth as criteria for separation. Similarly, the black-on-white pottery can be subdivided into smaller and smaller clumps on the basis of decoration, vessel form, vegetal or mineral paint, and other attributes, with pieces in the smaller grouping quite similar in all details. The extrinsic type cannot tell us what the intent of the potter, flint chipper, or bead maker was. If one asks, "What about the bead was important to the artisan at the time of manufacture?" the answer is, "We don't know." Archaeologists also often ask, "Was the type, as selected by the sorter, once equally well recognized or regarded as a separate type with prescribed uses by the aboriginal craftsman, or is the type merely a device of convenience for the sorter?" Usually it is probably the sorter's type rather than a valid cognitive type that the maker would recognize.

Although the ordering, classifying, and naming of types can be faulted for various reasons, no other procedure could possibly isolate and systematize all the specimens and allow inferences about technology, art, and culture contact or climax. Establishing types or using those established by others is an appropriate and inescapable procedure for the archaeologist.

Typological cross-dating of archaeological complexes depends on the existence of a series or sequence of artifact types of known age from one or more documented and dated sites. If one or more specimens of an already

dated and described ceramic or projectile point type is recognized at a site being excavated, the new site is presumed to be more or less the same age as the dated objects included in its strata. This technique is made possible by the extensive trade or exchange carried on over wide areas by prehistoric Americans. One of the best examples is seen in the Glen Canyon area of Utah, where some 1600 sites were reported by the University of Utah, but not one log or beam was datable by dendrochronology, and no radiocarbon dates were run. In the series of reports of that research, all dates of occupancy of the canyon are based on the ages ascribed to cross finds of named pottery types from the nearby Kayenta district of Arizona. The dates were known because tree ring dates are available from some of the adjacent Kayenta district sites where the types are dominant.

When cross-dating is done thus by means of pottery types, reasonable accuracy can be assumed because pottery can be fabricated by such different techniques and because it reflects so many other culturally determined choices that inferences about connections and relationships are quite often convincing. With other classes of artifacts, however, the credibility of claims about contemporaneity or cultural identity of two collections is greatly diminished. Many types persist unchanged for centuries, even millennia. Stone types are particularly unsatisfactory as indices of either time or relationship unless they are found in association with other materials.

There are several reasons for being skeptical of historical reconstructions or cultural connections based entirely on stone complexes. The first is that stone is not plastic. Although flint knappers can do wondrously skilled work, the number of possible forms is limited. Even more important, however, is the fact that for about two million years, chippable stone has been used almost exclusively for cutting, scraping, or chopping tools and (later) projectile tips. If the functioning of these utilitarian objects is satisfactory, there is little purpose in changing the form; therefore, styles persist. Adding this restriction to the brittle nature of the medium, it is obvious that the number of forms a chipped tool can take is limited. The forms of knives, arrowpoints, **axes,** or **choppers** are few indeed.

There are important exceptions to the above generalizations. Many chipped stone types appear to have enjoyed popularity over a short and known time span and usually occur in a uniform context; they are evidently reliable indices of time, area, and cultural association. Such types, however, are by no means as numerous as other more general and long-lived types. (Some short-lived types that have been used as index fossils, such as Folsom fluted points, will be described in the appropriate sections.) In any case, age ascriptions or other conclusions reached on the basis of chipped flint cross-dating should always be carefully analyzed as to kind, number, and diagnostic nature of the artifacts used in establishing the connection and the "transferred" age.

Seriation

Seriation is a procedure in which typology is employed to establish the chronology of a region or other study area. It is sometimes made very complicated, but it is basically simple. In certain situations seriation is useful for dating sites from an area where culture sequence and chronology are not known. It is largely based on the changes that are known to occur in artifact types. The changes, especially in ceramics, are in effect styles, often transient and short-lived. Or they may be due to technological changes that outmode objects with long histories. But short or long the styles slowly or rapidly go out of favor to be replaced by something quite different.

Prehistoric pottery or chipped stone artifacts can be arranged, or seriated, into a sequence based on the percentages of occurrences as they increase and finally diminish and disappear through time. Figure 1.5 shows how the percentages of an associated group

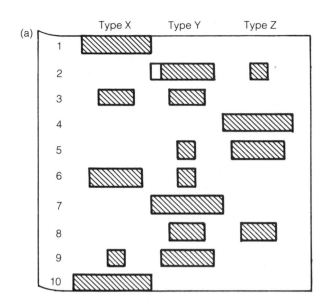

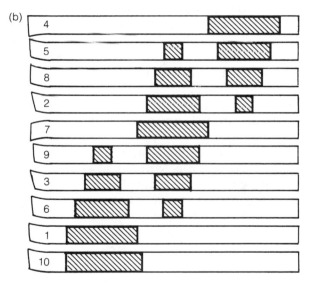

Figure 1.5 In this example, ten sites yielding only pottery types X,Y, and Z were discovered. (a) The collections from the sites were sorted, and the frequencies of each type at each site were recorded as a bar chart on graph paper. (b) The paper was cut into strips and arranged for best fit, thus creating overlapping sequences of continuous occurrence of each type.

of specimens are analyzed separately and recorded as percentage bar graphs, site by site. The result of the ordering of these bar graphs is that a series of ellipses or "battleship curves" are formed to represent gradual changes as the types lose or gain popularity. In seeking the best fit, that is, the smoothest curve that the percentages of the pottery types can be made to form, the bar charts need to be shuffled. When the best fit is achieved, it is assumed that a chronology has been achieved. But there is no way to tell late from early without some other data. At least two sites should be dated by ^{14}C, dendrochronology, or some other more-precise method. An excavation showing a local stratigraphic sequence with the layers yielding percentages that match one or two of the undated sites being seriated could also establish the chronological control.

The object of the exercise is to derive a relative chronology for a number of sites, or collection of artifacts, where ages or relationships to each other are not known. It is simple, easy, and so obvious that it may not deserve the space given to it here. But at an earlier stage in archaeological research, when fewer regional sequences were understood, seriation was spectacularly useful in establishing chronological control over large masses of material.

Yet another application of typology—but not with a chronological goal—has been developed in recent years. This application has to do with the study of use-wear patterns, and the object of the analysis is to detect the function of flint tools. Form is not at issue in this kind of typology. The study of use marks—that is, the microscopic striations caused by using a flint tool against wood, bone, or other stone—can be analyzed as to the direction of stroke or the quality of the material being cut, punctured, or shaved. Many students are interested in this aspect of lithic technology. They create types or classes based on use with names such as knives, projectile points, planes, **scrapers,** and so on. These are deduced not subjectively but on the basis of experimentation with identical tools made by the analyst and then used on the many materials available to the aboriginal user.

Having recreated the tool and used it as the makers presumably did, the analyst knows the strokes that were used and can identify use marks (scratches and striations) on the tool. This guides the determination of the use made of the aboriginally manufactured tool. Archaeologists have long assigned functional names to flint objects, such as scraper, drill, and so on, but the names were arrived at intuitively or subjectively. Names applied after use-wear studies are supported by experimental results and are doubtless more reliable.

Serendipity

Dendrochronology has uses other than providing a calendar for archaeology. Cultural events, such as the abandonment of Mesa Verde in the late thirteenth century can probably be explained by the long drought the tree rings record for that period. Earlier events in Anasazi history have been explained on the basis of droughts and other climatic events noted in the tree ring record. Dendrochronological data have also been statistically transformed into weather anomalies and maps of past climatic conditions. Since the 1940s estimates of prehistoric river flows based on tree ring records have permitted useful predictions about future modern runoff and river flow.

A serendipitous and nonchronological application of radiocarbon analytic techniques to the human diet has made a quite different contribution to culture history. A nagging question for more than half a century has been: When was maize introduced in the Southeast as a staple food? Claims have been made there for archaeological corn dating to before Christ, although such finds are not abundant so maize was not demonstrably a common food item. But an answer to the question comes from analyzing human bone. Like some other tropical plants maize takes up more ^{13}C and ^{14}C during certain phases of photosynthesis than do temperate zone plants. At the same time maize contributes slightly more ^{13}C than ^{14}C to those who eat it. Thus people with a heavy maize element in their diet have a disproportionate amount of ^{13}C in their bone collagen. This characteristic can be detected; the ^{13}C becomes a trace element. Human bone from Southeast sites has been tested, and on the present evidence of ^{13}C content, we can now say that maize, no matter when introduced, was not important in the southeastern human diet until after A.D. 900.

It should also be noted that if analysis of human bone reveals ^{15}N, beans were part of the diet. In the Southeast this occurred even later than the use of maize.

Obsidian also has other, nonchronometric uses. The chemical differences in obsidian that are a hazard in hydration studies offer surprising precision in the study of trade or exchange where obsidian is one of the commodities. It works like this: Each obsidian flow has a unique combination of trace elements. When samples are irradiated with thermal neutrons and analyzed by a spectrometer, the flow's chemical "fingerprint" is determined. No other flow has the same fingerprint. By means of this fairly simple procedure obsidian artifacts can be matched with quarry samples and the sources identified. This technique was used to identify Yellowstone obsidian at Ohio Hopewell sites; to identify two highland quarries as the sources of obsidian traded for several thousand years all over the Middle East, to isolate very detailed and precise data on primary sources in New Zealand and Melanesia, and to identify distant mountain sources for obsidian recovered in lowland sites in California.

Time and Space

Archaeology requires a mental feat that always seems difficult when first encountered: the simultaneous involvement with both time and space. That this should be dif-

ficult is somewhat surprising because all of us exist in, and cope with, a three-dimensional world with time seeming to flow past. Our experience in living makes us aware of past events and their relation to present, if not future, affairs; spatial relationships are just as well understood. Perhaps these dimensions are made part of the human mind so early that they fade into the background of consciousness. If this is true, it may explain the trouble students experience in recognizing both time and space when dealing with archaeological materials.

The problem is intensified by the specificity and unique contents of a single archaeological component. The collection is static, marking a frozen moment of time; at the same time, the objects make up the collection from a single spot. To solve the temporal and spatial relationship of a component to a similar collection, analysis shifts from the discrete to the abstract and poses altogether different problems of manipulation from those involved in studying a single collection.

Difficult or not the intertwined considerations of time and space enter into nearly every archaeological statement. Such judgments as "site A is contemporary with site B" or "site A is older than B" weigh evidence and make assumptions about time relationships. No question of culture A influencing or being influenced by culture B can be settled without some chronological framework and even knowledge of the time when one trait and then another appeared in either or both cultures under study. An interesting example of failure to find a solution to an archaeological question because of time is seen in the examination of the possibility of transfer (diffusion) of certain traits from Asia to Mesoamerica. No firm conclusions can be reached because the precise dates of occurrence in either area cannot be accurately ascertained. If the Asiatic traits developed 500 years earlier than the same traits appeared in America, the eastward influence is at least possible; but if the Asiatic phenomena are even ten years younger, the prospect of exportation to the Americas is ruled out and the question can be reversed: Did the traits move as a complex from East to West?

Culture Contact, Change, and Continuity

One of the most troublesome areas in anthropology is the understanding of the mechanisms of culture change. One mechanism, of course, is in the exchange of ideas, values, artifacts, language, or all of these when two expanding cultures come into contact, either directly through geographical contiguity or indirectly through visiting, raiding, or trading. Actually culture contact may be the easiest of the causes of culture change to identify. In archaeology the matter is somewhat troublesome because no actual behavior can be observed. Only the testimony of the objects and what can be inferred are at hand as evidence.

Archaeologists have written much nonsense about the effects of one culture on another, partly because several of the terms they use, including *diffusion, migration, replacement, competition,* and *survival,* are biological concepts and are not always appropriate when used to explain human behavior. They are appropriate for nonhuman species but fall short of adequacy in explaining what the human animal can do. When, for example, one finds ground squirrels occupying a given territory where fifty years ago none existed, the explanation that the species has migrated from elsewhere or that it has spread from a small center over a wider area is highly plausible. But if one finds a distinctive pottery style occurring over an increasingly wider area over a period of time, no such assumption about migration of either people or pots is automatically valid.

Pots, of course, can't move. They may be transported, but they reveal no evidence about how or why the carrying was done. Were the vessels moved in hand-to-hand trade or by direct export from the place of manufacture? More important, however, is the fact that a given fashion or style can achieve wider and wider popularity without movement of either people or pots. Knowledge transmitted verbally or visually would be sufficient. Nearly all explanations of migrations, population mixture or replacement, or progress of pottery or any other artifact across a land should be viewed cautiously. If the statements rest only on the evidence of pottery, arrowheads, or house types, the archaeologists just don't know. Much diffusion of culture traits or complexes in the Americas may have involved little more than communication between individuals from different tribes.

Diffusion also requires that an innovation be somehow compatible or have obvious advantages for the recipient culture. The spread of the horse over the Plains from tribe to tribe is an example of diffusion of a compatible new artifact and a complex of traits. The object (horse) was very useful to the recipients and was assigned an important place in the culture in accord with their values; as a beast of burden it replaced the dog. But even more important, it gave advantages in hunting and raiding and became a symbol of prestige and wealth. Both drastic and trivial changes in prehistoric Native American cultures must have often occurred in the same fashion, as an idea or complex of ideas (agriculture, for example) and the associated objects diffused to the limits of acceptance without necessarily involving extensive shifts of population or even of basic cultural values.

Archaeological finds reveal through artifact styles and types that contacts occurred and that one culture influenced another. What remains unclear and what will perhaps always be obscure is the mechanism of transport or exchange. Then, too, one may ask: Did culture A actually exert a significant influence on

B if the only evidence of contact is the presence of a few pots of a different style? That a few examples of a minor art would cause important change in an ongoing lifeway is unthinkable, particularly if the recipient culture B already possessed pottery and a knowledge of its manufacture. However, if culture B had hitherto not known pottery, adopting it could no doubt produce changes in the B culture pattern; these changes might then be identified as obviously caused by the new object and the associated technology. But even in such a case, one could not know *how* the first pots were introduced by culture A to culture B.

Whether the mechanisms of culture contact can ever be demonstrated through archaeological finds may be doubtful, but the fact of contact can be established, and its significance can be inferred. In interpretation one must separate (1) assumptions about mechanism from (2) the facts about artifact presence and (3) the cultural effects of that presence. One can be sure of (2) and make varying reasonable inferences about (3), but there is usually little certainty about (1). (One of the best-documented cases of actual migration of a sizable population is that of a Kayenta group that moved southward from northern Arizona to Point of Pines in central Arizona. Their new village is clearly different in architecture from others in the area and their handicrafts also reveal the Kayenta origin. Why the move was made cannot be proved of course.)

It is ironic that although archaeologists are strongly interested in stability, continuity, and change in culture, no robust theories about culture change have emerged from this interest. Most archaeological writing involves description of data and varyingly extensive comparisons with other sites or cultures. It often then moves on to statements about influences exchanged between cultures or evidences of culture change, but satisfactory theories about such change have not yet developed. Most archaeologists appear to use one of two assumptions about the nature of

change. The first is the idea that culture change is a gradual, uniform process that can best be described as complacent. The other view implies change in spurts, followed by periods of quiescence. The spurts would follow introduction or local invention of some technological or other innovation. Both views can be defended on the basis of archaeological findings.

The attempt to understand culture contact, change, continuity, and stability is engaging a large group of theoretically oriented young scholars, but one of the earliest attempts was made by a series of seminars in 1955. One session dealt with culture contact situations that could be observed in archaeological contexts. The seminar recognized and classified eight types of contact, the types being established on the basis of both logic and actual, well-studied examples. The types include situations where an intrusive culture is incorporated into the recipient one, where the intrusive one comes to dominate, where the cultures appear to coexist without marked influence in either direction, and others. The seminar made no attempt to explain why the results varied from case to case. Another session dealt with a specific case (the American Southwest), attempting to detect the traits intrusive over a 3000-year period and to isolate the cases of acceptance or rejection of traits and complexes as they were introduced. At the time the Southwest was the only culture area well enough known archaeologically to permit this kind of analysis. The Southwest seminar was a careful effort to outline culture history and explain culture change. Many of the contact types from the first session are exemplified in the Southwest study. The reports of the two sessions reinforce each other and can profitably be studied in sequence.

A third session of the seminars concerned itself with stability, a concept that archaeological data can illuminate empirically, although explanations must remain entirely inferential. This session was confined to sharply defining certain concepts and to suggesting a carefully developed hypothesis for testing, in the belief that archaeologically tested theories could ultimately contribute to broader anthropological theory. The major analytical concern was with the concept of *tradition*, a term that implies persistence of a culture trait or complex of traits over a significant spatial range and time depth. Persistence can, perhaps, be equated with stability.

One crucial caution must be made now lest it be overlooked. There is an unproved assumption that changes in details of the attributes of artifacts are an index to significant changes in other aspects of the culture where the objects had their original value. If the student discovers that over an 800-year sequence pottery decoration in a given culture became more flamboyant, ceramic technology became more efficient, and other developments related to this minor art appeared, he or she is immediately faced with the question: Is this an important culture change involving more than ceramics, or does it merely represent a slight intensification of an earlier valuing of pottery? The observed slight change in material specimens may equally well document a certain rigidity, arguing culture stability rather than culture change. How much change in subsistence pattern, architecture, or social organization can be claimed on the basis of prettier, fussier, or deteriorating pottery decor? If the changes can clearly be traced to another area some distance away, did the donor group that introduced new pottery designs have any other impact on the recipient one, particularly if both cultures are otherwise similar in overall culture pattern? Consideration of these points leads one to be very skeptical of sweeping conclusions about culture changes deduced from one class of artifacts. This does not mean that all statements about culture change found in archaeological monographs should be rejected; the evidence and its variety must be weighed against the conclusions. One question must always be asked: Does the change in artifact assemblage reflect a modification of the genius of the pattern, the structure, or the direction of a culture?

The problem in dealing with culture change is clearly one of scale. It is generally agreed that in any cultural system there appear to be slight deviations that require some internal systemic adjustments. Such small adjustments—perhaps to the temporary failure of a valued food resource—might lead to temporary or permanent changes in procurement scheduling. There is a cultural change, but its significance must be evaluated against the extent to which all the subsystems are modified or cultural values shift as a result of the original adjustment.

It seems reasonable to accept the fact of continuous but slight culture changes to maintain a balance or equilibrium with the natural and social environment as needs arise. It must further be accepted that only major changes in cultural behavior, such as a shift to farming or pottery use, will be detected archaeologically. Slight homeostatic changes will probably not be reflected in the record. The continual theoretical interest may be without merit or promise unless there can be agreement on exactly what change is, how it is detected and measured, and what is important about it. In any case, American culture history appears to document a continuum. The contributions of earlier cultures to the later ones are numerous, readily identified, and easily traced. It is more appropriate to view the American story as a gradual evolutionary one in which slight changes, perhaps millions of them, masked the shift from PaleoIndian foraging to the final farmers of the Northeast, South, and Southwest.

Classification

Classification of archaeological data can take several forms. One has been to build up an inventory or list of objects and customs distinguishing each recognized local culture and to arrange the cultures in their known or presumed order. On the strength of the inventory new data can be assigned by comparison to one or another of the known divisions in the cultural-chronological framework. Thus, the new material is absorbed or positioned in the local chronology. This is the most common approach to establishing control over a mass of unordered collections. The Southwestern classification, developed at the Pecos Conference of 1927, is of this type.

The Pecos Conference organized the remains of the Anasazi region into eight "periods." These periods, it was argued, were marked by sufficiently different material culture traits to make up distinctive complexes and warrant separation into periods. The separated complexes thus become statements about both time and trait associations. In the case of the Southwest, the Pecos classification suffered from the fact that it was created from scanty data; actual chronology was not known, and the system was extended to much too large an area. Worst of all, it was so welcome and needed that some students seized it as an eternal verity and a valid yardstick far beyond its appropriate geographic range. The classification lost its proper value as an aid to understanding and began to constrict thought by providing ready, if often incorrect, answers. Similar efforts in other areas of the continent have been briefly restrictive to a lesser degree.

The most common and useful type of classification is a more abstract ordering involving, by the nature of its terminology, some awareness of culture change. Here again the terms often carry implications of both time and stage of development. But in 1958 Willey and Phillips offered a synthesis of the prehistory of the entire New World. Their approach was to define "stages" of cultural development and to classify cultures according to stage. These stages could well be called culture "levels." The terms selected to designate the stages are

mixed in concept: Some are interpretive, while others are merely labels. The important aspect of the classification is that time span is not imputed to any stage qua stage. Time is another dimension. The stages of Willey and Phillips are Lithic, Archaic, Formative, Classic, and Postclassic; they will not be used in this book, but the stage concept is used because it is a helpful interpretive device. The separate traditions that can be recognized in the loosely described stages will be identified area by area. The stages used in this book are PaleoIndian (Willey-Phillips Lithic), Archaic (same as Willey-Phillips), and Climax.

A markedly different classification system is the Midwestern Taxonomic Method, credited largely to William C. McKern. That system was applied during the 1930s to the Plains and most of the East. The scheme is simple, representing another archaeological modification of a biological system. Taking account of neither space nor time, it consists of grouping or clustering artifacts and trait complexes that appear to be very similar or identical. These clusters of complexes are then compared on a slightly higher level of generality, and those that share a preponderance of traits are again grouped. Through several increasingly general groups, the system recalls the biological charts subsuming species under genera, subfamily, family, and so forth. The discrete single unit, called the component, was represented by the inventory of associated objects and traits recovered from one level at one site. Of course, more than one component occurred at a stratified site. Components were compared and grouped into abstractions called foci according to their degree of likeness. Each focus was compared with others nearby and eventually grouped with similar ones into a phase, and so on in increasingly broad and abstract general groupings.

The introduction of the McKern method led almost instantly to a useful classification of the hundreds of Midwestern and Plains sites that had been excavated and reported but were uncontrolled by any system. It soon became evident that the sites of a focus occurred in a closely knit distribution and were probably contemporary. Phases, too, showed quite limited areal spread. At the same time, components of one and another focus were recognized in stratified situations, and a relative chronology was developed. What actually happened was that by ignoring time and space in its concentration upon mere sorting and grouping, the McKern classification brought both spatial and chronological relationships into sharp relief. The success of the system was such that *focus* has now come to be synonymous with *local culture*. The other groupings have fallen into disuse, although the term *phase* is still used with a new genetic significance. Today it also has chronological implications, that is, one phase of a culture is followed by the next. Users of the McKern scheme ordered and gave meaning to the prehistory of about one-third of the continent in less than a decade, an achievement that marks the McKern taxonomic system as an important contribution to American archaeology.

Although all the classifications discussed above are extremely important in the history of archaeological development, they are of more value to the regional specialist or the professional scholar than they are to the beginner. None fully serves the intent of this book, which is to tell a story as coherently as possible, using any available ordering devices that will help make the story clear. In general the first controlling principle is chronology; the second is cultural likeness or typology. It is obvious that without the use of classifications developed by others, the present approach would not work.

It is necessary to return to the ambitious synthesis of Willey and Phillips (1958) to define some of the terms that will be used later and to touch on other points they make. From that book let us first consider their geographical units. The smallest unit is the *site*. This unit, of course, is the one the archaeologist works with; its size is extremely variable. The locality is also variable, but it is what we might call a community or local group. The region is likely to coincide with minor physiographic subdivisions where there is homogeneity of culture at any given time. The area is large, corresponding perhaps to the culture areas defined by the ethnographer. Willey and Phillips cautiously suggest that *locality* may be equated with *community,* while *region* may be thought of as *tribe;* this effort to give archaeological units a semblance of social reality was undertaken to bring archaeological units into some congruity with other anthropological concepts of what elements comprise significant social groupings.

Also useful are horizon and tradition. As seen elsewhere, *tradition* implies persistence through time. *Tradition* can refer to all the traits of an entire culture or can be restricted to a single complex. Thus, one could speak of the Pueblo Tradition, an agricultural tradition, or even a shallow bowl ceramic tradition. Tradition, then, is a vertical or chronological concept. Horizon, on the other hand, is a spatial continuity of culture traits or complexes that have wide geographical distribution and are known, or believed, to have diffused rapidly over the space where they occur. The notion can be thought of as a horizontal-spatial one, implying contemporaneity; horizon marker traits are normally thought of as coeval, providing time links from one region to another over an area of cultural similarity. Thus tradition recognizes the fact of regional cultural stability and persistence through time, while horizon is a practical tool enabling the student to spot close cultural relationships. Horizon markers also provide chronological fixes for developing regional and even areal culture sequences.

Archaeological Techniques

At some stage it is necessary to describe how archaeology is done, a matter much complicated by the fact that almost everyone is already convinced that the sole requirements are picks and shovels, strong backs, and a place to dig. Unfortunately this oversimplification is difficult to refute because at first blush fieldwork doesn't seem to require much beyond interest and leisure time. But fieldwork—the recovery of the artifacts and the noting of relationships—is of utmost and crucial importance because it is here that the control of the information begins and ends. Conclusions are no more valid than the raw information on which they rest; the data of archaeology are recovered from the ground. It is correct, however, to think of fieldwork as a series of techniques and procedures that are neither difficult nor profound. It is the invisible background of guiding concepts, assumptions, and scientific principles that the observer and recorder possesses as professional intellectual equipment that marks the difference between the archaeologist and the antiquarian or mere collector.

Most qualified archaeologists have lengthy classroom, excavation, and laboratory training. The laboratory is crucially important because that is where analytical skills and procedures are learned. Usually archaeologists learn in classes the content and sequence of various cultures: the Plains, the Southwest, or the Northwest Coast, European, and Asian archaeology.

Throughout the training the student becomes increasingly familiar with artifacts of all kinds; learns to think in terms of time, associations, and cultural complexes; and, one hopes, begins to see beyond objects (which at the level of the analysis are merely documents) to the outlines of a lifeway. Information to be culled from the mute testimony of the bones, potsherds, scraps of plants, stone tools, and structures coalesces into a pattern that is the archaeological reality. It is essential that the novice serve an apprenticeship under careful instruction in field research, that is, actual digging, instruction in recording procedures, and ultimately recording itself.

The record created during an archaeological excavation consists of written descriptive notes, tabulations of the **provenience** or source of artifacts, a photographic record of structural features, notes of phenomena (such as natural and cultural strata revealed in cross sections by trenching), and maps and sketches. Almost all those records have to do with associations of phenomena and the provenience of specimens. The purpose of the recording is to preserve the site and its contents in full context. The record is crucial because the site is destroyed by the very excavation that reveals its history and contents. The record developed by the archaeologist is all that remains. The quality of the notes controls the credibility of the interpretation of the site and its unique attributes. Clearly, the trained excavator-recorder not only carries a heavy responsibility but also must be a jack-of-several-trades, although there may be assistants to handle some of the chores.

Routine archaeological recording requires skill in mapping and photography, a knowledge of earth and soils and their physical attributes, some administrative ability and judgment, and endless patience coupled with a respect for detail. In the final analysis, therefore, fieldwork is done against a background of training that includes nearly everything touched on in this chapter. It all combines in the excavator's mind to form a framework of assumptions, concepts, attitudes, and skills that gives the archaeologist a posture entirely different from that of the relic hunter.

Today the archaeologist doesn't, as a rule, excavate a site just because it's there, although many have been dug thus opportunistically in the past. Modern archaeology is usually conducted on a rational basis; at minimum the contents of a site and a record may need to be *preserved*. Or a site may contain data (discovered during a sampling test) on a little-known local culture. Whatever the reason(s) may be, work isn't begun until some research scheme, plan, or design is developed to answer general or specific questions about that culture or its relationship to others. The excavator often has a bias: an interest in settlement patterns, subsistence, environmental factors, or other concerns. The research design will probably emphasize the special interests of the excavator.

Whatever the design, when an excavation begins the site is unique, and the excavator is ignorant of its contents. Ideally the excavator begins work as if entirely ignorant about what the new site will contain. Assuming ignorance of this particular deposit and taking every care to avoid anticipating that certain phenomena will be present encourages sharper observation. It leads to the discovery of subtleties of relationship that would otherwise be lost through a more complacent approach. Every site must be dug on its own terms. Unique in content, individual history, soils, microgeographical incidents, and the cultural and natural events or processes that have modified its contents after it was abandoned, the site dictates the procedures of its own inevitable destruction. Upon the archaeologist's astuteness and diligence in observation and recording rests the validity of the conclusions.

It is small wonder, then, that the first approach to a site is conducted cautiously. The first steps are usually sample cuts: either pits sunk into random (or selected) spots both on the apparent site and off its limits or a test trench dug from the outer limits partway to the center of the site. These tests reveal conditions such as the nature of the earth to be dealt with, the sequence of culturally relevant and/or natural soils, and many other details that help the digger understand the site and plan the excavation. The test trenches or pits are often called *exploratory,* a term neatly expressing their purpose and value. Based on the findings of the explorations, the systematic excavation operation can be done in several ways. (Manuals of procedures are legion and many special techniques exist. All such

books are useful, but none can possibly meet and cover all the exigencies of every problem the digger meets.)

After the first ideas about the contents of a site are gained from exploration, usually the next step is to remove, by careful cutting, the several layers of the site one at a time over a large area or even all of the site. Cutting is usually begun carefully at the edge of one of the exploratory cuts. *Carefully* does not necessarily mean either slowly or with tiny tools. Obviously, a 2-foot-thick layer of sterile topsoil overlying an ancient campsite could be removed with a bulldozer if reasonable care were taken to stop before reaching the layer containing the prehistoric data. In fact, a cardinal rule is that one always uses the coarsest tools that will do the work. That is, one does not use shovels if a bulldozer can be used safely, or a trowel if a shovel can be employed safely. The reasons are practical: Archaeology is slow at best; any steps that can accelerate the accumulation of data save priceless time for analysis or other excavation. Another reason is the overriding problem of funds. Archaeology is increasingly done by hired crews; time wasted on overcautious procedures translates into wasted money with reduced research findings per dollar. This does not mean that two days spent in laboriously tracing the edge of an earthen house floor with a trowel and brush are wasted or that removing fill over a fragile bone artifact grain by grain is improper. On the other hand, scraping away a large trash heap with a whisk broom or trowel may be senseless rote. Common sense—not exaggerated meticulousness—is an important ingredient in archaeological work. No procedure, whether "coarse" or "fine," should be followed unless its use is appropriate to the situation and it is focused on gaining some specific information.

In some situations, peeling layers from a large area is inappropriate or impractical. The removal of a large mound and the cleaning of a large complex of crumbled stone architecture are examples. There the common procedure is to cut slices vertically from top to bottom of the sometimes featureless cultural fill. This operation has the primary advantage of speed; at the same time, materials can be readily segregated as to layers if there are such, and there is no loss of stratigraphic data. In this technique, horizontal relationships can be kept clear only by making separate maps for every level. This is a major disadvantage because one never sees the structural features or other phenomena of an entire occupational level and their associational contexts at one time. The photographic record is, therefore, woefully incomplete; one relies entirely on maps and sketches for the spatial data. Most excavators combine the two basic horizontal and vertical cutting procedures and their many variations on every job, as dictated by the individual site and the data to be recovered.

There are many kinds of sites in the world. American archaeologists recognize as archaeological sites burial and substructure mounds, villages and campsites, cemeteries, refuse or midden heaps, trash pits, tombs, cave deposits, animal kills, irrigation systems, masonry and adobe structures, pit houses, earth lodges, and combinations of these. Each requires its own special procedures and precautions, but the available techniques are few so their flexible application is the key to fieldwork. It must be noted that it is easier to dig some purposeful construction, such as a house, tomb, or artificial earthen mound, than to uncover a randomly accumulated midden, trash area, or occupational deposit. Because purposeful construction, such as a post and mud house, reveals some system of logic or a pattern of behavior, its features can be anticipated and watched for to some extent. The random accumulation, however, reveals no plan at all; all relationships *may* be fortuitous, but they can never be assumed to be so in advance. The random deposit actually requires more vigilance on the part of the excavator; at the same time, this vigilance is less likely to be rewarded by cultural patterning.

It is easy to see that archaeology is not as simple as the shovel-and-strong-back school would have it. Indeed properly done fieldwork is frustratingly slow, tedious, and demanding; it should be performed only by the trained and patient person.

Although the archaeologist has full control in the field, the final report often involves the services of many technicians and scholars from other disciplines. The excellent book, *Science in Archaeology* (Brothwell and Higgs, 1970) exemplifies the range of ancillary studies undertaken to enrich archaeological knowledge. The volume contains sixty-one articles by scientists in other fields explaining their roles in sharpening anthropological analysis. The authors include dendrochronologists, mammalogists, botanists, metallurgists, radiologists, serologists, and other specialists. Even so, not all the special skills called upon are listed in that book. Cooperation by specialists in other fields is becoming more common, with the result that archaeologists must collect more varied data and solicit a wider spectrum of talent during recovery, analysis, and reporting. More importantly, these ancillary studies sharpen the perceptions of the excavators and permit subtler inferences; as a result, archaeological conclusions are becoming more precise and probably more valid.

Sharer and Ashmore's book *Archaeology: Discovering Our Past* (1987) is recommended for those interested in archaeological techniques.

Emergency Archaeology

The full story of any prehistoric American culture will never be learned. The practical problem of finding every location where some aspect of prehistoric human behavior has been preserved is enormous because there are so many. Beyond mere numbers is the problem of preservation. All archaeological sites are fragile in that they are only earthen or stone constructions, often buried under more earth. Erosion is pitiless and continuous; archaeological sites disappear before its destructive forces. Aside from erosion amateur and commercial collectors vandalize and destroy sites as they collect (see later section).

Site destruction also occurs because of modern construction. Each new reservoir, highway, airport, pipeline, or subdivision causes tragic losses. By 1945 construction in the United States had been so massive that the problem of salvaging the fragile prehistoric data thrown into jeopardy through site destruction during civilization's march led to the new concept of emergency archaeology. Emergency archaeology involves a thorough search (survey) for archaeological resources within a tract where construction activities are scheduled. Search of the threatened zone usually identifies representative sites of each cultural stage represented. Examples of each are then excavated. Such programs, usually government supported, have made spectacular contributions to knowledge. In some instances, the regional and even areal sequences have been dramatically extended or altered. Some idea of the magnitude of the salvage work is suggested by these figures: Between 1950 and 1970 there were reported in *American Antiquity* alone a total of over 675 emergency projects involving about seventy institutions. Some were as simple as trenching a proposed new access roadway into an airport. One involved survey and excavation over a reservoir location 200 miles long on a major river where hundreds of sites were found. By 1972 an informed estimate of federal salvage costs for emergency archaeology exceeded ten million dollars, to say nothing of private institutional costs and grants from philanthropic organizations. In the 1980s, however, public support of archaeological programs probably exceeds 200 million dollars annually.

Cultural Resource Management

Beginning in the 1970s the philosophy of emergency salvage of archaeological materials jeopardized by construction or development ceased to be the primary, or only, response to situations where site damage was threatened. The concept of mitigation (meaning to moderate, alleviate, or avoid) of the damage caused by construction became a major management goal. Instead of excavating every location that is threatened, mitigation calls for an ideal situation; the preservation and protection of archaeological sites in danger of destruction. Excavation, of course, also preserves the record but eliminates the entity it is "preserving." Mitigation may be the ultimate expression of the conservation ethic. An example of mitigation would be the modification or slight shifting of roads or pipelines to avoid archaeological sites. Only if no feasible manner of mitigation can be devised is excavation employed for the preservation of data. Of course, some projects have even been prevented or long-delayed until some constructive mitigation procedures could be devised. (See Chapter Seven for a fuller discussion of cultural resource management, hereafter CRM.)

Collectors and Vandals

Aside from the senseless and thoughtless destruction of sites through construction projects and the natural erosion of prehistorical sites, the archaeologist is faced with the work of the collector. The collector may be a hobbyist who vandalizes sites on weekends as a form of outdoor recreation. Such collectors are concerned with a hoard of relics, not cultural values, but their labors destroy as completely as if maliciously motivated. Commercial collectors are more systematic in their digging because their motivation is money; the more objects they discover, the better their income.

Commercial collectors may be agents for art dealers or sometimes for museums that value aboriginal objects but not their context. Or they may be merely entrepreneurs who loot archaeological sites in search of artifacts. Whole ceramic vessels are extremely salable at incredibly high prices. Buyers, who are probably making investments and expecting high appreciations in value, seem to increase as the objects become scarcer and hence more valuable.

The vandals are bold, unscrupulous, and often dangerous. Always they show utter contempt for the poorly enforced protective legislation, such as the recently strengthened Antiquities Act, and the even less effective legislation forbidding trade in antiquities between nations. Vandalism is not a new problem. The riches of Egypt were stolen and scattered in the nineteenth and early twentieth centuries. In Mexico and Peru the contents of ancient ruins and burials have been torn from context and dispersed to museums and art collectors around the world and are still for sale despite treaties against the trade. The trade in antiquities may eventually destroy more sites than the construction activities mentioned earlier.

The greed that fuels commercial ventures is powerful. Given the problems of policing the millions of acres of public lands, inadequate personnel, frequent administrative apathy, the token penalties for infractions when thieves are apprehended and brought to trial, and the boldness of the commercial pot hunters, there is little likelihood that vandalism will ever be controlled. The looters hold to the American concept of private property, and also that the ancient sites are natural resources on both private and public lands, and are therefore open to exploitation. In the face

of those ideas, the high rewards, and the unlikelihood of penalty, the control of this destructive "mining" of cultural treasures will remain difficult.

Of course public education helps prevent some people from entering the trade. But people who watch "Nova" and "Odyssey" on public television or read thoughtful editorials or articles in *Science* are rarely the ones guilty of the thefts. Nonetheless education is the only recourse I can see. It is hoped that the readers of this book will do whatever is in their power to prevent the criminal practice of robbing sites and help reduce the erosion of that part of the prehistorical American heritage. The artifacts, of course, are beautiful—clean of line and created with skill—but outside their original contexts their value as documents to be used in the reconstruction of past lifeways is diminished manyfold. They become instead scattered separate objects in homes, offices, or art galleries, where their beauty is rightfully admired.

Of course some sites are protected. A number of national and state parks and monuments preserve and interpret important sites. A few other important sites are being protected by the newly created Archaeological Conservancy, a nonprofit organization. In a variety of novel ways this group acquires title to properties where the sites lie, ranging from outright gifts of the land to purchase with grants from such sources as the Ford Foundation and the Rockefeller Brothers Fund, as well as contributions from the public. The Conservancy then transfers the title to some local entity for management, conservation, and, one hopes, interpretation. One can only applaud the concerned and innovative people who conceived and implemented this farseeing plan. They can't stop all the illicit trade, but the effort to ensure that outstanding examples of the remains of ancient cultures will be forever preserved deserves commendation and all possible support including financial donations. The famous Yellow Jacket site in Colorado is one of the many acquired by the Conservancy.

Careers in Archaeology

Today one can follow several specialties in archaeology. These are identified and defined by the Society of Professional Archaeologists (SOPA), which also provides the best available professional guidelines.

In 1975 SOPA was created by a handful of archaeologists deeply concerned about the poor training possessed by many of those doing environmental and compliance archaeological studies. The society's primary aim was to establish the minimum standard or level of training required for doing acceptable archaeological work in any specialty. It certifies individuals who can show proof of the necessary training, imposes an ethical code on its members, and to some extent regulates the members' professional behavior, withdrawing membership from any whose conduct violates the society's code of ethics.

For all specialties there is the same basic standard: at least an M.A. in anthropology or archaeology, twelve weeks of field work, four weeks of laboratory or curatorial experience under direct supervision, and evidence (often an M.A. thesis or a Ph.D. dissertation) of the ability to design and execute an archaeological project. Beyond this minimum—which some regard as insufficient—one must also document experience of a full year in the specialties, called emphases by SOPA, in which certification is sought. As of 1986 eleven specialties or emphases were listed by SOPA; the list is adjusted as conditions require. The 1986 list includes field research (excavation), collections research, theoretical or archival, archaeological administration, cultural resource management, museology, teaching, marine survey, historical archaeology, underwater archaeology, and archaeometric or physical and natural science laboratory research. A year's supervised experience, or more, in an area of emphasis usually qualifies the person having already met the minimum requirements. The above requirements, long overdue, have been accepted by most agencies and some consulting firms as their guide for the employment of archaeologists, which has improved the quality of research achieved by compliance and inventory projects. The demand for college and university teachers dropped in the 1980s, and jobs were very scarce for young archaeologists with M.A. and Ph.D. degrees. Those students turned to CRM and related positions, so the quality of CRM personnel improved along with the quality of the CRM research plans and accomplishments. The distribution of archaeologists in the work force is much different than one would imagine. In 1986 a survey conducted by the Society for American Archaeology showed that at least 15,000 Americans identify themselves as professional or avocational archaeologists and belong to one or more archaeological societies. A sample study of the professionals among the 15,000 showed that 20 percent were college professors, outnumbered by the 23 percent who were doing contract (usually CRM) archaeology; 30 percent were government archaeologists (federal, state, and local); and 18 percent were museum curators. And the demand for well-trained personnel seems to hold steady.

The individual aspiring to a career in archaeology can deduce from the SOPA requirements just listed that preparation is not a casual matter. Ideally, the individual should possess several innate qualities. Above-average intelligence is highly desirable, but attendance at a professional archaeological gathering will show that it isn't crucial. Curiosity, a bent for science, ability to deal with abstract ideas, and interest in nature are more necessary assets. A person with these attributes and a willingness to work has a good chance for success.

Just what college course one should follow is much debated. Many graduate departments prefer or even insist on undergraduate training in archaeology or anthropology. My own experience leads me to prefer a student with a broad academic or liberal background with some classroom experience in at least biology, mathematics, and geology, but above all training and experience in the use of language, far beyond the standard undergraduate patois. The qualifications established by SOPA make it plain that the archaeologists' chief tool is literacy—for writing, speaking, or instruction. A few anthropology courses at the undergraduate level are desirable but not at all crucial. The reasoning is simple: Archaeology is rooted in observation, a concern for relationships among data, clustering of attributes, how, and why. The more one knows about the environment and its forces, the broader one's knowledge, and that wider perspective probably means that more is observed and therefore more questions can be asked. Good archaeologists simply know more things. My concern with English is less with poetry (although archaeologists have written good poetry) than with descriptive, expository, even argumentative prose and a knowledge of words and how they go together to express ideas lucidly. Until the time comes to concentrate on the one or more emphases of choice, my advice is to stay general. Students should take their time, experience many things and enjoy their intensive learning years. What college or university to attend is often not decided rationally. Location, costs, even peer choices usually control the decisions about where one begins preparation for a career. There are good, excellent, and poor schools. The student can lay the groundwork for a sound career even in a school with low standards. When a graduate school is being chosen the decision is an important one. A school that emphasizes the desired professional track(s) is probably best, but there are many good graduate schools where one can guide his or her career toward one or more emphases even if the institution does not offer the specific training necessary. Remember that the library has books: They remain the best visual learning device available. One could

almost say that the choice of school should rest as much on the quality of the library as on the faculty.

None of what is said here is intended to be either for or against a career in archaeology. It is intended only as a guide along one route to achieving a goal.

Museum and laboratory positions can be exciting if sometimes tedious and repetitive. Chronometric and physical laboratories are interesting places to work, but jobs in laboratories open up slowly, so luck and patience are needed to find one. Fortunately most jobs today are widely advertised, as are field excavation and survey opportunities, so students should learn early to make a regular habit of watching the departmental bulletin board for what's available.

A final word is in order about field excavation work whether as a supervisor or as a shovel hand. The discomfort—dust, heat, and monotonous labor—is very real. Fieldwork is usually slow and nothing much happens on any particular day. Every exciting find—a burned house floor, a rich storage pit, an extensive and deep midden—is dug one shovelful or trowel scrape at a time, and the entire phenomenon is unveiled at a snail's pace. Some of the details—the design on a pot or the carbonized cordage that holds a charred house rafter or cross member together—can be exciting and challenging while one clears away the earth around it. But gnats, flies, and sweat in the eyes are more common than high excitement. In fact moments of discovery or new ideas come more often in the laboratory than in the field. To sum up, archaeology as a career is stimulating, challenging, personally rewarding, and overall downright fun, but romantic and glamorous it is not. Anyone who plans to be an archaeologist must have an early term at a field school or as a hired laborer on a dig. If the experience is too grim or totally distasteful, the individual can drop the entire idea of archaeology and look elsewhere for a lifework. The savings in money and peace of mind will be substantial.

The Social Uses of Archaeology

Archaeology is not just a concern with culture history or scientific theory building. Sometimes the culture historians and scientists lose sight of the variety of effects, both good and harmful, that archaeology has on society. But archaeology has real and measurable social values that can be identified. Because this book is perhaps the first systematic study of archaeology for many readers, a description of some of those social values are an appropriate inclusion in this chapter.

One must distinguish between the *uses* of archaeology—the way archaeology is used by nonarchaeologists for other than the reconstructions of past cultures—and the *contributions* made by archaeology and archaeological data to society. Some of the values here attributed to archaeology are a mixture of both use and contribution; therefore, the categories below are neither consistent nor all-inclusive but merely convenient.

The first use suggested is ideological and includes the political, the religious, and some spectacular lunacies. The second use lies with the humanities: esthetics, the human tendency to romance, the egocentric human thirst for knowledge of oneself, and the history of one's own kind. A third important function long served by archaeologists actually blends the ideological with the expansion of knowledge. It is found most noticeably in the archaeologist's current role of spearheading the conservation of the American heritage. Last is what the "pure" archaeologist usually sees as the major role—learning about and perhaps understanding events long past and thereby extending the frontiers of knowledge about human behavior. With the categories listed above, one can demonstrate the many enrichments to modern life that come from archaeology.

In the ideological realm we turn first to some political uses and abuses of archaeology. First to mind is the hideous blend of history, myth, and archaeology that Hitler (and scholars going back a century) proclaimed. In the nineteenth century, Kosina had demonstrated the "superiority" of Germans of all times in weaponry, art, and even music. In 1939 Professor Schneider proclaimed, "The best of what is German is Germanic and must be found in earlier times." With this foundation Hitler and Himmler created and justified the racist Nordic hysteria of Naziism and the Third Reich with its attendant genocidal horrors. That shameful use is well remembered. An equal, but less well known use of archaeology is that of China's Chairman Mao. Like earlier rulers of China, he systematically encouraged, even commanded, research into China's buried past. From the splendor of that archaeological past, such as the rich tombs of Prince Liu Sheng of the Han Dynasty and his wife Tou Wan, he drew validation for his now-displaced utopian state. Every peasant and common soldier was instructed to search for and report archaeological sites. In fact, it was soldiers who found and reported the famous tomb of Queen Tou Wan. Mao defined the role of archaeology in his modern China as a source of pride and inspiration thus: "Our nation has thousands of years of history: it has its good points and it has numerous valuable and rare and unusual objects. Make use of the old ways for present purposes and adopt Western ways for modern use."

Other less doctrinaire examples reveal that modern archaeology began in Europe for purposes somewhat resembling those invoked by Chairman Mao. In the sixteenth century, Gustavus Adolphus of Sweden, established the office of King's Antiquary. The Antiquary was not doing archaeology, but was establishing a national past for Sweden. Even earlier, Henry VIII supported the efforts of John Leland, his own Antiquarian, to save the monasteries that

Henry himself had despoiled. By 1586 Camden had written *Britannia*, celebrating the ancient glories, and had compiled an inventory of English ruins—churches, abbeys, Roman forts, dolmans, and Stonehenge—with an aim identical to the Swedish one, a search for British roots in the unwritten history of their land.

More beautiful and spectacular is the national pride that Mexico has carefully built around its past. The National Museum in Mexico City is for many the eighth wonder of the world, architecturally as well as in its content. Its lower floor, covering several acres, is devoted to the story of human occupation in Mexico and is filled with beautiful objects of gold, jade, crystal, obsidian, shell, ceramics, and stone that we have admired in art books and, if more fortunate, in the museum itself. The second floor, equally spacious, contains life-sized replicas of villages, courtyards, and farmsteads from every district (state) in Mexico. Busloads of teachers and children excitedly come from villages as far away as 400 miles to see the wondrous museum, but even more they come to find and recognize the gallery or alcove that displays their home district. Through archaeology, Mexicans identify with the splendor of their past and their modern stature.

Closer to home and on a smaller scale is the Makah Indian tribe's sponsorship of the excavation of the Ozette site near Aberdeen, Washington, where a few years ago an ancient Makah village was discovered. Like Pompeii it had been covered and preserved by a catastrophic natural event, in this case a massive mud flow. Beneath the mud, which had preserved everything in anaerobic safety, were the houses and all their perishable contents. The tribe, sensing that here were tangible evidences of its proud 2000-year-old traditional life as whale and seal hunters, helped secure a large grant of money for the site's excavation. It also provided a laboratory where the fragile waterlogged objects of wood and fiber could be preserved. The excava-

tions, fabulously informative in the amount and variety of objects, revived the Makah pride of ancestry. The tribe created a museum where the finds are exhibited and explained.

The final political use of archaeology I will note was in this country in the 1930s when the New Deal government sought to ameliorate the sickening paralysis that the Great Depression had brought to the nation. Among its programs was the Works Progress Administration (WPA), a form of welfare that gave work to thousands of unemployed Americans. The unemployment problem was most acute in the South. Somehow, partly because of efforts by the Smithsonian Institution, the WPA authorities were influenced to sponsor archaeological work there. Why? In the South there was a large pool of labor, only a few of the many archaeological sites had been sampled, and it was possible to work outside all winter. Moreover, archaeological work required only untrained workers with hand tools and a limited supervisory force. Also to be mentioned, and of crucial importance, is the fact that the availability of WPA labor marked an important moment, perhaps even the birth, of an archaeological conservation ethic. Thanks to a persuasive Kentuckian, Major William S. Webb, the Tennessee Valley Authority (TVA)—then engaged in transforming the Tennessee River into a series of vast millponds for the creation of electric power and drowning hundreds of archaeological sites in the process—was influenced to sponsor dozens of archaeological programs. Before the huge lakes filled, these programs salvaged a small percentage of the priceless data from sites of unexpected age and complexity. Thus the humane welfare purposes of the government, the building of a political dynasty, and the basic archaeological goal—more information about the past—were all served by the WPA program.

One of the earliest uses of antiquities for religious purposes was by Nabonidus, King of Babylon and probably the father of Belshazzer whose deeds are recorded in the Book of Daniel. Nabonidus conducted excavations within the sacred precincts of Babylon hoping to bolster his obsession that the Moon God was supreme and should head the Babylonian pantheon. Banished by the priests for his heretical actions, he continued to be absorbed in antiquities and theological speculations, ultimately devoting his time to temple building while Belshazzer wasted the empire. Modern archaeologists still consult the data compiled by Nabonidus.

Although there are others, I will cite only one more example of archaeological evidence used in a religious context. This more recent example is the Church of Jesus Christ of Latter Day Saints' (Mormon) use of Mesoamerican antiquities in validation of its dogma. The Mormon story involves the arrival by boat of immigrants from the Old World on the Gulf coast of Mexico, long before the time of Christ. The new arrivals, called Jaredites, are not identified as to origin but a later increment, called the Nephites, were called Israelites. The sites of La Venta, Tres Zapotes, Monte Alban, Uaxactun, and Kaminaljuyu are identified with the Jaredites, while scores of the later ones are credited to the Nephites. One author identifies the god Quetzalcoatl as Jesus Christ. The Mormon conviction that the Mesoamerican cultures are the result of Middle East immigration is bolstered by their imposing Christian symbolism upon Mayan and Mexican art. An example is their interpretation of a stylized tree at Palenque as their tree of life. Interestingly, the Mormon Church has for years supported an active research program in Middle America. Reports of the research are scientific and straightforward.

Another ideological kind of application, which can be called the spectacular lunacy, is a hodgepodge of archaeological and other data. The myths of Atlantis and Mu are old examples. The best-known recent ones are the best sellers *Worlds in Collision* and *Chariots of the Gods.* In both these books a mishmash of facts torn from context and fermented in sick

imaginings brought a mystic excitement to millions of readers and wealth to their authors. Archaeologists find it difficult to explain how such books mix and distort established scientific principles and the facts of world history. It is also frustrating because many readers reject the "dull grey facts" in favor of an exciting, albeit false, story.

Of more interest are some of the many absolute and tangible ways archaeology enriches the lives of modern people. The easiest value to recognize is how archaeology satisfies our unquenchable thirst for knowledge of ourselves and our past. In fact, the mere concept of age or antiquity excites most people and seems to provide its own justification.

As simple, nonarchaeological examples of the universal interest in the past, one can cite such historical novels as *Ben Hur* and *Ivanhoe,* or even the exploits of the pirate hero Captain Blood. In all these stories, historical data and vigorous action combine to make stimulating adventure stories, all the more exciting because they lie in some more romantic time in the past. In the same simple, but more archaeological frame falls the allure of historic buildings, famous battlefields, or ancient mysterious ruins: the Newport Tower; Yorktown, Virginia; or the inscrutable Sphinx.

Mingling with the merely "ancient" concept is another element, which may be called romance or romanticism, that intensifies the appeal archaeology has today. At world-famous Pompeii, near Naples, Italy, the antiquity and romance have an added element of the macabre when one understands the cataclysmic horror of the Mount Vesuvius eruption that smothered an entire city beneath a blanket of ash.

The tragic story of Pompeii has been slowly learned and documented entirely through archaeological work. Millions of people have visited the buried city where excavation has gone on since 1748. The city was buried in A.D. 79 and had faded from memory through the centuries. It was rediscovered under many feet of mixed volcanic pebbles, and Italian government workers began to uncover it. Slowly the enormity of the tragedy was learned as room after room and street after street were explored. They found here the skeleton of a laundress, collapsed by her tubs, there the body of a mother clutching her infant. A surgeon lay by his instruments, and a dog died writhing in death throes from the sulfurous fumes. Scores of people dropped in the streets as they fled the city and were buried in the papilla (pebbles of lava) and ash. As the hot ash continued to fall, it filled many houses and finally covered the city entirely. Perfect molds were left in the dense ash as bodies decayed; archaeologists poured plaster into the molds to make casts of people, animals, and objects. The casts capture even the facial expressions of the dying Pompeiians. Often deserted old cities are a wilderness of crumbling ruins, reduced to rubble as the elements slowly level the abandoned buildings; not so Pompeii. Its glories, preserved in a disastrous instant, are unfaded.

Another romantic craving that archaeology totally fulfills is the call of distant lands. An ever-fresh example is the Mayan discoveries made before 1840 by John L. Stephens. His work, *Incidents of Travel in Yucatan* with its beautiful engravings of Mayan temples, pyramids, and stelae (sculptured vertical monuments of stone) done by Frederick Catherwood, was a superb travel and adventure story in its own right. But its long-lived popularity came from introducing Maya prehistory to the civilized world. The author visited over forty now-famous Mayan cities; with the artist he suffered malaria, bedbugs and more dangerous pests, revolutionary disorders, and the discomforts of mule train travel in the jungle. Their many adventures, told with humor, pathos, and charming candor, are fascinating for readers even today. But neither hardship nor danger blunted their keen desire to find and accurately record the wonders of the vanished Maya. Through the magic of his pen, Stephens blended mystery, romance, and beauty into a backdrop for archaeological findings. His work

is one of the highest expressions of the several ways archaeology has served the craving of the public for more and more information about the past and the excitement of exploring it.

An overwhelming claim that archaeology has upon the heart of humans is the call of sheer, timeless beauty—in form, color, symmetry, or exquisite detail—seen in the public buildings, temples, tombs, and smaller art objects created in the past as they are discovered and restored by the painstaking hands of archaeologists. The art galleries and museums of the world display evidence of human artistic genius from many different extinct cultures, ranging from the Paleolithic cave paintings and engravings of Europe to the cast gold jewelry of the Incas, the enameled pins and brooches worn by Athenian and Roman nobles, and the austere statues of Egypt.

It is true that the earliest discoverers of Greek, Roman, Egyptian, and American antiquities and other art objects were not archaeologists but vandals and grave robbers. They served the wealthy esthetes who valued beauty itself; the intrinsic beauty of the ancient objects was, in those days, an adequate justification for collecting them. Even today many collectors see the yearning for beauty as an adequate justification for buying loot from rifled sites, tombs, or temples.

But to some extent archaeology developed as a profession out of that search for ancient art. Today the trained archaeologist continues to value art objects and more humble handicrafts, but they first serve as documents aiding the understanding and interpretation of ancient cultures. Nonetheless they still provide new thrills for the world of art. A New World example familiar to many is the famous wall murals of Bonampak in Chiapas, which yielded information for further understanding of the Maya culture. In films, popular magazines, and museum exhibits these murals continue to give esthetic delight to all viewers. European sites, such as Lascaux or the Cave of the Bulls in Altamira, reveal the sophisticated work of the prehistoric

Magdalenian artists of 15,000 years ago, as they portrayed the extinct large animals that the Stone Age people pursued for food. Treasure troves of knowledge for the archaeologist, in their dazzling beauty and rich realism they stand among the great art galleries, once magnets for visitors from around the world. Today people cannot enter the caves because of deterioration of the murals resulting from the pollutants brought by visitors. The temples of Catal Hüyük in ancient Anatolia (Turkey), the sculptures and mosaics of Egypt from before the time of Christ, and the architecture of Toltec and Aztec ruins in Mexico or Mayan temples in Guatemala are also often considered as much art as archaeology.

On a less heroic scale, ceramic, stone, and metal working and the carving of wood, bone, and ivory are preserved in archaeological settings. Even household utensils and tools are valid examples of folk art, treasured for their functional integrity and clean lines. The black-on-white pottery of the American Southwest, the intricate gleaming jades of Mexico and China, the bronze pins and tools of Babylon, even the sleek barbed harpoons of the Mesolithic hunters of northern Europe are all authentic art to modern eyes.

Archaeology makes one of its great contributions by offering understanding of world history. Through archaeology the histories of European, Near Eastern, and Chinese civilizations are known. The time and place of many inventions that combined to move humans from a simple hunting and gathering level of life into what we call civilization have been learned, and could only have been learned, through archaeological research. One can get another insight by asking what is the value of a museum of art, a natural history museum, or even a straightforward anthropological museum? What esthetic, educational, or inspirational stimulus or satisfaction do these public service institutions provide around the world? The answer is easy if one tries to imagine the many bare shelves and empty cases there would be in one's favorite

museum if every archaeologically derived object were to vanish. What would be missing? The statuary of the Mediterranean civilizations; the gleaming jewelry of Ur and Babylon; the gold, jade, and onyx objects and the sculptures and ceramic treasures from Mexico and Peru; the priceless porcelains of China; and the crude stone artifacts that tell the story of the slow cultural growth of Paleolithic people—all would be gone.

On a more practical note, museums and their archaeological contents can even be assumed to have gross economic value, simply because modern urban countries do not spend money on completely useless items. The very existence of museums enjoying public or private support or both constitutes a pragmatic argument for the general value placed by society on museums and their contents, including archaeology. The over 600,000,000 annual visitors to American museums alone offer impressive evidence for this argument. The millions of dollars spent for admission by visitors to museums and national prehistoric parks and preserves bespeak the implicit values individuals place on vicarious personal experience with other times and peoples and their extinct cultures.

Trivial perhaps, but in the same vein I mention the entertainment aspect of archaeology: the dozens of TV documentaries, such as those on "Nova" and "Odyssey," about the prehistoric past of many lands that grip the imagination of millions.

In conservation there is a fusion of all the archaeological contributions that have been identified. As every literate person knows, we have lately become painfully aware of the finite nature of our environmental resources. Out of this awareness came attempts to preserve a habitat suitable for human beings. Among our nonrenewable resources are prehistoric and historic locations, as well as the unique natural wonders of the land. Because the National Register of Historic Places attempts to inventory nationally significant historic and prehistoric sites, archaeologists early became important, even key, figures in that aspect of environmental protection.

As mentioned earlier, archaeologists were much in evidence in the 1930s, the period during which William S. Webb established salvage archaeology as a government obligation whenever its construction projects jeopardized the traces of prehistoric peoples. The concept of salvage again prevailed after World War II when the Committee for Recovery of Archaeological Remains and the Society for American Archaeology, strongly endorsed by the United States National Park Service and less vigorously by the Smithsonian Institution, saw to it that archaeological data would be sampled before the giant lakes being created along 800 miles of the mainstream of the Missouri River were filled. By the time the Glen Canyon dam on the Colorado River was begun in the late 1950s, the overt recognition of the need to salvage some of the cultural record was so strong that money for the Glen Canyon salvage was a line item in the national budget. And today the conservation concept is even stronger in the CRM movement.

Without denigrating the secondary uses and real contributions made over the years by archaeology, or its self-imposed scientific goals, I am constrained to say that the conservation ethic may be the longest-lasting gift from archaeology to society. Or it may be that the overarching value of archaeology is intellectual—not so much educational as inspirational.

Systems, Ecology, and Paleoenvironment

In closing this chapter, it is necessary to discuss at some length three important and related ideas that have greatly influenced all archaeologists. They provide the direction, perhaps even the bias, of this book and its contents. The first concept is systems theory. The second is ecology, a concept that is compatible with, but more limited than, systems theory. The third concept is paleoenvironment, a time-tied idea that aids in explaining archaeologically observed human behavior from the past.

Systems Theory

Strictly speaking, systems theory in its pure form probably cannot be applied to archaeological data. Systems theory (cybernetics) is defined as any "intercommunicating network of attributes or entities comprising a complex whole," a definition useless on the face of it. What the definition means is that a system incorporates a multitude of parts or segments, and all the parts influence each other in most complex ways. Viewing human culture as a system one can identify such major subsystems as food procurement, family life, religion, language, the natural environment, and many others that function as parts of the whole but are also subject to an infinite number of influences from other subsystems. A major component of human cultures is the environment and the resources of that environment, such as flora, fauna, minerals, and the overall climate. Changes in the total habitat might require corollary changes in the behavior of the humans who had adapted to an earlier set of stable conditions. The model thus calls for a dynamic system in which change is continuous. The changes in the habitat and the adjustments to new conditions throughout the system may be small, but sometimes the changes are large and possibly traumatic.

Inherent in the system are regulatory mechanisms called *feedbacks*, which are either positive or negative. Together they provide for a quasi-stability called *homeostasis*—that is, flexible enough to accept changes but accepting them slowly so that the entire system does not break down in the face of extreme new forces that appear suddenly. That overall changes occur through time can apparently be taken as a given condition. That a system can absorb and direct the changes, and preserve the nearly harmonic balance of all the divisive or cohesive influences felt by all the subsystems of the functioning whole is the crux of systems theory.

Considering human behavior to constitute a dynamic system, processual theorists—that is, students of such cultural change as can be seen in archaeology—see systems theory as providing a key to learning the causes of culture change. So far the applications of systems theory to archaeological data are few, probably because of the difficulty of knowing what effects the changes in the external (input) factors or the consequent internal stress would have on the many interdependent subsystems.

In a very limited exercise in applying systems theory to archaeology, Flannery (1973) attacked a perennial question in archaeology: What caused the development or origin of agriculture? Usually the origin of agriculture is charged to either discovery or experimentation and is thought to result from demographic pressures. Flannery says it was neither. He looks to the symbiosis between humans as food collectors and the species harvested, and then seeks to see what changes occur over time in technology and in the plants collected. His data are from the valleys of Tehuacán and Oaxaca in Mexico where the transition (from 10,000 to 4000 B.P.) from food collecting to sedentary agriculture has been charted archaeologically. He selected the food procurement system as most likely to react to new detectable external forces. From the larger procurement subsystem he selected six of many sub-subsystems; each dealt with one resource. The ones chosen were the harvesting of maguey, cactus, beans from tree legumes, whitetail deer, cottontail rabbits, and wild grass seeds. All the vegetable resources (and Flannery carefully gives details omitted here) are highly seasonal, so their harvesting must be tightly scheduled both because of the

period of fruiting and the competition of birds and other species for the same fruits. Grass seed collecting was originally no more important than any of the other five. The major seed crop was a foxtail grass (*Setaria*); a minor element was a grass we now call *Zea maize*. Maize is thought to have undergone a series of minor genetic changes very early. The result was an increased seed production by the species. Consequently maize became more important as a food source. Evidently it was encouraged and even planted to increase the yield. Thus more attention to maize required more time and some changes in the scheduling required by tending it and reaping the harvest. Through time and with the continuous evolution of the maize toward its present form, maize became fully domesticated by 4000 B.P. Around it had evolved a sedentary horticultural subsistence economy; changes in settlement pattern, social organization, and other subsystems resulted.

The initial slight genetic changes in maize that made it a more useful grain provided a "kick"—a minor deviance in the system. The deviance, being beneficial in providing more food, led to positive feedback in the system. And as maize became more important through the millennia, there was continuous rescheduling of other procurement, with the sedentary horticultural way of life as a product of the continuous "kicks" from maize production.

The upshot of the analysis is the conclusion that agriculture in Mexico originated as neither an invention nor a discovery, but as a long, drawn-out process involving a series of minor changes in the maize plant *and* the procurement system, as maize became more valuable and required a more elaborate and time-consuming technology. Along with maize, beans (*Phaseolus vulgaris*) also underwent genetic changes and became a more desirable food, as did squash (*Cucurbita*). They also contributed to the systemic changes that led to the agricultural system; the resulting changes in all subsystems transformed a hunting-gathering society into one of farmers.

There is much more to Flannery's thesis, but the part summarized here adequately demonstrates that systems theory can be successfully applied to archaeological materials. It should be noted that in the Mexican case, ethnographic analogies provide models of the several procurement subsystems, which are still practiced in the same valleys as well as in the western United States. In addition to clarifying the origins of New World horticulture, Flannery was chosen as an example because he worked both with real archaeological data and observed behavior, whereas other authors have confined themselves to more theoretical aspects of the advantages archaeologists can gain from using a systemic bias in research.

Thomas (1972) has made a different use of the systemic approach. He took Steward's (1938) famous subsistence model of the lifeway of the Shoshonean speakers of the **Great Basin** as a proposition to be tested. Steward had described a multiple subsistence pattern for the peoples of the Great Basin. Key staples were, seasonally, piñon nuts (autumn) and seeds of plants (summer). Thomas reasoned that the location of the staples would dictate the location of the settlements and, therefore, the location of artifacts that comprise some of the archaeological data. He then produced a flowchart that represented all the stops in the annual round as the postulated small bands (about twenty-five persons) moved from one environmental microzone to another as the seasons dictated. He next created a computer simulation program that he expected to indicate where among the ecozones of the Reese River Valley in Nevada the archaeological debris would be found *if* the Steward ethnographic model were correct. Thus he treated the subsistence pattern as a system and the Steward model a hypothesis to be tested by archaeological search *after* the simulation (which took account of seasonal vagaries, poor piñon crops, low grass yields, or an abundance of both). Thomas ran through the yearly round 1000 times and predicted where the

base and temporary settlements should be located. Field search verified the accuracy of about 75 percent of the predictions, a figure Thomas accepted as validating the Steward model. Other scholars are using the flowchart and simulation in similar efforts to use systems theory in their research.

Whether any archaeological systems models will or can take account of more variables for finer-grained reconstructions is doubtful. In a very careful review of the value of systems theory for archaeology, Plog (1975) correctly concludes that "concepts drawn from general systems theory have been used by archaeologists in asking old . . . questions in new ways . . ." He goes on to show that the questions and their antecedent assumptions are more precisely recognized or stated as a result of viewing culture as a system. Moreover, even an awareness of systems alerts the archaeologist to the importance of evidence of variations in societal organization. And, as the Flannery example shows, systems concepts "have been used to reformulate classical archaeological problems in useful ways"; the value of the systems approach seems thus to lie somewhat in direct applications, but even more in diffuse effects that lead to greater rigor and precision in interpretation and, probably, in fieldwork.

Human Ecology

The word *ecology* has, since its coining in the nineteenth century, been easy to define but difficult to interpret precisely. Its careless use by environmentalists as well as the transfer of its central idea outside biology has further eroded its original imprecision. According to a leading theoretical ecologist, ecology is "the study of the structure and function of nature," a far from precise statement. More simply, ecology deals with the complex interrelationships of species with each other and the environment. Thus an ecological community is a system. There are stable species communities or associations in the topsoil, in a cup of pond water, beside a stream, or in a mountain valley; indeed the entire world can be seen as an ecological community. The communities where species coexist are usually called ecosystems; ecosystems can be any size, of course. The larger the system geographically, the more complex it is. When humans, whose behavior is culturally rather than biologically controlled, enter the ecosystem, the complexities of the system are multiplied because the human presence *always* effects some changes in the natural balance whether intentionally or not. So we can say that ecology is less a science than a pervasive point of view; it is primarily an intellectual stance.

The term *cultural ecology* exists primarily in the vocabulary of the cultural anthropologist. It is an obvious redundancy. Any ecological situation involving humans is cultural, since most human behavior stems from the cultural system in which the individuals function. Thus most convincing cultural ecological studies have been carried out by ethnologists in situations where actual human behavior, as well as environmental forces and their complex relationships, could be observed and tested. Working only with the debris of cultural behavior the archaeologist must supply many inferences that will, perforce, remain unproved but can to a degree reconstruct the ecosystem of an extinct social group.

One specific example of success in using archaeological data to unravel a small portion of a vanished ecosystem had to do with the beginnings of horticulture in the eastern and middle United States. It began in the 1930s when examination of coprolites (human feces) from dry caves revealed that the use of many wild plants (called weeds today) for food was common as early as 4000 B.P. As data accumulated it was clear that among many weeds four were usually present in human coprolites found in dry Archaic cave sites. These were sunflower (*Helianthus anuus*), sumpweed or marsh elder (*Ida*), maygrass (*Phalaris Carolinia*), and giant ragweed (*Ambrosia trifida*).

Goosefoot (*Chenopodium*) is often found as well. It was also noted that the seeds of sunflower and marsh elder were much larger than seeds from modern wild plants; that circumstance led to the conclusion that those two species were probably domesticated. The same seeds are recovered (often charred) in the fill of Archaic open sites.

Whether the plants were consciously managed (i.e., whether seeds were selected from plants with certain characteristics such as high yield or being slower to release or scatter seeds than others of the species) or the changes in morphology were accidental cannot be known. What is important is that human intervention modified a part of the natural environment to human advantage. There were, of course, attendant changes in human behavior that care of cultigens would enforce. One change might be some form of tillage—the plants being able to thrive only in disturbed soils where competing plants were absent. Tillage would be a new food-getting technique that must be scheduled for early spring. Harvesting might not require a new technique, but better tools, such as wooden or bone sickles. (No such tools are reported from the Eastern Archaic, but they are found in the West.) Better storage facilities for increased quantities of seeds would be necessary. Whether the horticultural techniques were merely added to the food-getting repertory of procedures, or whether some hunting or gathering procedures were abandoned is not important. We may be sure that some adjustments in the cultural system would result from the necessity of tending crops even minimally. (A more-sophisticated example of human ecology, the application of systems theory to harvesting techniques and subsistence scheduling, has already been discussed).

Paleoenvironment

Another aspect of the study of prehistoric human ecology is the need to know the environmental constraints of the past. Perhaps the quickest clue to past environments is found in the vegetation. To prosper vegetation requires a combination of moisture, temperature, soil, and elevation above sea level among other things. For all common plant species the combination of environmental attributes and their range of tolerance for less optimum conditions is today well known. Given the knowledge of plants and their preferred environments, preserved plant pollens in the soil offer direct testimony to the plant populations of the past and therefore to the environment. It has become almost routine for archaeologists to take soil samples at their digs, from both cultural and natural deposits, so that **palynologists** can extract and identify the pollens included in the soil. Pollen from the natural deposits provide spectra of earlier and later plant communities. Bogs and lake beds offer a record of long sequences of pollen rain, giving a relative chronology of change in vegetation. Often, organic materials are recovered with the pollen core. If the organic material can be radiocarbon dated, the dates and the pollen record together can also tell when the vegetation existed. Thus, the environmental changes that led to shifts in kinds or percentages of plants can be reconstructed fairly accurately. Without chronological control the pollen record still portrays environmental changes—varyingly gross or fine—but with a chronology they provide data crucial to learning the particular prehistoric environment and suggest changing adaptive strategies in any prehistoric cultural sequence.

But pollen is not the only source of such information. At some sites vegetal food fragments are preserved because of very dry or very wet storage conditions. The anerobic environment of a bog or swamp prevents bacterial attacks on organic material. Also plant scraps or even seeds are often preserved by charring and may, therefore, be recovered from either wet or unprotected sites. Like pollen grains, the seeds can be identified after recovery by flotation or fine screening. On the face of it, these macrofossils reinforce the pollen count. But more important to students of human behavior, they show what species were selected from those available for use either as food or for raw materials.

Since about 1970 a new tool has been developed for delineating environmental conditions of the past. It is plant opal phytolith analysis. As botanists and others have long known, plants take up groundwater that contains hydrated silica and distribute it throughout the plant. At any point where the plant loses moisture, such as the leaf stomata, the silica is precipitated in the form of amorphous opal. Phytoliths are thus more abundant in the leaves and epidermis of plants. Grasses especially have many phytoliths. They have characteristic forms that correspond to the cell shape where the opal accumulates. However, the shapes vary according to the part of the plant, so that a phytolith from the stalk would differ from one from the leaf.

Like pollen, the phytoliths remain in the soil after the plant dies. The procedures for recovering the microscopic opals is similar to that used for pollen. But unlike pollen, which is formed genetically and is species specific, phytoliths offer a wide array of form in any one plant. To complicate matters further, some shapes are redundant, occurring in several species. However, there is a general correspondence of phytolith form (probably from the leaves) throughout one genus.

Thus it is possible to identify a phytolith from a panic grass, which differs from a fescue. With knowledge of the dominant grasses in a given location, an informed guess can be made about overall conditions when it was growing. The ability to use phytoliths for species identification seems distant. Nonetheless, some archaeological applications of phytolith analysis have been made, particularly in the Old World. Most American uses have focused on climatic change based on the vegetational shifts observed in the phytoliths. In one case a radiocarbon date was derived from the minuscule amount of carbon in each phytolith. One hundred pounds of soil were processed to recover enough phytoliths for the assay! Even though use has been limited so far, phytolith analysis can be expected to see increasing application as ancillary corroborative evidence in paleoenvironmental studies.

Another similar avenue to paleoenvironment has already been touched upon: the analysis of coprolites that contain the residue of foods actually ingested by prehistoric peoples. Like pollen recovery, these analyses of diet are not new, having been resorted to by occasional scholars since about 1900. But as interest in paleoecology and past environments becomes a more noticeable trend, more and more coprolite studies are being made.

Perhaps the most spectacular application of microscopic analysis of prehistoric diets was made on collections from the caves of the Tehuacán Valley; the results of this study gave Flannery a baseline forager diet for his account of the origins of Mexican agriculture mentioned above. The following dominant foods were identified: charred pochote root (ceiba or kapok tree), maguey (century plant), foxtal grass, two cacti, sapote (a fruit), and mesquite beans. Although these plants were important in the diet from 7000 B.P. to 1500 A.D., there were changes in emphasis, with some (*e.g.*, pochote) losing popularity through time. That change may not be real; more likely it represents small sample size for some of the strata. In addition to the plants represented, hair from ten mammals (cottontail rabbit being the most abundant), bones of small mammals, and feathers were recovered.

Following the Tehuacán study others analyzed a large number of coprolites from western caves. From Danger Cave were identified a list of vegetable species, including seeds of pickleweed (a compositae), bulrush (*Scirpus*), cactus, and other desert plants and shrubs. Small rodent bones were also present. In addition there were internal parasites—thorny-headed worm, pinworm, and tapeworm—and two specimens of the head louse—an ectoparasite. The diet could have been predicted on the basis of vegetable chaff and fragments of plants, but the coprolite analysis substitutes knowledge of actual meals for reasonable inference. Moreover, the quite specific data on parasites lends a new dimension to knowledge about the population. But more was observed than mere diet and parasites. In each coprolite were found tiny flecks of charcoal and very fine grit. Thus through analogy with the food preparation practiced by indigenous Great Basin peoples, we can infer that the seeds were parched by swirling them with live coals in a basket, and that final preparation involved grinding the parched seeds on flat millstones. The seeds that survived in the feces were those not crushed in the grinding, as the hard epidermis resisted the gastric juices.

From Nevada comes the analysis of coprolites from Lovelock and other caves near Humboldt Sink. Seeds and plant parts of desert vegetation were present, but the dominant items were seeds and fibers from bulrush and cattail. Not expected were the bones of the Lahonton chub, a fish about 4 inches long (genus *Gila*). A year-round heavy reliance upon the shallow lake was therefore postulated. This notion was in contrast to the usual assumption that the Archaic foragers all moved continuously from one food resource to another. Thus from one study there came important new knowledge about the procurement systems of the hunter-gatherer lifeway of the Great Basin, because the basin has been and still is dotted with rich marshlands that were quite obviously heavily used by the Archaic population. Although there are many examples of the contributions made by coprolite study, the above examples should suffice.

Chapter 1
Bibliography

Ashmore, Wendy, and Robert J. Sharer

1988   Discovering Our Past: a brief introduction to archaeology. Mayfield. Mountain View, CA.

Brothwell, Don R., and Eric Higgs (editors)

1970   *Science in Archaeology: a comprehensive survey of progress and research.* Rev. ed. Praeger. New York.

Childe, V. Gordon

1956   *Piecing Together the Past: the interpretation of archaeological data.* Routledge & Kegan Paul. London.

Dean, Jeffrey S.

1978   *Tree-Ring Dating in Archaeology.* Miscellaneous Paper No. 24, University of Utah Anthropological Paper, No. 99, pp. 127–138. Salt Lake City.

Deetz, James

1967   *Invitation to Archaeology.* Natural History Press. Garden City, NY.

This short book is a simply written excursion into some basic concepts in archaeology.

Fagan, Brian M.

1982   *In the Beginning: an introduction to archaeology.* 4th ed. Little, Brown. New York.

This book, or any of the subsequent editions, is highly recommended. Fagan has carefully and expertly outlined the reason for doing archaeology and the many conceptual tools and theories available to the archaeologist and has included many thoughtful passages on such things as cultural resource management and related items.

Flannery, Kent V.

1973   The Origins of Agriculture. In *Annual Review of Anthropology,* Vol. 2, edited by Bernard Siegel, Alan R. Beals, and Stephen A. Tyler, pp. 271–310. Stanford University Press. Palo Alto, CA.

Hodder, Ian

1982   *The Present Past: an introduction to anthropology for archaeologists.* B. T. Batsford. London.

In this book, Hodder emphasizes the importance of analogy in archaeological interpretation.

Michels, J. W.

1973   *Dating Methods in Archaeology.* Seminar Press. New York.

Plog, Fred T.

1975   Systems Theory in Archaeological Research. In *Annual Review of Anthropology,* Vol. 4, edited by Bernard Siegel, Alan R. Beals, and Stephen A. Tyler, pp. 207–224. Stanford University Press. Palo Alto, CA.

Sharer, Robert J., and Wendy Ashmore

1987   *Archaeology: discovering our past.* Mayfield. Mountain View, CA.

This is the best field manual for archaeologists that I have encountered. It contains some of the material found in Fagan but much more detailed information and instruction on the techniques of fieldwork.

Steward, Julian H.

1938   Basin Plateau Aboriginal Sociopolitical Groups, Bulletin 120, Bureau of American Ethnology. Washington, D.C.

Thomas, David H.

1972   An Empirical Test for Steward's Model of Great Basin Settlement Patterns. *American Antiquity* 38(2): 155–176.

Willey, Gordon, and Philip Phillips

1958   *Method and Theory in American Archaeology.* University of Chicago Press. Chicago.

This book has had a tremendous influence on archaeological thinking and has provided a series of classificatory terms by which the present book has been organized. The introductory chapter in this book is particularly recommended.

Willey, Gordon, and Jeremy A. Sabloff

1980   *A History of American Archaeology.* 2d ed. W. H. Freeman. New York.

It seems to me entirely desirable, even necessary, that anyone beginning the study of American archaeology should be aware of the history of the discipline: the struggling, almost ignorant efforts of the first practitioners and the gradual accumulation of enough knowledge to derive order, system, and coherence from the prehistoric data. Scholars today may tend to think that what we know today has always been known. The Willey and Sabloff book makes it clear how slowly and painfully this knowledge was won.

Human Conquest of the New World

Some perspective on archaeology having been developed in Chapter One, the task of this and later chapters is to unravel from the beginning the remarkable story of the human conquest of the New World, a virgin land uninhabited by humans until the waning days of the Ice Age.

The Setting, the People, and Their Heritage

The first, unrecorded, but most important event in the story was the peopling of the American continents. The early migrants were *Homo sapiens*—modern humans—coming from northeastern Asia. Proper questions would be: What were the environmental circumstances facing the migrants in their American quest? What cultural arsenal—shelter, subsistence pattern, toolkit, and social organization—did they possess? What were the climate and the resources they exploited in Asia? Then as today the climate of northeastern Asia is the least hospitable on earth for humans (except for Antarctica). Indeed, no one had even attempted to conquer the frozen wastes of Siberia (northeastern Asia) until some 25,000–30,000 or more years ago when a few intrepid Northern Chinese made the first tentative thrusts into that rigorous and dangerous land. They were hunters of big game (including mammoth), built sturdy huts, and had invented tailored clothing, if we can judge by the eyed needles archaeologists find in the debris of their villages. We can also be sure that environmental hazards would have ensured that the population was tough, hardy, and resistant to disease. We must assume that having survived the Siberian environment the discoverers of the New World were equipped with the appropriate cultural baggage—winter shelter, adequate clothing, and a range of subsistence techniques—for survival in the rugged conditions of the American Arctic.

Humans having evolved in Africa perhaps two million years ago during the Pleistocene geologic epoch, or Ice Age, it is necessary to review that phenomenon. Present evidence is that vast ice sheets partially covered the northern areas of both North America and Eurasia several times during the Pleistocene period. The ice was more extensive in North America than anywhere else on the globe except at the South Pole. The glaciers formed (for reasons not yet fully understood) in northern latitudes and continued to grow and advance slowly southward for thousands and thousands of years. We know the most about the last major ice advance in America. Known as the Wisconsin advance, its several lobes and oscillations have been well sorted out. Less is known of the preceding Nebraskan, Kansan, and Illinoian advances because each sheet not only carried earth and stones as it expanded and flowed southward but also planed the surface ahead of it, erasing some of the traces of previous ice masses.

The ice sheets, estimated to have been a mile deep at maximum, locked up thousands of cubic miles of water, which lowered world ocean levels no less than 300 feet. Thus, at the time of full glacial extent, the amount of the exposed land area worldwide would have differed greatly from modern times, particularly where the wide, shallow continental shelves had been freed from seawater. Figure 2.1 shows the increase in the North American landmass that resulted from lowered sea level during the maximum extent of the second major Wisconsin glaciation. The 300-foot drop in sea level would create the broad land connection with Asia called **Beringia** because the maximum depth of the Bering Sea today is only 180 feet. Of course, even minor glacial expansion would lower sea level somewhat. Much less than a 300-foot drop in sea level would expose some of the land bridge. Another important fact is that central and northwestern Alaska were probably never covered by ice.

Knowledge of the recent history of the ice comes not only from the geological record but also from extensive modern observations on the complex dynamics of today's Greenland and Antarctic ice caps. Glacial ice is not a static inert mass; on the contrary, it is constantly in motion. It flows outward as more ice accumulates at the center and its weight melts the bottom ice. The meltwater lubricates the infinitely slow movement of the mass as the high central part flows toward the edges; thus the ice moves ever outward. Where the terrain is rough, the ice rivers follow valleys and canyons just as water would.

There were three ice centers in North America: (1) the Labrador, centered in eastern Canada; (2) the Laurentide (the largest), centered where Hudson Bay is now; and (3) the Cordilleran, which flowed out from the mountains of western Canada. At their maximum extent the leading edges or lobes of the ice extended to meet and fuse with ice from the other centers. Thus when the central Laurentide ice touched the Cordilleran mass on the west and the Labrador on the east, there was a vast sheet of ice from coast to coast and deep into the United States as far south as Cairo, Illinois. At times the Labrador sheet covered all of New England.

To speak of Asian immigrants peopling North America on foot through Alaska with such a barrier in place is ridiculous. Some have suggested that boats could have been used or that the travellers followed the beaches. But boats haven't appeared that early in the archaeological record, and the beaches, which probably existed along central Beringia, would not have been continuous along the fjord-gashed coast of western Canada and southern

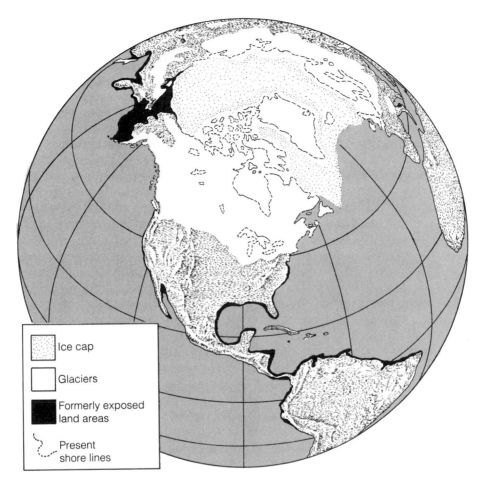

Ice cap

Glaciers

Formerly exposed
land areas

Present
shore lines

Figure 2.1 Extension of North American shorelines resulting from lowered seas during
the second major Wisconsin glaciation. Note land bridge across the Bering Strait
(Beringia).

Alaska. Those speculations are therefore rejected. Land entry is the more reasonable assumption. But the ice was not always there. As mentioned earlier, the ice sheets grew and melted in a rhythmic response to climatic factors still being debated. They retreated and even disappeared during warmer periods. As the ice masses shrank and their edges no longer touched, ice-free areas developed between the glaciers. Remember that as the ice melted, sea levels rose; during ice buildup sea levels dropped, and many shallow land masses were exposed, including parts of central Beringia or even all of it when the glaciers were largest.

Because all available evidence suggests that the immigrants were modern in physical type, the story of human entry into the Western

world is necessarily confined to the last half of the Wisconsin ice age, an episode that lasted only 60,000 years (some think even less). But we aren't certain of human population in northeastern Asia until well after the onset of the Wisconsin glaciation, so no reservoir of immigrants was available earlier anyway. To learn just when entry could have been made we must know the advance-retreat rhythms of the Wisconsin glaciers. Fortunately these are well understood, and their timing is well established. The time is set on the basis of many ^{14}C assays on buried logs and shells, as well as the painstaking correlation of many complex geological phenomena.

During the 60,000 years covered by the Wisconsin episode, there were four minor cycles of advance and retreat. Figure 2.2 shows

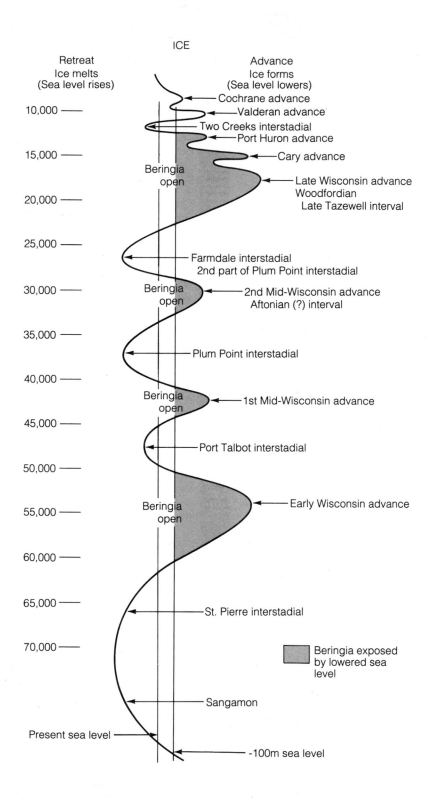

the cycles, both the advances when the ice covered the largest area and the retreats when the ice was partially or completely melted. The first advance began about 65,000 years ago, so that by 60,000 B.P. central Beringia lay exposed. Thus, eastern Siberia (western Beringia) was fused with Alaska (eastern Beringia). By 50,000 B.P. the ice began to melt, resubmerging possibly all of central Beringia. It was next briefly exposed between 45,000 B.P. and 40,000 B.P., and again for a longer time at 33,000 B.P. to 28,000 B.P. Finally it was open from 23,000 B.P. to 13,000 B.P., to be permanently submerged by or before 9,000 B.P.

With passage from Asia unhindered and easy for thousands of years during the past 60,000 years, the timing of the entry is established as one or more of the full or partial emergences of central Beringia. The earliest can be ruled out, because the human conquest of the Asian Arctic probably was not accomplished by 55,000 B.P. The period 40,000 B.P. presents a problem; the remains in extreme northeastern Asia (few, of course, are yet known) are not quite that old. On the other hand, Soviet arctic research is not yet extensive, and the full sequence may not be fully understood. Given present knowledge, however, the only possible time for an eastward movement of human population would be after 33,000 B.P. This timing fits the data because there is no American site reliably dated that far back. (There are several claims for earlier evidence of human presence, but all have been discounted for various appropriate reasons as will be noted later.)

For many years lack of information led archaeologists and geologists to believe that the Cordilleran and Laurentide ice sheets always overlapped for long periods at times of maximum advance. Thus Alaska would have been cut off, completely isolated from the lower United States by ice fields hundreds of miles

across and devoid of resources. Recent work has dispelled much of that thinking. It is now evident that the last major accumulations of ice (the last half of the Wisconsin episode) were not nearly as large as earlier ones. Moreover, Cordilleran ice advance was apparently not always, if ever, synchronous with the Laurentide; probably one advanced as the other retreated. Hence the two ice masses never touched during the last 25,000 years except possibly for 6000 years or less (between 20,000 and 14,000 B.P.) in northern British Columbia.

The movements of the western and eastern ice sheets during the Wisconsin has been likened to a giant zipper, closing from the north during advances and opening from the south during retreats. It is always possible, of course, that in the late Wisconsin the zipper never closed at all. One can therefore conclude that the path across Beringia and south to the Great Plains of the western United States was open to passage for about 80 percent or more of the time between 30,000 and 10,000 years ago. The probability of an open corridor from Alaska to the Great Plains changes the parameters for the study of the earliest Americans because it more than doubles the amount of time humans could have moved into the lower United States south of the ice fields. Until now, the supposed solid ice barrier was invoked to impose a 12,000-year maximum during which humans could have entered the United States (see Figure 2.3).

The geological data reviewed above is augmented by both palynological and paleontological findings. Both sets of information are scantier than might be desired, but both support the presence of an open corridor from Alaska to the United States during the late Wisconsin. The pollen record shows the northern part of the corridor (from the mouth of the Mackenzie River south to Great Bear Lake) to have been treeless, with the familiar dry steppe vegetation dominant. The condition for the lower Mackenzie Valley is described as steppe-tundra. There are fewer data

Figure 2.2 Ice advance-and-retreat rhythm during the Wisconsin stage of the Pleistocene, in years B.P.

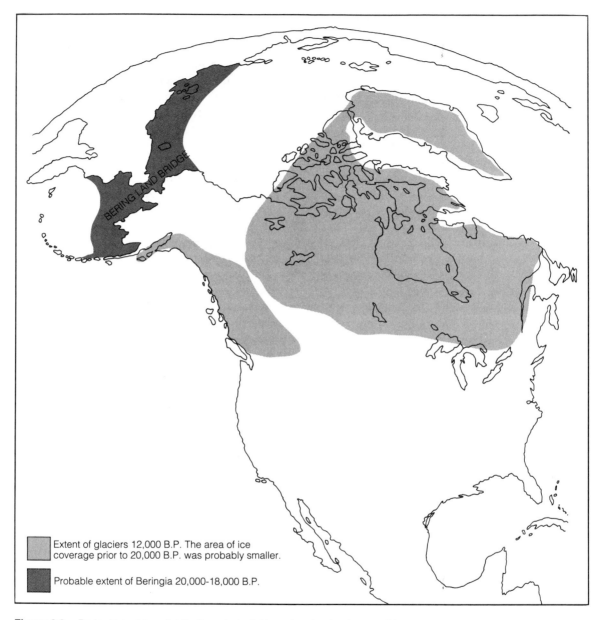

Figure 2.3   Beringia and the distribution of glacial ice, showing ice-free corridor.

for the southern segment (from Great Bear Lake to Great Slave Lake), but the conditions appear to have been similar, with perhaps more trees, especially spruce. The lower part of the southern segment is described as prairie or grasslands.

The paleontological faunal data come from only two locations, at each end of the corridor. One is Old Crow Basin in the extreme northwest corner of the Yukon Territory. Here mammoth, horse, bison, camel, and caribou had existed since mid-Wisconsin times or earlier. There are hundreds of specimens in fossil bone deposits all over the basin. The other evidence comes from the southern end of the corridor at Medicine Hat, Alberta. There, between two Laurentide glacial tills (approximately 17,000 B.P.), a deposit of mammoth, horse, camel, and dire wolf has been discovered. Such animals, of course, require a grassy habitat. Neither of those two faunal populations need be typical of the entire corridor. Both suggest that the faunal resources of the entire corridor would have been little different from those of Beringia.

Here three premises have been established that introduce the study of the adaptations of a human population to the New World and its varied environments: (1) The Native Americans were Asian in origin; (2) the entry might have occurred as early as 40,000 B.P., but later than 33,000 B.P. is more probably the correct figure; and (3) opportunity for human access to all the New World existed by that date.

Environment

The Asian migration to the New World has been presented above as if a crowd were merely waiting for central Beringia to emerge from the lowering waters to begin a casual stroll eastward. Such a picture is far from real. The climate of all of Beringia was arctic, but possibly more equable with smaller extremes of annual temperatures than now.

What environmental hazards would the (presumably) small band(s) of hunters have encountered as they moved east on the central Beringian bridge? What physical barriers were there? What were the food resources? The answer is that there was nothing new, all was familiar. The conditions across the new land of central Beringia were certainly the same as in northeastern Asia and central Alaska; evidently the climate and resources characterizing the entire vast area were essentially uniform.

The vegetation has been established as primarily a dry, cold steppe. Sedges, grasses, and *Artemisia* (sagebrush) were the dominant species, although patches of tundra (mosses and lichens) and clumps of dwarfed trees (birch and willow) were probably present. With central Alaska ice free over to the Mackenzie River Valley in the northwestern Yukon Territory, there would have been a continuous expanse of biotically rich terrain as much as 1000 miles wide and more than twice as long. The fauna was the same as in western Beringia: herds of herbivores, including mammoth, horse, bison, musk ox, and perhaps saiga (a giant antelope). The exploring bands were already familiar with the taking of such game.

The reconstruction above of the periods from 30,000 to 20,000 years ago of Beringian environment is based on evidence from the fossil bones of the extinct megafauna and the scores of pollen cores collected in both Russia and North America. Thus for Asians already adapted to the resources listed above and fully prepared to cope with the rigors of arctic weather, there was no hindrance to their slow expansion east and south. Why the people made their way to the unknown lands of the New World is, of course, unknown. They may have been the vanguard of an expanding population; they may only have been following game; or they may actually have been adventurous explorers meeting the challenge of the unknowns ahead of them.

What did the immigrants encounter south of the ice? We already know the Beringian environment; the next question is what were conditions to the south of the ice during the Late Pleistocene? West of the Mississippi Valley the environment was not greatly different from today's, although at the glacier edges there would still have been mixed steppe-tundra or forest (see Figure 2.4). As we have seen, vegetation is the clue to animal species and vice versa. As Figure 2.4 shows, the succession of continental biologic zones was the same 15,000 to 10,000 years ago as today; they were, however, much compressed because of the ice sheets. In the critical millennia

(a)

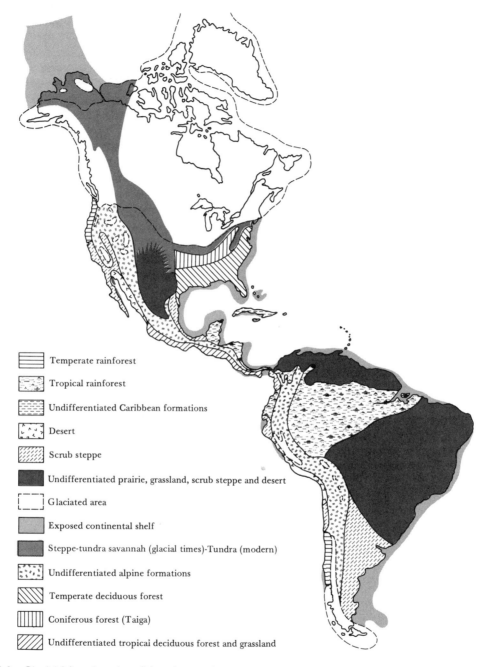

Temperate rainforest

Tropical rainforest

Undifferentiated Caribbean formations

Desert

Scrub steppe

Undifferentiated prairie, grassland, scrub steppe and desert

Glaciated area

Exposed continental shelf

Steppe-tundra savannah (glacial times)-Tundra (modern)

Undifferentiated alpine formations

Temperate deciduous forest

Coniferous forest (Taiga)

Undifferentiated tropical deciduous forest and grassland

Figure 2.4 Glacial (a) and modern (b) environments.

(b)

0   1000

Miles

between 20,000 and 10,000 years ago when the ice reached its final maximum, the high western plains were not a sea of grass but an even richer savannah, a grassland studded with clumps of trees. We can safely assume that prairie existed at the southern end of the migration corridor by 12,500 B.P. or earlier and the megafauna to be harvested were the familiar mammoth (found from Siberia to South America), horse, camel, and bison. Although species were different, the hunting techniques of the Arctic could probably have been readily adapted to the new species, which were initially unacquainted with the human predators.

The entire southern third of the continent was well watered. Springs, streams, and lakes were abundant. For example, studies of the high **Llano Estacado** of West Texas show that the flora were more heavily conifer (spruce and pine) during the Tahoka **pluvial**, which was a period of markedly cooler and moister climate from about 23,000 to 16,000 B.P. Fossil lakes (recognizable today as dry **playas**) and stream courses (now dry) testify to a well-watered land. In central and eastern Texas, what is now grassland is described as having been an open woodland deciduous forest with an understory of grasses, herbs, and shrubs until about 16,000 B.P. At the same time, between the pine and spruce forests of the Llano Estacado and mixed woodlands of East Texas there lay a broad belt of juniper and piñon parkland. Thereafter, many arboreal species disappeared; woodlands became parklands. By 6000 B.P. or earlier the treeless plains of today had come into being over most of Texas.

Nothing has yet been said about the country east of the Mississippi River and what it was like south of the Canadian ice. The contrasts there between today and 20,000–12,000 B.P. were far more extreme than in the West. At the greatest extent of the ice there were no Great Lakes, no New England, and no Long Island. The area was ice covered. The Blue Ridge Mountains of Appalachia were covered with **tundra,** and caribou fed in the Shenandoah Valley. In the same valley, owl roost pellets contained bones of such sub-arctic creatures as the arctic shrew, the pine marten, and the arctic hare. At the Saltville, Virginia, bone bed, dated at 13,400 B.P., there were caribou, moose, bison, musk oxen, mammoth, and mastodon; the most numerous bones were of mastodon.

When the last retreat of the ice began, it progressed rapidly. By 10,500 B.P. Labrador was free of ice. Spruce trees were gone from the Virginia hills, and the forests of modern times were taking shape. There were still now-extinct mastodon, musk ox, and giant elk in the Middle West and East, but most of the eastern fauna, especially that sought by humans, were modern species.

Thus environmental changes after 12,000 B.P. were rapid, even extreme. The changes in climate were reasonably correlated with withdrawal and final disappearance of the continental ice, except for the central Canadian glaciers and the Greenland ice sheet. A northward shift of the west-to-east cyclonic belt and jet stream created a warming trend. Vegetation followed the ice edge as ground and air temperature rose; precipitation generally decreased.

Extinction

Mention of megafauna always raises the question of extinction. Why are there no megafauna left? This reasonable query remains unanswered, but it has been the subject of much speculation. One favorite commonsense explanation is that changing climates and vegetation altered the regional ecology so greatly that the habitat no longer favored several species. Reduction or disappearance of the late Wisconsin precipitation would have rapidly reduced the amount of coarse grasses and reeds available for the bands of Pleistocene elephant (mammoth). That species could not adapt to a plains or desert ecobase; evidently the elephant population dwindled and disappeared in the West by about 11,200 B.P. The long-horned bison held on longer, but they, too, were gone by about 9500–9000 years B.P.

Another explanation is again a biological one. In the face of the postulated worsening climate and resultant increased stress the elephants may have dropped below the critical biological mass. In this view a deteriorating environment would ensure the disappearance of the species at a very rapid rate because it would lead to a minus birth rate. Disease has also been invoked as a cause. But the perennial favorite is that the human hunter, history's most efficient predator, administered the coup de grace in a phenomenon called overkill. This means merely that regardless of environment the kill rate exceeded the regenerative capacity of the species. If all or some of the other causes cited above were operative, the overkill toll exerted could well have been the final push to extinction.

All the theories of extinction, including overkill, have been debated for a century, but none are argued very convincingly. All the explanations overlook the well-documented fact that the end of the Pleistocene was marked by extinctions all over the world. Many species simply died out. Horses and camels in North America are good examples. One can get caught up in speculation on the matter, and there is no real evidence. But we have documented a drastic climate change; to this we only need add the presence of human bands, and the fact of rapid extinction. What follows—and this is what interests students of human history—are the culture changes that followed the climate changes and the loss of the big herd animals. For students of human behavior the reasons for the loss of species is to some extent a side issue. Of course if human hunters did apply the finishing touch to elephant extinction, it is probably the first in a long list of species extinctions that can be attributed to human predation. For the moment, however, the interest lies in the cultural adaptations necessitated by the disappearance of the mammoth and associated species.

The evidence is that elephant extinction was rapid, with long-horned bison (*Bison antiquus*) disappearing next. All the other species cited in the preceding paragraphs seem to have disappeared at about the same time or a little later than *Bison antiquus*. After about 8000 B.P. the megafauna of the West consisted of a somewhat smaller bison (*Bison occidentalis*) and modern species, including pronghorn antelope, elk, deer, and mountain sheep and goats. (The smaller modern bison (*Bison bison*) appeared much later.) In the East deer and elk were dominant. Because of different group behavior in the modern species human hunters had to develop new procurement techniques.

The preceding paragraphs are concerned entirely with the **Great Plains** and the eastern woodlands. However, a series of entirely different events characterizes the third of the continent west of the Rocky Mountains. The largest environmental province in the West is the Basin and Range Province. There the evidence of an early moist regime is indisputable and widespread. Prior to 14,000 B.P. the entire West was evidently characterized by large lakes and swampy areas formed by the lack of external drainage in the Great Basin. The overall vegetable resources, however, were the same 12,000 or 14,000 years B.P. as they are today; the vegetation was merely denser. The same can be said for the biotic environment, which can be generalized as a dry steppe; the dominant vegetation was sagebrush (*Artemisia*) with juniper and piñon communities on the many short north-south mountain ranges. Above the juniper and piñon forests were stands of spruce, fir, and pine. The entire region, however, was then much richer in subsistence resources because of the vast lakes and attendant aquatic vegetation, animal life, and water fowl. By 12,000 B.P. the megafauna harvested by the hunters were evidently the modern species known today. Although mammoth, horse, and camel fossils are found, no association with human activities has yet been demonstrated. Thus, over most of the West (as exemplified in the Great Basin) there existed the anomaly of a semidesert studded with rich and concentrated subsistence resources. (This is less characteristic of the eastern Plains.) As will be apparent in later chapters, this desert environment had important implications for the cultural history of the area where human adaptation to a series of specialized econiches was quite different from elsewhere in North America. The evidence is, however, that the Great Basin and the rest of the continent were occupied by humans after 11,000–10,000 B.P.

In summary, the population of the Americas is believed to have been derived entirely from Asia because: (1) there was there a slowly expanding population of *Homo sapiens;* (2) there was not the slightest physical barrier to the migration; and (3) the resources and climate of North America and Asia were identical at the point of juncture, imposing no problem of adaptation or cultural adjustment for the migrants. The migration is not thought to have been a steady flow of people. Nor is it reasonable to postulate numerous surges in the earliest stages of the process. As will be shown, there is some evidence for two or three population increments over a 5000- or 6000-year period. Probably only a few hundred individuals first crossed the Beringian bridge and slowly began to drift south and east around the edges of the ice. Their descendants, and any who followed, were cut off from return in a few millennia by the narrowing and final disappearance of the bridge, as the glaciers wasted away and the sea recaptured the exposed land. No informed scholar doubts today that humans reached the Americas from Siberia by the means and at the time outlined here. It is interesting that the Native American's Asian origins were recognized in 1589 on the basis of perfectly sound empirical evidence by Joseph de Acosta, a Jesuit missionary to the New World. All students who have examined the evidence, usually without knowledge of Acosta's work, arrive at the same conclusion.

Other Explanations of Human Presence in North America

Although the simple explanation above satisfies most of today's students on logical grounds, there are other views of the origin of Native Americans. The hardiest and longest-lived view has been the theory that the Native American was descended from the lost tribes of Israel. Many have embraced this idea; William Penn and Increase and Cotton Mather believed in the Israelite origin. One of its best-known proponents was James Adair, whose famous book about the Southeastern Indians (first released in 1775) was widely read. A literate Indian trader with headquarters in Savannah, Adair seized upon chance linguistic resemblances as evidence of Israelite origin. Linguistic evidence is indeed of tremendous importance in establishing cultural relationships, but to be accepted it must rest on clear similarity in syntax, grammar, word lists, and recognizable and preserved phonemic (sound) patterns. The objection to the evidence presented by Adair and others is not to the use of linguistics itself but to the citing of coincidental similarities in phonetics or meaning instead of structural similarities. Furthermore, this theory has since been negated because intensive scientific study has revealed no linguistic evidence of early Hebrew contact anywhere in the Americas. Moreover, no fruits, domestic animals, crops, artifacts, or cultural practices resembling those of the Near East have ever been observed in either of the Americas until after 1500 A.D. Complete lack of tangible evidence—such as the wheel, Old World grains, or domestic animals—makes the theory untenable, to say nothing of the commonsense problem of how a group of herders and gardeners with no recorded skills in seamanship could have voyaged to the Americas all the way from the dry hills east of the Mediterranean.

Similar claims that the Welsh, the Vikings, or the Phoenicians settled the West are based both on chance linguistic similarities and on legendary (as well as documented) later voyages of sailors from these countries. All these theories are equally groundless and arose before the development of scientific linguistics and long before anyone was aware of the length of time the Western Hemisphere has been inhabited. However, it is perfectly true that Norse sailors visited the Americas around 1000 A.D. They may even have influenced the cultures of the Northeast Coast Indian tribes, but we can be sure that the first American was not a stranded Scandinavian sailor.

Equally without foundation and verging upon the ridiculous are the hardy myths about lost continents such as Atlantis and Mu. The absurdity of the matter is manifest when Plato is identified as the inventor of Atlantis, a land "beyond." The legend has remained viable throughout the centuries and was given new life through a mystic cult that developed in the late nineteenth century. The myth is still with us, but no durable proof has ever been offered, despite hundreds of books on the subject. There is no geological, archaeological, or linguistic evidence to support the existence of the fabled Atlantis in the New World. Today Atlantis is generally believed to have been Crete, whose geological history and extinct Minoan civilization fit the legend very closely. Mu is a recently "invented" land; it may be taken even less seriously, if possible, than Atlantis.

Physical Anthropology of the Native American

Although the Asiatic origin of the Native American population is readily and widely accepted, there remain questions about the origin of the American Indian physical type. The once common classification of the several morphologically separable populations of the world into races is now regarded as an unrewarding exercise. Physical anthropologists now tend to speak of human variation and to explain it on adaptive, evolutionary grounds; they make no effort to describe races or varieties within races. Nevertheless, populations do differ in appearance. On typological grounds, the modern Native American population is regarded as quite distinct from other major world populations, with its closest phenotypic (physical) resemblances to the Mongoloid populations of Asia. Depending on whether one is concerned with the hemisphere as a whole or with detailed morphology of a tribe or a district, the Indian can be called either a homogeneous or a heterogeneous population.

But was the early American population so different from the Asiatic reservoir of *Homo sapiens* as it is now? Obviously not; once they were the same. What can be said about the appearance of the first Asians to migrate to North America? Almost nothing convincing or empirical can be offered. Some believe that the extreme variation in human form that led to the early recognition and description of varieties or races is a recent evolutionary phenomenon, possibly no earlier than 20,000 B.P. Other students of human variation argue that populations began differentiating 50,000 or more years ago. In any case, well-controlled ancient American skeletal finds are so few that there is essentially no evidence about the original **phenotype.** Moreover, the physical type of the ancestors of the Native American is a topic that seems to have no particular interest for students in recent years. The likelihood of abundant empirical data, such as actual skeletal material, is so slight that the entire matter may remain forever a matter of little concern, merely a question for speculation. The current lack of interest may stem from about 1950 when the emphasis of physical anthropological studies shifted toward human biology, variation as an adaptive evolutionary process, and genetics. In any case, we are left with theory and speculation.

The theories of original type deal with two questions. Where did the Native American stock evolve? What were the physical attributes of the parent stock or stocks? It must first be noted that physical anthropologists now tend to agree that the Native American evolved in place; at least there appears to be agreement about the homogeneity of that population. There is still debate about whether evolution was from a single stock or from the mixture of two or more slightly divergent populations after several modern physical types began to evolve.

Whether the theorist favors a polyhybrid origin or a single genetic stock usually depends on his or her conception of the nature of the migration. If the introduction of people is visualized as a frequent succession of waves or dribbles over many centuries, the notion of polyorigin seems the most plausible. But, if a small original population in a few closely spaced increments formed the seed stock, a single genetic reservoir seems more likely. Of course if the single seed stock were hybrid, the poly- or dihybrid view would remain valid. Informed opinion today favors one or two small groups as comprising the original, or founder, populations. From that founder gene pool the Native American physical type was created and stabilized. The Eskimo and Aleut, of course, constitute a separate wave of migrants who entered Alaska 5000 or fewer years ago. Their Asiatic origin has never been in doubt.

Whatever the genetic attributes of the parent stock may have been, the subsequent development must be understood as having taken place in a situation uniquely American. The human species was not numerous anywhere on earth then, but neither human nor subhuman forms existed in the Americas, and as a result there was no competitive human population. There was simply endless land filled with natural riches to be conquered by the tiny, arctic-hardened population of more-than-average toughness and viability. Culturally they were equipped with a knowledge of flint chipping; of making tools of wood, bone, and ivory; and of making skin-clothing. They probably sought big game and at the outset faced no adaptive problems as far as natural environment was concerned. From the Arctic port of entry, there lay ahead to the east and south increasingly varied environmental zones, more temperate climes, and varied resource complexes. As the original migrants roamed, expanded, and dispersed over the new land, the population remained thin. Phenotypic differentiation would have occurred in response to varied environments, and at the same time genotypic differences would have appeared in response to isolation, mutation, and genetic drift.

All the evidence supports the view that the early Americans and Asians shared genetic attributes. The teeth offer particularly strong evidence. Asian teeth differ in several ways from those of Europeans, and Native American teeth show the Asian traits. While there are a dozen or more distinctive details, there are five very obvious differences. First of these is the shovel-shaped incisor, which means that the back of the upper incisors (front teeth) are deeply troughed or scooped out and resemble a small shovel or scoop. In Europeans the lower second molar usually has two roots, but the Asian and Native American molars commonly have three. A similar difference is seen in the first lower molar, which has one root among Asians and Native Americans and two among Europeans. And the lower molars of North and South American and Asian natives have six cusps (or eminences for grinding), but four cusps characterize the European grinding teeth.

Whatever the evolutionary sources of the form of the teeth may have been, they are very stable. The five characteristics are consistently (but not universally) present in Native Americans. That cluster of **traits** has been called Sinodonty, a series of linked traits found only in East Asian and American native populations. The Eskimo and Aleut and the NaDene (the Indians of western Canada and the Navajo and Apache tribes), who first populated the Northwest coast and Western Alaska, share additional dental traits, including the single-rooted upper first premolar where the rest of the world has the two-rooted form.

On the basis of the distribution of the Sinodonty cluster of tooth traits it is argued that the basic complex first appeared in central Siberia in the Lena River Basin less than 40,000 years ago and that that population comprised the PaleoIndians who in turn were ancestors of today's Native Americans. The NaDene anomalies originated further east some time after 12,000–14,000 B.P., with the Eskimo and Aleut the most recent arrivals from the Amur River Basin, well east of Lake Baikal. Thus the teeth suggest a first migration, then a second one that brought the NaDene from the Amur Basin as early as 10,000 or more years ago, and finally an Eskimo-Aleut wave. Some students think the NaDene and Eskimo-Aleut arrivals were almost simultaneous, but the two waves suggested here conform to generally accepted ideas based on other data. The tooth studies provide strong evidence both for the Asian origins of the American natives and for the stability of genetic dental traits.

While the evidence from teeth is convincing, there are other lines of physical-genetic proofs of Asian origin. For example, in one recent study of several large collections of prehistoric skeletal material from nine Eskimo, one Aleut, and nine Native American populations, the frequency and association of twenty-four discrete cranial traits were compared. The comparisons were made by several statistics that express the morphological (in this case, cranial morphology) nearness or distance (similarity or dissimilarity) of all the populations to each other. The distances (differences) between the nineteen collections

studied were remarkably small. Accompanying the skeletal study above was a distance-nearness study of eight blood group systems and three serum protein systems from forty-five separate Eskimo, Asian Mongoloid, Chukchi, and Native American tribes. Some of the samples were large. The results fully supported the conclusions of skeletal study; in fact, the genetic distances shown were even smaller. Given such statistical nearness in the groups, the question of Asian origins is hardly worth further debate.

Although Asian origins are certain, the actual physical appearance of the members of the founder population is still a mystery. One hopes that further field research, particularly in Northeast Asia, will uncover human skeletal remains about 20,000 years old under good provenience control. Such a find would give the first reliable evidence of the probable physical appearance of the earliest Americans, and, conceivably, stem the floods of speculative prose the problem has generated. At present, however, the physical appearance of the first arrivals cannot be described. The few supposedly ancient skulls that have been found will be reviewed later in the chapter.

Many scholars have emphasized the essential homogeneity of the modern Native American that is due to the small gene input and the rigorous filtering effect of arctic conditions, and the sixteen million square miles of territory lacking human occupancy. The Native Americans at the time of first European contact were highly susceptible to measles, smallpox, and the common cold. This is cited as evidence of long isolation from the rest of *Homo sapiens*. The population is described as of stocky rather than gracile build (in both sexes) regardless of overall stature, which may be either short or tall. The extent of skin pigmentation is less than seen in the Old World, but the ability to tan is exceptionally high. The eyes are dark, the hair is coarse and straight, and body hair is scant in both sexes. Females often have the Mongoloid fold of skin over the eyes; incisor teeth are distinctive in the frequency of the shovel shape. Blood types A2, B, B Du, and r are lacking. The sickle-cell anomaly is not found. The Native American male is rarely bald, and the hair rarely becomes gray in old age.

Paleopathology

Interest in Native American paleopathologies has attracted several students in recent years. It is the study of diseases and injuries in prehistoric teeth, skeletons, and mummified remains. A couple of examples will suffice. One study of Plains sites lists healed fractures; periostitis, particularly of the lower leg (tibia); fusion of two or more bones; and osteoarthritis of the lumbar vertebrae and other bones. One sample showed that 50 percent of the skeletons had healed fractures; it has been suggested that the high proportion of trauma may indicate warfare.

A detailed study of a Fremont population from Utah showed that 50 percent of a large sample suffered from diseases, infectious and otherwise, that affect the bony structure, including dental caries, osteoarthritis, rheumatoid arthritis, osteoitis, trauma (fractures), osteoporosis, and ankylosis (hunchback phenomenon). Some of the diseases relate to diet and environment, as some appear to correlate with sedentary life and a greater reliance on vegetable foods. Certainly, the Parowan Fremont sample showed more dental and vertebral pathologies than the less-sedentary Salt Lake Fremont portion of the sample. (For more about diet-related pathologies, see Chapter Five.) Other studies have shown that as early as 8000 years ago, the archaic people of the eastern Great Basin were suffering from pinworm and thorny-headed worm, as well as body lice and, possibly, the liver fluke. The thorny-headed worm could prove fatal, as could the fluke.

In summary, we should remember that the presence of a unique human population in the Americas is a basic assumption. That this homogeneous population derived from an Asiatic population in the past 10,000 to 30,000 years is viewed as established; the "setting" of the genotype in isolation in North and South America is also seen as likely. However, it also seems reasonable that when and if skeletal specimens of the earliest population are discovered, they will not closely resemble the modern Indian. More likely the physical type will be of a type associated with the late Paleolithic stages of the Eurasian cultures.

Early Human Remains

If any portion of the above material on origins is true, there should be proof scattered over the two Americas in the form of preserved ancient human skeletons. Many claims of antiquity are made for many finds, but most such claims have not survived rigorous review. Some have proved to be quite humorous mistakes. Nebraska Man, for example, was announced on the basis of a tooth, which was soon identified as being from an extinct peccary!

Students vary greatly in their credulity, and there is perhaps no universally acceptable list of early finds. Among the early finds, some accept the human pelvis found near Natchez, Mississippi, associated with extinct fauna; Minnesota Man; the Torrington, Wyoming, finds; Browns Valley Man and Sauk Valley Man (both in Minnesota); Tepexpan Man (from Mexico); and the Midland, Texas, find. Acceptance of most of those specimens as early is based largely on the unwarranted assumption that **dolichocephaly** (longheadedness) and some primitive features of cranial morphology argue antiquity. Others, relying entirely on form, would accept an even longer list. All the finds cited above (and a long list from South America) were made, evaluated, and became varyingly controversial before any of the genetic studies cited above were done.

Today archaeologists are reluctant to accept most of these finds. In some cases the finds were made by people untrained in observation, and one cannot be sure of the context. In others a complete lack of either artifacts or extinct fauna precludes adducing even ancillary cultural evidence of age; in still others fluorine or other chemical tests are inconclusive. It seems by far the better part of valor to reject both those finds accepted on morphologic grounds only and those finds where the circumstances of discovery are uncertain or the technical observations inadequate. This leaves only the Natchez pelvis, which has been lost, and the Midland find in the continental United States. From Mexico, Tepexpan Man, a find widely questioned on the basis of poor field procedures, was later largely validated by a second study. The scarcity of human skeletal remains in the Americas may result from the accidents of discovery—the territory is large—or from the practice of cremation, which may be a very old one.

Midland Man

Frustrated by the failure of find after find to satisfy the rigors of scientific review, American scholars have turned with more confidence to the Scharbauer or Midland site in Texas, where what is now the most credible American skull was recovered. Confidence in the find does not stem from the clean-cut circumstances of the discovery. It rests, rather, on the exhaustive, dogged study of a very complicated situation made by a group of scholars searching every possible avenue for certainty of provenience. The Midland study has been called a model of working collaboration between scientists. Even more important, there would be no Midland Man

if it had not been for the alertness and good sense of an amateur, Keith Glasscock, who made the original discovery and called in the trained scientists.

The study was triggered by Glasscock's search for flint tools in a "blowout" in a cluster of sand dunes near Midland. Blowouts, which are common in the western Plains, are areas where the surface soils and successive lower strata are blown away until a resistant stratum is reached. They vary from a few yards to several miles in area. Many were formed in the western Plains states during the terrible dustbowl of the 1930s; continued drought and other factors caused vegetation to disappear so the wind could begin its plucking action. One feature of deflation, as this process is called, is that heavy objects in the area—stones, bones, artifacts, beer bottles, or old truck tires—do not blow away but settle down as the earth is blown from around and beneath them. When deflation finally ceases, the blowout floor is covered with all the objects that had originally been above it. All provenience control is therefore lost. The objects are all now merely surface finds; a beer bottle could be lying beside a mammoth tusk, or an iron wagon tire might encircle a rusty spur. Hence, even though blowouts often yield prehistoric material, they do not provide reliable clues about age or original association.

In the deflated zone Glasscock found a crumbling human skull lying partially exposed, apparently weathering out of a bed of gray sand. The blowout was one of several in the dunes. All had little islands and hummocks scattered over their floors. From these little knolls a series of geological events was deduced, but fitting the evidence together was a complex and tedious labor. Locality 1, where the skull was found, was cut quite deeply into resistant strata. Here the deflating process had removed two layers of sand to expose an ancient lake or streambed. The upper sands, already quite extensively studied by geologists, were first the Monahans, a loose, orange-gray sand that forms dunes readily, and next the rusty-red Judkins, which is more compact and resistant to erosion. Visible in some areas under the red component of the Judkins was a calcareous gray sand and, beneath this, an earlier calcareous white sand. The gray and white sands are either **lacustrine** or riverine deposits. The human skull, heavily mineralized, came from the gray sand, but there was no evidence that it had been intentionally buried.

To establish an associational context for the human bones, extensive excavation and field study were followed by a variety of laboratory tests. Before the work was finally done, the list of collaborators included (aside from the several archaeologists) paleontologists, photographers, chemists, physicists, geologists, a botanist, physical anthropologists, and a palynologist. The completed studies revealed that the gray sand, the layer that had contained the skull, was older than a Folsom complex found in the upper Judkins sands.

The complex correlations involved need not concern us here, but the result of the study was that the Midland skull was found to be more than 10,000, and possibly as much as 20,000, years old. Radiocarbon, fluorine, and uranium-daughter tests support the range of dates, as do the extinct mammal remains and other associations. The important thing to consider now is the skull. Entirely modern in form, Midland "Man" was a female about thirty years old. The skull is quite dolichocephalic and in other ways approximates the predicted morphology of the early population (Figure 2.5). There is nothing remindful of the generalized Native American pattern described earlier.

Tepexpan Man

One other skeletal find in the Americas is generally accepted as ancient. This is the Tepexpan find near Mexico City. There, after an elaborate experiment in the use of electromagnetic resistivity equipment to lo-

cate subsurface phenomena, excavation crews found a human skeleton. The explanation of its provenience is a masterpiece of vague reporting. It has been pointed out that the circumstances of the finding are so clouded one can never be sure whether the burial intruded into the late Pleistocene sediment where it was found, or whether it was included as the sediment was deposited. The issue is further confused by the fact that the individual, according to the physical anthropologists, does not differ morphologically from recent or even modern Indians. It has been opined that the Tepexpan skeleton is correctly assigned a terminal Pleistocene date (thus it is not intrusive) and may be 10,000 or more years old. Many accept this judgment and regard the specimen as evidence that the Native American had reached an essential homogeneity by that time. I hold that the issue remains in doubt.

In southeast Washington, near the mouth of the Palouse River, an interesting if enigmatic find is Marmes Man, recovered during emergency work before the flooding of a new reservoir. Two preliminary reports are tantalizingly cryptic. A thin artifact-bearing stratum was encountered in valley sediments. The stratum was beneath a layer yielding a radiocarbon date of 10,700 to 11,000 B.P., a date derived from shell. Fragments of three human skulls, all from young individuals, were recovered (Figure 2.6). On the basis of geological data, their age is estimated to fall between 13,000 and 11,000 B.P.

The three human skulls represented by the fragments have not yet been reported in detail. The preliminary statement, however, implies that there is nothing archaic in their morphology. I am inclined to doubt the age ascribed to the specimens on several counts: (1) The associated artifacts, especially the stemmed Lind Coulee point, are dated at the type site at 8700 B.P.; (2) the radiocarbon assay at Marmes was derived from shell, less likely to be accurate than a charcoal-derived assay; (3) the associated fauna was a large but apparently modern specimen of elk; and (4) the

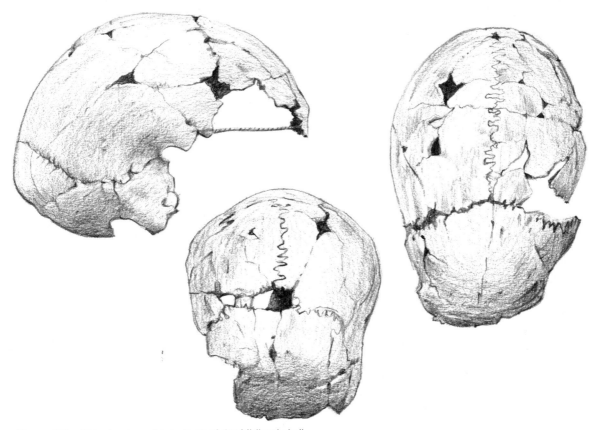

Figure 2.5 Side, back, and top views of the Midland skull.

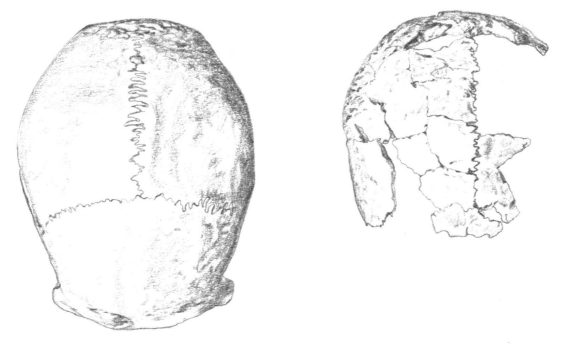

Figure 2.6 Marmes skull fragment.

delicate, eyed needle recovered is almost identical with two specimens from Hogup Cave dated at 6400 B.P. I do not challenge the validity of the Marmes find, only the imputed time range of 11,000 to 13,000 B.P. No other claims require review.

The Toolkit

Even more vexing than the problem of physical type is the question of the toolkit and overall technology possessed by early humans in America. It is obvious that the technology was suitable for an Arctic environment and the taking of big game. Very likely tailored skin clothing was standard. Presumably the stone toolkit would have been Asiatic in all respects, but we can make no definitive statements about the nature of the stone tools with which other utensils and tools were fabricated.

Despite our need to know the nature of the toolkit and the state of technology of the first Americans, nothing definitive can be said on present evidence. Although it is foolhardy to pursue the matter, it is necessary to point out a primary reason that we know so little. The problem lies in the assumptions made in the beginning of Early Man studies. It was presumed that whatever tool the earliest Americans were using would have been an Asiatic import. That comes down to the idea that the early fluted point technology associated with the Folsom and Clovis finds should have Asiatic prototypes, but no such prototypes have been found. Scholars may not even be worrying about the right questions. We need to know what tools the Asian migrants possessed at 25,000, 30,000, or even 35,000 years ago.

A European scholar, Müller-Beck, may have provided a reasonable answer. It is important to note that his views are several years old, having been first published in 1966 and 1967,

before any of the several American sites claimed to be older than 12,000 B.P. were discovered or reported. The scheme ran against popular thought and is still ignored by most American scholars. It is more persuasive today, however, in light of some of the finds discussed in Chapter Three. If we omit the subtleties of his argument, Müller-Beck's basic premise derives North American toolkits from Eurasiatic Paleolithic prototypes. He defines a Mousterian base, using the term *Mousteroid* to indicate that it is a pattern technologically remindful of the Mousterian of Europe, that is, the culture of the Neanderthals. At no point does he say that either the Neanderthals or the Mousterian culture of Europe got into North America. He is merely discussing a technological or typological complex, which does resemble the Mousterian complex well known to European scholars. The Mousteroid flint-working style or base provides a readily recognizable tool complex consisting of bifacially chipped **blades** or points, a big industry in **flake** knives, and flat flakes used for cutting and scraping just as they were flaked off.

After examining many collections in Asia and in the United States Müller-Beck says this complex is represented in America and could have been in the New World by 30,000 years ago. His first two maps (Figure 2.7(a)&(b)) show the Mousteroid tradition through Alaska and down into the Northern Plains by 28,000 to 26,000 B.P. The next two maps (Figure 2.7(c)&(d)) show the distribution of the bifacially chipped cultural kit all over North America south of Canada by 10,000 B.P. At the same time a later Paleolithic complex had spread over Siberia and into Beringia by 11,000 to 12,000 B.P. In order to distinguish it from the technologically different Mousteroid, Müller-Beck calls the later complex Aurignacoid, because it is remindful of the Aurignacian culture of Central Europe. It is characterized by slotted bone knives; polyhedral (many-sided) **cores;** arrows or harpoon heads; microflint tools; and narrow burins.

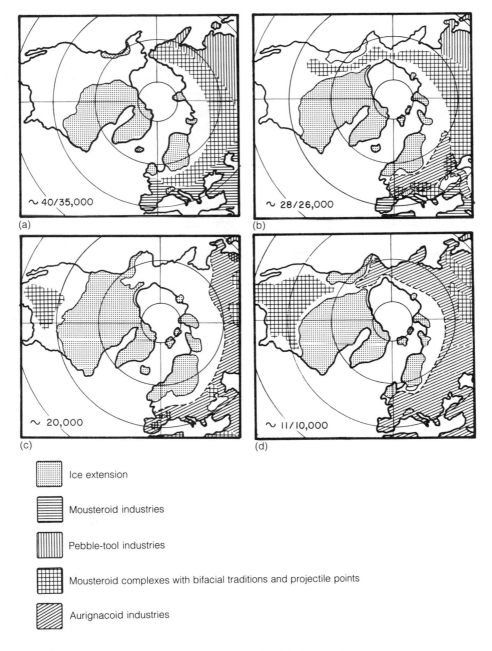

∼ 40/35,000

(a)

∼ 28/26,000

(b)

∼ 20,000

(c)

∼ 11/10,000

(d)

Ice extension

Mousteroid industries

Pebble-tool industries

Mousteroid complexes with bifacial traditions and projectile points

Aurignacoid industries

Figure 2.7 Distribution of Moustero-Aurignacoid cultures during late Wisconsin times: (a) at the end of the middle upper Pleistocene; (b) at transition between middle and late Pleistocene; (c) at maximum ice extension in late Pleistocene; and (d) at the end of the late upper Pleistocene, in years B.P. Note that map (c), designed in 1966, shows a solid ice distribution at 20,000 B.P., where an open passage is now thought to have existed.

There is also the matter of Diuktai Cave, and the so-called Diuktai culture of eastern Siberia, found along the Aldan River (35,000 to 12,500 B.P.) from Ezhantsy to Diuktai. The upper layers of the cave, dating to 12,690 B.P., yield an assortment of flakes, but bifacially chipped, triangular, leaf-shaped, and oval blades are also numerous in the large collection. It is suggested that the terminal Diuktai sequence in the cave may provide the artifacts from which the beautifully made, bifacially chipped tools of the American PaleoIndian evolved. But the terminal Diuktai dates are only a few years older than the fluted American points, so the timing may void the argument. However, some scholars regard the Diuktai and the earlier Kostenki II, far to the west in European Russia as prototypical of the Clovis tool forms.

To date most authors continue to see the well-chipped fluted points as uniquely American forms. That view has been reinforced by the realization that the tool traditions of the Alaskan cultures after 11,000 B.P. are the microlithic small cores and flakes, burins, and occasional bifacially chipped blades obviously derived from Asia but providing no link with the early hunters to the south.

The Aurignacoid nature of the Alaskan cultures after 11,000 is clear. The term *Aurignacoid* has also been used in connection with an early analysis of the late Paleolithic cultures of Japan. In a general way Müller-Beck identifies the PaleoIndians and the later Native American complexes found south of Canada as derived from the Mousteroid complex. Although Müller-Beck's ideas point toward a solution, it is clear that the question of the source or origin of the earliest PaleoIndian toolkit cannot be answered on present evidence. It is now time to consider the evidence we do have for human presence in the New World.

Chapter 2
Bibliography

Hopkins, David M. (editor)

1967   *The Bering Land Bridge.* Stanford University Press. Stanford, CA.

Hopkins, David M., John V. Matthews, Jr., Charles Schweger, and Steven B. Young (editors)

1982   *Paleoecology of Beringia.* Academic Press. New York.

Mead, James I., and David J. Meltzer (editors)

1985   *Environments and extinctions: man in late glacial North America.* Center for the Study of Early Man, University of Main Press. Orono.

Rutter, N. W., and C. E. Schweger (editors)

1980   The Ice-free Corridor and Peopling the New World. *Canadian Journal of Anthropology* Vol. 1, No. 1. University of Alberta.

The Early Cultures

Although the Beringian dry-steppe environment and the Asiatic origin of the human population of the Americas are reasonably well established, the toolkit the people carried can only be inferred. When early human studies began, it was assumed that the tools found with extinct fauna would be readily duplicated in Alaskan and Asian sites of the same or earlier age; that expectation was not sustained. After decades of search nowhere in Asia or South America have we found fluted points like those associated with long-horned bison and mammoth in the **High Plains.** And, as already indicated, the physical appearance of the early American population still cannot be described.

The early sites, therefore, give evidence only of human *presence,* not of the humans themselves. The evidence is found in artifacts of stone (and possibly of bone), in the use of fire, and bones of animals taken as food; all, of course, are perfectly valid evidence of human activity. It is on those tangible signs of human presence that the reconstruction of the human past must rest. Although there are thousands of locations—called sites—where humans have lived, worked, and hunted, only a few can be identified as ancient.

Because of the popularity of early human research, it became necessary to develop a set of criteria for evaluating the many claims. Of primary importance are the circumstances of "storage" of the artifacts and associated phenomena. A concentration of genuinely ancient artifacts is usually buried, sealed beneath one or more geologically formed strata. A break, such as an intrusion from above, that ruptures the sealing stratum renders the location suspect. Equally important is the inclusion of one or more diagnostic artifacts of types known from other sources to be early. Most early sites contain the bones of extinct animals. Thus a credible claim for an early location rests on (1) a buried, sealed—that is, undisturbed—situation; (2) diagnostic artifacts of known early age (which have the same purpose that index fossils serve in identifying geological strata); and (3) associated extinct animal bone. Since radiocarbon assays became available in 1950, a suite of radiocarbon dates is a most important fourth criterion. If a newly announced site meets those four criteria, it is regarded as valid and is thereafter used with confidence in reconstructing past lifeways.

Of course many extravagant claims are made for sites that do not meet the criteria. Many sites (some of putatively great age) are inexpertly dug by untrained people or carelessly dug by supposedly trained people in ways that blur the record and cloud their authenticity. Sometimes there are judgmental mistakes as well. An example are the pygmy mammoth sites that are perennially reported from Santa Rosa Island in California as ranging in age from 20,000 to 33,000 years. The finds are not rejected because of the age ascriptions, which are based on radiocarbon assays. They have simply never been fully reported; as a result the claimed association of burned earth, calcined mammoth bones, and crude flint tools or weapons cannot be assessed. The problem at Santa Rosa is that the excavators' enthusiasm led them to make overexuberant claims or misinterpret what they saw. Surface finds, isolated finds, single objects lacking any associations, or finds made by untrained observers remain dangling in time without cultural affiliation and cannot be used as evidence. Some of the tantalizing but unconvincing claims will be mentioned later.

Evidence Before 12,000 B.P.

One would suppose that during the passage across Beringia the travelers would have tarried to hunt and camp, leaving debris from game and scraps of flint, and that these locations would be frequently found in Alaska. There are none, although evidence later than 11,000–10,000 B.P. is plentiful and will be described.

A claim for one of the oldest evidences of human presence in North America comes from Old Crow Basin, at the edge of Beringia in the extreme northwest corner of the Yukon Territory. The basin was evidently a vast lake from about 30,000 B.P. until recent times. But before inundation caused by a natural (ice?) dam on the Porcupine River, it was filled with big game: mammoth, bison, horse, caribou, camel, and antelope. Many bones were deposited in the lake, and when it drained, the bones were dislodged to be redeposited in the eddies and on sand bars of the river. The area recently attracted geologists, paleontologists, and archaeologists, and now a great deal is known about the deeply incised Porcupine River and the complex sediments it has cut through.

Large collections of extinct mammal bones have been taken from the fossil beds of the Porcupine. A tool made of caribou bone was recovered from one bed where the bones showed signs of having been moved and redeposited by stream action. The tool is a carefully made flesher (for removing flesh from a hide) with several small teeth on the working end. There can be no doubt that it is an artifact. It was once dated at about 27,000 years B.P., with other bones in the deposit both older and younger, from 25,000 to 32,000 B.P. However, the ^{14}C assay was on bone apatite (a carbonate of calcium), which is now considered to be an unreliable carbon source. In 1986 an accelerator (TAMS) assay was conducted on collagen (organic material) from the flesher and other tools (of antler). The flesher's age was 1350 radiocarbon years, and the antler tools were less than 3000 years. So we dismiss the site as of no antiquity. This should warn those of us who forget the caution with which science requires us to temper our optimism.

Other Old Crow and Porcupine River localities yielded bones—particularly mammoth bones—that the archaeologists took to be broken purposefully by humans to create

tools. Usually the fracture spirals around the bone, a break that often makes quite a sharp edge (see Figure 3.1). The broken bones are believed to have been ad hoc, or expediency, tools. They were made for butchering and were discarded on the spot when the butchery was finished. A few bones are regarded as cores from which sharp pieces, also for cutting, had been flaked. In view of the convoluted arguments and experiments with modern bone involved in arriving at the conclusion that the bones were modified for hu-

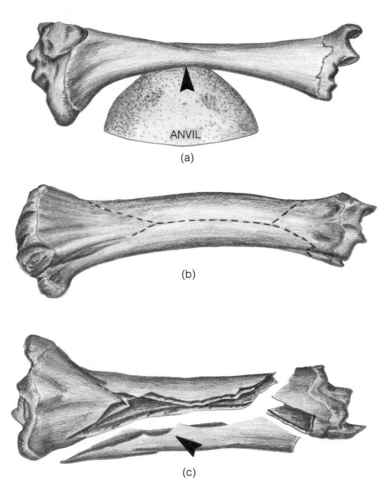

Figure 3.1 Bovid tibia before and after spiral fracture: (a) Arrow marks impact point; (b) dotted lines indicate fracture on dorsal side; (c) exploded ventral view of tibia—note the curved indentation and obtuse angle at impact point (indicated by arrow pointer).

man use; the fact that all the bone deposits are secondary, that is, transported at least once by water; the fact that very ancient bones in paleontological deposits yield bones with the same spiral fractures; and the complete lack of flint tools or scrap, charcoal, or other evidence of human presence, there is strong doubt that the specimens are tools at all.

The situation at nearby Bluefish Caves I and II was different in every way. Located some forty miles southwest of Old Crow, the caves contain apparently undisturbed layers of **loess** that include cultural debris and much animal bone scrap. The artifacts and bones were deposited while the wind-borne loess was being laid down over a period of 3000 years—from 15,000 to 12,000 B.P. There is no debate about the artifacts. They include microliths, a wedge-shaped core, a **chisel** (scraper?), and flakes of chert. The bones of mammoth, elk, horse, and caribou were found both outside and inside the caves. Many of the bones show cutting and scraping scars, probably made by humans during butchering. The exact dating of the artifacts is still hazy. The 15,500 to 12,950 B.P. dates are based on ^{14}C assays of the bone collagen. But on the basis of a correlation of bone dates with the loess layers, the excavator feels confident of a 12,000 date. Because the dates are by no means crisp and the association of the bones and chert **debitage** is uncertain, it is difficult to accept this find as fully valid. Additional work may provide more solid evidence.

The other evidence for very early occupancy lies south of the Canadian border, beyond the maximum extent of the ice. Sites that meet the criteria of being sealed, yielding artifacts with extinct mammal bones or evidence of purposeful fire, and dating by radiocarbon or other reliable techniques are rare. All of them are less than 20,000 years old, usually younger than the 16,000- to 14,000-year B.P. range. The artifacts of this group are flakes and crudely chipped bifaces as would be expected if they represent a Mousteriod tradition.

The Chopper-Scraper Tradition

Before discussing early sites in the Mousteriod tradition, a chopper-scraper tradition must be mentioned. It is unplaced in time, occurs sporadically over the United States, and is somewhat of an embarrassment to the archaeologists because its relationships to other cultures cannot be determined. One reason the collections become a problem is that they do not resemble the material from eastern Asia. Instead they are more like the southeastern Asia complexes labeled "choppers," which are assigned to a lower or middle Paleolithic tradition on the basis of typology. Most are percussion chipped and can be accurately described as both core and flake choppers and scrapers.

Prior to knowledge of the eastern Siberian cultures, the full evidence from Japan, or Müller-Beck's work, these crude congeries were believed by some archaeologists to be the early cultural stratum from which the later cultures had somehow evolved; the very crudity of the specimens spelled great age to some, but few scholars have adopted that view. Although there are many locations where thousands of the artifacts occur, none of the sites meet the minimal criteria for a valid site. Most of the chopper-scraper sites do not fulfill any of the conditions, because they are surface finds and as such lack chronological controls. They may be quite ancient, but no evidence other than great crudity can be produced, and crudity of technique is no guarantee of age. The known locations are largely in western North America. Generally the deposits are recovered from river terraces or lake beaches high above present water level or even in situations where there is now no stream or lake at all. Often, too, the specimens are heavily patinated or "varnished," leading to speculations of great age. It has been argued that the cumulative evidence of (1) location, (2) crudity, (3) varnish, and (4) other considerations can be safely taken as proof of antiquity. Most archaeologists reject or even ignore the entire matter. Some base their rejection on the lack of controls; others appear to reject the idea of a mid-Wisconsin emigration, to say nothing of the pre-Wisconsin dating that the typology of the implements would require.

Others scoff at the extravagant claims of the proponents, pointing out that comparable specimens can and have been recovered many times in buried or covered sites in clear association with well-developed projectile point series, **milling stones,** and other specimens known to be relatively recent. Still others ascribe the crude flaking to natural agencies such as frost or heat, claiming that thermal flaking of certain kinds of flint and chert resembles the results achieved by humans. They deny that these collections are even artifacts.

The problem came to early attention through work in the extensive deposits of these crude specimens in southwest Wyoming, especially on the river terraces on the Blacks Fork of the Green River. The Blacks Fork culture was described as displaying close similarity to the early and middle Paleolithic cultures of Eurasia. The investigator identified and illustrated a pebble industry, numbers of cores resembling fist axes, and extensive examples of Clactonian flaking techniques. Comparable collections were made for many years over a wide area, but no one has taken the claims very seriously. The claims have been disposed of by a reexamination of the Blacks Fork area where the artifacts were demonstrated to be quarry materials. In one excavated site (Pine Spring, Wyoming), they occur neatly stratified without change over a time range of 8000 B.P. to 1200 A.D.

Another location already mentioned that appears at first glance to be valid is Santa Rosa Island off the coast of California, where several finds have been made. Here dwarf mammoth bones found sometimes lying in red earth and deeply buried in sediment have radiocarbon ages ranging from 20,000 B.P. to over 33,000 B.P. No artifacts have been found in association with the mammoth bones, although chopper-scraper specimens do occur as isolated surface finds on the island. The mammoth bones are blackened, but by chemical action, not fire as has been claimed.

The early presence of humans on the island is attested by the radiocarbon date of 10,000 B.P. for two human leg bone fragments at the Arlington Springs site on the island. The bones were in a buried, once marshy, streambed. But the fascinating prospect of proving humans to have been preying on the evidently numerous little mammoths cannot be confirmed.

There are a wealth of archaeological sites and a long sequence on Santa Rosa Island, as well as an impressive array of radiocarbon dates on shell, charcoal, and other materials. The dates, however, do not apply to anything except the specimens themselves. A cultural inventory and details of recovery have not yet appeared. A visit to the island convinces one that if careful search and excavation were carried out, the prospects for finding artifacts and evidence of fire and extinct fauna in full association would be excellent. Many claims have been made, but the work has never been published. Therefore, as evidence of human presence earlier than 25,000 B.P., these finds must also be disregarded.

Time after time—at Manix Lake, Tule Springs, and other localities—either the finds are surface deposits, or the claimed association or age ascriptions dissolve in the face of rigorous reexamination. Some have said that the uncontrolled surface nature of the finds should be ignored because the materials represent a culture stage regardless of where found. It is sometimes claimed that although the accumulations are now on the surface, when deposited, they were on the same surface and were later probably sealed by finer deposits that are now eroded away. It is also argued that the specimens found on what is now the surface may represent one or more living areas in layers higher up in a sediment accumulation now entirely dispersed. Again no proof exists. The person who can lay all claims and doubts to rest (and remove the decades of inertia caused by doubt) by proving a certain period or time of origin for the chopper-scraper assemblage will have made a contribution to archaeology equal to any so far.

Another site near San Bernardino, California, Calico requires mention because of the considerable interest its alleged antiquity has aroused. Enjoying the spiritual backing of the late Louis S. B. Leakey, a large corps of volunteer workers has recovered from deep shafts in cement-hard fill a collection of scattered flakes that are claimed to be the work of humans. The site was visited by a large group of geologists and prehistorians in 1970, the operations were explained, and selected specimens were exhibited by the hosts. Any of the flakes—whether made by natural forces during the movement of the matrix (mudflow) or by humans—would have passed muster as a waste flake in a collection of **debitage**. However, there were no finished artifacts, no charcoal, and no particular concentrations of the flakes. There was no convincing evidence of structures (one circular arrangement of stone with no associated charcoal was called a hearth), and the objects were found up to a depth of twenty feet. The geological evidence is much disputed. The geologists estimated ages from 50,000 years to 1 or 2 million years B.P. for the formation where the objects lay. Tests of the matrix may reveal a true and different age for the sediments in which the flint pieces are found, but the question is not the age of the matrix but whether the flint objects are indeed tools, the product of human construction. Two reports have been issued. Neither is any more convincing than the site visit. So far I see no reason to call the location an archaeological site.

Leaving the acres of surface stones for later study by others, and in the hope that the age

and significance of the chopper-scraper complexes will one day be fully understood, we shall now examine some materials recovered under better-controlled conditions.

Related because of uncertain age to the chopper-scraper enigma are the scores of flint and quartzite quarries found across the continent. An exhaustive search revealed a series of quarries between Baltimore, Maryland, and Wilmington, Delaware, and at other places on the fall line at the inner edge of the eastern coastal plain. The deposits are cobbles or gravels at the scenes of extensive aboriginal digging and flint knapping. The number of crude specimens, which are identified as **blanks,** or half-finished tools, runs into thousands. These occur in lenticular accumulations called shop debris, where flakes, broken pieces, and rejected blanks are concentrated. The problem here and at many other quarries, such as the famed Spanish Diggings in Wyoming, is that the sites also contain pebbles sharpened on one end into well-made fist axes. All the quarries have been worked for thousands of years and thus have no affiliation with any one stage. However, the quarry debris and discarded flakes do resemble choppers and scrapers.

The quarry idea is attractive as an explanation for the chopper-scraper enigma because we know that deposits of good flint have been known and quarried for millennia. For example, the fluted points at the Shoop site in Pennsylvania are made from Onondaga, New York flint, more than one hundred miles away. Another example is the Alibates flint quarry in Texas, which was known and used by West Texas and New Mexican tribes for centuries. The largest and best-known quarry is the Knife River flint area in western North Dakota. The outcrop and production area is about 2000 square kilometers in extent, and the artifacts made from its flint are found all over the Plains and the Midwest. The area was evidently exploited over the full span of human presence (10,000 or more years). Obviously the quarries confuse the evidence and the arguments for the chopper-scraper tradition.

Concluding this section forces the admission that little has been established. The intent has been to mention a confusing array of objects, a plethora of claims, and an important problem yet unsolved. Neither the age nor the cultural significance of this complex can be settled here. The answer lies in the ground. For the moment the evidence favors the quarry waste as explaining the chopper-scraper objects.

The Early Sites

An early site more informative than Old Crow Flats is Meadowcroft Shelter near Avella in western Pennsylvania. The deposits in the shelter are colluvial (surface runoff) in origin. The site is located on the banks of Cross Creek, a tributary of the Ohio River. Although occupancy was more or less continuous, we are concerned here only with the next to basal layer, stratum IIa. One date of about 16,000 B.P. is ascribed to that layer. It comes from charcoal from the lowest fire pit in the stratum. Another is from a carbonized fragment of simple plaited basketry made from what appears to be birch bark; the dates for it are 19,650 ± 2400 and 19,150 ± 800 B.P. For many reasons those extreme dates have been challenged, but the date of 16,000 B.P. from the fire pit seems to be accepted by some.

There is a lower stratum (I) from which only charcoal has been removed. The dates from that stratum run from 37,000 to 21,500 B.P., but no cultural material such as chipped flint has yet been recovered there. From stratum IIa, however, workers recovered three prismatic flakes, one chipped biface with **retouched** edges, and one "Mungai" knife, which is nothing more than a flat prismatic flake that has been retouched on the edges (see Figure 3.2). The biface is not convincing as a precursor to the later fluted points as claimed. Except for the prismatic flaked knife,

the objects resemble other PaleoIndian finds from Fort Rock Caves in Oregon and Wilson Butte in Idaho. It should be pointed out, however, that the prismatic blades and the knife are similar to finds both at Blackwater Draw and the Lindenmeier location. The Meadowcroft site was evidently excavated with care and is the most nearly convincing of the early period sites reported to date. It has been repeatedly challenged because of (1) the very early dates; (2) the presence of only modern flora and fauna in the scrap; and more importantly, (3) the bits of bituminous coal in the fill. It has been demonstrated that coal can contaminate charcoal. Contamination would result in a greater-than-actual radiocarbon age assay. However, the artifacts, including the prismatic flakes, could well be as old as 13,000 or 14,000 B.P. The same artifacts from Fort Rock Cave and Wilson Butte are acceptable evidence of PaleoIndian presence. It seems that the claims of extreme age can be disregarded, however.

At the Fort Rock area of Oregon, a series of caves were excavated in the 1970s. The artifact take was scanty, but one cave (where an earlier partial excavation had revealed a rich Archaic assemblage) yielded many flakes and one bifacially chipped knife or point in a basalar stratum radiocarbon dated at 13,200 B.P. The associations of the finds have been questioned because excavation was done by arbitrary levels. This raises the question of possibly undetected disturbance of the deposits; the charcoal and the flint may not have been in association originally.

At Wilson Butte Cave in south-central Idaho, a flake that had suffered edge use damage, a bifacially chipped blade or knife, and two bones with cut marks on them were found in the lowest level. The ^{14}C date from associated bone scrap is 14,500 B.P.

Without putting undue emphasis on the matter just yet, it is necessary to mention that there is an increasing interest in the possibility of a prelithic or pre-Clovis bone tool in-

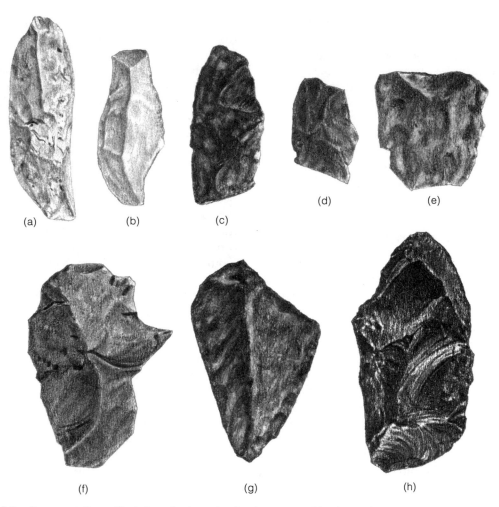

Figure 3.2 Representative artifacts from the lowest cultural stratum at Meadowcroft Shelter: (a)–(c) prismatic blades; (d)–(f) flaking detritus; (g) "Mungai" knife; (h) biface. Slightly reduced.

dustry. As more PaleoIndian kill sites are discovered and excavated, more bones evidently fractured "to a pattern" are being reported. Usually they are the strong, massive leg bones of elephant, horse, or bison. They are considered "expediency" tools for one-time use in butchering game and are not to be confused with the cylindrical bone or ivory rods or points widely associated with the Clovis fluted points and other tools.

The fragments are created by striking one of the long leg bones a heavy blow at about the middle of the shaft. The blow results in a spiral fracture that produces two pieces called choppers that are thought to have been used in dismembering a carcass; one piece at least has a sharp, pointed end (see Figure 3.3). Specimens from the Vore and Casper kill sites in Wyoming, the Jurgen site in Colorado, and Lubbock Lake and Bonfire Shelter in Texas have been studied and described. Sharp-edged splinters are also formed; these are called knives and can be sharpened by removing flakes as is done with flint.

Whether these bone chopper and knife fragments are tools or merely scraps remain-

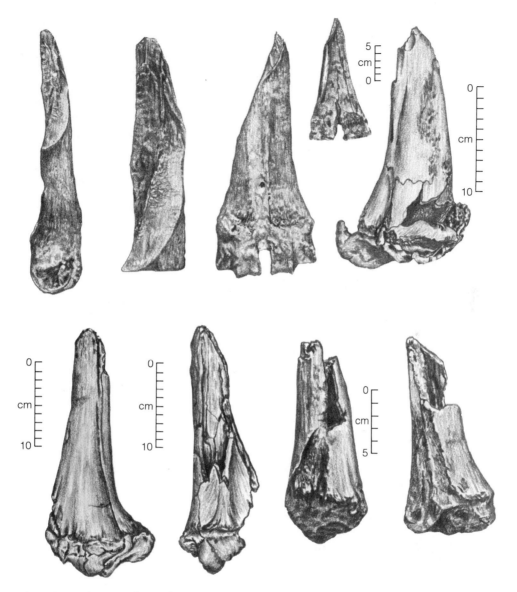

Figure 3.3   Long bone choppers. Scale given.

ing after bone marrow extractions is a real question, but definitive proof will be long delayed one fears. About all that can be done now is to direct attention to the increasingly frequent recognition of the forms and the increasing number of locations where they are found. The finds are claimed to portend an eventual recognition of a disposable bone tool industry that ran alongside and associated with the amorphous flake industry of pre-Clovis times and later. While many are skeptical of the idea, the patterning of the specimens or the occasional use-polishing of the choppers and the sharpening (by **percussion flaking**) of the bone splinters cannot be denied. The frequency with which they are being discovered recently (now that they are being noticed) and the fact that they are numerous where flint tools are not found, and vice-versa, argue that they are, in fact, manufactured tools. These artifacts continue to be viewed skeptically by many.

Mexico and South America

There is evidence of human presence south of the ice edge before 12,000 B.P. The site claimed to be oldest is in Mexico. At Tlapacoya, a few miles southeast of Mexico City, excavations were carried on at several locations for some eight years. At one, Trench Alfa, workers found three fireplaces surrounded by stones adjacent to a heap of animal bone scrap. The fireplace and food bones bespeak a reused camp on the pebble beach of a vanished lake, Chalco Chalco. The ^{14}C date was 21,700 B.P., made on charcoal from the hearth. Some of the fauna available were the now-extinct bison, mammoth, horse, camel, and antelope—the same familiar group (but different species) already encountered from Siberia southward. Two species of deer were represented in the food bones associated with the hearths; one is the modern Virginia deer. Black bear and sloth, to say nothing of shore birds and small animals, were also available. During the time of occupancy the area was shrubby and weedy, with amaranth common near the lake. Artifacts were scanty: three obsidian flakes, two pieces of worked bone, and many pieces of debitage. The andesite used for artifacts was local, beach cobbles of that material being available. This site is fully reported, and at the moment is the best documented of the very early locations. The evidence, however, is scanty and is viewed skeptically by some.

In Flea Cave in the Ayacucho valley of Peru a series of crude stone artifacts in a deep deposit are radiocarbon dated at 14,700 years B.P., the date coming from associated sloth bones. The artifacts were irregular uniface scrapers, a chopper, and prismatic flakes.

Farther south, in Patagonia, are the Los Toldos Caves. The basalar cultural stratum—level 11—of cave 3 yielded a large collection of stone tools. Included are large, thick flakes with retouched edges, large scrapers made from cobbles, and a few retouched triangular points made from flakes. The excavator regarded the points as Mousteroid in form. Associated were guanaco, horse, and camelid bones. Level 11 is dated at 12,600 B.P. This site was evidently carefully dug and crisply reported, making it quite credible. It puts human occupancy at the tip of South America a full 1000 years earlier than the well-known cultures of the PaleoIndians of the North American Plains.

On the coast of Chile the Monte Verde location offers evidence of occupancy between 12,100 and 14,000 years ago. In addition to scanty and amorphous flint material, the excavator reported evidence of contemporaneous house structures. Without denying the age of the site, it is possible to question whether the houses are actually associated with the early horizon.

At the other end of the continent at Taima-Taima in Venezuela a fragment of an El Jobo point and some used flakes were said to be found in direct association with a mastodon. The distinctive and early El Jobo point is very common in the district. It is a distinctive bi-point, lanceolate in shape, thick, and heavy and having blunt rather than sharp points on each end. A date of 13,800 B.P. was obtained from fragments of small branches, sheared or crushed into fragments some 1½ to 2 inches long. They are believed to have been in the stomach of the mastodon, which was a browser and would have routinely ingested such coarse materials. Scattered through the same layer of earth were other mastodon, horse, felid (cat), and glyptodont (giant armadillo) bones. The location should possibly be accepted at face value, but a full report has not been made.

Another South American location that seems to exceed 12,000 years in age is the Alice Boer site in Brazil. Still other sites believed to be the same or greater age are being reported.

As the evidence mounts for human presence in southern South America where people evidently foraged and had no biface projectile points, North American scholars may have to revise their thinking about the full cultural sequence of both the Americas. This rethinking must take into account the El Jobo and other bifaces and the evidence of big game hunting claimed for northern South America. It may be that the edge-worn chips and flakes of Wilson Butte and Meadowcroft are the North American evidence for the forager stage remains now being discovered in South America.

Because this book is about America north of Mexico, the South American evidence and the questions it raises will not be further pursued. (It is interesting to note that the ascribed radiocarbon age seems to carry the burden of proof in South America where sealed deposits, diagnostic artifacts, and extinct fauna are not always present.) On present evidence it seems that the South American sites are markedly earlier than the fluted points associated with Clovis and Folsom cultures in North America, but there are still no specimens strongly resembling the fluted points recovered in North America at 11,500 to 10,000 B.P.

After 12,000 B.P.: The Classic PaleoIndians

From 1926–1927 until the early 1970s there was an overwhelming time constraint on the study of the earliest people. For a number of reasons it was assumed that no one could have gotten south of the ice until the final melting was under way at the close of the Pleistocene. One of the reasons was that the glaciers were once understood to be one massive field of ice, unbroken from coast to coast above what is now the Canadian-United States border. Anyone who claimed evidence of earlier occupancy was ignored as a fool; an uninformed, undisciplined amateur; or a crackpot. Hence the increasingly frequent findings of extinct fauna associated with objects of human manufacture south of the Canadian border were deemed the oldest possible evidence of human occupancy. Such finds were termed *PaleoIndian*, which implied both great age and an ancestral relationship to the later population. Although for most students the findings described above have long since lifted the post-Pleistocene ceiling that inhibited research, the use of the term *PaleoIndian* is retained because it is widely accepted and familiar to everyone.

The locations to be discussed now have been carefully excavated and fully reported except as noted. They can be set in fairly secure geologic contexts, and the material is well controlled stratigraphically so context and provenience are definite. The first and best-known sites are in the Plains, scattered from Oklahoma to Wyoming and as far south as southern Texas. However, the distribution of evidences of PaleoIndian culture known today extends eastward from the Plains into New England and Nova Scotia. The Dalton complex of the lower Middle West and South (where fluted points also occur) is regarded as late PaleoIndian, although it differs in tool and weapon forms and, of course, ecological situation.

There are several named complexes and cultures to be described, but the shared criteria are simple and well known. The stage began when the most available big game was a series of now-extinct species: mammoth, long-horned bison, camel, and horse. It persisted through and beyond their extinction, with the latest sites yielding exclusively modern fauna. The PaleoIndians represented in the Western sites are broken into three sequent groups that are given culture names. The earliest is the Clovis, next comes the Folsom, and the latest is the Plano. Several slightly later Eastern complexes can be correlated, on typologic grounds, with the Clovis and Folsom divisions, and the Plano is represented in some places.

The generalized description of these subdivisions is short and scant. The Western sites yield bones, usually from more than one extinct animal. Tools include thin, fine-chipped, laurel leaf-shaped, biface blades or lance points; scrapers of various sorts; prismatic flake knives; and perhaps burins. They are most often kill sites rather than camps, so the full range of the artifact inventory may not yet be known. However, there are both campsites and kill sites.

Campsites are often elevated and may occur on dunes. The remains include hearths; broken, split, and charred food bones; chipping debris; and a full complement of flint tools, fluted or unfluted points, channel flakes (debris from the fluting process), hammerstones, several kinds of scrapers made from flakes, and random chips showing wear from use.

Kill sites occur on the banks of former fossil ponds or streams and are often at the base of a cliff or jump-off where the prey was stampeded to its death. All kill sites have been buried by subsequent deposition. The contents are restricted to the skeletons of animals and the few tools, including the fluted points, used in the killing and butchering processes.

A few sites are stratified, yielding evidence of two or even all three cultures from one station. MacHaffie in Montana, Blackwater Draw locality 1 in New Mexico, and Hell Gap in Wyoming are perhaps the best examples of well-preserved and recorded stratified sites. The long record at Hell Gap, however, was synthesized from two or three sites in the vicinity.

If it is possible to generalize so glibly about a 10,000 to 12,000-year-old culture stage that spans the transition from the Ice Age to the Recent, how do the three subdivisions differ? The Clovis was originally represented by only a few stations where all critics were satisfied about authenticity. The criteria for classification are that the kill always involved the mammoth (but not necessarily exclusively; see the discussion of the Lehner site below) and that one or more Clovis fluted points (Figure 3.4) are always found in close association with the bones. These lanceolate points are thin, 3 to 5 inches long, and about one-fourth as wide as long and have smooth, if sometimes large, percussion (?) flake scars and one or more short flakes removed from the base down the median portion toward the tip. These shallow flake scars give the characteristic "fluting." At present one would expect to recognize a western Clovis site from the association of mammoth bones and Clovis fluted points. Clovis points, or points closely resembling them, are known to occur over most of the lower forty-eight states, but only in the West are they associated with the mammoth.

The more numerous Folsom sites always contain remains of one or another of the large-horned extinct bison and the Folsom fluted point (Figure 3.5). The Folsom is lanceolate; made with delicate, **pressure flaking;** and thinned by the removal on each face of one long, thin flake almost to the tip. The points are distinctive and came to bear the name of the site where they were first discovered.

It was at Folsom, New Mexico, in 1926 and 1927 that the remains of twenty-three extinct bison (*Bison antiquus figginsi*) were uncovered in a box canyon with nineteen Folsom fluted points in undisputed association. This single find, dug with care and observed by competent scientists from several institutions and disciplines, set American prehistory on a new course. Beyond question, here was proof of

(a)   (b)

Figure 3.4   Clovis fluted points from near the Hell Gap site. Point (b) has been resharpened after breakage. Actual size.

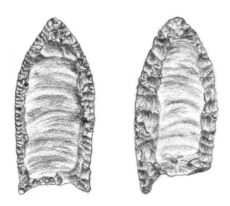

Figure 3.5   Folsom fluted points. Reduced.

the coexistence of Pleistocene fauna and tool-making humans. The impact of this one discovery, while not instantaneous, ultimately touched off a search for comparable finds that soon led to the discovery and acceptance of the even older Clovis complex. After the Folsom discovery (which stimulated search), Plano and Clovis sites began to be discovered in quantity.

The Plano diagnostic points, while varyingly leaf-shaped, are not fluted and show more variation in form than the preceding Clovis and Folsom fluted types (Figures 3.6, 3.7, 3.8, and 3.9). The fauna associated with the

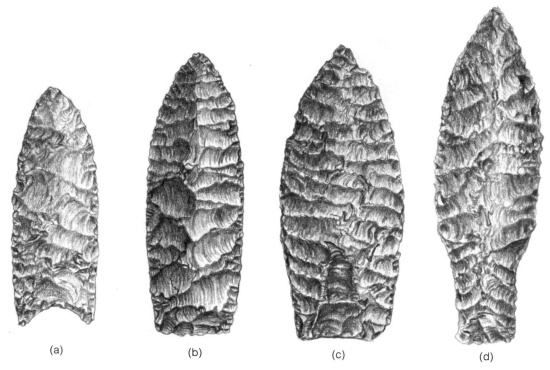

(a)   (b)   (c)   (d)

Figure 3.6   Plano points. (a) Plainview; (b) Milnesand; (c) Browns Valley; (d) Hell Gap. Reduced about one-third.

Plano specimens sometimes included modern species.

The Clovis Culture

WESTERN CLOVIS SITES   The best-known Clovis culture sites are Blackwater Draw near Clovis, New Mexico, and the Naco-Lehner-Murray Springs trio in extreme southeastern Arizona. There are no known precedent Eurasiatic forms for the beautifully chipped Clovis and Folsom points, so the fluting is believed to be exclusively a North American technique.

Blackwater Draw locality 1 was once a series of springs forming a large, deep pond with a marshy drainage channel. The sediment that eventually filled the spring and channel consisted of several contrasting lay-ers. The basal layer yielded elephant remains and the Clovis artifacts shown in Figure 3.10.

Additional work at the Clovis type site at Blackwater Draw showed that the Clovis complex can be characterized by another diagnostic artifact called the Clovis blade. This is a curved flake, prismatic in cross section, derived from a well-prepared core. There is no retouch. As Figure 3.11 shows, the preparation of the blade is a fairly sophisticated way of working flint. These blades were probably viewed as finished tools as they came from the core. They would have been used as knives or scrapers. Figure 3.12 shows how flakes are removed from a core.

The authenticity of the curved flake blades as being of Clovis provenience is strengthened by the occurrence of similar prismatic blades at a mammoth site nearby and at the Lehner site. Folsom specimens (dated by

Figure 3.7   Eden points from the Horner site. Actual size.

Figure 3.8   Scottsbluff points from the Horner site. Actual size.

TAMS at 10,260 B.P.) came from the next highest stratum, and the carbonaceous silt above it yielded Plano artifacts. The geologic processes were complex and have raised many questions, particularly about climate, but these need not detain us here.

Probably the most systematically studied of the Clovis sites to date is the Lehner location in Arizona. Equally well reported, but yielding less information, was the Naco mammoth site in Arizona. Both sites were brought to attention by laymen whose service to sci-

ence cannot be overestimated. Marc and Fred Navarrette discovered the Naco site; E. F. Lehner reported the site bearing his name. The sites are close together and very similar. Both are alongside a fossil streambed, sealed millennia ago by deposits of sediment. Both had been revealed by recent gullying. At both

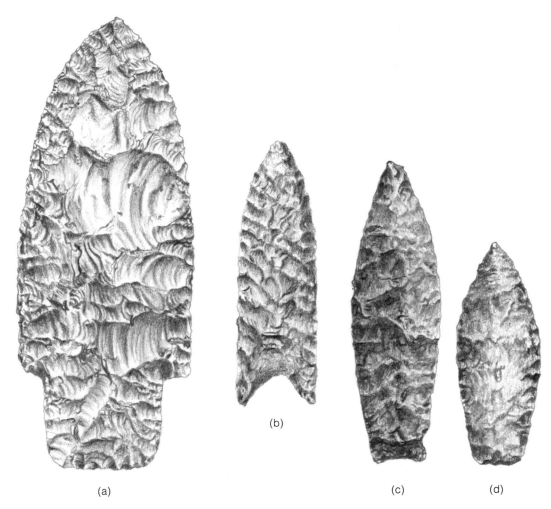

(a)

(b)

(c)   (d)

Figure 3.9 Plano points. (a) Alberta; (b) Jimmy Allen; (c) and (d) Angostura. The Angostura type appear to be merely small Agate Basin specimens. Reduced.

sites Clovis fluted points were in direct association with mammoth remains. At Lehner other extinct creatures—horse, bison, and tapir—were represented. There, too, was charcoal from a fire. Nine mammoth and the other animals are believed to have been killed and butchered on the spot. Figure 3.13 shows some of the flaked tools other than projectile points found. As already indicated, these authenticate the Clovis curved blade as belonging with the Clovis complex. Recent TAMS dating on twelve samples of the Lehner ma-

terial averaged 10,930 B.P. This seems to be younger than the average age for the Clovis.

Southeast Arizona may come to be known as "mammoth country" in view of two other locations, Murray Springs and Escapule, quite near the Lehner-Naco sites. At Murray Springs recent sediments sealed parts of two mammoth along with extinct bison, horse, camel, and wolf. Excavations revealed a living floor on which were some 3000 flint flakes and several Clovis fluted points. This was the first Clovis occupation zone discovered and rec-

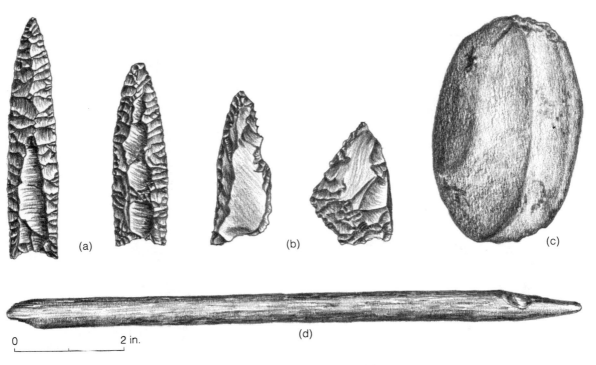

Figure 3.10   Artifacts from Blackwater Draw locality 1: (a) fluted points; (b) scrapers; (c) hammerstone; (d) worked bone. Reduced one-third to one-half.

ognized as such. The radiocarbon age of the find is 11,200 years B.P. At the nearby Escapule site excavators reported another incomplete mammoth associated with two Clovis points. Its age is estimated to be 11,200 B.P.

The Colby mammoth site in the Bighorn Basin of Wyoming yielded somewhat different data. Here in an **alluvium-**filled fossil arroyo a unique situation was observed. Although there were disarticulated mam-

Figure 3.11   Clovis blades from Blackwater Draw locality 1. Reduced.

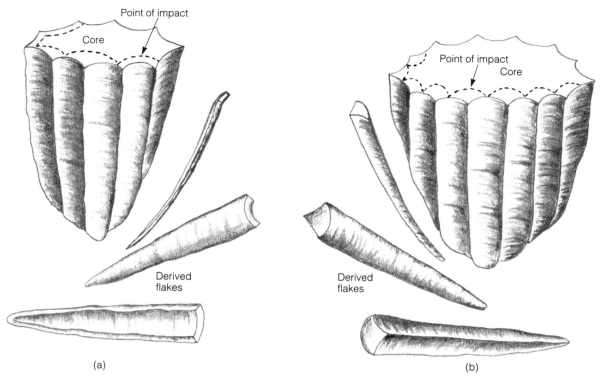

Figure 3.12   A core-nucleus technique for the production of flake blades: (a) lamellar; (b) prismatic.

moth bones up and down the old arroyo, there were also two neat heaps of stacked bones, each containing parts of three mammoth. In the better-preserved stack, part of the left side of a mammoth—ribs, scapula, leg bones, and the left half of the pelvis—lay on the bottom. Portions of two front quarters and a femur were next on the pile, and a complete skull was placed on top. Against the pelvis another scapula was leaning. Under the pile was a point called Clovis. It was not classic in form, but had basalar fluting (see Figure 3.14). Elsewhere on the site three other points were found during the excavation. No other artifacts were found except two "expediency" bone choppers, one made from the humerus of a mountain sheep or deer, and the other from the dense radius of a camel. Both are of the type believed to have been used for dismembering animals (see Figure 3.3).

The excavator suggests that the bone piles represent caches of meat for later use. If the kill were in the late autumn, the meat would quickly freeze (winter temperatures in the basin can fall to $-45°C$ ($-50°F$)). The idea that the meat was surplus and was allowed to freeze to preserve it is reasonable. Because only two bone tools and one point/knife were with the bones, the killing and butchering is presumed to have been at some other part of the site. There seems little doubt that Colby was a kill site. But this remains conjectural, the major portion of it evidently having been bulldozed away when a stock watering pond (locally called a tank) was being built. The two bone piles and the few artifacts are probably all we will learn from the site.

East of Colby in eastern Colorado the Selby and Dutton sites reveal nearly identical histories, physical situations, and stratigraphy.

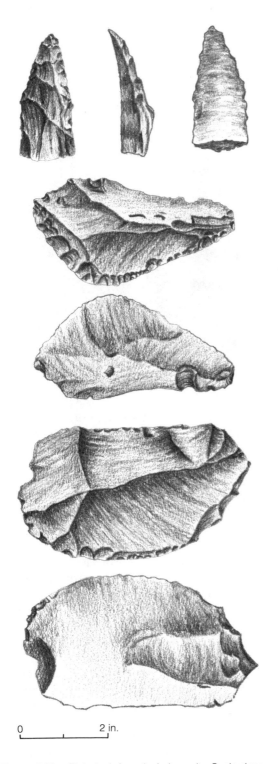

Both were small lakes with bone beds (with the same associated megafauna noted at other sites, plus sloth, deer, and antelope) in the lake deposits (sand, fine silt, and clays) that comprise a thick stratum above a thin layer of clay on the bottom. Except for one Clovis point and four scrapers made of flakes at Dutton, there were no flint objects. There were several of the expediency bone tools with the bone bed beneath the Clovis bone bed. The Selby site also yielded bone expediency tools. The tools are similar to the ones from Colby listed above and are compared to the Old Crow Basin bone tool collections. The authors postulate a pre-Clovis bone tool industry although no estimates of age are given. On the face of it, the sites appear to be of Clovis age.

A revisit to the long-known Agate Basin site has revealed a Clovis component, TAMS dated at 11,650 B.P. Now fully reported, the evidence indicates that the spot was a favorite location with campsites of Clovis, Folsom, and Agate Basin peoples. The Folsom level was TAMS dated at 10,690 B.P.

Other generally accepted Clovis sites include Domebo in Oklahoma, Miami and McLean in Texas, Dent in Colorado, and Iztapan in Mexico. There are other sites where mammoth remains are accompanied by non-diagnostic artifacts. The Union Pacific Mammoth Kill site in Wyoming is one of these. Here a mammoth had evidently been trapped in an ancient bog and possibly stoned to death with large boulders. Only two flint tools—not Clovis fluted points—were with it. The find may be authentic; the radiocarbon date is 11,300 B.P.

The Union Pacific site raises an interesting unsolved problem. Are these bog or marsh mammoth kills evidence of a deliberate hunting technique? Did the Clovis hunters search out drinking, feeding, or bathing animals and kill them there, where the clutching muck would hamper their movements? Did the animals seek water because they were badly wounded and feverish? Or were these animals mired and helpless through their own

Figure 3.13 Flake tools from the Lehner site. Scale given.

0   2 in.

Figure 3.14   Projectile points from the Colby site.

misjudgment and killed when discovered quite by accident by the hunters?

It has been seriously suggested that the usual "kill" site, where one mammoth is found in association with one or two Clovis points, is evidence not of a successful hunt but of a failed one. The argument is that the find records the escape of a wounded animal that finally died of loss of blood and weakness. The scattering of bones would have been the work of scavengers—wolves, coyotes, or cats. Whatever the answer is, most known Clovis sites are associated with fossil bogs and marshes, and some kills were clearly made in such locations.

MASTODONS   If mammoth were such preferred game, one wonders why mastodon, numerous in the East and found sporadically in the West, were not also taken. There have been scattered reports of mastodon and artifact associations east of the Plains, but the data have been inadequate or flawed in one way or another so that none have been fully accepted. One example is the Koch mastodon from the Pomme de Terre Valley in Hickory County in west central Missouri. Found in 1840 by a collector of fossils and analyzed a hundred years later, the evidence indicates that the associated artifacts were probably referrable to the much later Archaic culture. The mastodon skeleton was recovered from a strong spring location where the contents would have been mixed by the churning water action. From about 1965 to 1975 Koch's Spring and several others nearby (Boney and Trolinger) containing extinct and modern faunal bones were extensively excavated under little control. Based on the ^{14}C dates from the spring, the Koch mammoth was finally judged to have been about 30,000 years old; the artifact association was evidently fortuitous.

At Kimmswick, south of St. Louis, Missouri, mastodon and other bones were found in deposits in shallow ponds on a creek terrace. In the pond sediments, two mastodon, one above the other, were associated with two Clovis points and other artifacts. With the mastodon bones were several small animals, such as mice and marmot, that suggest a savannah habitat. The find appears to be the first credible mastodon-artifact association, but no age ascription is given. The sketchy preliminary report of the find leaves this site difficult to evaluate.

An aged mastodon has been discovered at Sequim, Washington. It lay in a glacial kettle (a depression formed as buried ice melted) buried in recent sediment. The animal lay on its left side; the right side was dismembered (by butchery it is presumed), and the bones piled nearby. Only one flake of stone was found near the heaped up bones. A rough cylinder of bone is said to have been imbedded in a rib and is identified as a bone point. With only a preliminary report, written early in the study of the site, the acceptance of this location must await further evidence.

A study of PaleoIndian settlement patterns determined a consistency of location of major early campsites in the central Rio Grande Valley of New Mexico. The area shown in Figure 3.15 is covered by aerial photographs. They were studied for likely camp locations (*likely* means situations similar to some where sites were already known to exist); the aerial photo survey was followed by field search. Thirty-three campsites were found along with twenty-six special use localities. The universal camp pattern for Folsom sites was a ridge location northeast of and overlooking a large hunting area. A water supply, often a now dry playa, was always adjacent. For Cody and other Plano locations, the sites were farther from the hunting area, with less uniformity in directional relationships. Because the nearby lakes had disappeared due to a general Altithermal warming and drying condition, the campsites were situated overlooking a stream. Thus, even in the matter of camp location, insights as to available game and changing climatic conditions can be gained.

The conclusion reached in the Rio Grande study was that the overriding consideration in camp location was water, not only for the human population but also for its megafaunal prey.

It is important to note that at several Clovis sites the projectiles are made of flint from the Alibates or Pedernales quarries. Those quarries were used for many years by successive groups. Either the Clovis and Folsom hunters went there as a group to get the flint, or they periodically sent task forces for it.

The big game hunters are also represented at two locations in Mexico. As already mentioned, at Tepexpan, in the Valley of Mexico a human skeleton was found in the same stratum as an articulated mammoth but not in association; no diagnostic artifacts were found. Because of careless fieldwork there was doubt (later somewhat dispelled) about the validity of this find, and little notice was taken of the discovery. Later, however, a mammoth with associated artifacts was discovered and reported under excellent control at Santa Isabel, Iztapan, also in the Valley of Mexico. With the Iztapan specimen was a knife vaguely resembling the Plano Scottsbluff type, but the ascribed date is about 11,000 B.P., somewhat early for that projectile type. Nonetheless, there is no doubt about the validity of the find. It is important because it documents not only the presence of mammoth hunters in Mexico but also the exceedingly rapid dispersal of the hunters southward as well as eastward from the presumed entry point in the northern Plains. A second Iztapan find also provided some chipped flint knives of nondiagnostic type.

EASTERN CLOVIS SITES The continental distribution and quantity of fluted points presents an interesting anomaly. Although the classic PaleoIndian sites occurring after 12,000 B.P. lie west of the Mississippi and Missouri Rivers, fluted points of several varieties are far more common east of these rivers (Figure 3.16). Several types, somewhat

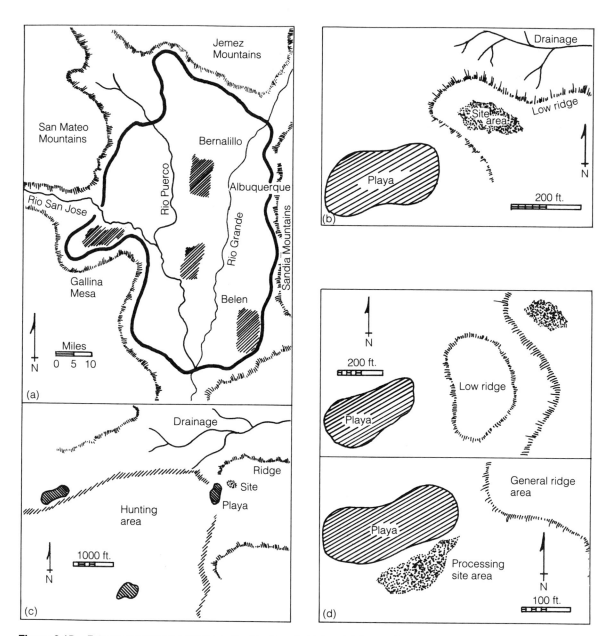

Figure 3.15 Folsom settlement patterns in the Rio Grande Valley: (a) the study area; (b), (c), (d) typical situations within the hunting area southwest (not shown in sketches (b) and (d)) of the elevated campsite, which overlooks the shallow lake (playa) and the hunting area.

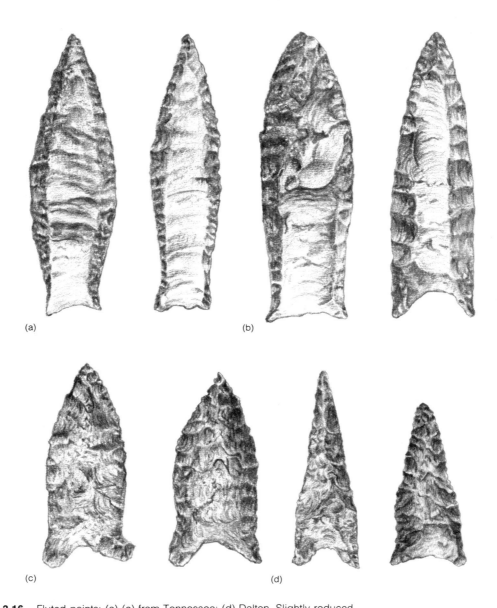

Figure 3.16   Fluted points: (a)-(c) from Tennessee; (d) Dalton. Slightly reduced.

variant from either Folsom or Clovis have been found in sufficient quantities to have been assigned local regional names. There are also several well-known eastern locations where many fluted points approaching classic Clovis in type have been collected. In eastern New York and in New Jersey, such sites as Port Mobil, Dutchess Quarry, West Athens, Kings Road, Potts, and Plenge are examples. Clovis fluted points come from most of these locations. Those from Plenge are particularly good specimens, as are those from Parkhill in Ontario. The scores of excellent Plenge site collections are particularly frustrating and largely useless because the only ones described are surface finds made by local amateurs and are, of course, undatable. There are also many other sites in the East such as Shoop in Pennsylvania and Williamson in Virginia, where scores of Clovis-style fluted points and much scrap from their manufacture has been known and recovered for years, but the artifacts dangle in time, again being surface finds. Williamson, however, is now known to have a buried segment.

Another site, Bull Brook, is near Ipswich, Massachusetts. It was discovered in the 1950s by W. C. Eldridge and Joseph Vaccaro, members of the Massachusetts Archaeological Society. (The gravel operations that revealed the site have since destroyed it.) While the microgeology of the site was puzzling in that no clearly discernible strata or old living surfaces could be detected, the artifacts and charcoal were buried twelve or more inches beneath the surface, and some 1000 specimens were recovered. They tended to occur in concentrations, as if discarded around preferred small camp spots. More than fifty fluted points or fragments were in the collection. The full inventory of specimens includes Clovis fluted pieces, which differ slightly from western ones; end scrapers with a spur; flake side scrapers of several sizes, including some that resemble the prismatic-flake Clovis curved blade; several sharp, pointed little **gravers;** drills; and the cores from which flakes were struck (Figure 3.17). The site is dated at about 9000 B.P., probably too recent by 1500 years.

At the Debert site in Nova Scotia, the assemblage resembles Bull Brook. There are 4000 artifacts from eleven living areas with associated hearths but no faunal associations. After averaging fourteen readings, the age derived from charcoal in the hearths is 10,600 B.P. Debert is a remarkably informative site. Like Bull Brook, it was a settlement, not a kill site, and was buried. At eleven locations there were concentrations of artifacts clustered around hearths. These locations are presumed to mark the site of shelters (perhaps open to the south)

with hearths near the north end of the flint-strewn living areas. At the time of occupancy, it appears that glacial ice was less than 60 miles away, and snowfields were as close as 5 miles. The periglacial environment, with an estimated mean annual temperature of 0°C (32°F), makes one suppose that the lengthy seasonal usage would have been late spring, summer, and early autumn, not winter. While no food bones were present, the target game is believed to have been caribou. The site, overlooking a then treeless, broad basin, was ideally situated for observing the herd movements.

Aside from the numerous fluted points that are not classic Clovis fluted and are now called Debert points (Figure 3.18), many other artifacts were recovered from the presumed living floors. The thousands of pieces include gravers; many scraper forms; forms called awls, drills, spokeshaves, and others; as well as much flint waste. There was an informative effort by the excavator to infer the "industrial" or functional uses of the several artifact classes, using four categories: (1) killing and butchery, (2) preparing consumable items (e.g., food), (3) processing raw material, and (4) making tools. The judgments were made on basis of form, edge wear, and chipping. There is not enough space to repeat all the interesting details covered in the report of what was a difficult and very important site.

A very recent find, 10,500 radiocarbon years old (TAMS), is the Vail site in Maine, just east of the Vermont border. It was discovered when the water level of a reservoir formed by damming the Magalloway River dropped well below normal to expose a wave-eroded area where whole and broken fluted points (some of almost classic Clovis style and some identical to the Debert specimens) were found.

Figure 3.17   Artifacts from Bull Brook. (a), (b) retouched blades; (c) **twist drill;** (d) uniface gravers; (e) fluted projectile points; (f) side scrapers; (g) end scrapers with graver spur at edge of blade. Slightly reduced.

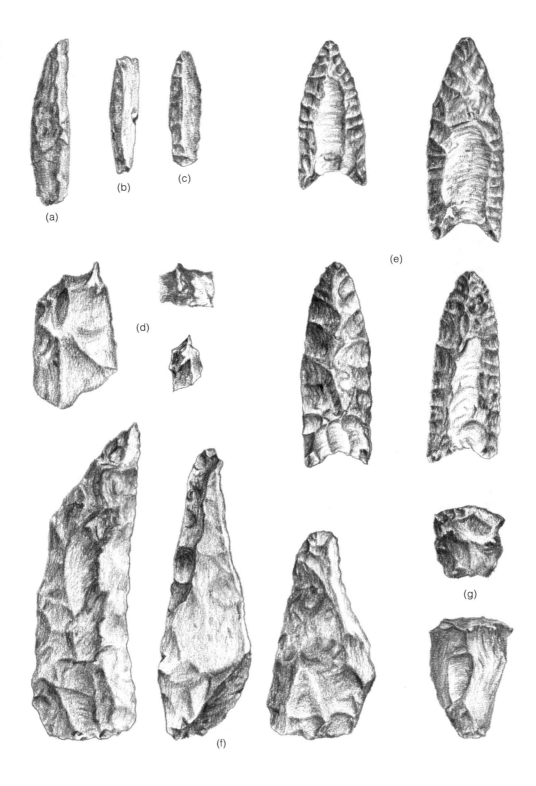

Figure 3.18   Debert point.

though perhaps 90 percent of the site remains, it was reinundated when the lake rose to its normal level, so what appears to be one of the richest eastern PaleoIndian sites cannot soon be revisited.

Since the Debert and Bull Brook locations were reported, several other PaleoIndian sites have been discovered and reported. Bull Brook II is a short occupancy site about 250 meters from Bull Brook. The tools are identical and are made of stone from the same quarry as Bull Brook. About 50 kilometers south is Wapanucket 8, where a PaleoIndian component essentially duplicates the Bull Brook assemblage. To the west, the Whipple site also produced fluted points, comparable to Debert, made from the same flints as those used at Bull Brook and Bull Brook II. The Whipple site yielded an average of 10,600 B.P., the same as Debert, with Vail of roughly equal age at 10,500 B.P. It is argued that Whipple, Wapanucket, and the two Bull Brook sites constitute a network (Bull Brook phase), and are contemporaneous at about 10,500 B.P., in the same range as Vail and Debert. Sites considerably farther south, such as Shawnee Minisink, fall in the same time range, TAMS dated at 10,570 B.P. The original dates from Bull Brook—only about 9000 B.P.—are probably wrong. Given all the evidence 10,500 B.P. is more reasonable.

Students working with PaleoIndian data in the Northeast have developed some interesting ideas. Their fine-grained studies have shown that early in postglacial times the landscapes would not have been tundra but woodland. It would have been a varied, patchy vegetation pattern with consequent differences in food resources. Based on lithic material, typologies of tools, and proximity, students have grouped the contemporary Bull Brook, Bull Brook II, Whipple, and Wapanucket 8 groups as a probable mating and possible work force network. The sites would thus form a sort of loose polity, although each would remain a social unit unto itself. The evidence also supports the notion of a low-

Like Debert, it was evidently occupied while the rugged interior of New England still had a tundra environment. About 200 meters from the campsite lay a kill site where a fluted point tip was found that fitted a base found at the campsite. Several hearths bespeak a long, or frequently repeated, occupancy, but the probably savage winters argue against a year-round base camp. In addition to making a collection of surface specimens exposed by wave action, a portion of the shallowly buried campsite was excavated. The location was elevated, downwind from a narrow canyon that opened into a wider valley. It is presumed that caribou were the preferred game and that they were ambushed as they fanned out over the valley from the confines of the canyon. There were a total of eight "hot" spots or activity areas (not all had accompanying hearths) where weapons were sharpened; none of the scrap indicated the fabrication of tools, merely sharpening. The tool inventory paralleled Debert in variety and presumed function. Al-

density population with high mobility so that the units of the mating network would often be in contact. Under this scheme the distinct social boundaries and closed mating network isolates would center around the better lithic sources. Debert and Vail are regarded as part of a similar cultural isolate.

Some of these speculations are reasonable. Proof of the mating network isolates is probably distant, but the evidence for a dynamic environment, where floral change was rapid and the accompanying faunal distribution was fluid is convincing. The absence of tundra would mean no huge migrating herds of caribou. Woodland game would have been the more solitary woodland caribou, moose, elk, and deer—animals that can be taken by the lone hunter or a small task force. Debert and Vail, however, because of their extreme northern location, would probably still have been harvesting herd caribou. The shifting of resources would lead to the suggested loose and fluid settlement pattern, or at least to a far-ranging hunting pattern, possibly out of a base camp.

Other recently described sites, such as West Athens Hill and Dutchess Quarry, were test excavated and revealed shallow but believable stratigraphy. At Dutchess Cave a questionable radiocarbon date of 12,500 B.P. was derived from a caribou bone allegedly associated with a fluted point. West Athens Hill was both a living and quarry site, but no hearths were observed. Dozens of point fragments were found. Presumably they were broken during manufacture. Thirteen fluted points are illustrated, but none is a classic Clovis although they are described as "conforming" to the Clovis fluted type. No other materials datable by ^{14}C were recovered. The flint scrap tended to be concentrated in what are called clusters. Many scrapers from the clusters show crushed and battered, hence dulled, working edges, leading the excavator to conclude that tools of wood, bone, and antler were manufactured here, as well as the basic flint forms. The site, on a hill, is believed

to have been a quarry, a living site, and a game-spotting location. There are several tools made of exotic flint from Pennsylvania, western New York, and Ohio, as well as from the distinctive local Normanskill flint. The clear implication is that, like those in the West, the eastern PaleoIndians were wide-ranging hunter-foragers. There are enough firm data to let us say without hesitation that there are both eastern and western PaleoIndian complexes that have similar toolkits and are almost coeval.

Another important eastern location is the Flint Run Complex. The site is about 50 miles west of Washington, D.C., on the south fork of the Shenandoah River. At Flint Run there is an extensive, stratified village or base camp, the Thunderbird site; a long-exploited **jasper** quarry; and flint-processing camps, one of which is the Fifty site.

Thunderbird has been the scene of the most extensive excavation. It is located on a long ridge a few hundred meters west of, and parallel to, the river channel. There are hunting camps and processing camps on fans extending out onto the floodplain. Debris occurs at "hot" spots (as at Debert and Bull Brook) on the terrace where structures or shelters of vertical posts are possibly associated with use surfaces and fired areas. These could be the earliest (10,900 B.P.) house structures in the Americas, but they are not clearly associated with the Clovis level of occupancy, most probably relating to the next or Archaic level; the evidence has been blurred by recent farming activity. A near-classic Clovis point and several other variant pieces were recovered from the lowest levels at Thunderbird. Above the Clovis finds are later Archaic levels. Other areas, apart from the structures, appear to be almost exclusively the result of flint-knapping activity; the evidence is in the presence of core fragments, and myriads of flakes created by pressure or hammer (baton?) blows. Like other such locations, the quarry sites yield largely cores, primary (percussion) flakes, and unfinished pieces labeled preforms. This is to say that production of half-finished tools went on at the quarries, which are located by outcrops of the chert or jasper.

The Flint Run investigators have gone rather carefully into the paleoresources of the region. Using a widespread series of pollen studies, they reconstruct the floral chronology of the Flint Run district in a familiar sequence. At 10,000 B.P., the mountain zone is characterized as having been tundra, and the foothills as spruce and pine dominated. There were extensive plateau grasslands, with the floodplain showing deciduous species and many extensive bogs. Except in one or two instances the bogs have long since been sealed beneath recent sediments. At 11,000 years B.P. fauna comprised the already familiar, now-extinct assemblage associated with tundra and **boreal** vegetation: mastodon, mammoth, caribou, two species of musk ox, moose, and bison. By 9300 B.P., or earlier, the animals were modern species.

At the Shawnee-Minisink site in Pennsylvania, TAMS dated at 10,570 B.P., a near-classic Clovis point and many other tools have been recovered, as well as good subsistence data, in what seems to have been a Clovis site. This project was fully reported in 1986. The Clovis level yielded fish bones and hawthorn seeds. This is the earliest North American evidence of fish in the diet; it was unexpected in a PaleoIndian context.

The Dalton Horizon

The existence and wide distribution of the Dalton point or knife and its associated tools has been known for many years. Found all over the Southeast—from Missouri to North Carolina and Georgia—its chronological placement has been uncertain, although kinship to the fluted points has been proposed. Because of its usual occurrence with the side-notched points of early Archaic affiliation, most students have regarded it as a form transitional from the fluted tradition to the Archaic. But now there are geologically sealed, stratified sites reported with pure Dalton assemblages. The age, based on ^{14}C assays, is 10,500 to 9900 B.P., slightly later than the Northeast sites just noted. That age makes the horizon essentially contemporary with the Folsom of the Plains.

The Dalton point sometimes has a shallow flute, but it is not **lanceolate** in shape (see Figure 3.16). Instead it combines the lanceolate and triangular shape. From a concave base the sides are nearly straight for about one-third of the length, and the remainder is a sharply triangular shape. Often the edges are thick and bevelled rather than thinned to a cutting edge. The cross section is a parallelogram rather than lenticular or lozenge-shaped. The bevelling is said to result from frequent resharpening of the tool. In fact, the type has been defined as basically a Paleo-Indian fluted lanceolate type with diagnostic resharpening. One wonders why only resharpened ones are discovered. Perhaps even when new they had the characteristic bevel. The Dalton Point is associated with many of the same tools found in Debert, Bull Brook, and Folsom sites. Notable is the distinctive "spurred" end-scraper (sometimes called scraper-graver), a variety of flake scrapers, and wedges (**pièces d'esquille**). Finding wedges so far south is unexpected. They are more common in the northern sites—Debert and Vail—where they are associated with fluted points.

Sites where Dalton materials have been found alone (i.e., unmixed with Archaic forms) are Rodgers Shelter in Missouri on the Pomme de Terre River; the Brand, Sloan, and Hawkins Cache sites in northeast Arkansas; and in the Haw River Valley of North Carolina. It is noteworthy that the Dalton people seem to have been the first to use caves and rock shelters in the uplands such as the Ozark plateau and the piedmont of North Carolina. The sites are rarely found in the river valleys, although their absence may be due to their being deeply covered by sediments. The upshot of new data and the firmer placement of the Dalton complex as being completely PaleoIndian at least in age, along with Debert and Vail, help establish the early spread of the PaleoIndians over the continent south of the ice before 10,000 B.P.

Evidently contemporary with the Dalton culture is the Little Salt Spring in west central Florida. The site, unique and enigmatic (if not improbable) in many ways, was under water. It is a sinkhole in the limestone over 175 feet deep. The surface basin has a steeply sloping bottom that opens abruptly into a throat that

expands like an hourglass more or less evenly to the silt-covered floor (Figure 3.19). About twelve meters down from the overhanging top of the narrow throat there is a ledge. Apparently the ledge, set deeply back from the mouth of the spring, was used more than once by humans when the water level in the spring was low. At least there was on the ledge a giant land turtle that had been killed by inserting a stick between the shells, presumably toward the heart. It was roasted, but the animal wasn't opened so the meat must not have

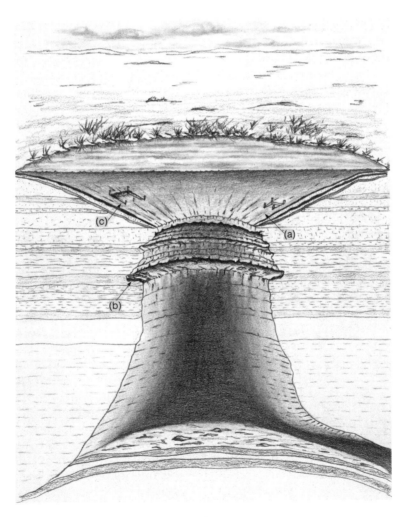

Figure 3.19   Little Salt Spring: (a) stake; (b) turtle; (c) fire pits.

been eaten. Bones of an extinct box turtle or tortoise, ground sloth, immature mammoth/ mastodon, and bison were also on the ledge. Around the lip of the sink or throat a series of stakes was driven into the sediment, and there were hearths higher up the slope toward the rim of the pool. No flint articles were recovered, but there were fragments of a throwing stick and a wooden mortar. The turtle bone was dated 13,450 B.P., the stake in the turtle shell was 12,000 B.P., and charcoal from one of the hearths was 12,100 B.P.

The presence of human evidence 75 feet below the current surface of the pool and small fires on the sloping basin bottom show that the water was much shallower 10,000 or so years ago. How the turtle shell was scorched by fire, and how the extinct megafauna bones got onto the ledge, undercut from the opening above, is not readily understood, and the excavators attempt no explanation. As mentioned, the exploration and limited excavation was done by divers; the site was, in fact, discovered by divers. The short and frustratingly incomplete 1979 report has not yet been augmented by a final analytic treatment.

In sum, the known stratified locations that have been radiocarbon dated securely place the PaleoIndian using fluted points in the East from 200 to 500 years later than the classic Clovis sites of the Plains. But so far the other fluted types in the East, such as the Cumberland, or the "eared" type called Quad, have not been found in controlled situations and are therefore not tied to specific dates. They are probably of the same age as the Clovis (and the Debert variants), but this is unproved.

The Folsom Culture

Slightly later than the western Clovis sites, and characterized by small projectile points with long, slender fluting scars, comes the Folsom culture. The inclusion of the Folsom culture as a separate section in this chapter is probably justified on the basis more of sentiment than of logic. But treating it sep-

arately here is more than a gesture memorializing the scientific breakthrough that followed the original Folsom find. The Folsom hunter evidently invented the cul-de-sac and surround technique for killing large numbers of game—usually bison.

There are several accepted Folsom finds, including Folsom itself and Level 2 at Blackwater Draw locality 1 in New Mexico, MacHaffie in Montana, Lindenmeier in Colorado, and Lipscomb in Texas. Newer finds include Hanson and one level of the Agate Basin site, both in Wyoming. Folsom fluted points are usually (although not exclusively) found in conjunction with the extinct long-horned bison. Most of these are kill sites where small herds of game were either trapped or driven over a fall. The radiocarbon dates cluster between 10,800 and 10,000 B.P.

Of the several sites Lindenmeier will be described at length because it is a campsite, rather than a kill site, and it yields the widest variety of material objects. The Lindenmeier site, just south of the Wyoming line in Colorado, is one of the most important of the Folsom sites. It was excavated in the 1930s and fully reported in the 1970s. Radiocarbon dates of 10,800 B.P. have been determined from charcoal collected some years after the excavation was done. Aside from its broad scientific importance, the site stands as a monument to the public-spirited amateurs— C. C., R. G., and A. L. Coffin—who found and called it to the attention of scientists.

Although there are several localities yielding artifacts and the work continued for several summers, the area of main importance to the story is a deeply buried, sloping stratum of black soil of high organic content, containing bones of extinct bison, modern forms of fox and wolf, and much workshop and campsite debris from a relatively continuous occupancy. On the basis of convincing geological and internal evidence, this stratum is interpreted as the shore and gently sloping bed of an ancient marsh or pond into which camp refuse was thrown. Later the broad valley was silted in by sediment from surrounding ridges and upstream until the surface was essentially level with no significant stream flow. When first discovered, the cultural stratum was buried about 2 feet deep near the original shore (?) and about 17 feet deep out toward the center of the pond. The material was revealed by a modern gully that eroded a deep channel to reveal the humus-rich stratum in the cutbank. The first excavation involved the cutting of a long trench down to the artifact and animal bone layer. No fireplaces, structures, or other evidence of village construction were found. The collection of stone artifacts, however, was rich and varied compared with other sites of this stage. In addition to small typical Folsom fluted points of chalcedony and other flints, there were several larger specimens (Figure 3.20).

In the typical Folsom point, after the fluting flake is removed, the edges of the blade are delicately retouched and, sometimes, ground or dulled toward the base. (This dulling of the edge is thought to have been necessary in order to attach the point to the haft). There is much waste flint in the deposit, including long, thin, flakes from the flutes, so the location is identified as a flint-knapping site as well as a much-used camp. In addition to the whole and broken Folsom fluted points found scattered in the debris, there were still some in association with partially articulated *Bison antiquus figginsii* bones. Elsewhere in the site artifacts were found in context with extinct camel and deer bones, as well as with bone from modern antelope. One mammoth tusk was also recovered. Among the flint tools were a variety of scrapers, including some well-made end or thumbnail types, where a thick flake is given a steeply beveled cutting or scraping edge on one end (Figure 3.21c). The small scraper with a graver spur also occurs. It is the same artifact often found at such early Eastern sites as Debert and Bull Brook. Side scrapers are often well-retouched flakes, with less uniform control of shape (Figure 3.21g). Some of the scrapers illustrated appear to be curved, prismatic pieces resembling the Clovis blade (Figure 3.21b). The Lindenmeier specimens show more battering and retouch on the cutting edges than those from a Clovis locality. The gravers are quite numerous (Figure 3.21a). These are usually random flakes on one edge of which a tiny, fine, sharp point (for engraving wood and bone?) has been worked with delicate pressure flaking. Some similar specimens with longer projecting points have been called chisels. Knives are broad, thin pieces with parallel sides and retouched edges, generally well made but showing nothing like the delicate skill of the fluted points. Even the flakes removed by the fluting process were used as cutting tools. Some very crude, ax-shaped, rudely chipped forms are called choppers. Other stone items include small hematite chunks used for pigment, grooved sandstone abraders or whetstones for smoothing and sharpening other tools, flat stones used as paint palettes, hammerstones, and some sandstone slabs (Figure 3.21f). Three or four eyed needles and an engraved bone disc (Figure 3.21d) were also found. The disc may have been an ornament or a **gaming piece.**

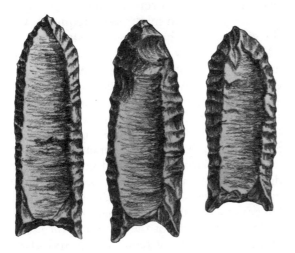

Figure 3.20 Folsom fluted points from Lindenmeier. Slightly reduced.

On the strength of the Lindenmeier collection it is possible to speak of a Folsom complex of artifacts; but of these artifacts, only the fluted points and the small scraper-gravers are sufficiently distinctive in form to have value in diagnosing either culture stage or individual collections as to affiliation. The snub-nosed scraper, a beveled knife form, the choppers, and the various side scrapers are found in many sites throughout the continent in other complexes.

The Folsom lifeway is not an exact duplicate of the one postulated for the Clovis. There is the already mentioned evidence of a new and efficient hunting technique, the cul-de-sac kill, as exemplified at Folsom itself. The technique was not only new but also suited to the prey. Bison blindly follow a leader. They are herd animals and not overly bright. The surround, while appropriate for bison, would not have sufficed for elephants who are intelligent, bellicose, and far more apt to charge the hunter than flee. The evidence suggests that the bison were driven into, or surprised by several hunters in, a cul-de-sac in the arroyo. Or the beasts may have been wounded during a drive and hazed into the trap, to be finished off in the box end of the gully. Such a technique seems to call for more than one or two hunters. It may bespeak intermittent group cooperation between hunters from several families, or it may suggest that the social group consisted of several families joined in a permanent band; at least a director of the hunt, either temporary or of some permanent status, may be inferred.

In portable possessions, camping pattern, clothing, shelter, and simple social organization (except during the hunt) the Folsom hunters no doubt greatly resembled their Clovis predecessors.

The new hunting technique meant a broadening of procurement technology and would require an entirely new set of procedures. That someone must have thought of it first is obvious. Trying the idea, however, would require planning. The technique would require a body of stalkers who would work cooperatively to drive a small herd of bison toward a previously agreed on trap or cul-de-sac. Once trapped, the animals would also need to be slaughtered by a cooperative effort. Clearly several bison cut off from the major herd and driven into the trap would provide tons of meat. All the group hunting activity above is new in the archaeological record. Very likely some form of food preservation, possibly drying, had to be performed by a fairly large labor force. Food drying might also have been an addition to the food technology.

The new kill technique would require someone with the power to organize and control the actions of relatively large groups of people. Therefore one postulates a social system in which a recognized leader with occasional power to command was essential to the success of the operation. (Of course, the authority figure may have had power only during the hunt as was true of the hunt "police" of the Cheyenne in historic times.) Thus the bare statement that a new food procurement technology was invented by the Folsom seems too simplistic. The cul-de-sac drive technique indicates that a relatively complex set of social relationships with one dominant figure had evolved from whatever the preceding Clovis social organization might have required. On the other hand, it has been suggested that the Clovis hunters were equally well organized and that there were organized work groups dispatched in search of needed materials. (For example, the Alibates flint and the Pedernales flint found at Clovis are from quarries more than a hundred miles distant from the site.) So it is probably an overstatement to say that the Folsom "invented" social control or the delegation of duties to task forces. But the evidence does suggest that these hunters of big game were not wandering helpless on the Plains or unaware of the necessity for cooperation in significant food getting and other endeavors.

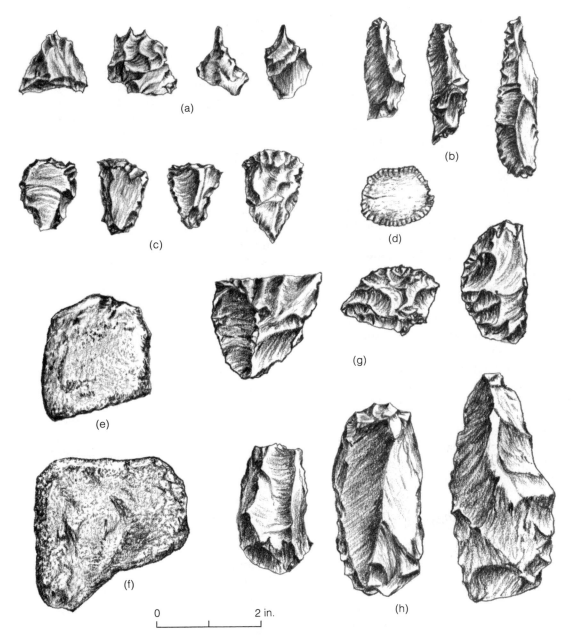

Figure 3.21 Artifacts from Lindenmeier: (a) gravers; (b) flake knives or scrapers; (c) snubnosed or end scrapers; (d) bone disc; (e), (f) smoothed sandstone slabs; (g) side scrapers; (h) quartzite scrapers. Reduced.

Western Desert Sites

Before leaving the fluted point hunters, it is important to mention that in recent years scattered fluted points, usually Clovis, have been found all over the desert West. They occur in Utah, Nevada, California, and Oregon, but they are usually surface finds and are not under good provenience control. Certainly there have been no reports of well-documented occurrences of fluted point with any datable charcoal or any of the extinct animals usually associated with the fluted points. But almost without exception the finds are located on the edges of, even on the beachlines of, old Pleistocene lakes known to have been in existence 11,000 or 12,000 years ago. Therefore it has been suggested by more than one scholar that the fluted points may represent not a big game hunting tradition at all but merely a projectile point tradition, and that the western specimens along the old marshes and lakes are referable to a Paleo-Indian focus on lacustrine (moist) environments and that the game were not large but small animals (birds, fish, etc.). Considerably more study and fieldwork needs to be done for this to become part of orthodoxy, but it is an interesting interpretation of the distribution patterns of the western points.

The Plano Cultures

In the East the record of the PaleoIndian story more or less ends with the Debert, Vail, Dalton, and related finds. But in the Plains as the PaleoIndian populations began to expand, the flint technology and point types proliferated. The crisp distinction between Clovis and Folsom is gone; the fluting technique in particular is lost. So the Plano designator is a catchall. Plano sites are numerous: Claypool in Colorado; Graham Cave in Missouri; MacHaffie in Montana; Allan, Lime Creek, Red Smoke, and Scottsbluff lower levels in Nebraska; Milnesand, Portales, and San Jon in New Mexico; Long in South Da-

kota; Bonfire, Damp Cave, Levi, Midland, and Plainview in Texas; Agate Basin, Allen, Finley, Hell Gap, and Horner in Wyoming; and several Canadian sites in Alberta.

Not all the Plano sites have been well reported, even though some are the type localities for certain named projectile or knife types. For example, the Finley site in Wyoming was extensively studied by geologists in the 1930s, but no full statement of the cultural debris has yet appeared. When research was first begun in the 1930s, all attention was devoted to the flint points or knives and the extinct faunal associations. If the points were not Folsom or Clovis types, they were described and named. The result was that for many years each excavated site lacking fluted points provided a new point type that was carefully described. The result was a wilderness of names and types; some of the specimens were not perceptibly different from some already labeled.

The confusion caused by the plethora of named point types was confounded by uncertainty about the ages of the sites where the types were recovered; they were simply deemed younger than Folsom, being unfluted. The primary problem, however, is with the points themselves. Like the Clovis points they all conform to a basic lanceolate or leaf shape. There *is* more variation in the proportions of the graceful lanceolate shape in the Plano types. The ratios of length to width can vary from 2:1 to 5:1, with 3.5:1 perhaps the average. But no Plano points have the medial fluting; the lack of that feature is to some extent diagnostic of the post-Folsom types.

Usually no reliable ages were originally assignable to the Plano types. But radiocarbon dating and continuous additions to the list of known sites have made it clear that many types, resembling one another but possessing different names, are contemporary. I would include Midland, Plainview, and San Jon as the first expression of the unfluted lanceolate point. Their imputed ages run from 10,500 to 10,000 B.P., only slightly younger than Folsom. And those points resemble each other markedly in length-to-width ratio. The quality of chipping varies, as do the details of chipping and shaping the bases. All appear to be edge ground and dull bladed on both edges from the base perhaps one-third of the distance up to the tip. There is no reason here to attempt the fine-grained analysis and detailed description of the many points and knives that would be required to satisfy the regional specialists about the exact point sequence of the Plano. The table below lists points, sites, and types in a chronology based on the analyses and biases of several authors.

Approximate Chronology of Major Plains Projectile Point Types

Time Before Present	Point Type
8000	Jimmy Allen
	Cascade
8500	Frederick—Firstview
	Cody Knife
	Scottsbluff
	Eden
9000	Alberta
9500	Hell Gap
10,000	Midland
	Firstview, San Jon
	Agate Basin
10,500	Plainview
	Milnesand, Folsom
11,000	GOSHEN(?)
	Clovis
12,000	

It is likely that a typologist confronted with a collection of Plainview, Firstview, San Jon,

Agate Basin, and Milnesand points would have difficulty segregating five uniform groups; the points would tend to arrange themselves in a continuum or gradation. All are lanceolate (though San Jon may have a slight shoulder as a result of heavy edge grinding), and most are well-chipped, with Midland the smallest and crudest. All seem to overlap in time or occur occasionally with Folsom points. The later types sometimes have narrow bases with pronounced shoulders, making the blade wider than the stem. The points found at Hell Gap, Alberta, and Scottsbluff are examples. The Cascade-Lerma points are anomalous because they lack the flat base, being double pointed; they are about 8000 years old and occur near the end of the PaleoIndian era.

The upshot is that only the Plains specialists can deal successfully with the regional variations in the fundamental lanceolate form of Plains projectiles. Moreover the many named types and the subtle differences between them have clouded our understanding and engendered useless arguments. It should be remembered that there is little evidence of culture changes from Folsom until the end of Plano times. Certainly changing styles in chipped flint points is not evidence of great change. The concentration on the kill technique certainly did not change.

Several hundred flint specimens, including thirty-two in the Plano tradition, were recovered from the Levi site in Texas. They include pieces resembling Angostura, Dalton, and Plainview specimens. There were also two Cascade or Lerma points and six resembling those found with the Iztapan mammoth in Mexico. Zone IV at Levi was the most productive, yielding exactly half the artifacts from the site. In addition to fifteen scraper types, ranging from well-made oval specimens to irregular flakes showing some use, there were three classes of burins, **microblades,** several prismatic flake scrapers and knives, gravers, five cobbles used as **manos,** one slab milling stone, and a solid bone or antler rod. This is the most extensive inventory yet reported for any Plano site. Zone II of Levi contained one basal fragment identified as a Clovis point and two projectile points that are reported as identical to Clovis points from Domebo. Two of the burin types were also represented in Zone IV. One can agree that Levi Zone IV may in fact represent a transition from Plano to Archaic, as do Graham Cave and other sites in Missouri.

Fauna from Zone IV are chiefly bison and deer, along with rodents, rabbits, and carnivores. Zones I and II also contained horse and tapir. Zone II is about 10,000 B.P.; Zone IV dates range from 9300 to 7400 B.P., with one sample, the deepest, yielding an inconsistent date of 6700 B.P.

Important data relevant to the Plainview— or at least to unfluted Folsom—comes from the Bonfire Shelter location in the Armistad Reservoir in Texas. It is a cave location kill site with three sealed layers of bone. Two of the bone beds yielded bison. Bed 2 contained an extinct form, either **Antiquus** or **Occidentalis,** and is radiocarbon dated at 10,250 B.P. Bed 3, dated at about 2800 B.P., of course contained modern bison. Plainview or Midland and Folsom points were recovered from bed 2. This location is an important one, in that it extends the range of two or three diagnostic projectile types much farther south.

The Eden point (Figure 3.7) is an especially well-made type, long and slender with smooth, even chipping and a strong median ridge. Occasionally the blade has a slight square shoulder creating a stem, and a squared base. Chipping varies; in some pieces the long, ribbony flake scars appear to extend across the entire blade, while in others the flake scars show that shorter, broader flakes were removed from each edge toward a median ridge. The overall form is altogether different in concept and execution from the preceding fluted forms, albeit equally well made. The similarity of Scottsbluff points to Eden is marked. The difference is in the slightly less precise chipping and the stubbier, less graceful blade

proportions, heavier shoulders, and shorter stem of the Scottsbluff points. That they bear different names should not obscure their probable relationship as variations on a common concept.

Another very important site, Horner, lies near Cody, Wyoming. It was dug in the 1950s, revisited in 1977, and reported in 1987. There were hearths or fire-stained areas, so it may have been a village, but this point isn't clear. Remains of 180 (probably modern) bison were found. Many specimens of both Eden and Scottsbluff points may attest to the contemporaneity and association of the two types. Other artifacts include scrapers, knives, engraving tools, choppers, hammerstones, and **rubbing stones.** Here, too, was found the uniquely distinctive Cody knife (Figure 3.22). This is a sharp cutting blade with an offset or angled stem; the chipping is very good, and the entire artifact is thin and smooth. Although size varies and blade-to-stem angles are different in some cases, the basic design remains the same. This knife has come to be regarded as a marker or index type. The radiocarbon dates, from charred bone and charcoal, place the Horner site at about 7000 B.P.

The Claypool site in Colorado yielded many Cody knives; Scottsbluff, Eden, and Plain-

Figure 3.22 Cody knife. Actual size.

view points; thumbnail scrapers; drills or perforators of flint; grooved abraders and whetstones; and other nondiagnostic items. The associated fauna are modern species, so Claypool supports the evidence from Horner.

The Lerma points of Mexico and Texas are equated with the Cascade points of the Columbia plateau areas. Both types show the Plano technique of chipping and smooth lanceolate form. The placement of the Lerma and Cascade points in the Plano grouping is done on admittedly technological grounds; the one or two radiocarbon dates falling at about 8000 B.P. support this placement.

Other probable Plano culture sites require no description here, with the possible exception of Milnesand, where a broad, lanceolate, stemless form of point or blade was recovered. This one seems to have wider distribution than some of the more distinctive types.

The fall or jump-off hunting technique, was added to the hunting repertory of the Plains tribes early in Plano times. It may be an improvement on the cul-de-sac of the Folsom. In any case, it persisted, along with the cul-de-sac and surround, as a basic technique from Plano times until about A.D. 1885. The term *jump-off* is aptly descriptive of this kind of hunt, and, as described by eyewitnesses in the nineteenth century, it was a colorful and exciting event. While the technique was simple in conception, success depended on many factors and required the coordination of a sizable group of people, close and skilled direction, and advance planning.

The principle seems to have been to direct a small herd of bison toward a precipice or arroyo in order to force the animals over the edge. The key to the process is that herd animals' usual response to the threat of danger is flight—often blind, unreasoned flight, which is called a stampede. The crucial beginning of a jump-off kill, then, involves turning (or luring with a decoy) a herd of a few dozen or more animals into the mouth of a wide, V-shaped trap formed by two long lines

of people or rock cairns or clumps of brush with people hidden behind them. At the mouth of the V the lines were quite far apart, and a few people behind them could drive the animals to enter the trap without suspecting the presence of other hunters. When the herd was within the trap, the hunters pressed close, frightening the animals into a faster pace, and the people in the lines of the V began to shout, brandish their weapons, wave blankets, and otherwise harass the running herd. The animals went deeper into the trap trying to escape the hunters, who were on all sides except at the small open end of the V. Terrified, the animals rushed toward the freedom promised by the end of the trap and so plunged to their deaths at the foot of the jump-off.

The procedures involved men, women, and children for stations in the trap and skilled "drivers" to divert a portion of a larger herd into the trap. The technique, of course, worked for hunters either mounted or on foot. Systematic butchery was carried out at the kill site. Evidently most of the hides were removed (the tail vertebrae are almost never recovered), and the carcasses were thoroughly dismembered.

At this juncture some other carefully excavated kill sites should be described to exemplify the wealth of information these sites contain. The first is the Olsen-Chubbuck kill in east central Colorado, not far from Kit Carson near the Kansas line; its age is 10,200 B.P. The kill occurred where a long, narrow gully (3 meters wide by possibly 2 meters deep) lay across the path of a bison herd stampeding down a steep hillside. Approximately 190 animals of both sexes and all ages were injured or killed in the trap. Butchery began immediately. In the course of the butchering (and during the kill itself) more than 60 tools—Firstview points, cobbles for breaking bones, and flint flake knives and scrapers—were lost or discarded.

Many of the bones were piled in order by heaps indicating that the butchery process

followed a consistent pattern. It was doubtless efficient and rapid. The bone piles showed
that after skinning and removal of the savory
hump meat, the forelegs and shoulder girdle
were removed, stripped of meat, and discarded. Next, the hind legs and pelvic girdle
were cut free, the meat removed, and the
bones discarded on the foreleg bones. Usually
in the scrap heap the hind legs lay above the
pelvic bones. Next atop the heap were chains
of vertebrae with skulls attached. Animals
wedged deeply into the narrow bottom of the
arroyo rarely showed any evidence of butchery, their bones being still articulated upon
discovery.

In addition to providing the details about
butchering techniques, the site allowed analysis of the age components of the herd: calf,
yearling, and so on. The chipped flint showed
that a wide range of raw materials had been
collected and used, including some Texas Alibates flint pieces. This reinforced the ideas
widely held about the wandering or trading
of the Folsom-PaleoIndian bands.

A number of bison kills have been discovered in Wyoming. One, the Casper site near
the town of Casper, is of interest because it
is not a fall but an unusual variation on the
trap or cul-de-sac technique. The site, dated
8000 B.P., was an extensive bone bed between
the horns of a fossil parabolic dune. The heavy
animals could not ascend the shifting sand of
the steep dune face. As they milled, their escape was cut off by the hunters between the
horns of the crescentic dune, and they were
slaughtered one by one.

This location also provided information on
herd composition; but the data suggest that
selective killing was practiced here, there being
more carcasses in the 0.6- to 2.6-year range
than a random herd would normally have.
Presumably the older animals were allowed
to go free. It is interesting to note that in sites
where the animal teeth are analyzed for age,
as at Olsen-Chubbock and here, they reveal
an October-November kill date. This suggests, as did the Colby elephant site, that kills

were organized after the weather had turned
cold, which reinforces the frozen storage idea.
Nearly all the associated points are of the Hell
Gap type.

There is also a report of a kill of yet a third
type reminiscent of Folsom. Here, in an ancient, very deep arroyo that ended with a
steep-walled "jump-up" or knickpoint forming an unscalable barrier, are the remains of
a kill of about one hundred bison. The technique involved driving several small herds
upstream until the animals were wedged
helplessly against each other in the narrow
gully. The date of this kill at the Hawken location (in extreme northeast Wyoming, near
Sun Dance) is 6500 B.P.

Aside from the detailed paleogeomorpho-
logical reconstructions made by the authors,
the site is the type site for a new point, here
called the Hawken side-notched. The form is
very similar to a distinctive Archaic style found
farther west in the northern Great Basin and
called the Northern side-notched. The points
are also similar to a contemporary and probably related Idaho series of side-notched points
called Bitterroot (see Figures 4.15 and 4.16).
The artifacts and the recent date remove this
site from the Plano list, but it exemplifies the
persistence of the mass kill strategy.

An interesting location reported recently is
the Owl Cave (also called Wasden) site in
southern Idaho on the Snake River Plain, a
cold, steppe-prairie environment amid lava
flows and buttes that have evidently been stable for 10,000 or more years. The site is a series
of large caves formed by the collapse of the
roof of a large lava tube. This natural trap was
turned to human advantage. Upon a layer of
roof spalls there were mammoth bones and
with them were three fragments of Folsom
fluted points. The radiocarbon date from a
bone that showed tool cut marks was 10,900
B.P., at about the extreme early end of the
Folsom time span. After another, more massive, roof fall, some 150 bison were apparently driven into the trap and butchered. The
date of this event was 8000 B.P.; the associated

artifacts were predominately Agate Basin types.

The Owl Cave Folsom deposit has yielded many expediency tools, including flaked mammoth bone fragments allegedly used as knives. There was also much flint debitage. In fact the Folsom part of the site is characterized as a flint workshop and bone quarry. It may be that the mammoth were killed after blundering into the trap, but the bison were probably stampeded over the lip of the collapsed roof.

The Arctic

The earliest cultural remains found in Alaska seem to be as old, or slightly older, than the Folsom of the Plains. But the tool remains of the first Alaskans are in no way similar to the delicately chipped fluted points and other tools of either the Folsom or the later Plano people. They are products of a different tradition that dominated eastern Siberia and Japan from 18,000 to 12,000 years ago.

The tradition in question is the "core and blade," which Müller-Beck called the Aurignacoid. The phrase refers to a very specific stone technology then found over much of Eurasia. It involves striking flakes of even size from carefully prepared cores of dome, wedge, or thick conical shape (see Figures 3.12 and 3.23). Many razor-sharp prismatic and quadrilateral flakes can be made with the technique. The flat flakes are also called **lamellar** (platelike) flakes.

In the Asiatic sites where the core and blade technique was first observed, the blades are common. The flakes were large. Some were used unmodified, while others were used as "blanks" from which end and side scrapers and bifacially chipped points and knives were made. At the sites over 10,000 years old, blades and chipped forms occur in about equal numbers.

In Alaska the assemblage is called the Paleoarctic. It was first described and named at the Onion Portage site on the Kobuk River. For an early Arctic site the artifacts were numerous, so good samples were recovered. But more important was the situation. The site lay upon and below a sloping bank or bluff on the Kobuk River, beside a caribou crossing evidently used for most of Recent time.

The site consisted of scores of thin layers of sands and earth washed from the bluff; in and between the layers were many thin cultural layers that had accumulated during intermittent, brief human use of the site. The alternating layers of wash and cultural deposit reached a depth, at one point, of about twenty feet. The lowest two layers yielded a collection (called Akmak and Kobuk) that included large cores, disc-shaped bifaces, ovate and elongated bifaces, and the small core flakes seen in Figure 3.12. The site was, and is, a landmark discovery because of its age of about 10,000 years, its depth, and the succession of later cultures in the upper strata. Its completely sealed circumstance is taken at face value.

Another important site, discovered earlier, is the Anangula, an islet off the coast of Umnak Island in the eastern end of the Aleutian Island chain. It was a surface site—evidently a blowout—where hundreds of cores and flakes were collected. The assemblage was a pure core and blade manifestation as Figure 3.23 shows. It was possible to locate and excavate a small, undisturbed area of the site; organic material was recovered and dated at about 8500 B.P. Although classed with the Denali site (see below), the flake blades are larger, averaging some 80 centimeters in length. The artifacts are more similar to those from the Shiritakii-Hattoridai site on Hokaiddo, Japan than to the Denali site. The general likeness to Japanese specimens was noted by the excavators.

Figure 3.23 Artifacts of the Paleoarctic tradition: (a)–(g) wedge-shaped cores; (h) blade core; (i), (j) core bifaces; (k) end scraper; (l)–(u) blades; (v), (w) fluted and incipiently fluted points. Reduced about one-third.

The Anangula's large cores and flakes are not typical; from Akmak times onward the cores and blades are small. Described as microblades, the flakes are often as small as 3 centimeters in length and 0.5 centimeter in width. They were too small to be hand held and used effectively alone. Evidently they were set in grooves on the edge of a piece of wood or bone; several blades set in line make a sharp knife or saw. Burins and gravers were also fashioned on the small flakes. Some students call the microblade industry the Denali. It is included here as a part of the Paleoarctic since the microblades were a part of that assemblage in the Akmak complex.

The sites that add the name Denali to the Paleoarctic tradition are clustered in the Tangle Lakes area south and a little east of Fairbanks. Several years were spent there in survey and excavation. Not all the sites are reported. While one radiocarbon date is claimed to be 12,000 B.P., most fall in the 10,000 B.P. or later range. This tight cluster of sites is on a fossil strandline of the Tangle Lakes. They occur in shallow soil that formed on a loess blanketing the shores. When the water fell to the present level, 30 meters below the old shore, another loess derived from the exposed lake sediments covered the habitation locations. Thus some of the sites were sealed. The investigator compares the sites with the Campus site that was dug in the 1930s and was correctly described as resembling the core and flake industries of Mongolia. Essentially ignored for about forty years, it can now be called Denali.

Microblades occur at dozens of other evidently early sites, including Girls Hill, Putu, Healy Lake, Dry Creek, Ugashilz Narrows, and Kogginang. The fluted points at Girls Hill and Putu deserve mention. A few scholars tend to see these points as the long-sought precursors of the Clovis and Folsom forms of the United States even though the chipping and control of the fluting is nowhere near as fine as that of the classic Clovis and Folsom points. But these fluted points occurred on the surface, so they are not dated and provide no real basis for postulating a fluted point horizon for Alaska. If a few were found in dated contexts, the case would become stronger. Lacking dates for the finds, it seems prudent to reserve judgment on their possible ancestral role.

At Healy Lake an enigmatic set of artifacts with Chindadu points occur along with the Paleoarctic complex. The points are small, thin, chipped stone specimens of triangular or teardrop shape. They are remindful of a few Japanese artifacts, but no other Alaskan examples have been reported.

The Denali is not crisply defined. It is too late in time to have influenced or contributed to the early culture of the hunters below the Canadian border and can be dropped from that consideration.

Settlements and Social Order

This chapter about the Paleo-Indian can be closed by touching on some of the reconstructions of PaleoIndian lifeways that have been attempted in recent years. The descriptions of the sites—Clovis through Plano—could well leave the impression that the big game hunters are thought to have harvested megafauna and little else. But at nearly every site described, except the ones reported earliest, smaller animals were also represented in the camp debris. The reason that the earlier reports ignored such evidence was probably that the excavators were careless by today's field standards or, more likely, were interested only in big animals and fluted points.

The picture of a single focus or focal subsistence has been misleading. Subsistence was undoubtedly more diffuse: A variety of vegetable foods and smaller game would not have been ignored. The tools found at the sites bespeak a wide variety of tools for making tools and processing foods. And all the evidence points to small bands of people who moved in a cyclical, planned way from one resource to another and returned time after time to familiar, favorite campsites. Some sites were evidently used repeatedly as base camps in locations that were favorable for both hunting and foraging. At Debert, Flint Run, Bull Brook, Hanson, Lindenmeier, and other Clovis and Folsom sites the toolkits, the concentrations of debris around hearths, and the wide variety of tools for specialized uses compel the recognition of a far wider spectrum of activities than endless hunts for big game. In addition to base camps, where three or four families gathered, there are several kinds of special-use sites. Quarries, flint-knapping sites, and hunting stands, to say nothing of single or mass kill sites, are examples of special-use locations.

As mentioned, base camps (sometimes incorrectly called villages) existed at Lindenmeier, Debert, Bull Brook, Hanson, Flint Run, and probably elsewhere. At Bull Brook and Debert particularly there were "hot spots" where flint objects and debitage were concentrated, with nothing between the use areas. At Debert the hearths were central to the debitage areas. At Hanson there were two hardpacked surfaces, carpeted in sand, that were interpreted as lodge floors. At both Debert and Hanson the flint tools were subjected to exhaustive functional analysis and were identified as saws, knives, scrapers, planes, chisels, gravers, and wedges. The inference that bone, antler, and wood were being used in the manufacture of other tools, utensils, and weapons is sound.

At the earlier sites perishable items were largely missing. Bones of the basic focal prey, if there were any, were not preserved, and there was no hint of vegetable foods. However, an early study of PaleoIndian sites in the southern Plains mentions the finding of seeds and evidence of storage. The Flint Run Complex, located along a fork of the Shenandoah River in Virginia, is distinguished by a series of sites that include living floors, many concentrations of flint-working debris from nearby quarries, and even clusters of just one class of artifacts. The Thunderbird site is an extensive stratified site in the Flint Run Complex. It is interpreted as a permanent (often used?) base camp where the resources, especially flint, were exploited, tools were refurbished, and domestic tasks were performed.

It seems clear that the term *foragers* or *hunter-gatherers* could correctly be applied to the PaleoIndians. Theory and ethnographic analogy have been applied to reconstructions of the PaleoIndian social organization by several authors. As is to be expected in such matters, the reconstructions vary, but some uniformities are apparent in the scholars' conclusions that: (1) The basic social unit was no more than two or three patrilocal families; (2) the seasonal range from resource to resource would perhaps have had a radius of less than 100 miles; (3) the range was a fully familiar territory; (4) many families aggregated in bands for communal hunts; (5) the task force personnel was flexible (for example, several families might gather on a hunt or as few as two or three persons might travel some distance to preferred resources such as a flint quarry); and (6) the social order was egalitarian with unrestricted access to all resources for all groups. On the other hand, in the Llano Estacado, the high southern plains of Texas and Oklahoma, there is little evidence of communal hunting. Most kills are singles, probably killed in ambush. At the Clovis (BW-1) site there were single kills all around the spring lake. For the entire Llano Estacado it is estimated that during Clovis times no more than ten basic family groups would have used the area.

All the studies of settlement patterns and types of site seem to agree that the base camp was always near water—a spring, arroyo, or canyon, where game would have been abundant because of water and vegetation—and always had a downwind overview and evidence of ancillary food resources. Such criteria would not control the kill, or other special-use, sites. The base camp can be identified by the rare evidence of varied food sources. For Clovis and Folsom sites debitage containing channel or flute flakes is considered key evidence of a base camp, because the manufacture was carried on there.

It is evident that science knows more about the animals killed, the flint-working ability of the PaleoIndians, and the details of the archaeological circumstances of the finds than about the social behavior of the people or their diet. One can predict that with archaeological interest now focused on broader interests, more will be learned about subsistence, settlement patterns, and possibly social organization. Except for some aspects of settlement preferences, data today are scant on such matters.

In the concluding words of this chapter, it is necessary to mention the problem of selecting sites used as examples from the increasing number of choices. Another problem has been the placement of the several stratified sites (Blackwater Draw, Lindenmeier, Hell Gap, Bonfire Shelter, Levi, and others) that contain two, three, and even more components. For example, Bonfire Shelter could also have been discussed as a Plano site; Hell Gap would fit in any of the three categories used here. If any logic has controlled the choices, it has been a weighing of the nature of the contribution the site makes to student understanding. It is fervently hoped that useful placements have, in general, been made.

In Chapter Four we direct our attention to the next continentwide cultural manifestation—the Archaic.

Chapter 3
Bibliography

The literature on the PaleoIndian is technical and professional in nature. Some of it is quite readable, however. Recommended are:

Fagan, Brian M.

1987 *The Great Journey.* Thames and Hudson. London.

This volume is highly recommended for students at any level of study. Smoothly and lucidly written, it is undoubtedly the best available treatment of the PaleoIndian. It deals with almost all reported finds—spurious or valid—in adequate, even detailed, analyses and is fair in evaluating them.

Frison, George C.

1978 *Prehistoric Hunters of the High Plains.* Academic Press. Orlando.

In this volume, Frison described Casper, Hawken, Glenrock, and many other kill sites more fully. There is also an interesting chapter on animal behavior.

Haury, Emil W., Edwin B. Sayles, and W. W. Wasley

1959 The Lehner Mammoth Site, Southeastern Arizona. *American Antiquity* Vol. 25, No. 1: 2–30.

This is a concise report of the discovery, excavation, and findings at the Lehner site. It is well done, reads easily, and has good illustrations.

Jennings, Jesse D.

1983   Origins. In *Ancient North Americans*, edited by J. D. Jennings, pp. 25–67. W. H. Freeman. New York.

MacNeish, Richard S. (editor)

1973   *Early Man in America: readings from the Scientific American.* W. H. Freeman. San Francisco.

This book is recommended. It is written in a very easy style and offers exciting descriptions of important PaleoIndian finds by the excavators themselves.

Wormington, H. M.

1957   *Ancient Man in North America.* 4th ed. Denver Museum of Natural History.

Probably now out of print, this book summarizes most of the PaleoIndian sites on record up to 1956. Pictures of excavations, artifacts, and an easy style make this book very worthwhile. Some of the locations mentioned are no longer regarded as important, but it remains useful as a wide-ranging introduction to the subject.

The Archaic Stage

At the outset it must be emphasized again that the concept of stage carries no connotation of time. The term *Archaic* is intended as a generalized designator (or shorthand term) for a lifeway, a subsistence strategy, and a social system. Wherever the Archaic is found—and it is continentwide—it was a hunter-gatherer mode of life. The population was small, probably increasing in density through time and, in its more complex, mature form in the East, contained many cultural elements that endured into the diverse cultures of the eastern woodlands after about 3000 B.P.

But to discuss the Archaic from place to place we need to specify the period of its dominance. The duration of the Archaic is highly variable; local or regional Archaic chronologies differ greatly. Most sources would date the beginning of the Archaic east of the Mississippi at 10,000 B.P. or a little later, with a terminal date of about 3000 B.P. In the Plains, however, it extended from 7000 B.P. to 100 or 200 A.D., and in the West from 9000 B.P. or earlier to about 1850 A.D. Obviously one can speak of the Archaic period only locally. In the same way, given the myriad of environments and the variation in resources, no one description of the faunal or vegetal species collected or the tools and weapons used can be offered for the continent. Even the differences between the preceding PaleoIndian stage and the Archaic cannot be crisply defined. In fact there appears to have been a rather lengthy transition period between them.

This transition period was a time of adaptation to new environments, especially in the East, as the arctic tundra, conifer forests, and caribou moved north, to be replaced by the deciduous woodlands that eventually blanketed the East from New England southward and west to the Mississippi Valley. In the Plains the climate was dryer, but the basic grasslands persisted; only the game differed as the Pleistocene megafauna disappeared.

The eastern Archaic lifeway developed in one of the richest and most varied ecological zones of the continent. There the Archaic peoples exploited a broad spectrum of plants and animals as had the PaleoIndian. By 4000 B.P. the population was fairly dense, large winter villages were reoccupied annually, and the subsistence pattern was one that seasonally exploited almost endless resources. Deer were taken year round, as were fish, turtles, and shellfish where available, and small game (turkey, squirrels, rabbits, muskrats, and opossums). Vegetal resources included the fatty nuts in autumn; berries, fruits, and grass and weed seeds in summer; and greens and bulbs in the spring. There is evidence of food storage at the winter villages.

In the Far West the population was much sparser, and both game and vegetal resources were less varied, but the same seasonal exploitation and orderly cyclical movement from resource to resource was the common pattern of life. Moreover, in a number of places vast marshes provided a microenvironment as rich as the eastern woodlands. Waterfowl, fish, and vegetal foods were available year-round. Some scholars think that permanent villages grew up around the shallow lakes and marshes, relying on these endlessly renewed resources.

Everywhere the stage was marked by increased variety in the toolkit, particularly in the development of new types of chipped stone points and knives with stems and side or corner notches. Many believe that these points were developed for use with the **atlatl** or spear thrower. The lanceolate forms of the PaleoIndian are believed to have been for thrusting.

As was true in PaleoIndian times, certain points or knives enjoyed wide popularity and seem to be fairly reliable time horizon markers. In the East a well-known sequence is found at most of the stratified sites from Alabama to New England. The Dalton (and local variants) points are always in the lowest deposits. They signal the end of the eastern PaleoIndian period and are usually thought of as marking the beginning of the transition to early Archaic. The age of the Dalton complex has been set at 10,000 B.P., a time when Folsom fluted points were (or were about to be) abandoned in the West. The early eastern Archaic projection point sequence was first observed at the Hardaway site in the headwaters of the Pee Dee River in the North Carolina piedmont. Earliest was the Hardaway-Dalton, followed by the Hardaway corner notched, the Palmer corner notched, three Kirk types, Stanly, Morrow Mountain I and II, and several later types. At the Icehouse Bottom site on the Little Tennessee River a similar series was recorded, beginning with Kirk and running up to Morrow Mountain, with St. Albans and LeCroy types between Kirk and Stanly (See Figure 4.1). At the Tennessee sites the Kirk level was dated at 9400 B.P. and the latest Morrow Mountain levels at 7000 B.P. Some of the same types (or comparable types with local names) are found in Alabama at about the same time and in New York a little later. The flint work is coarse and some of the types are hard for the novice to distinguish. The many local variations on the Dalton with bevelled edges are also confusing. (The broad distribution of specific eastern Archaic points is matched by the wide spread of certain points of the western Archaic.)

Figure 4.1   Eastern projectile point types from early (bottom) to late: (a) unnamed, (b) Iddins undifferentiated, (c) and (e) Morrow Mountain, (d) Savannah River, (f) Kanawha, (g) Kirk Stemmed, (h) Stanly, (i) St. Albans, (j) LeCroy, (k) Upper Kirk, (l) Clovis, (m) Dalton, (n) Lower Kirk. Scale given.

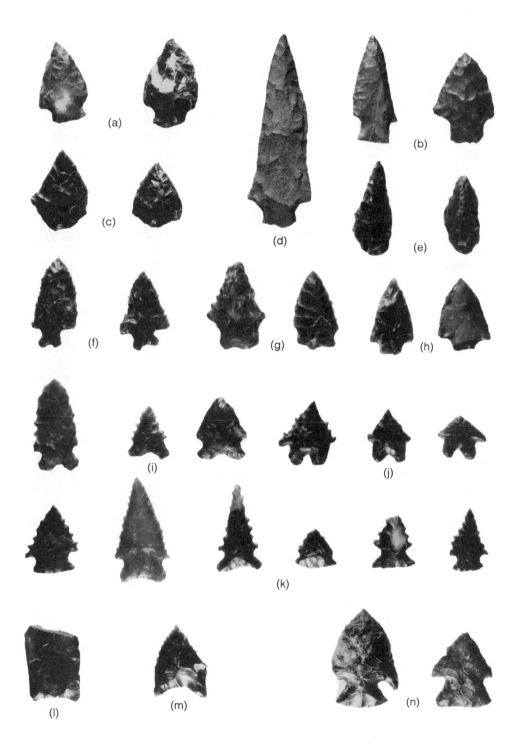

(a)

(b)

(c)

(d)

(e)

(f)

(g)

(h)

(i)

(j)

(k)

(l)

(m)

(n)

The facts of point distribution are difficult to explain. Were the newer types more efficient, or do they mirror a change in preferred game? Probably not the latter because wherever preservation of food bones is good enough for identification, deer is the dominant prey until historic times in the East. The change in chipped stone point "fashion" could hardly be explained by wide influence of a single band or tribe, given the assumed weak social organization at the time and the low population density. Whatever the cause, the successive popularity of point styles is an interesting problem.

The artifacts reflect a variety of technological skills. There is an increase in heavy ground stone woodworking tools necessary for successful exploitation of forest environments (**axes, adzes,** wedges, **gouges,** etc.); food milling equipment in specialized forms (**metates, mortars, manos, pestles,** etc.); stone vessels (important because they reflect greater permanence of occupancy than in the PaleoIndian period); and, in particular areas, ground slate points and knives, variously shaped polished atlatl weights, **plummet stones,** stone tubes or pipes, and stone beads. The chipped stone choppers and scrapers continue into the Archaic with little modification. The **drill** is very rare in PaleoIndian collections but is common in the Archaic. Although lanceolate forms continue, there is greater variety of points, with emphasis on stemmed, corner-notched, and side-notched forms, in that order. The presence of numerous forms—together and in quantity—of "rough stone" items (**hammerstones,** anvil stones, notched pebbles, saws, abraders, and whetstones) is considered to be a fairly reliable general criterion of the Archaic, as are masses of fire-cracked stones used in pit roasting and **stone boiling.** Bone, horn, and ivory **awls,** perforators, and needles (indicating basketry and/or skin working) or articles such as **gorges,** pronged fish spears, harpoons, and fishhooks (which attest to the harvesting of fish or other marine prey) are abundant in the Archaic, as are shell (especially for ornaments), copper, and **asphaltum,** which first appear in the Archaic. Formalized burials (such as **flexed burials** in round graves, partial cremation, use of red ocher, and inclusion of grave goods) and village site refuse accumulations (which, though small in horizonal extent, are often deep enough to indicate considerable temporal continuity) are considered important criteria of the stage; early evidence of houses and storage pits is generally lacking.

Obviously not all Archaic cultures would possess all the tools, equipment, or technology in the list above. The resources available over the continent vary tremendously, and the available equipment would be appropriate to those resources. For example, fishhooks would not be found in the Plains and there wouldn't be many axes, chisels, or gouges in the Great Basin. The list above should be thought of as a very general one, including all major and some minor items likely to be found during the Archaic stage in the appropriate environments.

It is important to repeat that the Archaic stage—the hunter-gatherer or hunter-forager stage is found all over the continent. In fact the Archaic stage, usually called the Mesolithic elsewhere, is found all over the world. Often described as exploiting a wide or even total spectrum of fauna and flora, it was the most successful lifeway ever devised by humans. Because in theory, if not in practice, all edible plant or animal resources were available for harvest, the entire subsistence mode was extremely efficient. It has led to the coining of the term *archaic efficiency* as a reasonable evaluation of an adaptation to the total natural environment. The local technology was, of course, closely geared to the resources of a limited area. We need only note the persistence of the Archaic as testimony to its effectiveness.

"Total exploitation," however, was not practiced. Not every edible food was collected. Considerable selectivity was exercised in the choice of subsistence species. Choices among resources are reflected in the archaeological record and have been universally observed ethnographically among modern hunter-forager groups.

An effort to explain this selectivity has led a few archaeologists interested in hunter-forager subsistence to borrow a biological concept that has survival or evolutionary implications and is usually called optimal foraging strategy or, sometimes, evolutionary ecology. Ethnographic research has shown that each group studied has a relatively short list of preferred or desired foods. These foods are harvested in order of preference. If one of the major preferred resources disappears seasonally or because of environmental change, those lower on the list are exploited. Rather detailed research has shown that the valued foods invariably provide the most calories for the least cost in collecting and processing effort. Those lower on the list simply provide fewer calories for energy expended in collecting and processing. Reduced to its simplest form, optimal foraging theory is an application in biology of the minimum effort and maximum gain so familiar in economic study. Minimum effort–maximum gain theory can be reduced for hunter-gatherers to a statement that the food gathered will be tasty, nutritious, varyingly abundant and hopefully close to hand.

What seems to be basic, then, to hunter-gatherer subsistence is selectivity. The choices are based on nutrition and caloric reward. The archaeological record abounds in evidence of this characteristic. A couple of examples will illustrate both the seasonal and the opportunistic nature of the procurement system.

In the Illinois Valley archaeologists have discovered that the Archaic population exploited the migratory waterfowl rather heavily. The Illinois-Mississippi Valley, of course, is a flyway for migratory waterfowl as they go north in the spring to breed and rear their young and return south in the fall with the summer brood added. Large quantities of nuts

were also taken in that area, as were turkeys and deer. Both the turkeys and deer fed on some of the nut crops. Fish and deer were probably taken year-round, while berries, tubers, and greens were collected during their growing season. Artifacts for capturing and processing these resources abound in sites such as Indian Knoll in Kentucky and Eva in Tennessee, which are in similar environments. Since the resources were so predictable over such a long period of time, the toolkit, while increasing in variety to reflect the growing population, does not change very much.

Meat supplies in the Great Basin were markedly sparser. Rabbit hunts occurred in the fall, rabbits being most numerous at that time of year. Antelope were harvested periodically by means of drives, but the recovery rate for an antelope herd is slow so antelope were not a regular item of diet. In the Great Basin and many other areas known to ethnologists, the major portion of the Archaic diet was vegetal: seeds, tubers, roots, and berries that could be collected and stored. Interestingly enough, the vegetal foods were rarely the most preferred food. Wherever subsistence habits have been studied, meat is the preferred food. Nonetheless, the diet remains largely vegetal in most of the foraging cultures that have been studied ethnographically.

But there is more to archaic efficiency than mere seasonal exploitation of the most desirable foods. The implications of the concept of efficiency are legion. Efficiency in exploitation implies new techniques of food preparation and a broadened range of raw materials. One basic innovation is the use of some form of mill for crushing or grinding hard-shelled kernels or nuts. The slab millstone and the small upper millstone or mano were used over the West for the grinding of grass seeds from several species. In the East a stone or wooden (?) pestle was used in stone and wooden mortars to grind nuts and possibly smaller seeds. The mill simultaneously made available new vegetal foods and necessitated new cooking techniques such as those required for making cakes, loaves, or mush.

The use of plant fibers made possible the development of textile arts, with the result that mats, baskets, and bags were created from resources previously unused. Coiled basketry required a few new tools, such as the bone or wooden awl used in stitching. The availability of baskets expedited gathering, transport, and storage. Mats may imply a notion of greater personal sleeping comfort and the wrapping and storage of objects, or they may only have been for bodily warmth or funerary gear. In the West the flat, shallow, **winnowing basket** was an essential and highly practical piece of the equipment needed to prepare grass seeds for use as food.

Fibers were also used for cordage in making nets to catch fish, rodents, and even fowl. The cordage may have partially replaced skin and sinew in many things. The variety of devices for taking game of every size may also have increased.

What archaic efficiency implies, then, is a technology using many raw materials not clearly present in the record of the Paleo-Indian cultures, in a series of inventions or innovations. Technological advance, of course, leads to specialized rather than all-purpose tools (for example, three sizes of snares in a single design for large, medium, and small rodents of similar habitats), and increasing skills would lead to refinements in food collecting and conceivably to other special tools.

Eastern Archaic

Early (10,000 to 8000 B.P.)

Until recently dealing with the Early Archaic in the East has been complicated by the fact that there were so few excavated and reported sites. Those that were known were widely scattered, and no consistent pat-

terning or clustering of artifacts defined a recognizable complex. Work has accelerated since the late 1960s, particularly in emergency excavations behind the dams creating reservoirs, and a large inventory of sites now offers comparative data. As a result of comparison (and at risk of oversimplification) one can say that a series of diagnostic projectile point or knife types characterize the Early Archaic more or less over most of the East and into the Midwest. The associated ^{14}C dates run from about 10,000 B.P. in the South to about 8000 B.P. in New England, while they average a little later west of the Appalachians.

The timing, the repetition of a somewhat similar sequence of points, and the extensive distribution has led to the postulation or definition of an Atlantic Slope Tradition to which the Early Archaic sites belong. The varyingly distinct types are usually found in this order: The earliest are Kessel and Charleston (and Big Sandy I) at slightly less than 10,000 B.P.—evidently contemporary with terminal Dalton. Next comes the Kirk (9000 B.P.), which have corner notches and, frequently, serrated edges. In the next 2000 years there occur the bifurcated stemmed types St. Albans and LeCroy; the short stemmed Stanly; and, by 7400 B.P., the Morrow Mountain and Kanawha types. (For typical examples of these point types again see Figure 4.1.) Those types can evidently serve as horizon markers (see Chapter One) and as a basis for assigning dates to an artifact assemblage not datable by ^{14}C or other means.

Stone artifacts are about the only evidence to document the Early Archaic. Animal bones and other organic materials are rarely found because they are dissolved or decayed by bacteria and rainfall carrying the weak acids from decaying humus percolating through the soils. But when organic materials were charred, of course, they did not decay because charcoal is chemically very stable.

Some important early sites are Icehouse Bottom, Harrison Branch, Calloway Island, Rose Island, and others on the Little Tennessee River; Modoc Rock Shelter in Illinois; St. Albans in West Virginia; Hardaway in North Carolina; Stanfield-Worley in Alabama; the lower levels of the Thunderbird site at Flint Ridge in Virginia; Rodgers Shelter and Graham Cave in Missouri; and a few sites in New England that seem to be later by some years than the Early Archaic sites in the south.

Icehouse Bottom is one of several newly reported sites on the Little Tennessee River in Monroe County, Tennessee. The excavator believed that there were very early Archaic sites along the river but that they were deeply buried under flood sediments. It was reasoned that the sites would be just above or just downstream from topographic features that would constrict flood runoff waters. The deceleration of stream velocity and ponding caused by the constriction would result in deposition of much of the sediment load upstream from the constriction. At the same time the turbulence below the narrows would create bars, that is, rapid deposition of silt because of the decreased water velocity in the eddying currents. Five locations were selected for a test of the assumptions. Icehouse Bottom was one site found just downstream from a short narrow segment of the channel.

The test was conducted by backhoe trenching. When cultural material was found as deep as eight or nine feet, excavation was done by hand, with the backhoe used only to remove the noncultural overburden. The cultural layers were as much as 15 feet thick, so the maximum trench depth extended to some 23 feet in some spots. The cultural record extended from 9200 to 7000 B.P., spanning Early into Middle Archaic. The dates were derived from charcoal bits recovered by water screening from the culture-bearing strata. The finds, except for textile impressions and charred nut hulls, were stone—some 95,000 pieces, of which 3000 were tools with the remainder debitage.

The successive levels were labelled according to the dominant type of chipped points or knives in the levels. The earliest was the Kirk, next were St. Albans, LeCroy Bifurcate,

Stanly, and the latest, Morrow Mountain dated at 7000 B.P. As mentioned, these labels are no more than the names of projectile point types that have been in use by eastern scholars for many years (see Figure 4.1).

There were over 300 circular fireplaces scattered on all levels. On the Kirk levels they tended to be "prepared"; that is, clay was brought from a nearby quarry and used to model a base or hearth for the fire. Most often in the upper layers no hearth was made. The fire was merely built in the spot desired with no further ado. A number of the prepared clay hearths had distinct basketry impressions, always manufactured in the **twining** technique. Except for three out of twenty-nine, all the basketry-impressed hearths were in the Early Kirk layers. The significance of impressing basketry into the soft clay of the hearths is unknown.

No food bones were recovered, probably because of the moist, acidic conditions where they lay. But even vegetal remains were scanty, seeds being almost nonexistent. Charred acorn shells were found from Kirk times onward, as were hickory nut shells, which were dominant in most layers. By about 7000 B.P., during Stanly times, walnuts appear to have been used. Walnuts became the most popular within a few centuries after their use began.

Although Icehouse Bottom and other nearby early sites were little more than sampled due to the time limits on the work (they were part of the Tellico Dam reservoir salvage program), their record of the Early Archaic confirms and extends previous knowledge of that time period in the Tennessee region. Now submerged, the sites cannot be revisited.

In Alabama, where many Archaic sites have been found and excavated, Russell Cave is well known. It lies on a small tributary of the Tennessee River near Chattanooga, Tennessee. Excavated intermittently and never fully reported, Russell Cave contained a wealth of Archaic data. There were actually two caves, but only the upper one had been used as a camp. The lower one contained a perennial stream. The cultural deposits were 14 feet deep. The earliest were dated at 8200 B.P., and the site was occasionally occupied until nearly historic times. One infant burial from the base layers dated to 8500 B.P. The projectile points at that level were of Early Archaic type, but there is no mention of Dalton points. Above were Middle and Late Archaic levels when the use of the shelter was heaviest. After the Christian era, uses of the shelter were rare, merely temporary stays by hunting parties.

Another important Archaic location in the eastern United States is St. Albans in West Virginia. Preliminary reports are that the site contains some 35 feet of alternating cultural and natural layers. The lower levels were sampled with an auger. The lowest provided charcoal dated at almost 10,000 B.P. Of the total depth 19 feet have been excavated. Located on the Kanawha River on an ancient natural levee the site has been inundated, with concurrent deposition of sterile silt, countless times in its long history. The cultural zones are thus well-sealed, and it is one of the longest dated artifact series in eastern North America. The artifacts recorded partially duplicate the record at Hardaway and Icehouse Bottom.

The Stanfield-Worley Bluff Shelter is another informative southern site located in northern Alabama near Tuscumbia. The circumstances surrounding its excavation merit mention. It was discovered by amateur members of the Alabama Archaeological Society and excavated with funds raised by the Archaeological Research Association of Alabama, Inc. The University of Alabama provided tools, equipment, material, and supervision. Labor was volunteered by students, Boy Scouts, members of the Archaeological Society, and other interested parties. The list of donors and participants contains over 300 names. Again the amateur archaeologist is to be thanked and congratulated.

The site lies next to a stream under a large overhang 40 to 50 feet deep and some 200 feet long. It contained four separable strata. These

are labeled zones A through D, D being the lowest. Zone D was sealed by a sterile silt layer, zone C. Zone A yielded pottery; zone B was Late Archaic, lacking pottery; zone D was early, yielding Dalton points and a small collection of scrapers. The radiocarbon age of zone D was about 9300 B.P. The Dalton (zone D) deposit thus accumulated at, or even slightly earlier than, the time the Plano cultures were beginning to differentiate from the preceding PaleoIndian hunter base.

Although the artifact yield from the Dalton zone was small, seven familiar types were recovered. The types were three variants on the Dalton type (Nuckolls, Colbert, and Greenbriar), Big Sandy I, Hardaway Side Notched, Beaver Lake, and Stanfield Triangular. (As discussed later, The Big Sandy point type was originally named from the upper or latest level of the Eva site, but the Big Sandy I points at the Stanfield–Worley site were 2000 to 3000 years earlier. The misidentification stuck, so the Big Sandy I type is now firmly established in archaeological reporting as an Early Archaic type.) Despite the various names, the non-Dalton type points are not widely different. They are all essentially triangular, with concave bases. The chipping is reasonably smooth, but the overall impression is one of crudeness. The Big Sandy I is important because it has irregular side notches, a detail of form that becomes very common in later Archaic types.

The collection also includes some well-made little gravers (Figure 4.2), the familiar small flakes upon which a tiny, sharp point is prepared by careful chipping. Comparable gravers are included in all the early collections wherever they were noticed and saved by the excavator. Being small, rude in outline, and unknown in America until recent years, it is likely that thousands of gravers have been overlooked and discarded during the decades of excavation. Additional flint tools included long, flat flakes with secondary chipping around the edges to make knives or scrapers. Other, better-modeled scrapers made from

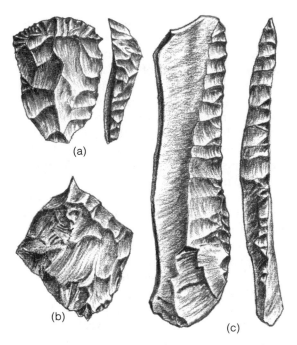

(a)

(b)

(c)

Figure 4.2 Artifacts from the Stanfield-Worley Bluff Shelter: (a) scraper, (b) graver, (c) flake knife. Approximately actual size.

thick flakes were rectangular, oval, and triangular in shape. The Dalton food bone scrap, well preserved under the shelter, was predominantly white-tailed deer with terrapin, turkey, and squirrel represented. No tools indicating a concern with vegetal foods were noted.

Although zone D may have been a living site, no hearths or living surfaces were identified. In zones A and B the artifact take was heavier and can be readily correlated with other reported later sites. Zone B was most heavily used; there were many storage pits and several basin-shaped hearths containing ash and charcoal. Storage pits and hearths are characteristic of zone A as well. The deposit was shallow; the total site depth varied from 5 to 7 feet, with zone B averaging only 6 inches in thickness. Sites in Tennessee (Nuckolls) and Alabama (Quad) yield large collections of materials duplicating the Dalton complex—gravers, variants on the Dalton point, and many

scrapers made from prismatic flakes very like the Clovis knives.

The Early Archaic is, of course, represented in other places. At the Thunderbird and Shawnee-Minisink sites, the smooth transition from the fluted point levels to the Archaic is recorded. The projectile points that were chronological markers in the Piedmont are found here in the same order, and the familiar scrapers and gravers, are present as well.

The Early Archaic is also represented in New England at such sites as Neville and Weirs Beach in New Hampshire. The dating falls a little later in that area, and sites that are clearly Early Archaic are by no means abundant. Current wisdom is that the advent of modern woodlands was delayed in New England because the glaciers of the Great Lakes and Labrador regions receded more slowly than those to the west. Food resources were therefore much scarcer because the conifer forests, which provide few food resources, remained dominant. With nothing to attract them, the Archaic population only became significant in New England after 7500 B.P. when weather was milder and biota more varied.

Early Archaic is not clearly represented at all in most of the Great Lakes region. Only the late PaleoIndian stone types (i.e., Plano types) are represented there, and they persist until about 7000 B.P. A few sites in the Great Lakes area, however, have yielded both Plano and Early Archaic types, which suggests that the Archaic tools were replacing the Paleo-Indian ones and that there was some overlap of the two tool traditions. For a time the Plano projectile types dominated south of the lakes. One can conclude that the Early Archaic per se is largely confined to the Southeast and that the eastern Archaic lifeway developed in the South and expanded northward with the spreading deciduous forests. Thus Middle and Late Archaic sites are common over all the states, but the earliest forms are not.

What can be said descriptively about the Early Archaic is largely limited to what can be learned from the chipped stone, which is scanty. For example, except at Shawnee-Mini-sink, Icehouse Bottom, and a few other scattered open sites, subsistence is largely inferential. Some sites yielded limited amounts of animal, fish, and vegetal fragments, but no **milling stones** were found. The toolkit of knives; gravers, or **burins;** scrapers; and the infrequent adze or axe forms, however, do testify to a considerable industry in wood, bone, and hide. Basketry, or at least twined textile, is evidenced at Icehouse Bottom. Most authors emphasize that the Early Archaic is little more than a slow transition, little different from PaleoIndian in subsistence focus or toolkit, except that in the South the fluted point style disappeared in favor of the Dalton types, which in turn also disappeared.

In the short descriptions above the paucity of solid interpretive facts is evident. The Early Archaic is known almost entirely from the chipped stone tools used by the people. Except for the lack of fluted points, the tools and their presumed function do not seem to differ from the tools of the fluted point makers. It is assumed that a hunting-gathering subsistence mode was standard, but evidence of the animals and vegetal foods taken is largely lacking.

So we move on to the Middle and Late Archaic where slightly better data are available.

Middle (8000 to 6000 B.P.) and Late (6000 to 3000 B.P.)

In order to save space and avoid redundant artifact lists, the distinctions between Middle and Late Archaic will be largely ignored. Many of the sites to be described have both Middle and Late components, frequently not recognized during excavation. Those that are known to be late can be recognized by the dates ascribed to the sites. Although there are artifacts typical of the Late Archaic—for example, copper objects, terrapin carapace and pebble rattles, and a wealth

of imported shell—the crowning distinction of the Late Archaic is the initiation, possibly the invention, of food production, which is discussed at the end of this section.

It is possible to speak of Middle and Late Archaic not because there were dramatic changes in lifeway but because there was an observable broadening of the spectrum of resources exploited and the addition of a few new items of technology. The tool inventory began to include more ground stone tools such as axes and adzes. Bone tools such as awls used in basketry are found, implying the making of coiled basketry. Where they were available, freshwater mussels were collected. The quantities of shell in the midden accumulations imply that shellfish were important but were by no means the only food item. Fishhooks testify to a developing freshwater and ocean fishing industry. Again it seems that the best evidence of this phase of Archaic development comes from the South, the Atlantic coastal states, and the Midwest.

If it is correct to think of Early Archaic as essentially an extension of the PaleoIndian, Middle Archaic should be thought of as the real beginning of the richness that characterized the fully evolved late stages of Archaic. And many of the traits that characterize the high cultures of the continent can be identified in incipient form in the Archaic cultures.

In the southern states the diagnostic Middle Archaic point appears to be the Morrow Mountain type. It is characterized by a basically triangular form, with convex rather than serrated sides; a short, blunt rudimentary stem; and nonsymmetrical shoulders. In no way does it resemble the Kirk or bifurcated stemmed forms of St. Albans or LeCroy. The Morrow Mountain type and its chronological placement were recognized during the Hardaway research mentioned earlier. It was once misidentified as the Gypsum point, a late type from the West.

The Middle Archaic is represented by the middle layers of Hardaway in North Carolina, St. Albans in West Virginia, and Stanfield-

Worley and Sanderson Cave in Alabama, among others. Perhaps the greater amount of Middle and Late Archaic data came from the excavation of many huge shell mounds—some with a twenty-foot depth of deposit—along the Tennessee River during the TVA salvage digs of the 1930s. Unfortunately the digging was done with such gross controls that the basalar Middle Archaic materials were not always segregated. But at the Eva site the objects associated with the Middle Archaic were segregated and recognized. It merits a careful review.

The Eva site is in western Tennessee. It is now an open location on a natural levee along one of the long-abandoned channels of the lower reaches of the Tennessee River. The site reveals four significant strata. The lowest, stratum V, is dated at 7200 B.P. Strata V and IV yield artifacts of the earliest or Eva component. They are regarded as early Middle Archaic. Stratum III is sterile earth completely sealing the underlying strata IV and V. Stratum II is the Three Mile component, and stratum I is the Big Sandy, a late phase. On all levels there were many animal food bones— all of modern species—and on all levels deer accounted for 85 to 92 percent of the bone. Other animals were bear, raccoon, opossum, turkey, and fish. In Three Mile times a heavy occurrence of mussel shell accompanied by a decrease in deer bone represents either a broadening of the subsistence base, a decline in the available number of deer, a climatic change, or perhaps all of these. No shell debris was found in the Big Sandy layer. So at Eva deer was apparently the year-round staple, and we can assume that the hunting technology was primarily aimed at this prey. Deer were more than food sources; they provided antler and dense, solid bone for a variety of tools and an occasional ornament, sinew for tough cordage or thread, and hide for clothing and other leather goods. In all periods, the rich acorn, walnut, and hickory nut crop of the area was probably harvested, but no evidence other than anvil stones from stratum

V and **nutstones** from stratum I argues for the use of nuts. The artifact complex was rich and varied, with the fewest types coming from the Eva (strata V and IV) layers. The greatest variation, and perhaps specialization, occurs in the stone tools.

The tools point to specialized uses, most of which can be identified with hunting. One was the atlatl (an Aztec word), or **throwing board** or spear thrower (Figure 4.3). It was usually of composite manufacture, consisting of a springy wooden shaft about 2 feet long, fitted with a tough hook of antler, often with a weight mounted toward the center of the shaft (for balance or better whip action), and a shaped handle or grip with finger loops. The atlatl itself was an important technological advance. With it the spear could be thrown farther and with the same or greater accuracy as with the unaided arm. Its use implies open glades in the woodlands because it could not be employed in dense growths of timber or undergrowth.

The resilient antler tips or tines were used for the delicate work of retouching flint. The large number of awls is often taken as evidence of much leather working, but the awls were more probably used for making baskets. They are always common in sites where basketry itself is preserved; basketry and weaving are found in Archaic sites wherever dry conditions of deposit permit their survival. The failure of basketry to survive in eastern sites either in the open or in damp shelters is due entirely to the conditions of local storage.

There were human burials associated with all levels. A total of 180 were recovered. Forty-seven of these were infants or juveniles, with the remainder adult. Eighteen large dogs were given formal burial as well. Fourteen of the dogs were from the Three Mile level. None came from the Eva level. Usually the dogs as well as the human bodies had been placed in prepared pits; 75 percent (both human and dog) were in the fully flexed position. Most came from the Three Mile level, with only seventeen humans from the Eva level. Some-

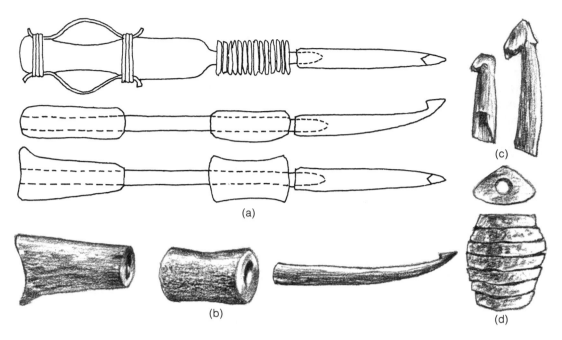

Figure 4.3   Atlatl parts from Indian Knoll: (a) restorations; (b) atlatl handle, weight, and hook; (c) atlatl hooks; (d) shell atlatl weights.

times a grave would be dug through an earlier interment, which would scatter the older bones.

An astonishing thirteen (13 percent) of the adults are said to have survived past the age of sixty, five even passing seventy. For aboriginals to survive to these ages is unusual. The five over seventy were all male (see Chapter Five on the health advantages of a foraging lifeway over that of sedentary farmers), and nearly half of the females had died before age thirty. They were small, with delicate bone structure, averaging 5 feet 2 inches in height. Males were larger, heavily muscled, and big-boned, with a mean height of 5 feet 6 inches. The crania were high-vaulted, **mesocephalic,** with medium-heavy brow ridges, wide malar bones, and some **alveolar prognathism.** Shovel-shaped incisors occurred but were not dominant. They became more numerous in the later levels. No cranial deformation was noted. This physical type corresponds closely to the few other Archaic populations that have been studied. Certain peculiarities of genetic

nature were noted in the Eva site population, such as the large canine teeth found in the later levels. The excavators concluded that the basic homogeneity of the skeletal remains from all levels in the site argues for an isolated and stable gene pool over the life of the site. A similar stability of the same basic physical type was observed at Indian Knoll, to be described later.

At the Eva site the toolkit provides a glimpse of a technology geared to a series of staple foods in what was probably a semipermanent settlement or base camp. Deer was the dominant food and meat source, providing raw material for tools and hides for clothing as well. The awls and needles speak for basketry, tailored clothing, and footwear. The atlatl, presumably a more efficient hunting tool, was also present. Stone—**mullers** and nutstones—was used in processing vegetal foods. Fishhooks of bone and antler, antler hide scrapers, tubular bone beads, stone pendants, and a wide variety of flint types, including Morrow Mountain points were also found (Figure 4.4).

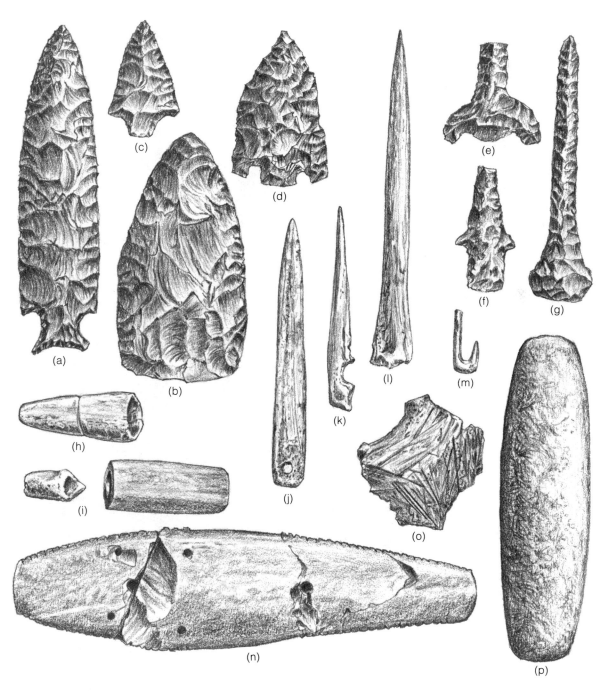

Figure 4.4 Artifacts from the Eva site: (a) Benton point, (b) bifacial blade, (c) Morrow point, (d) Eva point II, (e) and (f) stemmed drills with Eva base, (g) drill, (h) tubular pipe, (i) atlatl hook and weight, (j) bone needle, (k) and (l) bone awls, (m) bone fishhook, (n) gorget, (o) sharpening stone, (p) pestle. Variable scale.

Red **ocher** in lumps and as powder smeared on some objects was common. From other Middle Archaic sites such items as turtle carapace rattles, antler atlatl hooks, atlatl shaft weights (including **bannerstones**), and possibly the bell-shaped pestle for processing vegetal foods in wooden mortars can be added to the artifact inventory. Flat milling stones, presumably for processing vegetal foods, have been found at Modoc Rockshelter in Illinois and Doerschuck in North Carolina.

Still another rich Archaic site is Indian Knoll in western Kentucky. Although the stratigraphy, undoubtedly present, was not noticed, the site is a classic example of the shell-mound Archaic station. The sites of the Lauderdale focus in northern Alabama were also fine examples. Indian Knoll lies on the banks of an old channel of the Green River. It is about 2 acres in extent (450 feet long by 220 feet wide); shell and earth had accumulated to a maximum depth of 8 feet. An incredible amount of cultural debris was recovered. Artifacts exceeded 55,000 in number, and some 880 skeletons were found. (An earlier excavator had removed several hundred other burials.) The burials, including twenty-one dogs (which were diagnosed as being right-footed!), were in more than half the cases tightly flexed in round wells or pits (Figure 4.5). Most of the others had been laid on the ground and covered. Many of the human burials had grave offerings and ornaments with them, and most individuals had been smeared with red ocher pigment at the time of burial. In physical type these people were very like those described from Eva; they were also quite a homogeneous population.

As at Eva, food animals represented in the midden show an overwhelming preference for deer (23,100 pieces of deer bone out of a total of 25,570 bone pieces recovered), although raccoon, opossum, dog, groundhog, wildcat, and a few rodents were also taken. Turkey and goose were the favored birds. Drumfish were taken and mussel shells were numerous

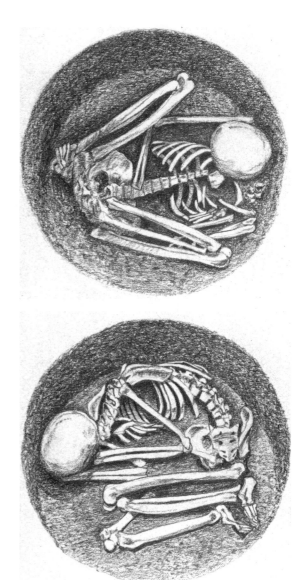

Figure 4.5 Round grave burials at Indian Knoll, Kentucky.

on all levels, indicating that this mollusc probably served as a minor staple.

The artifacts were scattered randomly throughout the fill, although sometimes clusters or caches of almost identical pieces were found, as if the maker or owner had hidden but never retrieved them. There is a bewildering variety of tools made from every material. The list of artifact classes the analyst prepared runs over 100 items.

Throughout the site were prepared clay floors that are presumed to have been living areas. Many fire-reddened zones on these floors marked the hearths. Around the fireplaces were the charred hulls of walnuts, acorns, and hickory nuts in great quantity. Scattered molds of vertical posts set into the clay floors around the burnt areas suggest rude windbreaks or covered shelters; more careful excavation might have revealed house patterns. In fact later excavations at other sites unearthed similar clay floors with an arc of posts at the clay edges. Some of the floors of these obvious dwelling structures had been repaired or renewed, which suggests frequent reuse or long, continued use of the house.

Artifacts can be divided into broad categories based on materials used and manufacture. These were **chipped stone, ground stone** (smoothed), bone, antler, and shell specimens. Chipped flint objects included quantities of points, usually well chipped and divided into stemmed, side-notched, and corner-notched types. Stemless ovoid or triangular, probably hafted, knives 3 to 4½ inches long were common. Drills of winged and expanding types were numerous, as were a variety of scrapers made from thick, sometimes prismatic, flakes. Including fragments there were over 13,000 flint specimens in all. Today the archaeologist would have split this collection into many more types, probably giving them specific type names. Ground stone includes atlatl weights of prismatic and bar types, grooved axes, grooved **mauls,** hammerstones, pestles (usually conical), milling stones (**lapstones**), **cupstones** or nutstones (slabs with numerous shallow pits 1 to 1½ inches in diameter), a few stone beads, and miscellaneous items such as whetstones and slate discs. Two thin sheets and one bar pendant of copper were found in graves.

Bone awls of many styles, including thousands of splinters, were recovered. Ulnae of deer and other animals, cannon bones, and tibiae were all used for awls. Flat, spatulate objects were also numerous. Fishhooks; thin, slender pins or **bodkins,** some with flat heads; tubular beads; larger bone tubes; and other bone tools were also found. Thirty-two rattles made from box tortoise shells with pebbles inside came only from graves. Perforated canine teeth, possibly used for necklaces, and beaver-incisor engraving tools round out the list of bone specimens. Antler was used for atlatl tips and handles, bone-flaking tools, and projectile points.

Shell was a favored material for beads (discoidal, tubular, and spherical), rings, **gorgets,** pendants, atlatl weights, and knobheaded pins. Gorgets and pins were made from Gulf of Mexico conch shells which, of course, had to be obtained through exchange, as did the several examples of clusters of *Olivella* shell sewn on robes or used as beads. Representative specimens of the items cited above appear in Figures 4.6 and 4.7.

The Lauderdale focus sites of Alabama are as rich as the Indian Knoll deposit. The similarities between them are numerous and obvious. Although the deposits span a long time range, the only report of the Alabama collection made no effort to separate Early from Later Archaic complexes. Some of the sites were as much as 16 feet deep and covered many acres. Along with such sites as Turtle Mound near New Smyrna, Florida, the Lauderdale and Indian Knoll sites offer conclusive evidence of permanent dwelling places for many people over centuries of use. (In many cases in the riverside locations, thin deposits of silt occur throughout the sites and seal off the lower layers. These silt bands are taken as evidence of brief periods of extremely high water that required temporary site abandonment.)

Some of the items found at Indian Knoll assume a certain importance. These are the

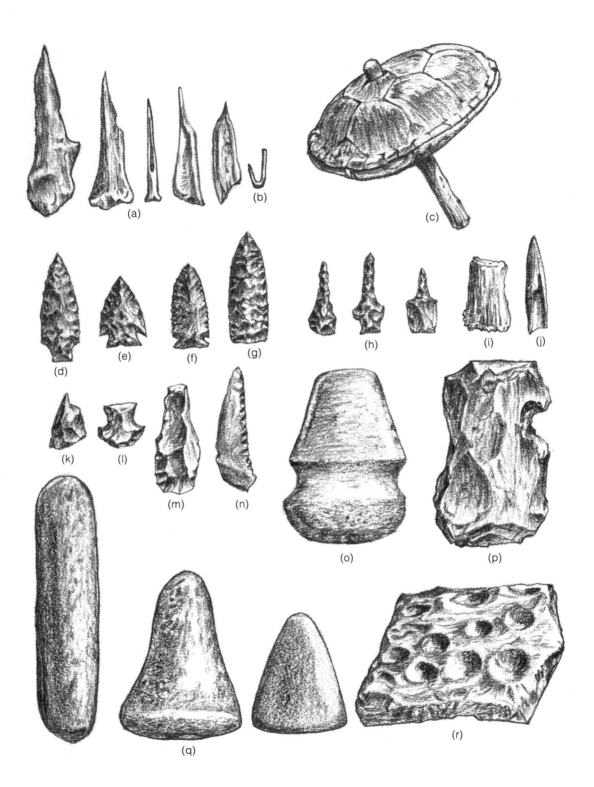

(a)   (b)   (c)

(d)   (e)   (f)   (g)   (h)   (i)   (j)

(k)   (l)   (m)   (n)   (o)   (p)

(q)   (r)

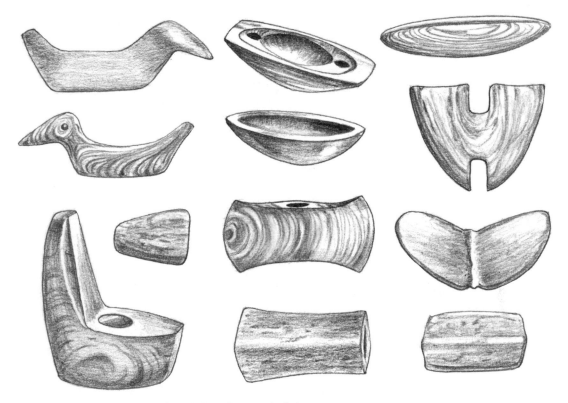

Figure 4.7 Stone atlatl weights. Slightly less than one-half size.

scraps of copper and three species of marine shells. Assuming that the copper came from the Great Lakes region as finished items and that the marine shells came from the Gulf of Mexico, we are confronted with adequate proof of long-distance procurement. The exotica were valued enough, probably as symbols of status and prestige, that journeys were made to collect or trade for them. The items presage an important event: the beginning of a trading network that apparently persisted until European contact. The carefully dug graves and inclusion of extensive grave goods

◀ **Figure 4.6** Artifacts from Indian Knoll: (a) bone awls, (b) bone fishhooks, (c) terrapin carapace rattle (restored), (d)–(f) projectile points, (g) blade, (h) drills, (i) antler atlatl handle, (j) antler projectile point, (k) graver, (l)–(n) scapers, (o) grooved ax, (p) notched limestone hoe, (q) pestles, (r) nutstone. Variable scale.

reveal attention to a burial ritual that marks an increase in cultural complexity. The beads, carefully carved hairpins and bodkins, and use of red ocher are evidence of the prevalence of ornamentation. The tortoise shell rattles imply ceremony and possibly medical and ritual practices.

The Riverton culture of east-central Illinois along the Wabash River moved the study of the midland Archaic in an interesting direction. It is a local culture confined to the Illinois side of the Wabash Valley in Crawford and Lawrence counties. As interpreted by the excavator, the settlement system for the Riverton sites reveals a seasonal shifting of the population from a major settlement to a series of five special use locations: The settlement was occupied in winter, the transient camps in spring and autumn, and the base camp in summer. *Hunting-gathering* camps and *biv-*

ouacs are postulated on the basis of scanty surface debris, but none of the bivouac, or hunting camp, sites was excavated and studied. Settlements cover 2 to 3 acres and reveal postmold patterns (houses?), clay-floored areas, burials, and many domestic utensils; all bespeak permanency. The transient camp are also extensive, but they reveal none of the structural features suggesting permanence. They have a quite different set of artifacts, all indicating short-term use. Base camps resemble the transient camps in many ways, but the dietary emphasis is different.

Although the Riverton sites (Riverton, Swan Lake, and Robeson) yielded radiocarbon dates between 3500 B.P. and 3100 B.P., the age of the culture is probably 4000 to 3000 B.P. based on the full artifact inventory, which resembles that of Big Sandy, the latest stratum at Eva. The Riverton sites are deep midden accumulations containing much mussel shell. The amount of shell varies, but it is present in all levels. Major terrestrial mammal foods were deer and turkey, with turtle and migratory birds also important in the base and transient camps. In the settlement diet neither turtle nor migratory birds loom large. (At every site there is an interesting, probably coincidental, fluctuation in animal food bone; when the proportion of deer drops, the turtle use increases. Did the unsuccessful deer hunter work off his frustration by stalking the slower turtle?) The preference was for yearling or even younger deer. One-third of the specimens were of this age range.

A further example of the middle Archaic sites is Black Earth, one of a cluster of sites in the Carrier Mills district of Saline County, Illinois. These sites occur on a series of ridges around Pleistocene Lake Saline in southeast Illinois just west of the Wabash River Valley. Lake Saline was a series of shallow lakes covering many square miles. At certain times of the year or in dry years they would have been little more than swamps. Quite evidently, the people who occupied Black Earth were exploiting the swamp, a remnant of Lake Saline

that even today lies west of the site. The swamp has undoubtedly always been there. The site is dated from about 6000 to 5000 B.P. It can thus be called terminal middle Archaic. The soil is rich, deep, and black. There was no perceptible stratigraphy, so four arbitrary zones were established in the deep midden. There was evidently considerable activity at the site; $1\frac{1}{2}$ meters of earth had accumulated even though it was a low ridge location beside the ancient lake. The artifacts were exceedingly numerous. For example, there were over a thousand chipped stone objects. They were nearly all carefully made bifaces; the commonest forms were the Matanza and Big Sandy II types.

There were a number of grooved axes, but the dominant ground stone artifact was the flat slab (metate?) and the familiar pitted slabs called nutstones. Bone and antler tools were exceedingly numerous. Deer was the most common bone source, although birds and turtles provided the raw material for some objects. The list includes awls, pins, needles, fishhooks, and turtle shell tools and rattles. Awls made up 70 percent of the collection. This suggests a heavy basketry industry, but no preserved pieces were reported. No house structures were observed, although there was mention of possible postmold patterns. The structural phenomena were confined to pits of four kinds: deep cylindrical pits, probably used for storage; shallow pits that were essentially basin-shaped charcoal concentrations, possibly used in the processing (smoking) of hides; shallow basin-shaped clay concentrations whose use was not speculated upon; and shallow, oval, basin-shaped pits, possibly used in subsistence-related food processing (but not storage). The products taken or harvested included nuts (hickory nuts, acorns, walnuts, and hazelnuts) and seeds (80 percent were hackberry, wild bean, wild grape, and persimmon). The faunal remains were numerous, 37,000 pieces of bone being recovered. From them seventy-seven taxa of terrestrial and aquatic animals were identified. The list includes turtles, small mammals or deer, migratory waterfowl, and fish. This list of floral and faunal foods shows a diverse immediate environment and an equally thoroughgoing exploitation of the animal habitats associated with the swamp, shoreline, and lakeshore, as well as the drier, upland, wooded and grassy habitats. The authors conclude, understandably, that this was a multiseasonal site with animal resources available on a year-round basis. The site also contained a large burial ground from which over 150 burials were recovered. Of these 124 were complete enough to permit careful study. A few individuals were in definable pits; the rest appeared to have merely been laid on the ground and covered. Of the 124 burials mentioned 34 had associated artifacts. The individuals with artifacts accompanying them were adult males.

Like many others the site seems to exemplify a rapid and complete shift from highland resources to the opportunistic use of new aquatic species in the bottomlands. Aside from this quite understandable broadening of the subsistence base, the Middle Archaic was not marked by great cultural change. Of course there was an increase in aquatic resources because the Middle Archaic coincides with the middle Holocene climatic regimen when stream flow decreased, the river valleys were aggrading, and varied bottomland vegetation was able to establish itself.

Archaic sites have also been dug in the Middle West. Here shell is often absent, and there is a reduction in, or complete absence of, shell as a raw material. Otherwise the artifacts are quite familiar. An example is the Faulkner site in extreme southern Illinois, an open site on the edge of the Ohio bottoms. It yielded eleven burials and an assortment of flint tools. Bone and shell were missing, having probably long since decayed, as had the human skeletons except for the faintest residual outlines. The projectile points, knives, and scrapers, including gravers, are of already familiar types. There were also milling stones (described as mortars and grinding stones). In a comparison with the stone inventory from Indian Knoll, there is a close sharing (61 percent) of comparable traits. Presumably, the resemblance would have been even closer had there been other than stone artifacts to compare. The Faulkner site also contained a series of trash-filled pits. Some had been used as roasting pits and had fire-reddened earth and fire-cracked stones at the bottom; others were burial pits. Though somewhat earlier, Faulkner can be grouped with the Riverton culture.

Another important site is Rodgers Shelter. It lies in the lower reaches of the Pomme de Terre River of southwest Missouri. It is located on a terrace under an extensive overhang and was investigated prior to the filling of the Harry S. Truman Reservoir.

Possibly the greatest importance of Rodgers Shelter comes from the fact that it contained a complete record of human use from 10,500 B.P. (the Dalton period) to 1000 B.P. It was extensively investigated over a number of years. The final report is still in preparation although some important data have been released. Rodgers was used intermittently during the Early and Middle Archaic periods and had its heaviest use during the Middle period. It was used for the processing of **hematite**—that is, the creation of red ocher powder presumably for ornamental use—the processing of vegetal foods, and extensive flint manufacture and repair. Walnut hulls suggest is was occupied during the autumn and into the winter.

The camp was also, of course, a hunting camp. There is evidence of the collection of catfish and suckers from the river, and toward the end of the occupancy, mussels became an important food. Cottontail and deer were collected earlier, along with turkey and many smaller mammals such as opossum. So the shelter demonstrates the same multifaceted subsistence base we have come to expect from the wide-ranging Middle Archaic populations.

Because of the environmental bias adopted by the excavators at the beginning of the research, a wide variety of environmental data was collected. These data included depositional history (the sedimentation), some pollen analysis, and a study of the freshwater mussels and snails that give precise clues about temperature, among other things. Small mammal remains and botanical remains were also collected. The data strengthened the understanding of Holocene climate in that region. From 11,000 to 8300 B.P., or early Holocene, the environment was cool and moist, and there were deciduous forests. The topography was a little more pronounced, that is, more rugged than earlier, and was subject to rapid erosion. From 8300 to 5200 B.P. was the so-called Hypsithermal, which is the equivalent of the western Altithermal. The Hypsithermal implies reduced precipitation, lowered river levels, and tall grass prairies at or near the Rodgers Shelter. After 5200 B.P., vegetation moved toward what we have today, but severe hillslope erosion was detected in the period from 6300 to 3600 B.P. Extensive erosion has been stipulated for the Altithermal of the West as well.

Analysis of the archaeological data has been exceedingly painstaking and detailed. The flint specimens were examined microscopically and other ways to establish functional classes. But the authors made a second step using the functional classes to establish what they called behavior indicators. The identification of the major activities at the site were in part derived from these studies.

Near Rodgers Shelter, along the same terrace a few miles upstream, was a location known as Phillips Spring. Phillips Spring repeats the Rodgers Shelter sequence after about 7800 B.P. While it is not yet fully reported, it is regarded as a base camp. There are storage pits, well-defined floors, hearths, and many areas where concentrated debris marks work areas. However, the main reason for introducing Phillips Spring here is the fact that squash and gourd remains were recovered; they are dated at 4200 B.P. At the time of reporting this was the earliest occurrence of these presumably tropical plants in the Midwest.

The presence of squash or gourd parts (seeds, rind, and peduncle) in archaeological contexts is usually interpreted as firm evidence of horticulture because the modern squashes are cultigens requiring human intervention for propagation. Because squash and gourds (*Cucurbita*) are generally regarded as tropical, not North American, in origin, they are assumed to have diffused from Mexico (or been imported) as cultivated species.

Since the Phillips Spring finds, however, cucurbit rind fragments from the Koster and Napoleon sites in Illinois have been TAMS dated at 7000 B.P., quite early in Middle Archaic times. Given the early date and the fact that there is one (possibly two) native cucurbit, the assumption that cucurbits mark the advent of horticulture can be questioned. The fact that the native cucurbits today are self-propagating raises even stronger doubts about early cucurbits as cultigens. Like the early archaeological specimens, which are essentially gourdlike, the fruits of the native gourds have thin rinds, many edible seeds, but no flesh.

Some gourds that were used as containers for other substances have also been found. A proposal has been made that the gourds were first employed by shamans as rattles used in curing or magical rituals rather than as food. In any case cucurbit finds are not numerous. About thirty instances—dated from 7000 to 3200 B.P.—have been reported. If used for food they were not important. If used only for rattles or containers, a natural wild source should provide enough for the shamans. For the moment it seems reasonable to discount the cucurbits as positive evidence for horticulture.

Eastern Agricultural Complex

The question of squash and gourd remains leads directly to a review of probably the most important single accomplishment of the Late Archaic. For several years evidence has been accumulating that the first agriculture practiced north of Mexico was by the Late Archaic peoples of the East using indigenous plants. This practice, fully and completely documented, can be viewed as an important cultural increment. The gardening and food preparation technology practiced in the East is not only ancient but also completely different from the one practiced in the Southwest. In the East from the earliest times, the ground was prepared and planting was done with the hoe, a very efficient tool. The digging stick or **dibble agriculture** of the Southwest was evidently unknown. The grains—first seeds and later maize—were hulled by soaking in lye leached from wood ashes. It was crushed in wooden mortars not on the milling stone (metate) of Mexico and the Southwest. The ground meal of the East was often used as mush rather than bread, cakes, or the familiar tortilla.

The common species grown by the eastern gardeners were plants now regarded as weeds. They are called *cultivars*, which, unlike *cultigens*, are wild plants that respond to nurture and encouragement by producing more and larger fruits (seeds) but are not modified enough genetically to lose the ability to propagate and survive untended in the wild. Cultigens, on the other hand, are so altered genetically that they cannot propagate unaided. They survive only with human intervention. Maize, sunflowers, and cucurbits are probably the best existing examples of plants that depend totally on human aid for survival. The sunflower of today is a very tall plant with a single flower about a foot in diameter at the top of a sturdy stalk. (It is popularly called a Russian sunflower but was probably developed somewhere in the United States during aboriginal cultivation.) It is an important crop today and depends on human care because the seed head no longer shatters to disperse the seed. The multiflowered wild form was collected as early as the middle Archaic.

At least four cultivar species were being cultivated in eastern North America by 3500 B.P. The major native species were the sunflower (*Helianthus annuus*) now recognized as a cultigen, marsh elder or sumpweed (*Iva annuus macrocarpa*), giant ragweed (*Ambrosia trifidia*), and maygrass (*Phalaris caroliniana*). Four more genera—pigweed (*Amaranthus* sp.), knotweed (*Polygonum*), lambs-quarter (*Chenopodium* sp.), and little barley—are sometimes included in the list of plants cultivated at this time.

The presence of a gardening technology means, among other things, that when maize was later introduced into the cultural system, it was readily incorporated into existing technology for scheduling, tending, harvesting, storing, and processing of grains. When we encounter it in the archaeological record by perhaps 1100 or 1000 B.P., we know there was no significant adaptive adjustment necessary in the agricultural system. It was probably regarded as just another, but highly productive, grain.

The evidence for this early prehistoric agricultural system comes from many sites in the Midwest. Ash Cave in Ohio, Salts and Mammoth Caves and Newt Kash Hollow in Kentucky, and the Ozark Bluff Dweller sites in Arkansas, all yield the same species associated with Late Archaic archaeological materials. In fact the Ozark Bluff Dweller sites were where the complex was first discovered and eventually analyzed and reported. Oddly enough no one paid much attention to the association of a wide variety of perishable objects of prepottery times in that cave. One reason, perhaps, is that the caves had not been excavated with any precision, and the exact association of the cultivars with the early material was not observed. And at that time no one suspected the 10,000-year time depth for the early eastern cultures.

The Northeast

Research with the Archaic began much earlier in New York and New

England than in the South. Several traditions have been identified. Early Archaic sites are rare but have been reported, including Sheep Shelter in Pennsylvania, Wards Point in New York, and the Neville site in New Hampshire. These sites all yielded examples of the Kirk, LeCroy, and Stanly projectile points. Thus the Atlantic slope tradition is represented, but the dates are later. For example, at the Neville site, a projectile point type (the Neville point) described as similar to Stanly, dates to less than 8000 B.P.

MARITIME TRADITION   In the extreme Northeast—Maine, Nova Scotia, and Labrador—a maritime adaptation developed early in Middle Archaic times. The technology was specialized for harvesting sea mammals and fish. One of the earliest sites is the L'Anse Amour site located near the Labrador-Quebec border. It is a burial location—one of the earliest American burial mounds of record. While grave goods from a single individual buried in a single mound are scarcely a sound base for postulating a specialized culture, the objects found with the burial are suggestive. The burial was made in a large, round pit some 5 meters in diameter, but the burial was toward one side, not in the center. The pit was about 1.5 meters deep and was filled with sand; the low mound was covered with a thick pavement of river boulders. With the burial were a walrus tusk, two large knives chipped from pink **quartzite,** a walrus ivory harpoon line holder, a tapered bone pendant, some caribou ulna projectile points, a whistle made of bird bone and some graphite chunks. Red ocher had been smeared on several artifacts. Two charcoal samples from beside the burial yielded radiocarbon ages of 7500 and 7250 years B.P. The importance of this location is not the limited insights it offers about the maritime specialization, but its evidence of the age of the maritime focus. It marks the beginning of the Maritime Archaic subsistence.

A more recent and more informative site is Port au Choix, a cemetery on the gulf of St. Lawrence in Newfoundland, only a few miles from the Labrador coast. It is a discontinuous concentration along about a mile of sandy, raised beach 6 meters above present water level. The sand is alkaline, making for good preservation of perishable materials. Of four locations tested, locus II, where fifty-three well-preserved burials were recovered in a sealed layer, was the most informative. The cultural layer was beach sand and shells. It was sealed by a calcareous stratum that was created by the chemical action of acids (from a surface layer of humic soils) on limestone slabs over the burials and the **calcium carbonate** (shell) in the sand. The acid soil also gives evidence that the conifer forest that is present today had covered the site for millennia. The inference is that the area was not forested when it was used as a cemetery. No accompanying village has been found. Despite the lack of any living sites, the grave goods give us a good understanding of the subsistence base.

The burials were in a flexed position in pits, lying on the left side, or were bundles of bones; there was no particular directional orientation. Artifacts were found with most of the burials. Many burials were "sealed" with a limestone boulder, perhaps to keep animals from disturbing the burial during decomposition. There was no pattern in amount or kinds of grave goods that could be correlated with either the sex or the age of individuals. Red ocher was smeared on the grave walls, the body, and the associated artifacts.

The inventory of artifacts is amazing in its variety. There were long knives or lance points of ground **slate,** carefully made, quite symmetrical, and hexagonal in cross section. Chipped stone items were rare. Knives and lance points of bone and whalebone and harpoon heads of antler were common. Fish **leister** points, **beamers,** scrapers, eyed needles, awls, and carved animal effigy combs, were all fashioned from bone. Beaver teeth, set in handles, were used for cutting and carving. Axes, adzes, and gouges were made from tough stone—they suggest extensive manufacture of wooden tools and objects.

Ornaments and ritually (?) employed artifacts were numerous. They include carved bone and antler combs and hairpins, often with a bird or other zoomorph carved on the end. There are whistles and rattles, **bone tubes** and beads, shell beads, and pendants. A carved stone effigy of a killer whale is an exquisitely real representation, not so much in its detail as in the clean taut lines that capture the essential action of the animal leaping from the water. Also with the burials were teeth, jaws, claws, and beaks of seal, caribou, deer, dog, wolf, fox marten, sea otter, gull, and great auk. It is presumed that some of the animal parts had been in now-decayed medicine bags or bundles. From somewhere the people collected amethyst, clear quartz, and **calcite** crystals, as well as colored pebbles, all of which were found with the burials.

The age ascriptions of the Port au Choix cemetery range from 4300 to 3200 B.P. The burial pattern exemplified there has long been recognized in Maine, New Brunswick, and along the St. Lawrence as far as Quebec. In many locations acidic soils have dissolved the bones, but the ocher-filled graves, the slate knives and points, harpoon parts, gouges, and axes clearly affiliate the so-called Red Paint people of Maine with the Maritime Tradition.

LAURENTIAN TRADITION On the face of things the Maritime Archaic stands alone, but some think it may represent a highly successful adaptation to ocean resources by an inland, woodland tradition called the Laurentian (although the dates from L'Anse Amour, of course, do not support that view). The Laurentian occurs from New England to the Great Lakes in both the United States and Canada. An early phase of the Laurentian is the Vergennes, dated at 5200 B.P.: later than

the L'Anse Amour site but earlier than Port au Choix. Certainly its artifact inventory nearly duplicates the Maritime one, regardless of which is earliest (Figure 4.8). The same lance points, knives, and plummets occur, and all are made of slate. A new item is the **ulu** or rocker knife that is not yet reported from the Maritime area. A characteristic flint point called Otter Creek is usually found with the assemblage. Otter Creek points are flat or slightly concave based, broad triangular points with convex sides and shallow side notches. However, it persists in vogue for some time, so its occurrence is not confined to the Vergennes phase. There are also end and side scrapers. The label Vergennes is restricted to assemblages that include the slate artifacts that comprise the "core" traits.

To the south, the Brewerton phase of the Laurentian Tradition is better known. The phase actually seems to have been established by the excavator primarily to accommodate two rich Late Archaic sites (ca. 4000 B.P.). Brewerton is clearly a late Vergennes manifestation. The two sites were Robinson and Oberlander 1. Both were large, long-used locations with extensive deep deposits of refuse. The artifact series is quite varied. Listed are many chipped flint forms; some were distinctive points, including the Otter Creek points also found earlier with the Vergennes. There were ground and polished stone items, including winged bannerstones (atlatl weights), plummets, gouges, adzes, and **celts.** Bone was used for awls, gorges (double-pointed bone splinters perhaps used as fishhooks), and fish leisters (multipronged spears). The tools imply extensive industries in hide, bone, and wood. There was heavy reliance on hunting, but fishing was also important, as were nuts and other vegetable foods. Except for the two type locations the Brewerton sites were small. Probably the two large ones were base camps, and the Brewerton was only a small local manifestation concentrated in Ontario and northwestern New York.

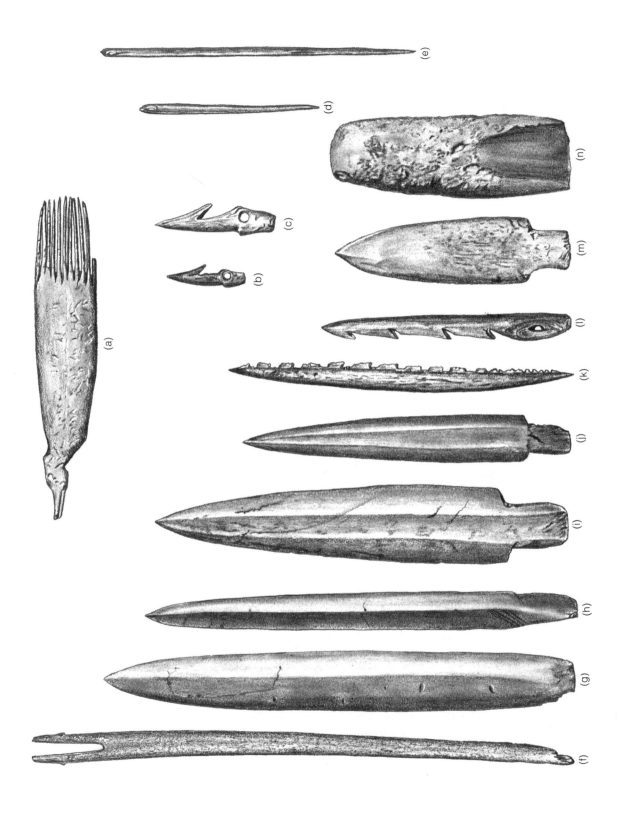

(a) (b) (c) (d) (e) (f) (g) (h) (i) (j) (k) (l) (m) (n)

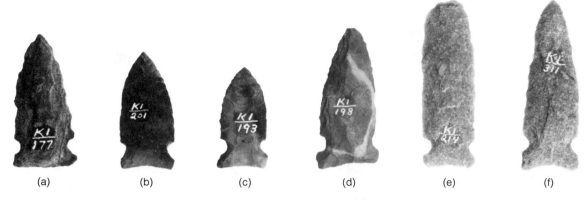

Figure 4.9 Otter Creek points.

A third phase of the Laurentian is called the Vosburg phase. It is little different from the others except that there is a corner-notched point added to the basic Laurentian styles, including the side-notched Otter Creek type.

A later (sub)tradition called the Piedmont is also included in the Atlantic Slope Tradition. It is best known by the Lamoka phase which coexisted with the Brewerton, dated at 4500 to 4000 B.P. Largely limited to the Genesee valley, it has a list of material traits quite alien to New York. It resembles the midcontinent Archaic seen at Indian Knoll, the Lauderdale sites, and the Savannah phase in Georgia far more than it does the contemporary Brewerton. But of course it shares some items with the adjacent cultures, such as small, narrow-stemmed projectile points. Restricted to the Lamoka are the stone pestles and bun-shaped mullers; thick-walled, basin-shaped stone mortars; and a highly diagnostic beveled edge adze, as well as many celts, which were used as axes (see Figure 4.10). Bone objects were very numerous. The list includes

◀ **Figure 4.8** Typical artifacts of the Maritime Archaic: (a) wooden comb with merganser duck effigy handle, (b) and (c) bone harpoon points, (d) and (e) bone needles, (f) harpoon foreshaft, (g)–(j) ground slate lance or spear points, (k) leister point, (l) leister or harpoon point, (m) slate point, (n) stone gouge.

flutes and whistles, awls, needles, and bone tubes; gorges and fishhooks were especially common. Spearpoints, bear or wolf tooth pendants or necklaces, bone pendants and scrapers, beaver tooth tools, and pendants and other objects of turtle shell were also found. Antler tools and notched stones that may have been net sinkers were common. In short the artifacts indicate a heavy emphasis on fishing and hunting, and the charred hulls of nuts, especially acorns, show an equal reliance on vegetable foods.

The artifacts and aquatic focus of the Lamoka represents one of the clearest expressions of the late Atlantic Slope Tradition even though freshwater molluscs were not used. Later phases are the Sylvan Lake, Squibnocket, and River. These occupy a very small area, share general traits such as narrow-stemmed points, and are regarded as being further evidence of southern influence on the local cultures.

A final tradition is the Susquehanna. It is late in time (about 3700 to 3400 B.P.). Aside from its apparent southern relationships the Susquehanna is notable for a new tool or utensil type: the carved steatite (**soapstone**) bowl. **Steatite** occurs in southeast Pennsylvania, along the Potomac and James Rivers in Virginia, in the Carolinas, and in Massachusetts. The bowls were carved from the soft stone,

Figure 4.10 Stone artifacts of the Lamoka phase: (a)–(g) Lamoka points, (h) ground stone celt, (i) and (j) ground stone beveled adzes, (k) stemmed spearpoint, (l) pecked stone pestle, (m) chopper, (n) muller and milling stone. Scale given.

which has good heat-retention properties. Usually a shallow oval or rectangular with rounded corners, the bowls were thick-walled and about 12–14 inches long by 8 to 10 inches wide. The interior was smooth, but the exterior might be either rough (showing carving marks) or smooth. Flat lug handles were carved on one or both ends. Common at Susquehanna sites, the bowls date to 3500 B.P. or earlier, well ahead of ceramic vessels. Their wide distribution attests to extensive trade and their popularity. One presumes they were a luxury trade item. Molded ceramic bowls of the same shape, but thick and poorly made, developed later. Neither the shape nor the pottery persisted, having had short popularity and limited distribution. By 3000 B.P. a ceramic style appeared that involved coiling and crushed

rock temper. It was quite different in appearance and made by a new technology (see Chapter Five).

The best known and last of the northeastern Archaic phases is the Orient. The Orient also had limited distribution in New Jersey, Long Island, upstate New York, and Massachusetts. Because the known sites are mostly cemetery locations, little is known of the day-to-day life. The burials were cremated, as in some other northeastern Archaic cultures, so the grave goods are the only source of information. The graves were deep pits sprinkled with red ocher. Grave goods included distinct, "fish-tailed" points, defaced and **killed** (ceremonially damaged by breaking out the bottom) steatite bowls, and gorgets.

As the descriptions above suggest, the analyses and groupings students have made of the northeastern Archaic tend to be unrealistically restrictive. The study has resulted in extremely fine-grained distinctions based on many material and intangible inferred traits and in the naming of an incredible number of quite local cultures. Earlier studies appear to have placed much more emphasis on the local distinctions than is evident in the more recent analyses from the South and West. Some of the differences may be due to the mental set of the investigators. But some may be real. Each local culture may reflect a slightly different adaptation to one or another of the varying New England environments, which do offer different resources. Nonetheless one cannot help noticing that except for changing projectile styles, the traditions are more similar than different. Lamoka of the Piedmont Tradition, however, does show a different cultural inventory. It seems to mark another strong infusion of southern traits.

The consideration of the eastern Archaic can be closed with mention of the important early Neville site on the Merrimac River near Manchester, New Hampshire. Here a small sample from an unusually deep site was salvaged by amateur excavators before construction of a bridge. It was unexpectedly informative in re-

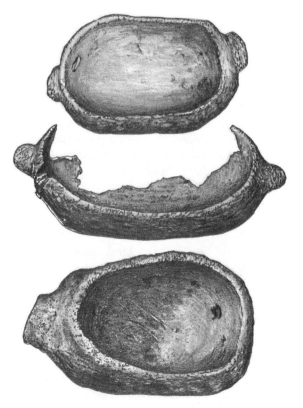

Figure 4.11 Steatite bowls. Top specimen 40 cm. long.

vealing deposits nearly 8000 years old. The basalar layers yielded points similar to the Stanly and Morrow Mountain of the Carolina piedmont. Its age, cultural connection far to the south, and stratified content make the Neville site a key to further understanding. The site was beside the Amoskeag Falls where anadromous fish were taken, and the harvest must have been huge. No bones remained, but the soils of the lowest cultural area show high concentrations of mercury (which some fish retain in their livers), so the assumption that the site was a fishing station and the fish harvest heavy seems quite defensible. After the initial early use, the site lay abandoned until Late Archaic times when it evidently served as a transient camp rather than just a fish-harvesting location.

Aside from establishing the early arrival of southern Archaic in the Northeast, the Neville site contributed to the formation of the concept of Atlantic Slope Tradition as a widespread, stable Archaic base. It can be recognized as early Middle Archaic from Massachusetts to Florida. At least the diagnostic Neville-Stanly and Stark-Morrow Mountain projectile types occur throughout. In the sequences of projectile types, there appears to be a development from the Early Archaic through to Late Archaic.

The Boylston Street Fishweir in Boston is unique and deserves special mention as one of the first successful multidiscipline studies in modern American archaeology. Built about 4500 B.P., the 2-acre fish trap was discovered in 1913 during excavations for a building. Renewed construction in the 1930s provided the opportunity for a detailed study. The weir had been constructed of vertical sticks 4 to 6 feet long, sharpened on one end with a stone axe, and driven in clusters into a blue clay bed. Then bundles of brush were forced down between the stakes, forming a loose fence. Most stakes formed rows, but other stakes occurred at random without any pattern. Probably the tops of the stakes were below water level at high tide and were well in sight at low tide.

Construction involved considerable time and effort, and continuous maintenance was required. An estimated 65,000 stakes were required for the 2-acre enclosure. Two layers of brush and many repairs show that the bay was silting up so it was necessary to place new brush on top of the old as the first layer was partially covered and would not hold the fish.

The permanent fish trap or weir, reported by early European observers along the Atlantic Coast as far south as Florida, was a highly efficient food-gathering mechanism. The historic traps were usually built in tidal flats or rivers where tidal action was strong. Fish were diverted into the trap by straight "leaders" of wattle. The leaders might be in a V leading directly to the trap mouth or might be perpendicular to the flow of the current. When the tide receded, the entrapped fish were gathered, either in nets or with spears. Of course fish could also be left in the trap until needed.

The Boylston Weir is important less as a weir per se than as evidence of concerted building effort and constant maintenance work by a nearby community. It gives another insight into the exploitation of an inexhaustible food supply by members of a permanent settlement, as well as a possible hint about social controls. The cost in effort would have been too great for casual or infrequent use; maintenance may have been scheduled by an authority figure.

Weirs, often made of brush, are still quite common on the New England coast and they, too, require quite constant maintenance. No doubt the designs are aboriginal, having been learned from the coast tribes by the earliest European settlers and perpetuated until today.

The Old Copper Culture

One of the enigmas of the upper Great Lakes Archaic is the copper-using culture found on both sides of the Great Lakes in Wisconsin, Michigan, and Ontario. For perhaps 2000 years this area was the location of an industry unique for its time: the collection or mining of free, float, or vein copper and the fabrication by alternate beating and annealing (heating) of a wide range of tough, durable tools and weapons. There have been problems with dating the industry, but it seems now that the years 5500 to 3000 B.P. bracket it. Thus it would equate in time with the Vergennes and Brewerton phases. The objects manufactured include rat-tailed tanged points of lozenge shape and long daggers or bayonets with bevelled edges very like the slate pieces of the Maritime cultures. Many square, four-sided awls; gouges; large fishhooks or gaffs; harpoons; "rocker" knives that would be used like the slate ulus; adzes; socketed spear points; and other tools were found (see Figure 4.12). The ornaments found were finger rings, pendants, bracelets, beads, and arm bands.

Fewer than a dozen sites are known. All of them appear to have been primarily cemeteries. The copper items are often recovered as grave goods, so the assumption is that the copper had a ritual or symbolic value beyond the utilitarian. The chipped flint points associated with the burials lead to the placemer: of the Old Copper Culture in the Laurentian Tradition. Burial practices varied; **bundle, extended,** flexed, and cremated have all been observed. With only a mortuary complex, a suggestion of trade, and scanty flint pieces to go on, the full significance of the copper industry remains obscure.

What is perhaps most important about the Old Copper culture and its beautiful and sometimes fragile artifacts, is the extensive trade that began at this time. For example, slender copper awls presumed to have been obtained from the Old Copper country were found in graves at Indian Knoll. The facts of interregional trade, probably following waterways, having been established so early, should be kept in mind. From this time onward, copper evidently became increasingly valued by the aboriginals of the eastern half of the continent. One might say that from Old Copper times on, the use of copper—for utilitarian objects and later for personal ornamentation and (probably) symbols of rank or office—expanded.

The Poverty Point Anomaly

In the lower Mississippi Valley there exists a puzzling, anomalous culture that deserves mention as we leave the Late Archaic of the East. This is the Poverty Point culture of which over 100 sites are known. Two important ones have been excavated: the Jaketown site on the Yazoo River in west-central Mississippi and the Poverty Point site in Louisiana. The Jaketown site was occupied for more than 3000 years no doubt because of its especially favorable location. The concern here is with its lower, Archaic level. The Poverty Point site appears to have been occupied only during the Archaic stage, with radiocarbon dates covering a 3300 to 2200 B.P. range, somewhat later than the Archaic persisted elsewhere. Both sites have a rich and standard Archaic complex of stone tools. Objects include tubular pipes of clay and stone; sandstone whetstones and saws; adzes; small celts; atlatl weights of several types; hematite plummets; steatite and sandstone vessels; numerous heavy, stemmed, and notched chipped points; and assorted scrapers. The usual traits are the "Poverty Point objects" and an extensive microflint industry.

The Poverty Point "objects" are nothing but clay balls of a unique sort. They are thought, on the basis of good evidence at Poverty Point, to have been used in stone boiling cookery in a land devoid of stones. These **cooking balls** are made with no great care. A handful of plastic clay was merely formed into a ball of cylindrical or biconical shape in the hand or between cupped palms. Fingermarks made during the compression and shaping were not obliterated. The clay objects, which occur literally by the millions, were then fired to a bricklike hardness.

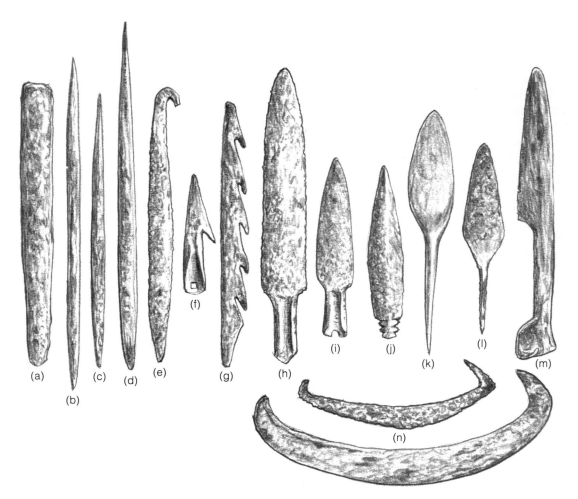

Figure 4.12 Old Copper artifacts: (a) chisel; (b) and (c) awls; (d) and (e) punches; (f) and (g) harpoons; (h)–(l) spear points; (m) knife; (n) crescents, probably knives. Slightly less than one-half size.

Even more unusual at the two sites was the microflint work. The industry involved the striking of tiny (1-inch long), prismatic flakes from egg-shaped flint nodules or cores in the manner already noted in the Arctic core and blade and the Small Tool Tradition of Alaska and Canada. From the flakes were made perforators, end scrapers, side scrapers, and needles. The microflint industry in itself is not news, but to find it so early in the lower Mississippi Valley is unexpected.

The Poverty Point site is also characterized by vast earthworks composed of five concen-tric octagonal ridges covering so large an area that they were not at once recognized as ar-tificial. There was also a pyramidal mound and possibly a large bird effigy-mound. There may also have been low conical mounds at this site. The fill of the low ridges contains village site debris showing no lensing or load-ing. While the earthworks are reminiscent of Hopewell, they are older than the Ohio works and their relationship is unclear.

The combination of no cultigens and no clay pottery, with the construction of mounds means that the entire Poverty Point complex defies acceptable placement in the larger framework of southeastern prehistory. We leave it for later research to decipher.

The radiocarbon dates from southern sites are consistently earliest, so the Archaic seems to have been flourishing there before it was well established in the Northeast. The lag can perhaps be attributed to the fact that the northern forests, being largely coniferous, were not attractive to the hunter-gatherers, and that significant population expansion awaited the transition to game-rich deciduous forests like the ones in the South.

It should be noted that the terminal stages of this final phase of the eastern hunter-gatherer stage can also be described as a lengthy transition. A number of traits and behavior patterns can be seen interacting together to create a sequence of higher cultures that dominated the East until the last ones were extinguished by settlement pressures after the European presence was established. Some have said that by definition the Archaic ended when pottery was introduced, organized religious mortuary cults appeared, and horticulture began to be practiced rather extensively. But to end the stage by definition is far too simple. Not until 1000 A.D. did the universal eastern subsistence pattern lose some of its hunter-gatherer emphasis. Those data will be introduced in proper context in a later section. But the new ideas—pottery, horticulture, mound burial of the dead, and trade in exotica—did not appear simultaneously or at one place.

The Plains

The Archaic developments that are easiest to follow are those in the broad midsection of the continent between the Rockies and the Mississippi River, from the plains of Saskatchewan and Manitoba to the Texas Gulf. This area encompasses the vast Missouri, Pecos, Arkansas, and Red River drainage basins. More simply, it includes the western woodlands and the Great Plains. At site after site the artifact finds reveal a period of transition from the Plano artifacts of 9000 to 7000 B.P. to Archaic tool types already distinguished in the eastern woodlands.

One of the best known of these sites is Graham Cave in Missouri. While there are some contradictory statements about the details of the cave, it is clear that the basal layer yields radiocarbon dates ranging from 9700 to 8000 B.P. The cave fill was an accumulation of earth, ash lenses, and living debris over 7 feet deep. In the lower levels the artifacts were of Plano type, or rather of types resembling the Plano. There was one Dalton point. The dominant projectile points or knives were lanceolate. In the second level (the levels were arbitrary 1-foot cuts) the Plano objects were mixed with those of eastern Archaic type. There were large lanceolate and triangular blades; stemmed and deeply corner-notched points or blades; drills; ovoid and thumbnail end scrapers; flake scrapers; grooved axes, manos, and milling stones; nutstones; a shell pendant; a split bone awl; hammerstones; and an impression (in clay?) of twined weaving. One piece of coiled basketry was also recovered. Bone needles, tubes, spatulas, ulna awls, **antler flakers** and **wrenches,** and a perforated wolf canine tooth were also found. In other areas of Missouri—Table Rock and Pomme de Terre (e.g., Rodgers Shelter) reservoirs—the eastern Archaic is readily recognized at scores of sites.

In Oklahoma a series of Archaic complexes that can be correlated with sites in Missouri in the Table Rock area, as well as with eastern Archaic sites, have been identified. One complex is called the Grove Tradition. Both Middle and Late Archaic are represented. The characteristic Grove inventory is synthesized from several sites, some of which contained over 12 feet of accumulation. Even though none of the sites was large, the depth of accumulation and the change in artifact lists and frequency are taken to indicate a long period of use or frequent reuse. The excavators report the large corner- and side-notched points, with contracting-, parallel-, and expanding-stem blade or point forms also common. The blades are broad and often have serrated or bevelled edges. End and side scrapers, drills, choppers, and grooved axes are also part of the assemblage. The slab milling stones, manos, and mortars indicate the use of plant foods. In the Late Archaic level, about the same complex exists, with bone awls and flaking tools and some objects of shell also reported. The original work was done in the 1950s. There has since been more work, and the phases are better defined and more fully described.

The Archaic stage is represented all over Texas (e.g., the Levi site). There appears to be a transition between, or blending of, the eastern and western Archaic. That blending is best seen in the Balcones phase as it links, through its artifact complex, the eastern and western Archaic.

Moving west and north from Missouri, Arkansas, and Oklahoma into the Plains, the reported Archaic sites are less numerous, but those available provide more evidence for the blending with the western Archaic, as can be seen quite clearly in the Texas manifestations. The best-known sites are Signal Butte in Nebraska, McKean in Wyoming, and Pictograph Cave in Montana.

The most fully reported of the High Plains sites is McKean. Here on the Belle Fourche River was a large, open, well-stratified site in the reservoir area behind Keyhole Dam. It was located near the river in the lee of a protecting ledge of sandstone. The upper level is radiocarbon dated at 3400 B.P., the lower level at perhaps 5000 to 6000 B.P. The analysis emphasized the trait similarities shared by the two levels at McKean and one or more complexes at Pictograph Cave, Signal Butte, and Ash Hollow in Nebraska; several early Utah sites; and Birdhead Cave in Montana. Several diagnostic projectile points were recovered from level I (the lower), which was separated from the upper level by sterile soil. One was a slender, lanceolate type called the McKean point. McKean points are short—2 to 3 inches long—with both base and stem incurving gracefully from a wide midportion. Deftly pressure chipped and usually with a deeply indented concave base, these are quite distinctive pieces. Other types, many with indented or deeply notched bases, with stems or side notches, also occur. Two of these types, the Duncan and the Hanna, are regarded as having diagnostic value in both cultural and chronological contexts (Figure 4.13). Most of the blades and points are smaller and better made than is generally true of eastern Archaic material. There were also snubnosed end scrapers; **spokeshave** scrapers; random flake scrapers; round, retouched flake scrapers; and numerous ovoid blades of good workmanship. Manos and milling stones were also present. Bone tools were absent, but three tubular bone beads were found. The food bones indicate deer and bison to have been favored prey, but the sample is very small. At some sites there are bison kills.

The depth of the site is variable, the lower stratum being from 1 to 4 feet below the surface. Thirty-four hearths were associated with the lower level. Most of these were irregular lenses of discolored sand and charcoal flecks. A few others were small, shallow basins in the sand lined with small slabs of stone. Charcoal flecks and sand filled the basins. The slabs and peripheral sand were reddened from the heat of continued use. Two cache pits and one human skull burial were also associated with the lower level. The original work at McKean was done in 1954. Since then the artifact complex has been recognized at scores of sites all over Wyoming, and in the Canadian provinces of Alberta, Saskatchewan, and Manitoba. In Canada the dates are younger than at the type site.

In Montana there is an important sequence that begins with PaleoIndian debris, proceeds through the Archaic, and carries into proto-

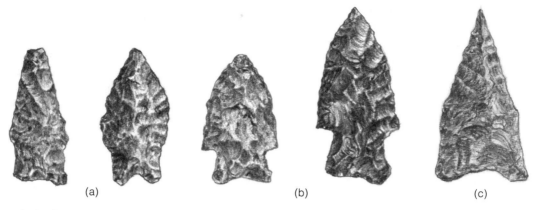

Figure 4.13   Plains points: (a) Duncan, (b) Hanna, (c) Dalton (first called Meserve). Slightly reduced.

historic times at Mummy Cave. A brief report tells of finds of potential importance to the understanding of Plains Archaic. The location, on Blackwater Creek of the North Fork of the Shoshone River, a few miles east of Yellowstone Park, was a dry cave containing cultural and natural fill more than 25 feet in depth. The radiocarbon ages range from about 9250 B.P. to 1580 A.D. The stratigraphy is under perfect control; sterile layers alternate with the thirty-eight occupational layers. Layer 1 is basalar; layer 38 is the topmost. The sterile layers are alluvial in origin, as the creek periodically flooded the cavern. The cave is important on three counts. The long sequence of chipped stone points repeat the sequence from the Plains from what may be an unfluted Folsom (in layer 4) on up through the Plano lanceolate types. By about 7000 B.P., side- and base-notched points appear (layer 17). They are apparently of western Archaic type, but the authors see them as more nearly resembling points from locations farther east in the Plains. In layer 30, at about 4420 B.P., the debris includes tubular bone pipes, coiled basketry, cordage and netting, leather scrap, animal (food) bones, and milling stones (metates). The same variety of materials is found again in layer 36, which also includes McKean points. The similarity of the artifacts to those from sites within both the Plains and the Great Basin leads one to assume that the culture is a western complex blended with Plains material.

Western Archaic

West of the Rockies an environmental setting quite different from the woodlands of the East and the game-rich Plains posed a different set of adaptive problems for the Archaic populations. Archaeologically the western Archaic is probably better understood than the rest of the continent, perhaps because, except for the more complex cultures of the Southwest, there was nothing else for archaeologists to study. The chronology of the area is firmly established based on hundreds of ^{14}C assays that extend from 11,000 B.P. to 1850 A.D. in some areas.

But the West is too large and the time span is too great to allow for facile generalization. When humans first arrived—12,000 to 10,000 B.P.—the region was cooler and moister than it is today. By 10,000 B.P. environmental conditions were generally about like today, although still slightly cooler and moister. But the climatic fluctuations of the West are notorious. From 7000 to about 4500 B.P., conditions were hotter and drier than today. Human populations were perhaps reduced, but the area was not depopulated. Beginning at about 4500 B.P. the conditions were again much like modern times, but there have been cycles of drier and wetter climate that may have made for short-term hardships, as they do today. Although fluctuations have occurred, the general trend since 4500 B.P. has been toward drier climatic regimes. Climatic forces, of course, control the abundance and variety of biota, and hence the food resources available for human use.

But the mere fact of drier or wetter trends is misleading. Foraging humans do not exploit half a continent. They use the resources of a very small area—a series of adjacent microenvironments. The environment of any location is determined by latitude, altitude, soils, and local topography, and in the West these provide an endless variety of locations where humans prosper. The only plausible way to understand human use of the West is on the local or site-specific level. The paleoenvironment of many locations has been reconstructed from fossil pollen, fragments of plants, elevations, fluctuation of plant zones (derived from pollen and macrofossils in pack rat middens), bones of small animals, fossil lake beaches, dune activity, old soils, and varying tree ring widths in preserved timbers. Knowledge of microenvironments is possibly even more important to understanding human history in the West than in the East, because moisture in the West is chronically scanty.

Here we will consider three cultural provinces, the Great Basin, the **Columbia Plateau,** and California west of the deserts. These correlate only roughly with natural physiographic zones. The province that has attracted the greatest scientific attention is the Great Basin, an inland basin with no external drainage. It is now understood as a mosaic of habitats where many subsistence strategies were practiced by Archaic peoples. There were (and still are) scores of spring-fed lakes, large

marshes, and extensive aquatic zones along the few major rivers. The marsh habitat was very productive—fish, waterfowl, seeds, and tubers—and we find permanent base camps that relied heavily on those lacustrine resources. But many resources occurred in patches—grass seeds, many tubers, small and large mammals—and their procurement required a mobile lifestyle, involving a cyclical seasonal movement from one resource to another. The Archaic lifeway geared to the desert characterized a vast area—much larger than the physiographic Great Basin (see Figure 4.14). That way of life has been called the Western Archaic. It is found from eastern Oregon and southwestern Idaho through Utah and Arizona and onto the Mexican plateau, as well as in eastern and southern California.

In California as in the Great Basin a variety of environments led to an equal variation in exploitive patterns. However the basic cultural uniformity seen in the Great Basin is missing.

North of the Great Basin lies the Columbia Plateau. The human use of that area was much modified by the extensive lava beds and the presence of three strong rivers: the Columbia; the Snake; and, in Canada, the Fraser. The vast runs of spawning salmon in these rivers offered a limitless quantity of storable food, a resource exploited for thousands of years. Sites are rare in the lava beds.

First to be described is the Great Basin. As indicated earlier, the distribution centers in, but is not confined to, the physiographic Great Basin, and the culture is recognized over a much wider area (Figure 4.14). Wherever it occurs, the climate is characterized by low moisture and wide temperature extremes. Elevation variation is also marked.

In the valleys the vegetation is most often sagebrush and grasses. The abundance of plants varies greatly in response to local moisture, and the faunal populations vary with the vegetation. Many mammals are small; rodents and rabbits predominate. Antelope and mountain sheep were the commonest large

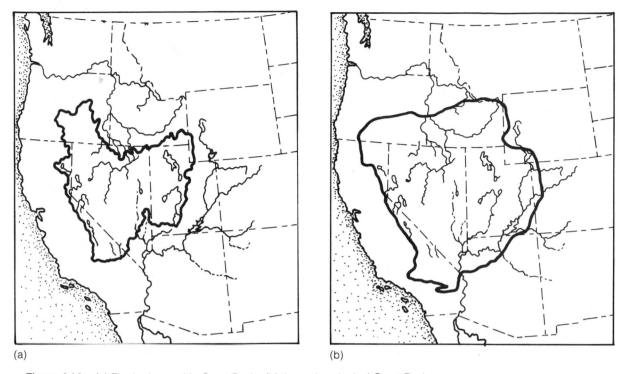

(a)　　　　　　　　　　　　　　　　(b)

Figure 4.14　(a) The hydrographic Great Basin; (b) the archaeological Great Basin.

animals, with a normal number of predators—most often bobcat, coyote, and badger. The valleys can be described as shrub desert or as dry steppes. But in the endlessly repeated north-south trending mountain ranges the biotic zones change rapidly with increases in elevation. The steep flanks of the hills are covered with piñon and juniper with patches of sage and grasses. Above this are the pine forests, and above the pines are aspen and fir. At the higher elevations both deer and bighorn sheep were available as were larger rodents such as marmot, porcupine, and, rarely, beaver. The piñon groves were a rich source of food since the nuts provide both fat and proteins. For reasons not well understood, piñon were rarely a part of the diet until after about 5000 B.P., but they were heavily exploited after that time.

All the varied resources of the many environmental niches, from the valley floors between the ranges up to the mountain tops,

were readily available for exploitation. Thus, despite the undeniably deficient moisture of the region (although effective moisture increases with elevation), the land provided a diversity of resources (many seasonal) for hunters and gatherers. Harvesting, of course, meant moving from one resource to another in a cyclical wandering round. The round would be similar from year to year, because the major foods were vegetal and did not move. Game availability would vary with annual precipitation, recency of last harvest, disease cycles, and perhaps other factors.

The austerity of the environment outlined above is only partially correct. The basin is studded with shallow spring-fed lakes. These are often at the point of transition from foothills to valley floor. A few small but permanent streams also empty into the valleys and often flow as far as the valley edge all summer. The permanent ponds, marshes, and seeps are rich in food resources, including migratory and resident waterfowl and aquatic plants. The margins of the ponds and marshes support other plants that yield both fruit and seeds.

Wherever lacustrine resources existed, they were heavily exploited. In some very rich areas, notably Humboldt Sink (where the Humboldt River ends, having no outlet to the ocean), it has been argued that the lake and marshes were exploited exclusively for many months of the year, with people going out into the desert on short collecting trips but returning to a lakeside base camp. There were, of course, many marshy oases smaller than Humboldt Sink that could also be heavily exploited. What emerges is a foraging lifeway most often geared to a fairly broad, if patchy, spectrum of resources that persisted for many millennia. But survival was less grim than arduous. The resources were (and remain) sparse and scattered and had to be collected. The choice of resources to be procured was probably a function of many factors mentioned earlier, such as nutrition, availability, and costs in labor of collecting and processing. Subsistence was not quite on a day-to-day, hand-to-mouth basis. Nuts and seeds, dried fish, and, perhaps, dried meat were stored, but generally speaking the food quest occupied part of each day. Thus the focus of the western Archaic is the same as already seen in the eastern Archaic. The difference lies in the sparser and less-varied resources of the West and the correspondingly lower density of population.

It is necessary to mention one of the first and highly influential reconstructions of the fluctuations of Basin climate because it occurs in all the literature and has already been used in this volume: that is, the scheme proposed by Antevs in 1948. Of course many subtleties in the record eluded Antevs in his pioneer research. But although its details have been challenged, its fundamental accuracy has never been in question.

Three basic climatic regimens were recognized and remain the standard. These stages of climate—the Anathermal (cooler and moister than now, from about 11,000 to 7000 B.P.), the Altithermal (markedly hotter and drier than now, from 7000 to 4500 B.P.), and the final Medithermal (similar to today, from 4500 B.P. to the present)—were remarkably accurate. They were based on a wide variety of studies and a broad data base ranging from studies of Great Basin sediments to Great Plains loess deposits to the clay **varves** left by Scandinavian glaciers. Modern studies merely modify and elaborate on the many regional deviations from the generalized trend that Antevs outlined. They do not destroy his findings or the evidence. The basic terms *Anathermal*, *Altithermal*, and *Medithermal* will be used as appropriate in this and other sections.

An early definition of the basic western Archaic culture is appropriate here. The list includes such traits as an intensive exploitation of selected species; small-seed harvesting and consequent special cookery of mushes and cakes; fur cloth; woven sandals (sometimes hide moccasins); the atlatl and dart; a wide variety of small projectile points; knives (both large and small); flat or basined millstones and cobble manos; crude tools called **pulpers;** choppers and scrapers; wooden clubs; tubular pipes or sucking tubes; vegetable **quids;** twined basketry technique first, with coiling soon added; and a high valuing of *Oliva* and *Olivella* shells traded from California. From the western Basin there is a more-detailed list of long-persistent core traits, many late in time, involving specific artifact types. This list includes deer-hoof rattles, medicine pouches (which persisted to modern times), twined matting, scapula grass-cutting tools, perforated bone or antler wrenches, bird-bone whistles, cane arrows with hardwood shafts (late), wooden-handled flint knives, L-shaped scapula awls, digging sticks, solid-shaft **fire drills,** wooden fire-drill hearths, and coiled and twined basketry.

Before beginning a discussion of the sites, it should be mentioned that there is a uniformity of point types in the West comparable to the long sequences noted in the East. They are not always horizon markers because some occur over a long time span. Figures 4.15 and 4.16 show the types and the chronology.

Among the first sites to be reported were several caves in eastern Oregon, Roaring Spring, Catlow, and Fort Rock being the most important. Together, and usually under good control, the several Oregon caves yielded twined basketry; string; matting; sandals made from tule; fire drills; L-shaped awls; thin milling stones and manos; many atlatls and dart shafts; bone bars (for flaking flint?); bone beads; and a wide variety of projectile points of triangular, notched, and stemmed or stemless lanceolate types. The chipping is usually fine, and the pieces are not large. Many end scrapers and other scrapers made from flakes are also found. One of the seventy-five woven sandals from Fort Rock Cave was radiocarbon dated at 9000 B.P. The frequent sealing of the cultural remains in these caves by ancient volcanic ash and tephra gave evidence of quite early habitation of the desert area, and the excavator made a claim of great age. But at the time (ca. 1940) scholarly consensus denied the possibility. With the use of the radiocarbon dating technique in the 1950s, when scores of desert sites yielded dates of more than 8000 B.P., the original interpretation was firmly established.

Considerably after the Catlow-Fort Rock research was done, a rock shelter site (in Oregon) called Dirty Shame was excavated. The Dirty Shame cave is located in a deep canyon with a southern exposure, which made year-round occupancy possible. It is almost certain to have been occupied year-round after about 2500 B.P.

The site itself covers a period from 9000 B.P. to 1600 A.D. There is, however, no evidence of any sort of use from 5850 to 2750 B.P. The deposit within the cave was about 15 feet deep and was rich in artifact materials. The many early chipped flint specimens were long and lanceolate in form whereas the specimens of the middle period were largely the

familiar western types (Figure 4.16): Elko eared and side-notched; Humboldt; and the blunt, tapered-stem Mojave types. In the upper levels were the small, triangular-notched and stemmed types such as Rose Spring. There were also flat slab flake knives or saws, which also occur at sites farther south in the basin, and many many forms of stone drills. The flint specimens suggested a considerable industry in wood, bone, and probably hide, and the wealth of perishable objects supported the suggestion. The perishable materials included basketry, mats, soft bags, two types of sandals (familiar from Catlow and Fort Rock caves), wooden and sheephorn knife and scraper handles, rabbit skin robes, and many other tools of wood and bone, including a flute made of cane.

Many of the baskets were decorated: On one an *Olivella* shell bead was found. The cave was particularly rich in evidence of the subsistence pattern. It was the expected foraging pattern, and it testified to a balanced diet. Throughout cave history the major game species were deer, jackrabbit, cottontail, marmot, and big horn sheep. Some antelope apparently were also taken. A further list of foods was identified from coprolites (dried human feces). There were small mammals of several species, antelope (identified from the hollow hair), crayfish, shellfish, fish, insects, sunflower and goosefoot, much prickly pear, sego lily, wild onion, wild rose, and chokecherry. Plants collected were available from late spring through summer and well into the autumn. As could be expected, some changes were detected in the dominant vegetation and hence in the overall environment. But in general the resources seemed to remain more or less the same. However, pollen cores from mountain marshes and plant scrap (macrofossils) in the cave fill told of changing environments. During the Altithermal, for example, there was a dominance of sagebrush (*Artemesia*) over the grass that dominated before and after that period.

Nonetheless excavators judged the lifeway to have been stable. Artifacts and diet showed

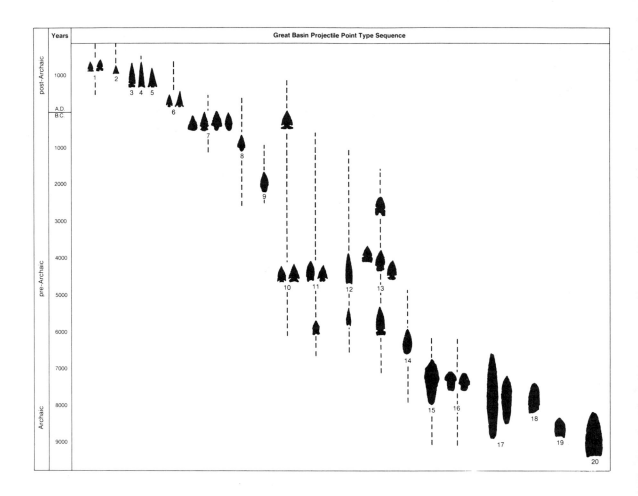

Figure 4.15 Temporal distributions of recognized Great Basin projectile point types. Projectile point outlines are placed on dashed lines, representing temporal span at the times of maximum popularity. This chart is a generalization; in any given area within the Great Basin, the types present and their temporal occurrence may vary. Type name (and alternate names) are: (1) Desert Side-notched series (Desert Side-notched, Uinta Side-notched, Bear River Side-notched); (2) Cottonwood Triangular; (3) Bull Creek Concave-base; (4) Parowan Basal-notched; (5) Nawthis Side-notched; (6) Rose Spring–Eastgate series (Rosegate series: Rose Spring Corner-notched, Rose Spring Side-notched, Eastgate Expanding-stem, Eastgate Split-stem); (7) Martis series (Martis Triangular, Martis Corner-notched, Martis Stemmed-leaf); (8) Gypsum; (9) McKean Lanceolate; (10) Elko series (Elko Corner-notched; Elko Eared, Elko Side-notched; Elko Contracting-stem); (11) Pinto series (Gatecliff series, Little Lake series, Bare Creek series, Pinto Square-shouldered, Pinto Sloping-shouldered, Pinto Shoulderless, Pinto Willowleaf); (12) Humboldt series (Great Basin Concave-base series: Humboldt Concave-base A, Humboldt Concave-base B, Humboldt Basal-notched, Triple-T Concave-base); (13) Large Side-notched (Northern Side-notched [Bitterroot Side-notched], Hawken Side-notched, Rocker Side-notched, Sudden Side-notched, San Raphael Side-notched); (14) Cascade; (15) Large unnamed stemmed; (16) Large stemmed (Great Basin Stemmed series: Lake Mohave, Silver Lake, Parman series, Windust); (17) Hasket 1 and 2; (18) Scottsbluff; (19) Folsom; (20) Clovis.

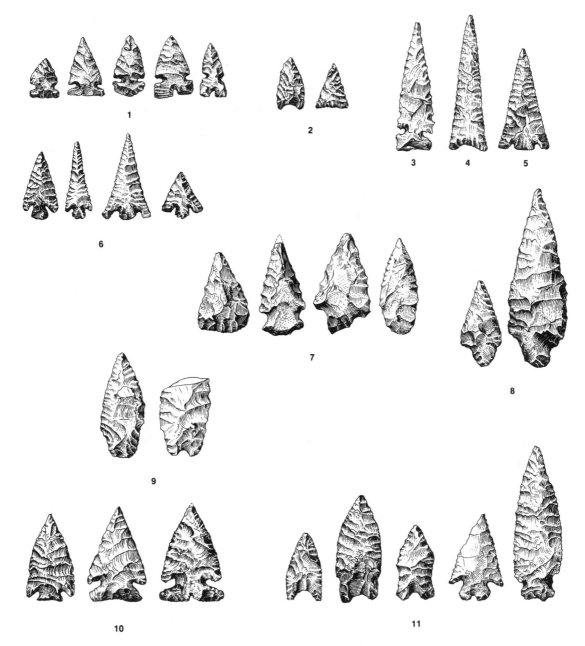

Figure 4.16 Examples of Great Basin points. The numbers are keyed to Figure 4.15. Figure continues on page 154.

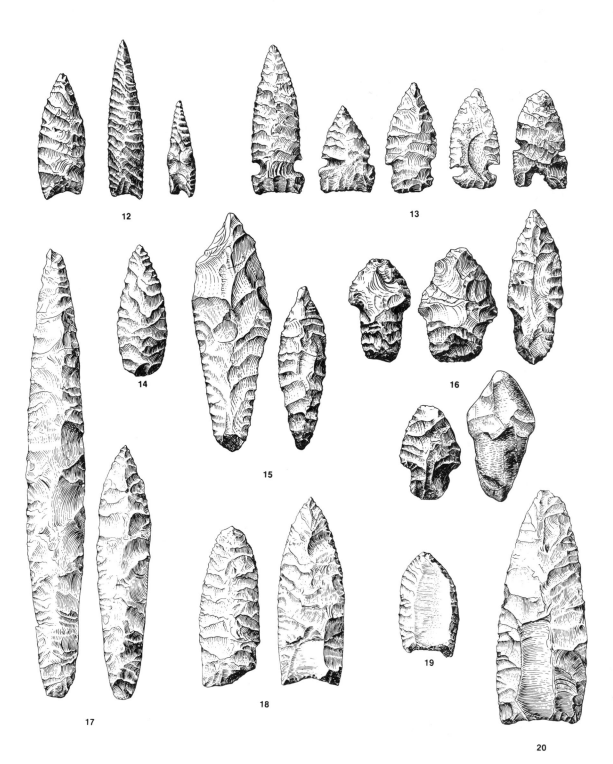

Figure 4.16 (*continued*)

only minor fluctuations over time. Most remarkable, and indeed unique, were the two or three grass-thatched houses (wikiups) built inside the cave after 2700 B.P. (see Figure 4.17). They are interpreted, and we can probably agree, as being evidence of year-round occupancy during the last 2000 years of the cave's use. Altogether the site appears to have been well-studied and lucidly reported, although in segments. No complete report is available, and, I believe, none is expected.

In order to establish what might be called the continuity of the annual round, ethnobotanists working in central Oregon have provided a very interesting diagram of the annual round of the historically observed Harney Valley Paiute, here reproduced as Figure 4.18. Note that the aboriginal names of the months are related to subsistence phenomena (for example, April and May are indicated as Indian potato month; May and June as salmon months). The times for collecting various foods are also indicated. This ethnographic analogy closely fits the dietary findings at Dirty Shame and dozens of similar dry cave deposits all over the Great Basin. For our purposes, we can probably assume that the historic foragers of the basin, the many local Paiute tribes, were pursuing a lifestyle and annual round that

Figure 4.17 Dirty Shame wickiup as reconstructed from excavation data.

differed only in detail from those of the prehistoric foragers.

Southeast of the Oregon caves are a series of sites in Utah. Of these, the best known is Danger Cave on the western edge of the Great Salt Desert. This wide-mouthed grotto was the scene of intermittent human use from 10,300 B.P. or earlier until recent time. It overlooked several spring-fed bogs. Its portal was choked by midden by about 1 A.D., so later occupants, including historic Paiute, were able to camp only in the slight shelter of the hooded overhang.

Cultural accumulations reaching a depth of 13 feet represented six periods of use (Fig. 4.19). Most of the fill was mixed chaff (from pickleweed) and dust from the salt flats where the pickleweed grows. The latter was harvested for its seed, which was parched, milled, and eaten. The debris yielded many artifacts and food bones. With good stratigraphic control, it was possible to see the invention or adoption of new tools as time passed, with the greatest variety occurring in level V. Over sixty knife and projectile point types and over twenty scraper classes were isolated. The radiocarbon age of level I was about 10,300 B.P.; that of level II, 9700 B.P.; level III, 6600 B.P.; and level IV, 5400 B.P. Samples from level V ranged from 4000 B.P. to 20 A.D. The samples came from within the cave well back from the portal. Materials from the front of the overhang would probably show quite recent dates. (It is now evident that a sixth layer was present and even identified in the cave portal during excavation. It should have been segregated but was lumped with level V during analysis. Therefore, Figure 4.19 has layer VI added.) The presence of ceramics and small triangular projectile points is evidence that the cave was used until after 1400 A.D.

There was an increase in classes of artifacts from early to late levels. For example, there was a shift in basketry techniques from 100 percent twining at 9700 B.P. to 15 percent twining versus 85 percent **coiling** by 4000 B.P.; the hemp (*Apocynum*) used for cordage was

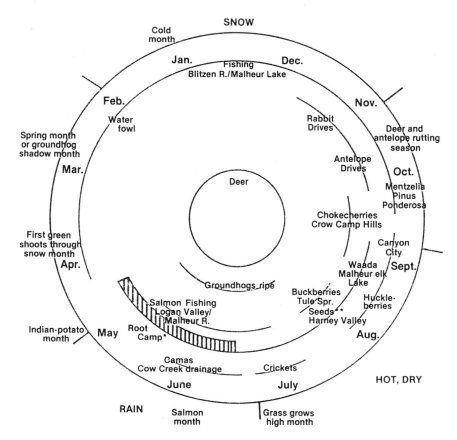

Figure 4.18 Harney Valley Paiute seasonal round.

replaced by greasewood bark during the last two levels. Level II and later levels show an early preference for the small- to medium-sized, triangular, stemmed and notched points, with the larger lanceolate or pear-shaped styles gaining in popularity in later layers.

Danger Cave yielded over 1000 flat milling stones and fragments, over 2000 chipped stone pieces, hundred of manos or **handstones,** over a hundred pieces of coiled and twined basketry (and one piece of coarse cloth resembling canvas), netting, horn, bone, wood, antler, shell (including species from the California coast), leather, and minerals such as **mica** and ocher. The cave was an actual living site where many wornout tools, weapons, or utensils were discarded, as well as food bones

and other scrap. Hundreds of exhausted **quids** of fibrous vegetal material that had been thoroughly chewed were found on all levels. All the quids were stems of the desert bullrush. They may have been chewed for food, juice, or flavor, but since the fiber was used in cordage, the leaves may have been chewed to separate the fibers or for both purposes. Quids are common in many cave sites.

Many famous sites near lake shores seem to have been used as cache or storage spots (for example, Lovelock Cave) rather than as dwelling places. As a result Danger Cave has a wider variety of utilitarian objects, while the cache sites contain perhaps more "valued" materials (Figures 4.20–4.22). Among the debris at Danger were various scraps of wood and plants that were used in fabricating bags,

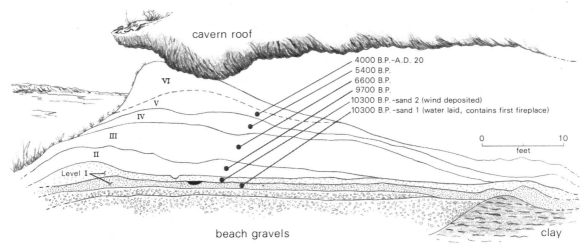

Figure 4.19 Cross section of Danger Cave, Utah. Dates shown are conservative estimates averaged from radiocarbon assays by three laboratories.

nets, knife handles, and other objects. The sixty-five plant species identified from 4000 pieces of artifacts and scrap in the debris are all still found in the area. Animal species used as food included antelope, bison, mountain sheep, jackrabbit, wood rat, dog (?), bobcat, and desert fox. The mountain sheep was the commonest big game. A few pieces of elk (?) antler were found, but no bones of the big cervids were identified; all these food bones are from modern species.

An interesting corroboration of the diet of the Danger Cave dwellers as reconstructed from the archaeological collections comes from an analysis of the coprolites from the cave. The study identified charred pickleweed, cactus pad epidermis in quantity, tiny charred cactus spines, leaves and seeds of the salt bush, bullrush, rabbitbrush, and two or three kinds of animal hair, including antelope. All samples contained cactus scrap, pickleweed fragments, charcoal, and grit. The grit came from the fine-grained milling stones used to grind the charred pickleweed seeds. Unexpectedly the coprolites contained the eggs and specimens of lice and ticks and the egg sacks of internal parasites such as pinworms,

roundworms, and thorny-headed worms. Insect legs and wings have also been recovered from coprolites. This testifies to the antiquity of the practice of collecting, charring, and storing grasshoppers and Mormon crickets, which was done historically by the Gosiute of western Utah.

About 40 miles east of Danger Cave and separated from it by the sterile expanse of the Great Salt Desert, Hogup Cave lies on the southwest flanks of the Hogup Range. This site, with $14\frac{1}{2}$ feet of cultural fill, spanned over 7000 years of time—from 8350 B.P. to 1470 A.D. It is a larger cavern than Danger, with a similar exposure opening southwest over the salt flats. The Desert Hills, where Danger lies, are visible from the Hogup portal.

Except for Hogup's later beginning date, Hogup and Danger replicate each other in many important ways, including both artifact and climatic evidence. The Hogup data are rendered more informative, however, by the excellence of the analyses of ancillary data by nine specialists in other fields of science. The participating scholars' findings and opinions were blended into the cultural interpretation, but more importantly they give detailed

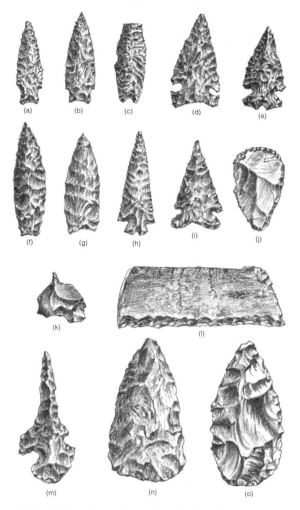

Figure 4.20 Lithic artifacts from Danger Cave: (a)–(i) projectile points, (j) scraper, (k) graver, (l) slab knife or saw, (m) drill, (n) basalt knife, (o) obsidian knife. Reduced about one-third.

environmental data (especially with respect to climate) that are very likely correct. For example, examination of the plant macrofossils in Hogup Cave (the Hogup fill was largely vegetal, as in Danger) layer by layer, identified forty-six plant species that were collected and used for food, fuel, cordage, tools, and probably other needs such as medication. All but one of the species occur today in the vicinity of the site; none is more than 40 miles away, with most quite near. It was concluded

that any climatic change was subtle. The subtlety was explored. Based on plants, combined with the incidence of animal species in the sixteen cultural layers, the conclusion was that where the salt flats now are there was a shallow lake from ca. 8350 B.P. until 3200 B.P.—a 5000-year span. During that time the weather was warmer (an estimated 1° C higher mean temperature than today) except for a period when conditions were briefly cooler and moister at about 8000 B.P. The findings above are supported by dietary, palynological, avian, and mammalian studies, as well as the archaeological evidence itself.

In addition to duplicating many artifact classes from Danger Cave, Hogup yielded several unusual items. Among them were the bootlike Hogup moccasin, some tiny "horned" feather and fiber fetishes, and several engraved stones (Figure 4.23). Some twenty elk teeth, perforated for suspension and highly polished from wear, had been a necklace or other ornament.

There is good evidence that after the shallow lake had been reduced to a series of sloughs and marshes, there was a lacustrine aspect in the Hogup economy. Aquatic birds, and rushes, including rhizomes, were heavily represented in the edible food inventory. The lacustrine phase ends abruptly at about 4250 B.P.

The sixteen occupational strata at Hogup were separated into four phases: unit I, represented by layers 1 through 8 (8350 to 2200 B.P.), unit II (2250 B.P. to 400 A.D.), unit III (400 to 1300 A.D.), and unit IV (1350 to 1850 A.D.). Unit I is characterized by a heavy reliance on vegetal foods, varied game animals, and aquatic birds. This unit shows the most intensive human use of the Hogup location. Unit II shows a decline in wild seed foods (and in milling tools) with an increase in big game taken, pronghorn and bison becoming the commonest species. Unit III marks the evolution of the Fremont culture from the Archaic base, while unit IV is equated with the Shoshonean speakers of historic times. The units are believed to mark significant culture

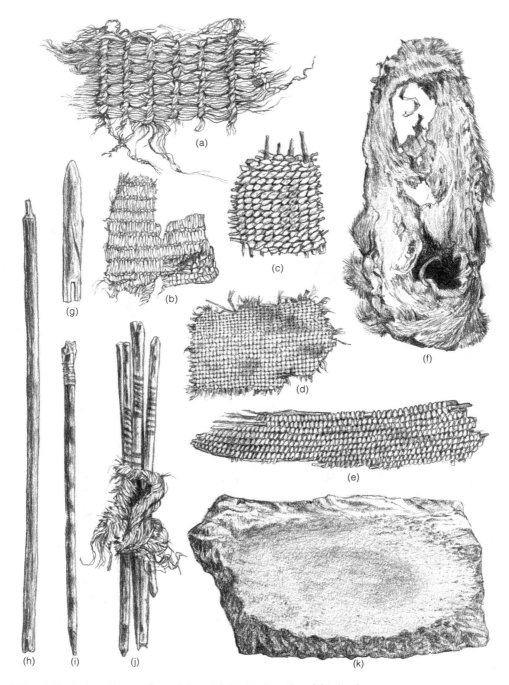

Figure 4.21 Artifacts from Danger Cave: (a) and (b) twined matting, (c) twined basketry, (d) coarse cloth, (e) coiled basketry, (f) hide moccasin, (g) wooden knife handle, (h) dart shaft, (i) arrow shaft with broken projectile point in place, (j) bundle of gaming sticks, (k) milling stone. Variable scale.

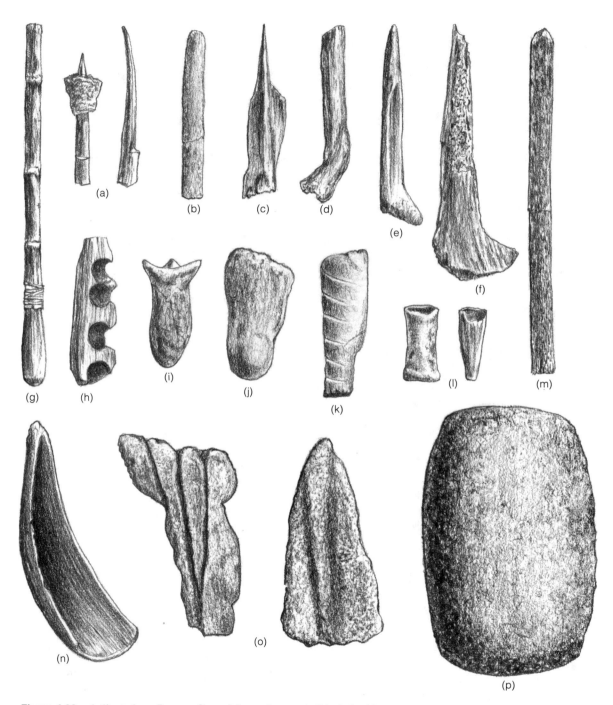

Figure 4.22 Artifacts from Danger Cave: (a) wooden pegs; (b) worked bone; (c)–(f) bone awls; (g) fire drill; (h) fire drill hearth; (i) clay effigy, probably a kit fox; (j) clay effigy; (k) worked bone; (l) bone **tinklers**; (m) worked bone; (n) horn spoon; (o) abrading stones; (p) mano. Variable scale.

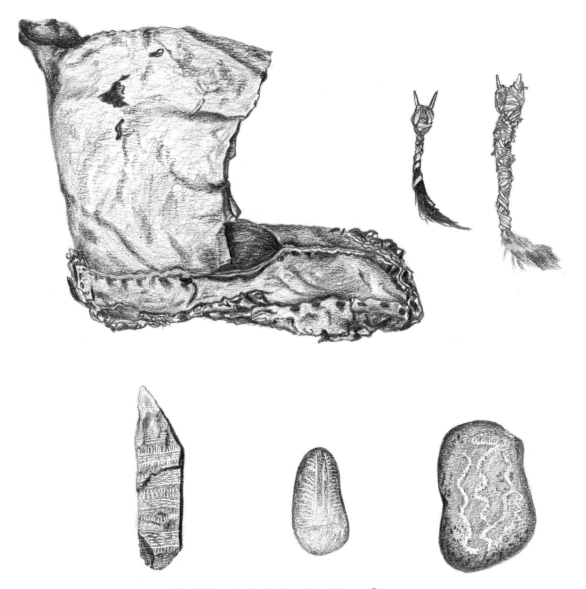

Figure 4.23 Moccasin, feather effigy (?), and etched stones from Hogup Cave. Reduced.

changes. The changing environment, the shift in chipped flint types, the evident changes in preferred foods, and more subtle considerations figure in the conclusions. They link the climatic and resource changes with the cultural changes. Similar changes can be noted, but less sharply, in the Danger Cave artifact lists. The Hogup Cave report is a balanced blend of data and interpretation and is recommended reading for anyone interested in either human ecology and adaptation or the desert Archaic.

In addition to the sites just discussed from the eastern Great Basin, two other important Archaic sites have been located and excavated far to the east in the Colorado Plateau. The first of these is Sudden Shelter at an elevation of 7200 feet above sea level on the flanks of the Wasatch Plateau near Salina, Utah. Although it was a deep, well-stratified site containing a wide variety of artifacts, its chief importance in this context is that it was very carefully excavated: Twenty-two occupation strata were discovered and individually removed, and what was learned is of regional importance.

Probably because of the elevation and the severe winters there, Sudden Shelter was evidently a summer base camp throughout its use from 8400 to 3300 B.P. Activities included the manufacturing of flint tools, seed gathering and processing, and hunting. Because the fill was a little damp, the preservation of perishable objects other than bone, which was abundant, was poor. The deposit was 4 meters of limey colluvial fill, the first occupancy being essentially on the bedrock of the wide overhang. The twenty-two cultural strata more or less divided themselves into three major units of accumulation: the first and earliest (I) seems to have extended from 8400 to 6300 B.P. Evidence contained within it indicated that the subsistence items most often taken were deer and porcupine with few vegetal products. Stratum II lasted from 6300 to 4600 B.P. Subsistence as well as artifacts changed during this period. Cottontails and mountain sheep were the major meat food while grass seeds were the dominant vegetal resource. In the final period (III), which lasted from 4600 to 3300 B.P., the dominant meat food was again the mountain or bighorn sheep while the vegetal food was amaranthus, grass almost entirely disappearing. From the sedimentary record, the snails included in the fill, and other sources it was demonstrated that stratum I was moist and cool, stratum II markedly drier and warmer, and stratum III more moist and equable.

Of most importance, however, aside from the demonstration of climatic shifts, was the occurrence of some well-known, widespread projectile points in rather tight chronological clusters. In stratum I the Pinto, Northern side-notched, Humboldt, and Elko series were dominant. In stratum II the Elko continued but in diminishing numbers, while two side-notched, locally named types rounded out that kit. In stratum III the dominant projectile point was the widely distributed contracting stemmed Gypsum point (see Figures 4.15 and 4.16). It is interesting that this sequence seems to be well controlled at this spot and yet the dates of most of the types identified at Sudden Shelter are markedly older than the dates of the same type specimens found in the western Great Basin. This seems to support those who maintain that the eastern Basin was inhabited earlier than the western. In terms of today's climate and resources, that makes considerable sense.

A hundred or so miles east of Sudden Shelter, deep in the Colorado Plateau is Cowboy Cave. Its setting is entirely different from Sudden Shelter's. It is only about 4000 feet in elevation and lies on the edge of the canyonlands of Utah in a steppe environment; that is, grass and sage in a red rock (Navajo sandstone) setting. Although the site repeated the sequence of projectile points already noted at Sudden Shelter, its contribution lies in its wide range of artifacts and the presence of maize in its upper levels.

The cave is also interesting in that it was used earlier by herbivores. A layer of animal dung about two feet thick underlay all the cultural materials. Analyses of the dung and the specimens of hair, bones, and other identifiable animal parts led to the certain identification of five species. They were bison, which was dominant, elephant, camel, horse, and sloth. Elk may have been there as well. Bison hair and two elephant tusk tip fragments made the identification of those two species beyond doubt.

The cultural use of the cave began at about 8600 B.P. and extended to about 450 A.D. But it was by no means continuous. The first occupancy lasted only about 600 years. Then there was a hiatus of nearly 1000 years and a second 900- to 1000-year occupancy (stratum III). Another gap of over 2500 years was followed by stratum IV when the cave was used for some 440 years. After another 1200- to 1300-year break an occupancy of 510 years, ending at 450 A.D., was recorded. There is no ready explanation for this occupancy record. It may or may not tie in with climatic fluctuation. The long gap between stratum III and stratum IV, however, is about the time of the Altithermal and covers over 2500 years, so possibly these breaks indicate some drastic kind of environmental change. Aside from the questions it raises, the most important aspects of this cave are wide variety of artifacts recovered and the importance ascribed to some of them by students of Great Basin prehistory. There were, for example, a number of clay figurines from the earliest levels right to the top. Little painted sandstone slabs and many incised stones are a strong link to the Great Basin. There were also many of the **wicker** animal figurines found in ceremonial contexts in the Grand Canyon and Great Basin. Here they are found broken, battered, and discarded in the fill, which indicates a day-to-day secular use rather than the ceremonial or sacred use usually ascribed to them. Interestingly, they first occur at about 3500 B.P. as do those long known from the western basin.

The usual tools of wood and bone occur, including fire drills and **fire hearths,** spindle whorls, string and stick snares, projectile points, arrow and dart shafts, and much cordage and basketry (Figures 4.24, 4.25). All these things, of course, are more-or-less standard, but the upper or fifth stratum seems to be the expression of the terminal Archaic, which came to be called Basketmaker II in the Four Corners area to the southeast of Cowboy Cave.

To the west, there are numerous important sites, including a cluster around Humboldt Lake in west-central Nevada (Lovelock, Leonard, Humboldt). Together the sites offer a fairly complete inventory of the artifacts. They contain the remains of a people whose subsistence focused on the many lacustrine resources of the shallow, fluctuating lake.

Lovelock—a large, irregular cave opening out onto fossil Lake Lahontan—was one of the richest sites in the West. It was nearly filled with huge roof spalls weighing many tons and had been used primarily as a cache site. Lovelock and Humboldt Caves were dry and, though sometimes occupied, were used mainly for caches. Being late in time (about 4500 B.P. to 1850 A.D. for Lovelock and 1 A.D. onward for Humboldt), the varied artifacts were used in a climate very like that of today. The special items showing lacustrine focus include **tule** reed duck decoys dated at 2000 B.P., fishnets, and two types of fishhooks, to say nothing of several dried suckers and chub found in Humboldt Cave caches. Other artifacts are more familiar. These include well-made baskets, both twined and coiled; scapula and sheep-horn sickles; fiber sandals; tubular pipes; flint knives with wooden handles; bow fragments, and other evidence of the full exploitive round (Figures 4.26 and 4.27). Objects very similar to those from Danger Cave include the L-shaped awls, fine netting, atlatl foreshafts, fire drills and hearths, woven skin blankets, horn spoons and wrenches, as well as a number of chipped-flint tools.

Humboldt was particularly rich, yielding thirty-one caches. Most of the cache pits were lined with well-preserved basket fragments. One cache contained what appears to be a **shaman's** kit. The inventory from Humboldt lists the following classes: duck decoys of tule reed; feather bundles (in fourteen caches); sickles of mountain-sheep horn; horn wrenches; scapula sickles or grass cutters; bone awls, including the L-shaped one cut from a scapula and other types; bone needles; fishhooks of two types (both composite); digging sticks; fire drills and hearths; many composite arrows and parts; dart shafts; shallow cottonwood bowls and slabs; wooden knife

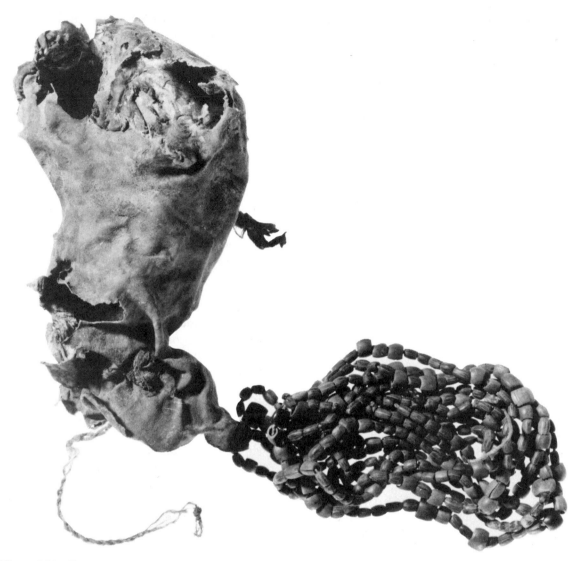

Figure 4.24 Fawn's head medicine bag from Cowboy Cave and the necklace found inside it. The necklace is made from wild plum and silverberry pits and juniper berries.

handles; chipped flint points, knives, and scrapers; hammerstones; wicker and coiled basketry (766 pieces of coiling represented 213 baskets); flexible and rigid twined basketry (the flexible bags are of a type called Catlow Twined, described from the Oregon caves); cordage of all kinds and sizes; fiber sandals; feather robes; string aprons, pine nut and *Olivella* beads; bone whistles and tubes; tubular stone pipes; and many fragmentary miscellaneous items. At neither of the above sites was the mano or flat millstone reported, although many occur on nearby open sites around Humboldt Lake. The food bones found

Figure 4.25 Wicker figurines, painted and etched stones, and clay figurines from Cowboy Cave.

SCALE (cm)
0 1 2 3 4 5

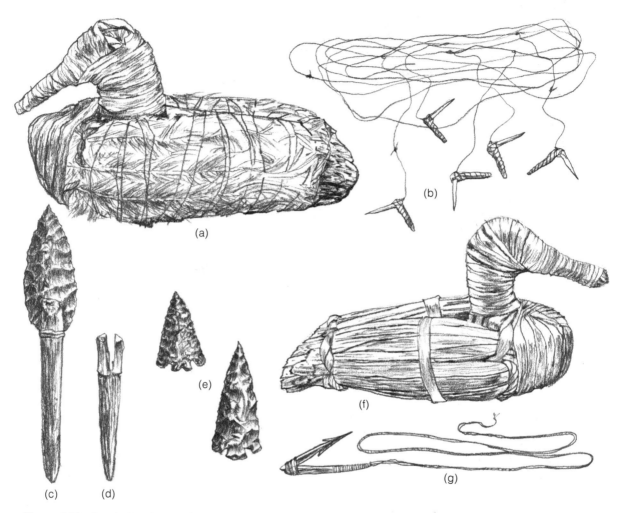

Figure 4.26 Lovelock culture artifacts: (a) duck decoy of tule reed and duck feathers, (b) fishhooks on a **setline,** (c) hafted knife, (d) knife handle, (e) projectile points, (f) tule duck decoy, (g) bone fishhook with wooden shank and twined line.

in Humboldt Cave show that grebe, pelican, heron, swan, goose, duck, hawk, and raven were taken, as were mountain sheep, deer, jackrabbit, badger, fox, bobcat, marmot, several rats and mice, and muskrat. At Lovelock the mammal list was longer, with weasel, skunk, mink, beaver, wolf, cottontail, and antelope added; all the species are modern. Raw materials for perishable tools were derived from scores of plants—*Apocynum* (hemp), rush, cane, various grasses, greasewood, wil-

low, cottonwood, and other species—already cited from Danger Cave. Quids were also numerous.

The objects from Lovelock were more numerous and varied, being recovered from forty cache pits as well as from the fill, but the range of classes is about the same as at Humboldt. The Lovelock culture has been divided into an early-middle-late sequence covering about the last 4000 years. The list emphasizes perishable materials, so it is not easy to apply

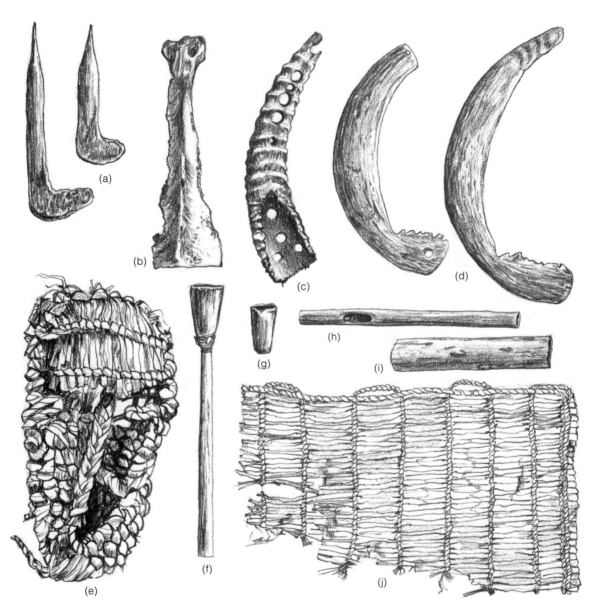

Figure 4.27 Artifacts of the Western Archaic Tradition, California-Nevada area:
(a) scapula awls; (b) scapula grass cutter, 9 inches long; (c) worked sheet horn; (d)
worked mountain sheep horn sickles, 10-¼ and 13 inches long; (e) tule sandal; (f) and
(g) tubular stone pipes (f with stem); (h) bird-bone whistle, 6 inches long; (i) pelican-
bone tube, 4 inches long; (j) twined tule mat. Variable scale.

to most sites, but the classes correspond rather neatly with the perishable things found in the upper two layers of Danger and Hogup Caves.

Farther south, near Las Vegas, Nevada, Etna Cave yielded completely typical artifacts of textile and flint in scant quantity but in a good state of preservation. The cave also contained a series of stick figurines of game animals, many impaled upon a spear or lance through the chest cavity. These remarkable little figures have been found in several places along the Grand Canyon and have been radiocarbon dated. The dates cluster around 3500 B.P.; the Etna Cave specimen falls at 3750 B.P. As mentioned, others of a battered and broken but slightly more elaborate construction technique were recovered from Cowboy Cave in Utah; their use continued until later in time.

A very interesting site excavated recently is Gatecliff Shelter, located in Monitor Valley almost in the center of Nevada some 20 miles west of the Reese River Valley. The site was excavated with extraordinary care. Some eight years were spent in the excavating process. The shelter work was part of a much larger project, which was the study of the entire Monitor Valley. The study was aimed at understanding the past and present environment and the details of human adaptation to those environments. A cadre of specialists were concerned variously with all aspects of geology, paleontology, sedimentation, and botany. The record of the research pertaining to Gatecliff Shelter is detailed almost to tedium but very thorough, leaving little about the setting unknown.

The shelter itself, a fairly large cavern overhung by a ledge, contains some 10 meters of fill, the upper 7 containing cultural material. A number of individual strata were collapsed into four major stages. One interesting thing was that during the period the Altithermal prevailed the sediments indicated quite wet episodes as well as the drier ones anticipated by the definition of the Altithermal. There were sixteen cultural horizons, which were divided into five named phases.

The period of occupation extended from about 6000 B.P. to probably 1500 A.D. or, perhaps, even into the historic period. The phases are defined in temporal or chronological terms. Each is named and is defined by flint projectile point types that already have established time spans attributed to them. Therefore, the phases are chronological, characterized by points used as chronological markers. The five phases are:

1. Layers 16 (the basal layer) to 12, which are labeled the Clipper Gap phase and dated from 6000 B.P. The phase is characterized by Humboldt concave base points.

2. Layers 11 through 8 are called Devils Gate and dated from 4000 to 3000 B.P. The phase is characterized by Pinto and Gypsum types.

3. Layers 7 through 4 are called the Reveille phase and dated from 3500 B.P. to 500 A.D. The phase is characterized by Elko eared and corner-notched points.

4. Layers 3 and 2 are the Underdown, which extends only from 1 to 300 A.D. This phase is characterized by the Rosegate series.

5. Layer 1 is called the Yankee and dated from 300 to 500 A.D. The phase is characterized by the Desert side-notched and Cottonwood triangular points (see Figures 4.15 and 4.16).

The importance of the site lies less with its content than with the behavioral data (the use of space, activity areas, etc.) that were obtained by careful clearing of occupational floors and mapping of all objects found on those floors. Of the several layers, 8 and 9 in the Late Devils Gap and Early Reveille phases show the heaviest occupancy observed at the cave. It occurred at about 3000 B.P. Layer 8 was the scene of great activity. Flint tools and objects were made in the rear of the cave, and the debris was discarded there. Sandstone milling slabs were made in quantity out nearer the front. The millstone scrap or debitage is everywhere, but most of it is concentrated just inside the drip line. Over 2000 fragments of bighorn sheep bones and many cottontail bones were also close to the portal, both inside and outside the drip line. Awls and drills testified to domestic tasks, such as basketmaking, hide working, and the manufacture of wooden tools and implements. These artifacts were toward the front of the shelter like the sandstone debris. Most of the activity took place around the several hearths in the shelter, although some of the flint work was done deep in the rear of the cave in an alcove on the west side.

Among the artifacts were over 400 incised stones (such as came from Hogup and Cowboy caves) whose use, purpose, and importance are still subject to much debate. There were over twenty shell beads made from *Olivella* and abalone. Wooden tools and objects of all sorts, such as fire hearths and drills, snares, and weapons, were common.

Turning southwest from the basin, a putatively Early Archaic variant is the Cochise of southeastern Arizona and southwestern New Mexico. The earliest level is called Sulphur Spring and has only been reported from the type site. Its validity has been challenged because the objects did not accumulate at the site. The entire deposit is clearly alluvial, so the artifacts were probably redeposited by stream action. The apparent association of the artifacts with extinct fauna—horse, mammoth, dire wolf—as well as with modern bison, antelope, and coyote is merely evidence of random stream mixing.

Later in time, the Chiricahua Cochise is reported from several locations. Dated at 7000 B.P., it shows a somewhat fuller complement of artifacts, including milling stones and projectile points. Latest is the San Pedro stage, which endures until the introduction of pottery. The stonework in all stages is crude and shows a general similarity to other complexes

of the southern area. It seems possible, through both stratigraphy and typology, to show an ancestral relation of the Chiricahua to the Mogollon of the later Southwestern cultures. Most would agree, but the usual caveat about basing conclusions on the typology of stone artifacts should be mentioned. With the Chiricahua Cochise one should include the Concho complex in Arizona, Lobo in New Mexico, and the Rio Grande-Atrisco sites near Albuquerque.

At Tularosa Cave, where many classes of perishables were preserved, the transition from Late Archaic to Mogollon is documented. There was probably some loss of control of provenience in certain areas during excavation, but the sequence from the lower Chiricahua Cochise stage up into the Mogollon culture of the Christian era can be accepted, except as noted later. In the prepottery or Cochise levels the stonework was of the same type as elsewhere in the Southwest. The perishable items were innumerable; Tularosa was one of the richest sites in the West.

From the prepottery levels came the milling stone and small mano; coiled basketry; exhausted quids; fiber sandals of wickerwork and leather; moccasins; bone tubular beads; cordage and traps; net bags; cradles; fire drills and hearths; atlatls and darts; chipped points and knives; choppers and hammerstones; drills; gravers; abrading stones; short, stubby bone awls; wooden knife handles and trowels; wooden and bone dice; pigment; skewers; **wooden cylinders;** and other familiar classes. Specimens of thirty-nine natural floral species exploited for food, tools, and raw materials were recovered. Of these the food plants included yucca seeds, cacti, walnuts, various grass seeds, and sunflower and desert primrose seeds. In addition, the prepottery levels are said to have yielded maize, beans, squash, and gourds. But the association of the cultigens with a nonpottery level more likely results from a loss of stratigraphic controls and the mixing of two discrete cultural levels.

An open site, well-dug and well-reported, is

Cienega Creek, where the Chiricahua Cochise can be seen to evolve through time into the later San Pedro.

In the extreme southwestern portion of the Great Basin a great deal of amateur as well as professional research was sparked by the PaleoIndian excitement of the 1930s. Many surface surveys were conducted but relatively little digging was done. However, no reliable synthesis had been made of the many sites until recently. Or perhaps one should say so many syntheses had been made that they could not be correlated. The problem was compounded by the extravagant claims made for the extreme age of some of the complexes. So although there are many reports, the facts about the area haven't been well known. Currently, however, there appears to be some agreement about the sequence of events there.

The California deserts, of course, lie in what is now southeastern California. The area is dominated by the Mojave, Colorado, and Death Valley deserts. These three now-hostile locations show ample evidence of long, if intermittent, human use. Here, as at Gatecliff Shelter, the sequence is geared to temporally diagnostic common western projectile point types. For the Mojave area, the chronology covers about 11,000 years. The earliest is the debated and uncertain San Dieguito complex, which is dated from 11,000 to 7000 B.P. (see Figure 4.28). The next, and possibly better understood, is the so-called Pinto occupation, which is characterized by several types of Pinto points. Generally these points (see Figure 4.29) are small and crudely chipped; some have parallel sides, and some tend toward the triangular. Indented bases are common as are eared and side-notched bases. The small size and possibly the crudity of the work are the diagnostic attributes. The Pinto occupancy of the desert seems to have been confined to about 7000 to 6000 B.P., and then the sites were abandoned. But following an increasingly wet period, it is believed the Pinto people returned to the desert. At no time was the use of the area heavy. Presumably, the people were hunters and gatherers although no milling stones have been positively identified as part of the artifact assemblage.

From 4000 B.P. until about 500 A.D., the Gypsum period is much better represented and much better known. The climate was considerably more temperate. The projectile point types associated with the Gypsum period include the familiar Elko eared and Elko corner-notched points, as well as the contracting stem Gypsum point. In some locations, the Humboldt concave base is also part of the collection. A well-known Gypsum period site is Newberry Cave at the south end of Troy Lake Basin in California. The contents included many perishable and nonperishable artifacts. The stonework included Gypsum, Elko eared and corner-notched points, scrapers, and heavy choppers. A fire drill hearth, cordage, sandals, an atlatl hook and dart shafts, foreshafts and butts, and a tortoise shell were also recovered. There were also numerous items that were probably ceremonial, such as feathered plumes, several split-twig figurines more crudely made than those from farther east, quartz crystals, and painted stone. The cave itself was lined with pictographs. Other Gypsum artifacts include manos and milling stones, as well as the mortar and pestle, shaft smoothers, small incised slate and sandstone slabs, sandstone tablets, and slate tubes (possibly pipes). The abalone rings, beads, and ornaments from central California, and *Olivella* shell beads show there was considerable trade with the California coast and a fairly widespread settlement of the area. The millstones permit the inference that the economy was based on nuts and seeds.

The final two periods, Sarasota Springs and prehistoric-historic Shoshone, round out the picture. Sarasota Springs shows some continuation of Gypsum artifacts, but in several places there is evidence of slight contact with the Anasazi cultures to the east in such things as pottery and turquoise.

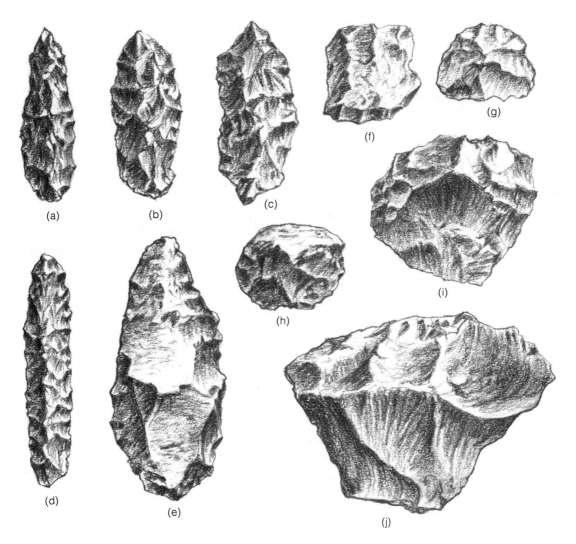

Figure 4.28 San Dieguito artifacts: (a)–(e) knives; (f)–(i) scrapers; (j) chopper. Reduced about one-third.

In connection with the Mojave Desert and the San Dieguito complex, the somewhat hazily described Western Pluvial Tradition should possibly be mentioned. The tradition is described as one focused on the many lakes and marshes in the western and southwestern Basin of 11,000 to 9000 years ago. Subsistence was presumed to have been by means of hunting mammals and wild fowl and gathering vegetable foods other than seeds. No milling stones were present. The toolkit was not very complex or varied. There were the Lake Mojave points, chipped stone crescents, scrapers of many kinds, drills, hammerstones, and gravers. The age is estimated, but it is believed to go back to at least 11,000 years ago because occasional examples of fluted points are found in the same settings, that is, along the banks of old Pleistocene marshes and lakes. Hence it is argued that the Western

Figure 4.29 Pinto points. Reduced about one-third.

Pluvial tradition coexisted with the fluted point hunters of big game and is as old. Actually the Western Pluvial tradition seems to be nothing but a term substituted for the San Dieguito assemblage.

Probably the best known of the San Dieguito sites that are claimed to typify the Western Pluvial Tradition would be the C.W. Harris site on the San Dieguito River only 15 miles from the ocean. The artifacts were recovered from a gravel conglomerate more than six feet below the river floodplain. Technically similar to the Lake Mojave collections, the artifacts include leaf-shaped knives, bifaces, short-bladed shouldered points, a stone crescent, engraving tools, choppers, cores, and many types of scrapers. Another site that is believed to represent the Western Pluvial Tradition is in Clear Lake Basin. This location has been only superficially examined, but it is evidently quite deep (over 5 meters), and nine separable occupation levels are visible. The oldest, according to a charcoal ^{14}C assay, is 11,250 B.P. At that level there were hearths, obsidian artifacts, bone from both birds and fish, and freshwater clam shells. Most important, perhaps, were the twenty-five burials. They were flexed and had with them lanceolate, lozenge-

shaped bifaces of obsidian and chert, pointed stone artifacts, pointed bone artifacts, and a couple of enigmatic ground stone slabs or tablets. The burials dated 10,500 B.P., but the dates may be suspect (even though they do agree with the charcoal date) because they were made on collagen from human bone itself. Although the site yields a quite different artifact collection it is labelled as another manifestation of the Western Pluvial Tradition. However, the utility of the tradition is questionable.

We turn now to the Archaic cultures in the western two-thirds of California. Those Archaic cultures of California outside the Great Basin do not greatly resemble the western Archaic we have been describing for many pages. There is a maritime specialization along the coast. This is not surprising given the optimal and opportunistic exploitative stance now recognizable as a hallmark of the Archaic adaptation over the continent. Here in California, as well as the East, there is marked variation in resources and an equal variation in regional lifeways and their subsistence foci. Because local distinctions can be so readily drawn, the extensive literature tends to split cultures rather than combine them. Nevertheless a series of broad patterns has been described and will be used here. In most cases, whatever stance the early Archaic people adopted continues up into historic time (as was true of the Great Basin, except for the brief flowering of the Fremont culture in Utah).

The western half of California being considered here has abundant resources, being considerably moister than the lands east of the Sierra Nevada. Generally there were endless oak forests and thickets, deer apparently abounded, and maritime resources were exploited in all coastal and riverine situations. In fact, the maritime focus was dominant in northern California, and the cultures there were similar in most respects to, though less elaborate than, those of the Northwest coast.

The richness of the environment, especially the oak groves with their huge acorn crops and the attendant populations of deer, permitted the establishment of year-round settlements and the heaviest population after 1 A.D. in the West. The lifeway was quite stable as well. It was so stable, in fact, that the corn agriculture and ceramics introduced from the Southwest were never adopted except peripherally. Presumably this occurred because the long-established acorn-fish-deer subsistence pattern was fully reliable and satisfactory.

In western California, there was evidently a much greater concern with the dead. Many were buried in mounds, others in extensive cemeteries. An analysis of the grave goods of these many cemeteries has led some scholars to suggest that there was in California a social complexity quite unlike the simple egalitarian societies usually posited for most of the western Archaic and quite at variance with the simple and relatively stable technology the archaeology reveals.

Several lines of evidence have been invoked to suggest a long-lived, ranked society with dominant lineages. First, there is the demonstrated density of population after about 1 A.D. There is considerable trade in shell beads and obsidian, and most important, there is a differential distribution of costly grave goods between individuals in any given cemetery. In fact, there is even a concentration of individuals with much grave goods as opposed to the rest of the cemetery where such goods are lacking. That evidence, along with a reexamination of the ethnographic accounts, has led to the speculation or suggestion that the heavy, possibly crowded population had led to the development of a relatively complex system earlier here than anywhere else in North America as far as we know. It is postulated that some individuals or lineages were able to manipulate social or political systems and in that way extend their individual influence well beyond the limited tribal or ethnic limits. If systems such as trade in obsidian or in the several prized species of shell did exist, one must assume that there

were alliances between powerful individuals in quite distant locations. The archaeology actually seems to support that view. Precise proof, of course, will be difficult to come by.

Southern Coastal California

The earliest of the southern coastal traditions is the Encinitas. It includes many local complexes, such as Topanga, Oak Grove, La Jolla, Little Sycamore, and the Channel Islands. These complexes vary in their artifact content, and the earliest period is dated from about 7000 B.P. The milling stone is the marker. But hunting and fishing did not necessarily diminish, so the addition of the millstone simply indicates that another set of resources was being exploited. Sea mammals and coastal mollusks were also taken for food. Actually, this period marks the local beginning of the wide exploitation characteristic of the Archaic. The artifacts continue to include the crude chopping, cutting, and scraping tools of the San Dieguito. Also present were bone awls and beads, atlatl hooks, and shell beads and pendants. Weaving and basketry are known from impressions in asphalt (used widely to affix handles, attach beads to other objects, etc.). The millstone and shell in various forms, stone discs, and the unusual cogstones are characteristic up and down the coast. The cogstones are merely heavy perforated thick stone discs with coglike projections all around the perimeter, of unknown function. Projectile points are rare, but burials, which are usually reburials, are numerous. They are often flexed with the head toward the north. Cobblestone cairns were erected over the graves when any attention was paid to the deceased. Grave goods were rare (Figure 4.30).

One of the best known and longest lived (from 7000 to 5000 B.P.) of the southern coastal California cultures is the LaJolla, a milling stone assemblage. The inventory is scanty and

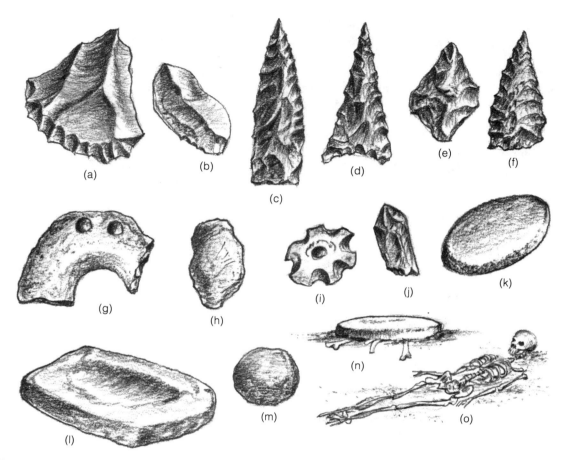

Figure 4.30   Characteristic traits of the Topanga culture: (a) and (b) scrapers, (c)–(f) projectile points, (g) and (h) ornaments, (i) stone cog, (j) worked quartz crystal, (k) stone disc, (l) metate, (m) mano, (n) reburial under metate, (o) extended burial. Variable scale.

not uniform, but pebble choppers; grinding implements (either mortars or the flat slab); large, poorly chipped points; flake scrapers; stone discs; shell beads of disc shape; spire-lopped *Olivella*; and both flexed and extended burials, as well as reburials under rock cairns, are more or less shared features. The staple of subsistence was either acorns and seeds, shellfish, or both, with hunting common to all facies.

The Campbell phase followed the Encinitas as early as 5300 B.P. It was characterized by one more new technology: the hopper mortar and stone mortar and pestle and the development of acorns as a staple food. The hopper mortar was a basket attached with asphalt to a rock outcrop; a pestle was used inside it to crush the acorns. The function of the hopper, of course, was to hold the crushed acorns as they were churned up and down by the pestle movement. Many shell and bone ornaments, and projectile points were part of the material culture. There was heavy hunting of both land and sea mammals, and fish were also taken.

Central Valley

From the southern coastal region we move north and east into the rich central valleys that lie between the coast ranges and the Sierra Nevada. So far the known sequence is relatively short. There are reasons for this: Since the central valleys drain from both the coastal ranges and the Sierra Nevada to the east, alluvium is very deep. The earliest remains, as we saw in the Little Tennessee River Valley, are probably deeply buried. At the time of the first historic knowledge, the valleys were a virtual paradise for foragers. There were marshes, lakes, streams, and prairies where elk, deer, pronghorn antelope, sheep, rabbits, other animals, and countless waterfowl were available. Three phases overlapping in time have been recognized in the valleys. Of course, there is an ill-defined earlier occupancy ending, perhaps, at 5000 B.P. Then we encounter the Windmiller phase, 4750 to 2250 B.P., the Berkeley, 3500 to 1500 B.P., and the Augustine, 1 A.D. to historic time. Most of what we know about the Windmiller pattern has been learned from the many large burial mounds. The characteristic artifact is the mortar and pestle (Figure 4.31).

Dependence on nuts and acorns seems to have begun during Windmiller times, and evidently it was never discontinued. Using acorns for food involved more than crushing or grinding the nuts. After milling, the meal had to be leached to remove the astringent tannin found in the raw acorns. This process involved soaking and rinsing the meal in water. There were countless baked clay balls presumed to have been used in lieu of stones for stone-boiling in baskets. There were many projectile points of several kinds, many of them large. Fish leisters, fishhooks, nets, and line sinkers all attest to heavy fishing activity on the streams. The fish bones recovered are largely sturgeon and salmon. There are some smaller fish remains as well.

Another hallmark of the Windmiller and, of course, later cultures, are the **charmstones.** They are shaped like plumb bobs and well made of alabaster, marble, or magnetite. Some are highly polished. Although called charmstones, they may equally likely have been net sinkers. There were also cylindrical needles

or pins of slate, basketry, many shell ornaments, and shell applique. The shell was usually fastened or fixed with asphalt to the object being decorated. There was considerable use of steatite for beads. Interestingly (and this never changes throughout the rest of the California sequence) there was extensive trade: Obsidian from both coast range and Sierra Nevada quarries, shell from the coast, and quartz and alabaster from the Sierra Nevada have been identified.

The burials (except very old females, which were flexed) were extended in the supine position in cemeteries. Many of the sites show that more than 50 percent of the graves contained grave goods. There is no sex or age distinction as to which burials have accompanying grave goods. This has been interpreted as indicating a social status that is ascribed rather than achieved. The orientation of the burials—with their heads to the west-southwest toward the setting winter sun—has been interpreted as evidence of winter burial. The burials were made at the more-or-less permanent settlement. If, as is proposed, the Windmiller people went to the foothills and into the Sierra Nevada in the summer (and the grave goods distribution does indicate this), probably the permanent villages were largely deserted in summer. The notion of summer abandonment is to some extent confirmed by the distribution studies that have been made. They show a seasonal occupation in the Sierra Nevada; at least typical artifacts and cairn burials are found there. Undoubtedly the villagers returned before autumn for the acorn harvest.

The Berkeley phase or Consumnes culture occurs in both the central valley and on the coast, especially near San Francisco Bay. The diagnostic artifacts are chiefly ornaments of shell, steatite, and slate, charmstones being common. There are also well-flaked, large lanceolate points with concave bases. The same points show up in the Borax Lake culture to the north, as will be mentioned. Shell beads were profuse and varied greatly in shape

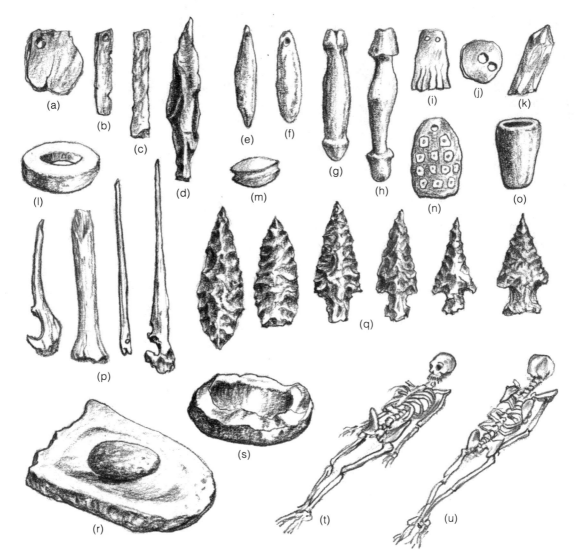

Figure 4.31 Artifacts of the central California Windmiller culture: (a) **biotite** ornament, (b) and (c) slate ornaments, (d) "bangle," (e)–(h) charmstones, (i) shell ornament, (j) shell disk, (k) worked quartz crystal, (l) steatite bead, (m) clay object, (n) shell-inlaid turtle carapace ornament, (o) stone pipe, (p) bone tools, (q) projectile points, (r) metate and mano, (s) mortar, (t) and (u) extended supine and prone burials. Variable scale.

through time. That variation has been used occasionally to establish chronology.

Little need be said about the Augustine phase. It is the period when the basic outlines of the historic cultures take form, including the heavy reliance on acorns as a staple food.

It is now possible to say that after about 5000 to 4500 B.P., the early California cultures show very similar evolutionary development, except for the northern California coast. The mortar and pestle seem to be ubiquitous. They occur everywhere west of the Great Basin. It seems entirely possible that in the Sierra Nevada, pinenuts were also harvested. They, too, could have been processed in the mortars. In all cases where there is information, the harvesting of game and fish was variably important but never absent.

Northwest Coastal California

The earliest northern California coast material, at about 6000 B.P., is called the Borax Lake. It is very poorly known, being characterized only by several heavy points, lanceolate bipoints, and lanceolate points with an indented base. The millstone with pebble mano, and the mortar and pestle complete the list of recovered objects. But by 500 A.D., the Gunther phase was widespread. It had a mollusk, fish, and sea and land mammal subsistence orientation, as well as the mortar and pestle. The remains have been recovered from large shell mounds also used as cemeteries.

The shell mounds contained tens of thousands of mollusk shells, and the artifacts were numerous and specialized. One of the most common was the toggle harpoon fitted with harpoon points of bone and chipped stone. Woodworking was evidenced by stone adzes, axes, and chisels. There were bone awls, antler wedges, and spoons made of mountain sheep (?) horn. Not hitherto encountered are effigies of animals (called zoomorphs) made of several kinds of stones, steatite bowls, and large ceremonial blades of red and black obsidian. These all reveal great skill in sculpture and stonework. The same objects are interpreted as evidence of conspicuous consumption of wealth. The obsidian blades in one collection were identified as originating in two quarries, one 200 miles away, the other over 300. We find also the flanged and offset pestles that imply continued use of vegetable foods. There were net weights, baked clay figurines and bone hairpins. The similarities of the Gunther lifeway to the rich and more elaborate coastal cultures as far north as British Columbia are quite clear. The connection with the historic tribes along the coast is equally obvious.

Deriving the basic cultures of California is a complex task. Each of the phases or patterns discussed above has subsumed within it several locally named cultures. Given the fact that many California sites have been excavated and varyingly well reported, it is still true that the reported material is rarely compared with that of adjacent districts. Each excavator or reporter has tended to name the sequent manifestations differently, and the coordination of these many sequences is difficult. Among California students, there has also been a tendency to revere the detailed differences in artifacts: Beads are an example. The concern with minutia has been allowed to override the obvious similarities in the basic adaptation displayed by the California prehistoric peoples.

The evolution of the central and southern portions, as well as the interior northern part, has been essentially the same. Subsistence is based on the exploitation of waterfowl, fish, nuts, deer, and, where available, sea animals. It seems to the outsider that the acorn-game resource base was the dominant factor in the development of California cultures. Certainly, the area was rich in resources, possibly even as rich as the eastern woodlands, but the resources differ. It should also be noted that most of the patterns dated after 500 or 600 A.D. are usually interpreted as prehistoric manifestations of the tribes historically observed in those locations over the state.

The Plateaus

In this section the Columbia Plateau, the Snake River Plain, and the Interior Plateau of southern British Columbia have been combined. As is generally known the entire region of the Columbia Plateau is unique in North America in consisting of extensive lava flows deeply incised by strong-flowing rivers such as the Snake, Columbia, and Okanogan. The rivers are the key to the archaeology. Many of the lava fields are badlands; there appears to have been a tendency for aboriginal use to be concentrated along the water courses, and in many cases a riverine subsistence focus appears early in time. This is most typical of settlements along the Columbia River itself.

Most of the available data result from emergency excavations conducted behind the dozen or more reservoirs that now cover the valley floors behind the dams that obstruct the flow of the Columbia and Snake. Here as elsewhere the salvage nature of the research has had its own effect. The pressure of time in emergency archaeology, as job follows job, often prevents early reporting. River valley research also results only in river valley data, so that even the explored areas where data have been accumulated could be typical only of the restricted territory and special resources of the rivers not of the plateau as a whole. But the occupancy of the lava fields was expectably scanty, so it is believed that the intensively worked river areas adequately sample the plateau archaeological story. At least there is a general correspondence in the contents of many sites. The syntheses now available use the river valley data as typical. In fact, all the sequences of the Plateau are in remarkable agreement in many important ways. For example, the earliest segment of the chronologic sequence (i.e., before 8000 B.P.) is vague as to typical artifacts or representative sites everywhere. The cultures of the second segment of time—7500 to 5000 B.P. or later—are usually shown as complacent, with little change through time. More variation and trait accretion seems to mark those after 2500 B.P., when the culture pattern that was observed by ethnographers in historic times, began to emerge. All authors agree on heavy Great Basin influence being recognizable in the artifact inventory, especially during the middle period; some see the local variations beginning at this time. The late cultures are far richer, having a wide variety of new artifact classes that contrast greatly with the smaller inventories of earlier times. The enrichment of the later cultures is believed to represent the penetration by Pacific Coast or more northerly cultures (or ideas) into the plateaus. For example, the Salish tribe is usually credited with contributing the new cultural elements and the strong trade economy that characterize the northern tribes of the plateaus in the historic period.

The cultural chronological sequence used by most authors was developed as a result of several excavations in southeastern Washington on the lower Snake River. Its easy applicability over all the interior plateau testifies to the general similarity of the prehistoric environments and the adaptations made to them. It should be noted that the historically reported dependence of the indigenous groups on the aquatic riches of the Columbia River and its tributaries is merely the historical end-product of a lifeway at least 8000 years old, or so the archaeology suggests. In fact, interpreting the prehistoric objects collected and phenomena observed usually invokes ethnographic analogies.

The four basic phases are the Windust, 10,500 to 7500 B.P.; Cascade, 7500 to 5000 B.P.; Tucannon, 5000 to 2500 B.P.; and Harder, 2500 B.P. into historic times. The Windust is represented at numerous locations: Lind Coulee, in Washington; Five-mile Rapids, near Dalles, Oregon; Milliken, on the Fraser River in British Columbia; the Marmes Rockshelter site in Washington; and Windust Caves. At many of these sites the later phases are also represented. For example, at Five-mile Rapids the archaeological deposits record continuous use from the beginning at 8000 B.P. until the nineteenth century.

The cultural inventory of the Windust Phase includes large, lanceolate and stemmed points, large scrapers, so-called pulper **planes** (which are obviously nothing but the cores left after flakes have been removed), scraper planes, choppers, and knives. The millstone or mortar is absent or rarely encountered. Many of the locations are at places where, in historic times, vast quantities of salmon were taken and dried for trade and winter use. Occasionally, there are curved prismatic blades and burins. Bone atlatls, awls, and necklaces have also been recovered. The game taken includes seal, deer, elk, beaver, jackrabbit, and antelope—all of modern species. Stones with encircling grooves used perhaps as **bolas** or net weights occur (Figure 4.32). The edge-chipped pebble chopper is another diagnostic artifact.

The Cascade phase (7500 to 5000 B.P.) shows many technological additions. At such sites as Five-mile Rapids and Wildcat Canyon and others on the Columbia and John Day rivers, salmon bone and mussel shells in quantity attest the heightened use of the fishery and the harvesting of riverine resources. While many of the tools of the Windust phase continued in use, two projectile points—the Northern side-notched and the double-pointed Cascade—were added. The Northern side-notched type is similar in form and is chronologically equivalent to the Elko series of the Great Basin. It also resembles the Hawken type from the Plains. Large quantities of fish bone show how important the fisheries were becoming, possibly because of technological improvements in harvesting. Both mortars and millstones provide evidence of the use of vegetable foods. Pithouses appear. The houses and the heavy harvesting of salmon hint at the beginnings of sedentism and the establishment of historic settlement and subsistence patterns by at least 6000 B.P., or earlier. The Tucannon phase is little different, except that the stone points are smaller and triangular with contracting stem or deep corner-notches; grooved or notched stones are somewhat differently made and very common; there are hopper mortars and pestles, as well. Bone and antler wedges are new, as is a bone shuttle for making nets. Subsistence was still based on the salmon, but big game, elk, deer, antelope, and mountain sheep were also taken.

In the Harder phase the riverine exploitative technology grew strong. The settlements grew in size, and the houses were larger and possibly more substantial. The hopper mortar and accompanying pestle, for processing camas lily bulbs marked an increase in the vegetable diet. The broad-notched blades gave way at this time to small, triangular points with long stems and deep corner-notches. They mark the end of the lance and atlatl as the bow and arrow were introduced and became popular. The bow and arrow provided a superior weapon because of greater range and the rapid fire attribute. The toggling harpoon, both one piece and composite, was another new device for taking game. The full range of choppers, knives, scrapers, and other stone tools were used as before. The well-made circular (20 to 25 feet in diameter) houses were semisubterranean with basin-shaped floors and, usually, a central fireplace (Figure 4.33). The wooden frame was covered with skin, mats, or both.

The Harder phase, or its locally named equivalent, is richly represented at several sites. Wildcat Canyon on the Columbia River and Mack Canyon on the Deschutes, Harder on the lower Snake, and Umatilla Rapids on the Columbia at its confluence with the Umatilla River are among the better-reported sites. Umatilla Rapids has not been fully excavated, nor is it likely to be. The deposits are as much as 10 feet deep extending for over a mile along the south bank of the Columbia. Some thirty houses with basin floor, central fireplace, and elevated benches around the walls have been identified. Houses had been built over earlier ones, so the number of houses observed archaeologically is no real index to the original population of the village. It does testify, of course, to long-term use of a favored location. The major use of the site extended from about 3600 B.P. to the nineteenth century. Lewis and Clark actually visited the village in 1805 and 1806. They described a town of some fifty "lodges" and an estimated 700 people who had gathered for the spring salmon run. Although the chief occupation occurred toward the end of site use, the earliest remains

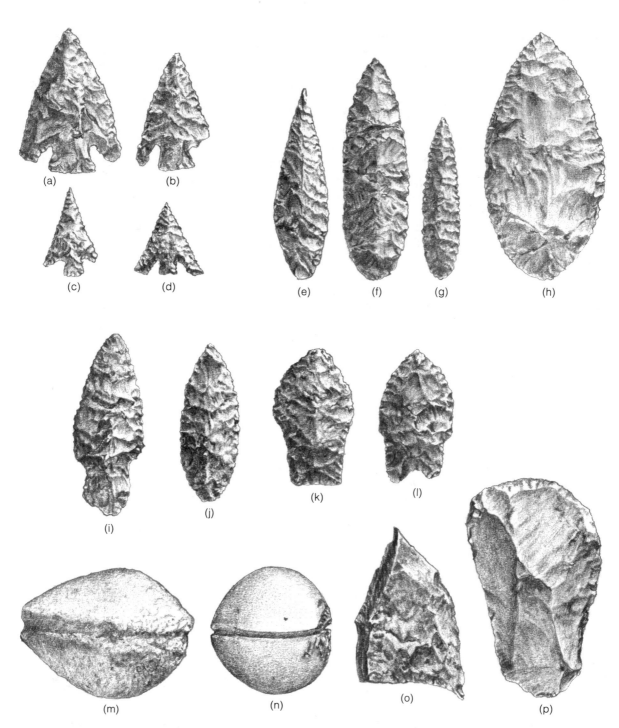

Figure 4.32 (a)–(d) Harder phase projectile points; (e)–(h) Cascade phase lithics; (i)–(p) Windust phase artifacts. Variable scale.

Figure 4.33 Artist's reconstruction of a Harder phase pithouse from the lower Snake River region.

discovered there lay beneath the Mazama ash testifying to 7000 years of occupancy. The Mazama ash came from the massive 7000 B.P. eruption that created Crater Lake in southern Oregon. In fact, most of the early sites so far excavated in Oregon and southeast Washington reveal a varyingly thick stratum of Mazama ash. Objects below it are, of course, over 7000 years old; finds above it are later. That same ash blanket has been used as a chronological marker by archaeologists since the 1940s. It was dated after 1950 by radiocarbon assay on organic materials directly beneath or included in it. The same ash can be chemically identified in Idaho and Utah as well as in bogs and other deposits over the rest of the Northwest.

The Harder site on the lower Snake River in southeastern Washington gives its name to this phase. It is not entirely typical of the phase, however. There were some thirty pithouses arranged in two rows alongside what may have been a street, but they were larger than usual. One had been rebuilt or refloored four times, but the artifacts, except for chipped flint objects, were scanty even though the midden was quite deep. Only a few mussel shells and scattered fish bones imply a riverine subsistence. A few scattered bones of bison and elk were also recovered. The many projectile points were largely small, triangular, delicately chipped forms, often with deep corner notches. They, at least, are typical.

Well down on the Columbia only a few miles east of Five-mile Rapids (Dalles, Oregon) lies the Wildcat Canyon site. The data were excavated from 1959 through 1967 but lay neglected until the 1980s. When finally reported (by others than the excavators), the materials proved to span about an 8400-year period from 8500 B.P. to about 1800 A.D. The Mazama ash provided the familiar marker sealing the earliest levels of occupation. Although all phases are represented at Wildcat Canyon, the heaviest use was from 2500 B.P. to about 100 A.D. That level, of course, is referable to the Harder phase (locally called Wildcat), which contained a number of pithouses, some of which had been built on top of earlier ones. Many had been refloored several times. They were generally round, but some were square with rounded corners. There are fireplaces varying from central, stone-lined, and paved pits to mere open fires and scattered ash located toward the pit edges. Some of the houses were sunk as deep as 3 feet into the ground. Diameters were from 15 to 20 feet. At the site were five deep earth ovens. They are large pits filled with fire-darkened rock, probably chunks of **basalt.** The ovens were for cooking camas and other bulbs. A large cemetery contained some fifty flexed human burials, with no standard directional orientation. There were other burials scattered over the site, some in abandoned houses. Interestingly, there were also six dog burials. They were large, almost identical in measurement to modern Siberian sled dogs. Many of the artifacts were found with the many burials or on house floors in what are presumed to be segregated work areas.

Artifacts other than the familiar small projectile points, knives, drills, and scrapers, included notched net sinkers, mauls, pestles, milling stones and mortars, bone (largely awls, including the L-shaped scapulae awls found all over the Great Basin and Plateau), harpoons, and shell beads of local mussels as well as coastal *Dentalium* and *Olivella*.

Before leaving the plateau it is perhaps useful to mention more explicitly the thriving trade with the interior along the Columbia and Snake Rivers to the coast and other localities. In historic times the Dalles, another name for the Five-mile Rapids, was a rendez-vous for native and white traders. While the horse was present by then to make land transport easier, some movement of goods continued by water. Trade at the Dalles in the nineteenth century certainly involved all of Oregon and Washington. Figure 4.34 shows the tribes involved and the commodities exchanged.

Source Area	Items
Upper Columbia and western Plateau	camas bulbs, hazelnuts, huckleberries, beargrass fibers, basketry, tule mats, dried berries, hemp, stone artifacts, freshwater shell ornaments, hemp twine
Middle Columbia–lower Snake River	salmon, camas bulbs, baskets, hats, freshwater shells
Northwest Coast	marine shells, dried salmon, salmon oil, deerskins, wapato roots
Great Basin	edible roots, skin lodges, elk and buffalo meats
Klamath River	wocas lily seeds, elk-skins, beads, shells, bows
Great Plains	catlinite clay and catlinite pipes, buffalo skin tents, painted buffalo hide bags, pemmican, buffalo horn and robes, parfleches, dressed moose skins, buffalo bone beads, feather headdresses

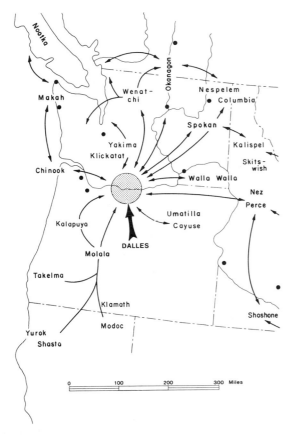

Figure 4.34 Major groups historically involved in trade at the Dalles, Oregon.

pic peninsula. Because it is permanently wet due to the intermittent presence of the tidewater, the preservation at the site was excellent. Well-woven flat bags and conical hats of cedar bark, gill nets of cedar bark with stone sinkers still attached, wooden and bone codfish hooks, and huge halibut hooks were recovered. The halibut hooks are shaped exactly as they are today except that they are made of wood instead of metal. The halibut hooks, along with halibut bones in the midden, are adequate evidence of ocean-going bottom fishing as one harvesting technique. Wooden pieces include a long-handled knife with an inset side blade that was still sharp enough to cut up fish.

At Ozette, west of Hoko on the Pacific side of the Olympic peninsula, a treasure trove was encountered. There at the site of a recently abandoned Makah village there was discovered a massive mudflow that some 500 years ago had engulfed and crushed a half dozen cedar plank houses with shed, rather than ridgepole, roofs. The mud had preserved everything perishable within the houses. Excavating meticulously with tiny water jets, the archaeologists recovered wooden boxes, figurines of bone and wood, cedar canoe paddles, boat-shaped wooden bowls, and human effigy bowls (the bowls being carved into the abdomen of the human effigy). There were loom parts, large boxes (one with a thunderbird design), harpoons with mussel shell blades, wooden and whalebone clubs, and an otter tooth encrusted effigy of a carved dorsal fin of the killer whale (Figures 4.35, 4.36). Whale vertebrae with harpoons embedded and many whalebone objects speak to the same organized whaling that was practiced historically by the coastal tribes.

North from Ozette in British Columbia, the limited study of the coastal and riverside archaeology shows early remains comparable in age to the northwest Plateau just summarized. Some students view the early artifacts as so similar that the British Columbia re-

On the coast of Washington, Oregon, and northern California, extensive remains document an exploitation of the sea as early as 2500 B.P. and possibly earlier. The people there used ocean-going craft, built cedar-planked longhouses in permanent settlements, and made extensive use of cedar bark and milkweed fiber for cordage. They fabricated wooden objects from many tree species, and made stone, bone, and ivory tools, weapons, and ornaments. One of the earliest of these sites was Hoko in extreme northwestern Washington. It is a midden location in the tidewater zone on the banks of the Hoko River. The Hoko, of course, empties into the Straits of Juan de Fuca on the north side of the Olym-

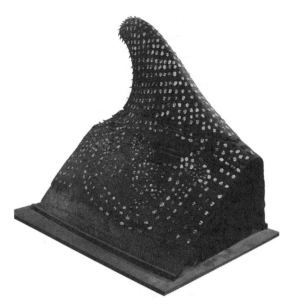

Figure 4.35 Wooden effigy of killer whale fin decorated with sea otter teeth (from Ozette).

mains are lumped with the Windust and Cascade phases, that is, the Paleoplateau. It is true that large lanceolate and large side-notched points occur early. Generally, however, the Canadian specimens are more carefully chipped, and there is more variation in form than in the Windust. Other students see the early material as quite different from that of the Plateau proper, resembling the Paleoarctic already described. The dispute can't be settled here, but the Paleoarctic similarity seems quite marked.

Remember that the Paleoplateau artifacts include the projectile points, the edge-chipped pebble chopper, occasional burins, and large prismatic knives or flakes struck from polyhedral cores. The same technique has already been noted in the Aleutian/Alaskan material very early where, in some cases, it is dominant. The blades and polyhedral cores are remindful of the Paleoarctic assemblage, although the microblades are generally absent. But in the Lochnor-Nessikip location on the Fraser River several sites reveal a history of possibly 8000 years, with the basal layers dating to about 7500 B.P. There are lanceolate and notched points, but they are accompanied by a few microblades and cores. This location was evidently a favored salmon-fishing station. But then, during the middle period at Lochnor-Nessikip, the microblades are abundant. Woodworking tools, such as adzes or celts, wedges of antler, rodent-tooth chisels, and stone mauls attest to a wood industry on a significant scale. By 3500 B.P., deep, semisubterranean pithouses exist as they do elsewhere on the Plateau.

At the Milliken site near the mouth of the Fraser, there is an early zone (dated, it is said, to 9500 to 8000 B.P.) where the artifacts are the expected leaf-shaped point, ovate chipped knives, pebble choppers, scrapers, and burins. All this sounds exactly like the Five-mile Rapids Cascade collection on the Columbia and suggests that the Cascade phase began earlier than the 7500 B.P. ascribed. Although the site itself is beside a long rapids and is a strong fishery today, no mention is made in the report of the discovery of salmon bones.

Additional information comes from the Namu site, located at the mouth of the Namu River on the British Columbia coast, more or less midway between the northern tip of Vancouver Island and the southern end of the Queen Charlotte Islands. Lying in the historic Bella Bella territory, the site contains a 9000-year history. The ^{14}C dates run from 9140 B.P. to about 1500 A.D. Two adjacent sites, Roscoe and Kisamet Bays, replicate the later components at Namu.

Aside from its depth—10 feet—and long time span, the site contained some interesting data. The lowest component, Namu I, contained an exclusively microblade-microcore industry, dated from 9000 to 7200 B.P. From 7200 to 4500 B.P. the deposit contained the large, crudely chipped biface points and pebble tool-chipping debris attesting the presence of Paleoplateau influence by that time. The microblades were still present in abundance. The thick clay and humus-rich fill (black matrix) containing Namu I also yielded food

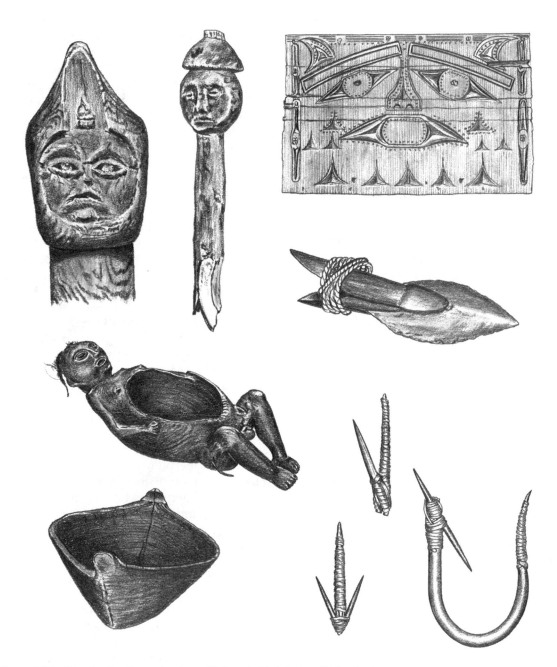

Figure 4.36 Wooden bowl, wooden box with thunderbird design, fishhooks, harpoon head, and effigies from Ozette.

bones of land and marine fauna: salmon, seal, sea lion, bear, deer, and beaver. No bone tools were recovered. At 4500 B.P., however, there is a change. Shellfish were added to the diet, so the fill becomes largely shell. But an extensive bone industry and new stone tools also appear, and the mix of land and sea animal prey continued. Because the interest here is in the early component, we leave Namu noting that it testifies to the presence of the Paleoarctic and Paleoplateau and their blending by 7200 B.P.

The Namu data support the conclusions reached at sites to the north where the Paleoplateau artifacts appear later, and to the south where they are earlier. In fact at Kodiak Island and the south coast of Alaska the blend of the two traditions has evolved into what is called the Ocean Bay Tradition by 6000 B.P. The collections are unremarkable; there are still leaf-shaped, percussion-chipped blades of Paleoplateau types as well as microblades. Additionally, a single stone lamp, presumably fueled with mammal fat, and several barbed bone harpoon heads have been found. The food scrap contained the bones of sea mammals, water birds, several kinds of fish, sea shells, in association with caribou, bear, and other land mammals. The open ocean creatures taken were the albatross, cod and halibut, and such sea mammals as sea otter and porpoise. The taking of such species testifies to the existence of ocean-going canoes at that time. The evidence suggests a heavy coastal specialization by 6000 years ago or earlier, comparable to the eastern Maritime Archaic.

The Ocean Bay complex (Figure 4.37) is well-represented on Anangula Island by 6000 B.P., later of course, than the famous core and blade site there. In the Aleutian chain, the Ocean Bay is followed (by 5000 B.P.) by the Aleutian Tradition, characterized by stone lamps, barbed stone harpoon heads, and a variety of fairly well made chipped slate knives, and points in many forms (see Figure 4.38). The long maritime adaptation of the Alaskan cultures was now well established.

At the same time (5000 B.P.) to the east and south, the distinctively new Kodiak Tradition was developed. Along with chipped pieces, the technique of polishing slate after chipping appears. The polished slate forms include the rocker knife, or ulu; long lance heads or knives and stem points; stone lamps; and barbed bone harpoon heads (Figure 4.39).

South from Kodiak Island to the Queen Charlotte Islands, the cultures and sequences are unclear. But farther south at Vancouver Island and the Straits of Georgia, there are sites yielding ground slate tools and showing a subsistence focused on maritime resources, as is the Kodiak Tradition. Called the Straits of Georgia Tradition, it is contemporary with, or slightly later than, the Kodiak at 5000 B.P. (see Figure 4.40). The associated objects (barbed harpoon heads and wedges; awls and fish leisters of bone; and long ground slate swords, daggers, or lance points) and predominantly sea mammal bone food scrap, show that open ocean hunting continued as the major subsistence practice.

By 3000 B.P. further developments of the southern maritime Georgia Strait Tradition are seen in the Locarno and Marpole phases. The chipped stone points continue as do microblades and their distinctive cores. From slate, there were **earspools, labrets,** polished celts and adzes, and well-polished slate points and knives, including (later at Marpole) rockerlike ulus noted earlier. There were also chipped slate points, toggle harpoons, barbed harpoons, and wedges and lance foreshafts of antler and bone.

The now large sites are to be found on oceanside locations. The food scrap contains both sea and land mammals. There is evidence that by 1 A.D. they were building the large cedar plank houses so common later. Also by this time, there was sculpture in antler and stone. The graves reveal social distinction in that some have rich grave goods of *Dentalium* shells, disc beads, and copper plates. Thus, the intensive maritime exploitation common at historic contact was merely

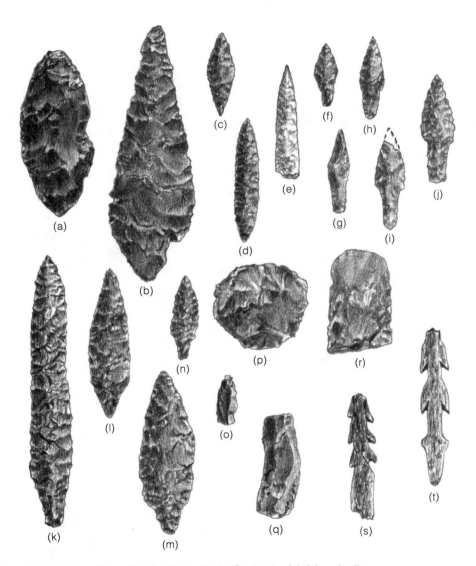

Figure 4.37 Artifacts of the Ocean Bay Tradition, Alaska Peninsula: (a)–(n) projectile points and knives, (o) and (q) blades, (p) discoidal core, (r) adze blade with polished bit, (s) and (t) bone harpoon dart heads.

the elaboration and diffusion of a lifeway and a series of technologies that had their origin in the Aleutians, South Alaska, and Northwest coasts.

An Ethnographic Sketch

The historic end product of seven or eight millenia of evolution, the Northwest Coast tribes have excited popular and scientific interest for many years and for many reasons. Distributed from Alaska to northern California, they occupied a zone of enormous natural riches, although the resources tend to diminish as one moves from north to south. The northern tribes—Haida, Tsimshian, and Tlingit— probably enjoyed the greatest concentration of marine plenty. In the opinion of many, those

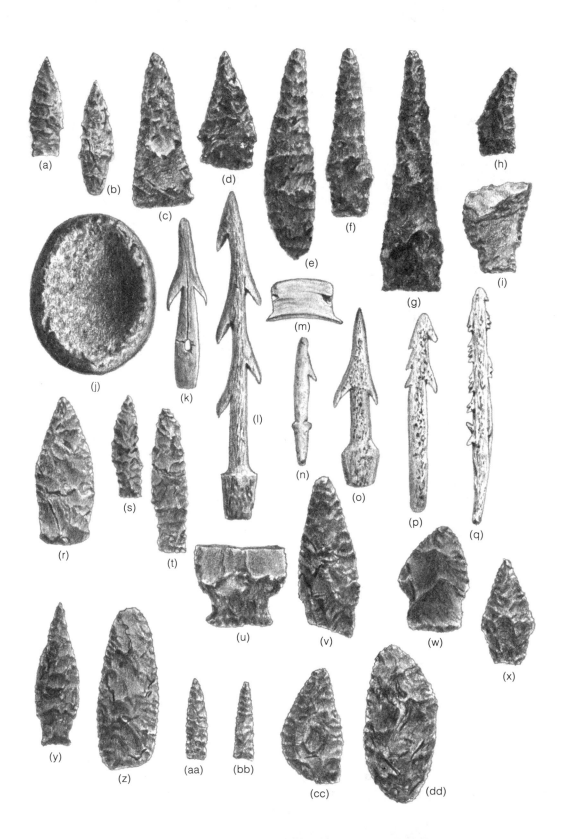

(a)

(b)

(c)

(d)

(e)

(f)

(g)

(h)

(i)

(j)

(k)

(l)

(m)

(n)

(o)

(p)

(q)

(r)

(s)

(t)

(u)

(v)

(w)

(x)

(y)

(z)

(aa)

(bb)

(cc)

(dd)

tribes represent the apex of the maritime pattern of life.

The adaptation is remarkable in having a very complicated system of rank and class based on wealth in material objects (on a strictly hunter-gatherer level). Neither domestic animals (except the dog) nor agriculture was practiced or perhaps even known. It has been labelled the "highest" development of all the foraging cultures. The most obvious evidence of this "high" development lies in the stratified social system already mentioned; the rich mythology and ceremonialism; the superb craftsmanship in wood; and the bold, unique art styles.

For foragers the Pacific Coast is one of the earth's most favored spots. The mild, equable climate results from the presence of the Japanese current, which tempers the coastal weather. The moist, warm environment encourages lush vegetation: rain forests of large trees with an understory of berry thickets. Dominant in the forests are red and yellow cedar, which are easily worked and carved. Large land animals such as bear and deer are abundant. But the true abundance is in the sea. Staple foods of the Northwest coast tribes were salmon, halibut, herring, and cod, with whales an occasional target for hunters.

But the main food, salmon, was not always present. Salmon are anadromous: Hatched in freshwater streams, the tiny hatchlings soon go to the ocean where they mature. After three or four years, the adult fish (now 20 to 70 pounds and more) return to spawn in the stream where they were hatched. The annual salmon run occurs in early autumn. Hundreds of thousands of fish churn the stream as they forge upstream. That was harvest time for the tribes. Every able-bodied person worked—

catching, gutting, splitting, and drying or smoking the fish. Each household prepared and stored literally tons of fish. Berries, too, were harvested in summer and autumn and preserved by drying or packing in fish oil. Halibut, an open ocean species, was available more or less year-round, but winter storms prevented continuous fishing. Thus during summer and autumn there were surges of abundance when large surpluses must be collected, processed, and stored. The seasonal abundance of food and their processing techniques made the remainder of the culture possible, partly because subsistence was assured and there was less food quest and more leisure during winter and spring.

In those slack seasons artisans and artists created the fabled carved and painted art of the Northwest. Art was almost exclusively ornamental; nearly every utensil, weapon, and house—as well as masks, headdresses, and ceremonial gear—was decorated with the family crest. The depictions were generally of real or mythical animals (Figure 4.41), among them the thunderbird. Many designs combine animal and human features into anthropomorphic forms. The distinctive style blends realism with a series of conventional treatments. One convention is that all parts of the creature being depicted must be shown. On a flat surface the head would be central with half the body and two legs to the right, the other half to the left. In effect, the animal is split in the dorsal-ventral plane and spread out flat. On a box or fiber hat, or round object, there was even greater distortion, but all parts were represented. Also each animal was executed with standard identifying features. For example, the beaver was usually shown with prominent teeth; round nose; broad, flat tail; and perhaps a stick in its front paws. A killer whale had a heavy head, a blowhole, and the distinctive sharp dorsal fin. The raven had a long, straight bill; the eagle a hooked beak.

The individual units of art carry heraldic messages of lineage and rank; they are called crests. The crests, emphasizing mythical

Figure 4.38 Artifacts of the Aleutian Tradition: (a)–(i) and (r)–(dd) stone projectile points and knives; (j) stone lamp; (k) and (l), (n)–(q) bone harpoon or spear heads; (m) ivory labret. (a)–(q) Umnak Island; (r)–(dd) Chignik region, Alaska Peninsula. Much reduced.

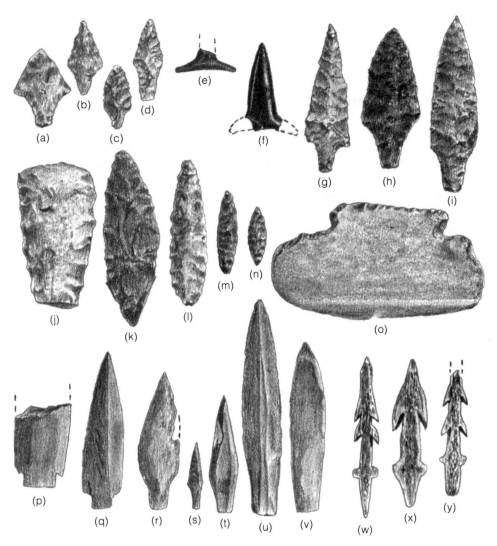

Figure 4.39   Artifacts of the Kodiak Tradition, Alaska Peninsula: (a)–(d), (g)–(i), (k)–(n) chipped projectile points and knives; (e) and (f) labrets; (j) adze blade with polished bit; (o) polished slate ulu; (p)–(v) polished slate projectile blades; (w)–(y) bone harpoon heads. Much reduced.

ancestors, appear on everything that belongs to a person, from totem poles to carved horn spoons. All property is private. The crest can be likened to a European coat of arms, which carries similar explicit claims of ancestry and rank.

Work in wood displayed the same skill and ingenuity seen in the art. The cedar served virtually every need. It was used for the huge plank houses that were often 20 by 60 feet or larger (Figure 4.42) and for canoes made of single logs up to 60 feet long and capable of carrying sixty people and tons of freight. Wood was also used for boxes, pails, crests, the intricately carved totem poles, and most domestic utensils. Some of the boxes

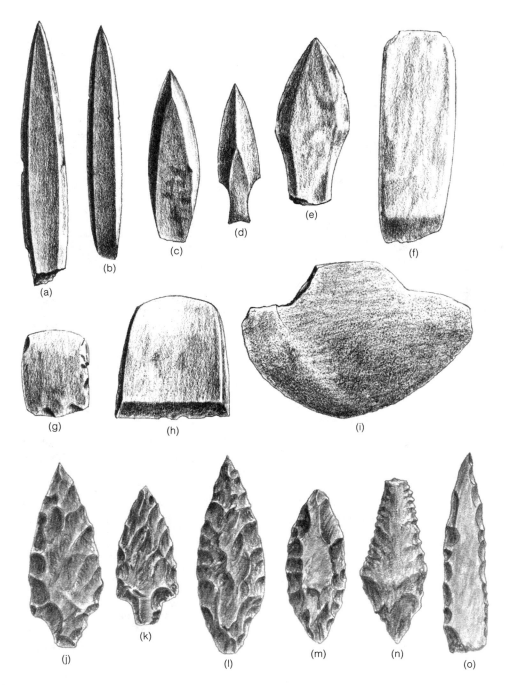

Figure 4.40   Artifacts of the Gulf of Georgia Tradition, from the Fraser Delta region: (a)–(e) ground slate points, (f)–(h) polished adze blades, (i) ground slate ulu, (j)–(n) chipped stone points, (o) chipped and ground point.

Figure 4.41 Painted bentwood box, Tlingit tribe. The design is not the split animal, but an abstract portrayal of a mythical being. The shells inset on the top are opercula of sea snails.

were so tightly fabricated that they were leak proof and were used to store fish oil and other liquids. The wooden chests or boxes were also used for storage of food, clothing, weapons, ceremonial gear, and most other items.

Perhaps from the almost inexhaustible resources and the surpluses of goods that rewarded households that worked hard, there developed the concept of wealth. Wealth was measured in ornately decorated blankets (of sea otter skins, fiber, and hair), personal and household objects, the grandeur of the house and its carving, and all other highly visible items. The greatest wealth of course was possession of a "copper." That was a shield or plaque of beaten native copper sheeting, ap-

propriately decorated. Wealth was never hidden but always displayed because it enhanced prestige.

The most ostentatious use of wealth was the potlatch (a Chinook jargon word meaning "to give"). This intriguing practice is difficult to understand. To the European observer, the potlatch was a pointless squandering of treasure. Given at a house building, funeral, initiation ceremony, in honor of a son, and other occasions, the potlatch involved inviting guests, feasting them for days or weeks, and finally distributing gifts—food, blankets, boxes (empty or full of food), dishes, carved spoons made of sheep horn, and so on—until the pile of goods the host had accumulated over a period of years was gone. The host was demonstrating his wealth and his family's strength and position. Thus, the purpose of the potlatch was to validate or enhance status. It can be best understood as a function of the complex social system. There were hierarchies within the classes, so that everyone had a ranked status.

Basic to the social system were the two kinship groups called moieties that divided the society or tribe. They constituted matrilineal marriage groups and were competitive with (and sometimes hostile toward) each other. Marriage partners came from the opposite moiety. Since descent was in the female line, a father's children belonged to his wife's lineage and moiety. Each parent, of course, remained a member of his or her own moiety and owed loyalty and assistance to it. Since wealth and position were so important, society was further divided into classes with status within any class dependent on inherited position within the lineage and wealth, which could be inherited or acquired through hard work and the potlatch. Each person, therefore, was ranked in relation to every other person in the group. The classes were chiefs, nobles, commoners, and slaves. Chiefs were actually nobles but stood apart as dominant. Dominance was less political than social, rest-

Figure 4.42   Authentic Tlingit plank house, constructed by Tlingit CCC workers in the 1940s under the supervision of Viola Garfield.

ing as it did on rank, wealth, and personal attributes; the chief's power was largely confined to his own kin group.

Chiefs gave the potlatches. They invited guests to the affair from outside their villages, setting a date months or years away in order to accumulate the requisite amount of goods. His family and lineage worked, hunted, traded for, and created fine objects during the period of collecting. The invited guests were members of his wife's moiety. At the actual ceremony, the guests were seated by rank and the distribution began. Everyone got something appropriate to his or her rank. At the end, no goods were left; and the host was temporarily fully impoverished, although richer in status. He might also have more property such as a new house and thus really be more wealthy

in consequence. If the potlatch were for his son, the son now had status in his own lineage because of the generosity of the father. It must be understood that there was reciprocity. The newly impoverished chief would be a guest at other potlatches and receive appropriate gifts; he might even receive some—was a dynamic force in the society—an avenue of achieving position and an incentive to industry and thrift—and constantly reinforced the values of the group.

From tribe to tribe there were variations in the rules governing the potlatch and when it was given. Space does not permit detailing these nuances. What is given here merely attempts to show the central role that the institution of the potlatch played in Northwest Coast tribal life.

The Arctic and Subarctic

Although they are often treated as a separate entity, the inclusion of the Arctic and the Subarctic in this chapter is consistent with the concept of the Archaic hunter-gatherer subsistence pattern. Although these hardy Arctic foragers arouse one's admiration for their successful adaptation to one of the world's most hostile environments, it remains true that they were almost exclusively hunters. They survived on the harvest of sea and land mammals, birds, and fish. With scant and short-lived vegetation, there was no storable vegetable resource as a cushion for hard times or lack of game. Animal life provided food, clothing, shelter, and even fuel. Indeed, along the coast it was necessary to comb the beaches for driftwood to make needed tools and implements.

All Arctic prehistory up to the present is a saga of efficient foraging where many rich resources known in the temperate zones are lacking. At the same time artifacts show little resemblance to the Archaic of the more temperate zones except for the Palisades and related northern Archaic cultures of Alaska. European, Canadian, and United States scholars have studied the Arctic for more than a hundred years. Even so, while the cultural sequence is known as a result of that research, the data are scanty. The spotty nature of our knowledge is entirely referable to the Arctic vastness, the few short weeks of the summer field season, and the ever-present difficulty of transportation.

The Arctic cultures of Alaska were evidently little influenced by those found in the area below the Canadian border (except for the northern Archaic). On the other hand, much of Canada has been responsive to influences from both Alaska and below the United States border. Canada will therefore

be treated separately after this discussion of the Alaskan-Aleutian story.

The Arctic has an enormous extent, with thousands of miles of coastline, hundreds of islands, and long inlets and stretches of open water, to say nothing of tens of thousands of square miles of landmass. Alaska itself can be divided into three geographic regions (Figure 4.43):

1. Southern Alaska is mountainous and heavily glaciated. The mountain ranges are geologically younger and lower in elevation in the western part of the Alaskan peninsula and in the Aleutian Islands than the Cordilleran ranges to the east. Volcanic activity has been frequent; at least forty-seven eruptions have been recorded in Alaska since 1760.

2. The broad valleys and low mountain ranges of the interior are in sharp contrast to southern Alaska topography. The Yukon River is the most extensive drainage system of the interior, heading into southeast Yukon and finally flowing into the Bering Sea at Norton Bay.

3. North of the Yukon Valley lies the Brooks Range, which provides a barrier between the interior and arctic Alaska. This large mountain range, an extension of the Rocky Mountain system, is rugged and barren. It ranges in altitude from 9000 feet near the Canadian border to 3000 feet at its western end, near the Chukchi Sea. The 8-mile-wide range offers one principal pass, the Anuktuvuk, to the Yukon Valley. The Arctic Slope, north of the Brooks Range, is a crescent-shaped tundra. The coastal waters are shallow, and the land is flat, with innumerable shallow lakes. The frozen tundra of the winter becomes swampy and impassable in the summer.

The Alaskan climate varies widely, from the mild, moist weather of southeast Alaska

Figure 4.43   Alaska and Northwest Coast.

to the dry, bitter, windswept Arctic Slope. The mountains of southeast Alaska intercept moisture-laden winds of the Pacific, causing abnormally heavy snowfall, with the result that the glaciation of Alaska has been con-

fined essentially to that area. The effects of the Japanese Current account for the mild climate of the southern Alaska coastal belt. The Aleutian Islands remain cool in the summer, with more-or-less continuous rain throughout the year. The climate of the interior of Alaska is continental. The winters resemble those of the Plains states.

North of the Aleutians, the Japanese Current is dissipated in the Chukchi Sea, so its effect is not felt north of the Pribilof Islands. From October to August the Arctic Ocean is locked in ice. The Arctic Slope is windswept, but summer and early autumn are fairly mild. Spring and late autumn afford the best conditions for movement on land. **Permafrost** solidifies the land of the entire Arctic Slope and about half the Yukon Valley, as well as small areas in southern Alaska.

The flora of Alaska is alpine. The interior, especially along the waterways, has large spruce forests mixed with balsam, poplar, and birch. The milder climate of the south permits the growth of hemlock, while willow shrubs, grasses, mosses, and lichens thrive on the Arctic Slope. Animal life is plentiful throughout the entire area. The sea yields salmon, halibut, cod, crab, sea otter, sea lion, seal, walrus, and whale. Bear, moose, elk, and numerous small, fur-bearing animals abound in the interior, while countless caribou once inhabited the Arctic Slope and interior.

After the Paleoarctic (see Chapter Three) had ended about 8000 B.P., there is no archaeological evidence of habitation in Alaska proper (see Figure 4.44). The gap in the record may be referable to the accidents of discovery or may represent a climatically caused absence from the area. But by 6000 B.P., a toolkit identified as Archaic, and perhaps influenced by a population from somewhere in the western United States, appears in the interior of Alaska and British Columbia and on the northwestern coast of Alaska. Called the northern Archaic, it was first discovered on Cape Krusenstern at the Palisades sites (Figure 4.45).

Based on the evidence below, Cape Krusenstern is evidently of considerable age, although the age ascription was inferential until the work at Onion Portage, described in Chapter Three. The Archaic complex consists

of small, side-notched, and stemmed points crudely chipped from flint. As Figure 4.45 shows, the pieces resemble more southerly Archaic specimens. Moreover, the Palisades flint collection had been exposed so long that it showed cortical change or decomposition, although this alone cannot constitute evidence of antiquity.

What makes this complex interesting is its location near a series of parallel beaches where, in horizontal beach "stratigraphy," the remains of modern Eskimo houses occur on the present beach, with older cultural remains (known from other stratigraphic situations to be earlier) on former beaches farther and farther inland. With the sea so important to Arctic dwellers, the beaches are the preferred dwelling sites; but in areas with the right conditions beaches "recede" inland as new ones of gravel are built up by heavy seas. The new beaches then become dwelling sites. Through the centuries the older remains become increasingly distant inland from the currently occupied beach, and a time sequence can be built up on the basis of the horizontal relationship of the materials. Figure 4.46 shows Cape Krusenstern, the parallel beaches, and the location of the Palisades, Norton-Choris, and Denbigh Flint finds made there. Scholars have relied on the same kind of horizontal beach stratigraphy elsewhere in the Arctic.

Following the Palisades, came the Arctic Small Tool Tradition. It includes the Denbigh Flint complex, the Denbigh being one of the type assemblages. First described from a shallow but well-sealed deposit in extreme western Alaska on Norton Bay, a long-known but ignored congeries of Arctic types and flint techniques was rediscovered beneath evidence of later and already described cultures. The Denbigh complex consists of chipped crescent blades or knives, blades or points, delicate little burins made from fine prismatic flakes, other burins from large irregular flakes, flake scrapers, harpoon blades, faintly fluted points, and some lanceolate blades remindful of Eden points (Figure 4.47). Noteworthy are

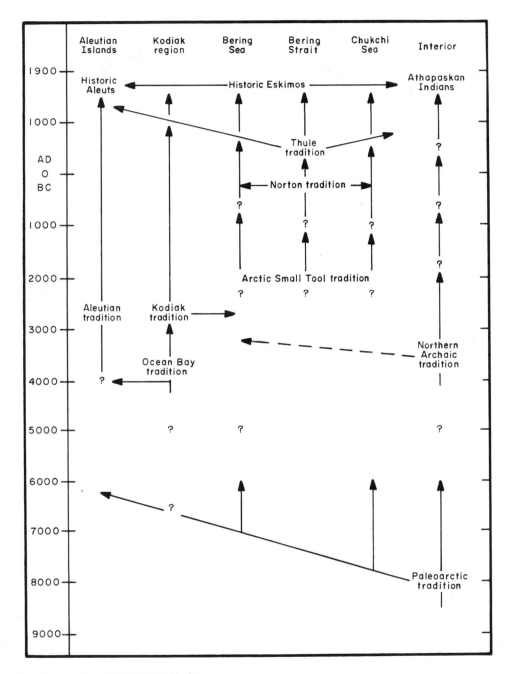

Figure 4.44 Major cultural traditions in Alaska.

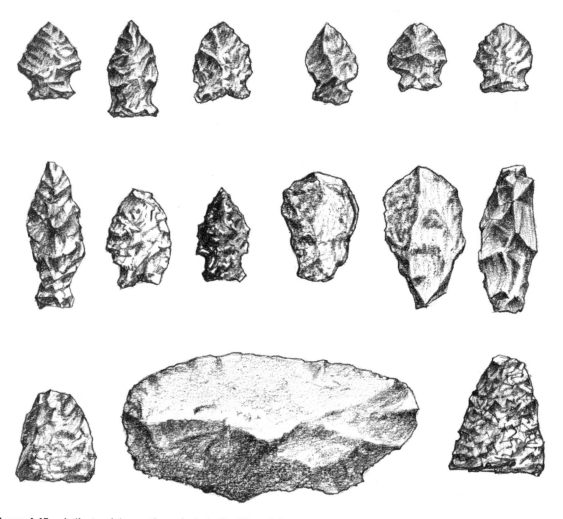

Figure 4.45   Artifacts of the northern Archaic Tradition. Palisades site, Cape Krusenstern. Reduced one-third.

the fine ripple diagonal flaking and the use of prismatic flakes. Aside from the stratigraphy, at the time of its discovery the Denbigh site was very important because it provided a time depth for the Arctic cultures by yielding radiocarbon dates of about 4000 B.P.

The Arctic Small Tool Tradition has a wide distribution. It extends eastward from Alaska into the Canadian provinces and on to Greenland; evidently it is an ancestor of the Canadian Dorset cultures. The finds are distributed along, and deep inland from, the shores of the Arctic Ocean. It is also found on the east

and west shores of Hudson Bay and the coastal islands. The hallmarks of the culture (with regional formal variations, of course) are the microblade, burin, projectile points, and scrapers found at the Denbigh site. The sites are thin; the best stratification is probably at the Onion Portage site. In its first occurrences, the Arctic Small Tool Tradition evidently had an entirely interior or land mammal (caribou) orientation. In later periods, there was coastal or maritime adaptation; it has been suggested that the eastward spread of the culture was by migration of peoples, rather than

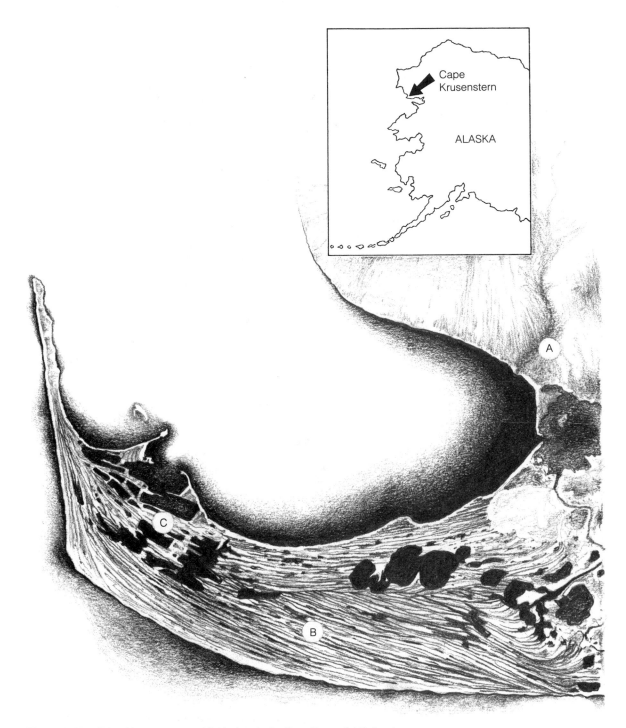

Figure 4.46 Cape Krusenstern and loci of early Arctic cultures: (a) Palisades,
(b) Norton-Choris, (c) Denbigh Flint.

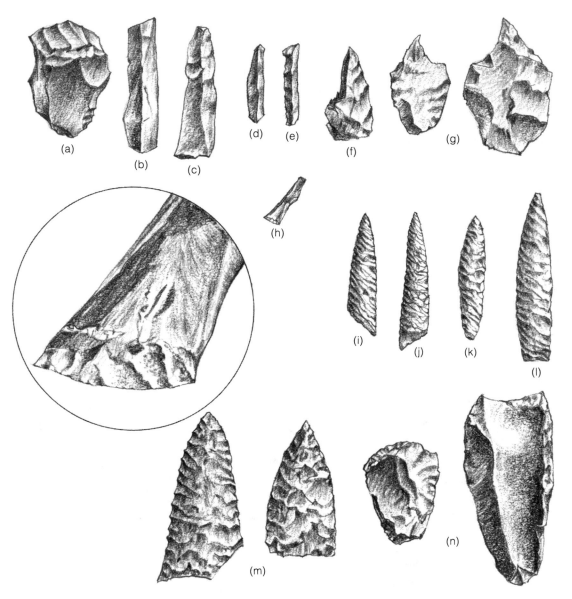

Figure 4.47   Artifacts of the Arctic Small Tool Tradition, Denbigh Flint complex: (a) microblade core, (b)–(d) microblades, (e) burin spall, (f) and (g) burins, (h) burin spall and much enlarged view of retouched cutting edge, (i) and (j) sideblades, (k) and (l) projectile endblades, (m) large projectile (possibly harpoon) blades, (n) scrapers. Reduced about one-third.

the diffusion of a tradition. The dispersal of the Arctic Small Tool peoples has been linked to climatic change by several scholars. They disagree, however, about whether the climatic shift leading to the rapid spread of the tradition was a warming or a cooling trend. In any case, it required an adaptation to land animals (mainly the caribou) and fishing.

A large collection of artifacts (dated after 4000 B.P.) was recovered at the Chaluka site in the eastern Aleutians, testifying both to the intense exploitation of the sea and some Kodiak influence, although the Aleutian Tradition seems to be dominant. The food scrap recovered at Chaluka indicated that those cultures exploited the whale, walrus, sea lion, seal, sea otter, and many birds (at huge rookeries), as well as many species of fish and shellfish. The game extended "from whales to whelks." The richness of the land was not reflected in the artifacts, which were numerous, specialized, and well-manufactured, but not elaborate. The art is simple, albeit distinctive in some aspects. Slate was chipped, not rubbed or ground. At this early date, persistent traits include harpoons, fish spears, pronged bird spears, chipped ulus and knives, lamps, fishhooks, and bolas. Skin boats, atlatls, lamellar flakes, and woodworking are present. After about 4000 B.P. Arctic prehistory is the story of those cultures that are largely dependent on sea mammal hunting and a technology of considerable complexity.

In a limited area on the northwest coast of the Bering and Chukchi seas, new developments are seen after 3000 B.P. They evidently developed from the Arctic Small Tool Tradition. Called the Norton, this tradition includes several separately labeled local cultures. These are the Choris, which is the earliest; the Norton at about 3000 B.P.; the Ipiutak and Near-Ipiutak; and others. By 2500 B.P. to 1 A.D., the Thule culture had developed from the Norton with many artifact types carrying over from the earlier culture. The term *Thule* includes materials once labeled Okvik, Old Bering Sea, Birnirk, Punuk, and Thule itself. From Norton times onward the sea mammal orientation dominated the life recorded by the archaeology. The emphasis on whaling grew with time.

The Norton and Thule peoples lived in seaside locations. They built sturdy, semisubterranean houses of rocks, whalebone, and driftwood, usually covered with sod and lined with skin. The houses had long, downward sloping entryways with a deep "cold well" at the lower end and a trapdoor up into the house. Tools and weapons became highly specialized for the maritime hunting. For example, there were different harpoons for seal, walrus, and whale. Skin boats used in fishing were the one-man **kayak** and the open, skin-covered dinghy or **umiak.**

The Norton seems to have spread widely along the northern and Pacific coasts where it persisted for several centuries after the Thule had taken form. It was characterized by flint items of several types reminiscent of the Arctic Small Tool Tradition except that the microblade industry had disappeared. The site at Cape Krusenstern (where the sequence runs from Palisades to modern Eskimo deposits) exemplifies the Norton culture (see Figure 4.48).

The Norton objects are characteristically crude and rough, revealing nothing of the artistic qualities of the later traditions. Only the chipped stone was well done, although some care was taken with the coarse and simple pottery. One might hope that the Norton pottery would shed some light on the origins of the pottery of the eastern United States, but this hope is apparently vain, primarily because pottery appears later in the Arctic than in the eastern woodlands. For some reason, most people are surprised that any pottery should occur in the Arctic, perhaps because ceramics were once thought always to accompany agriculture. The Norton pottery is frequently not well fired but is surprisingly sturdy. The usual vessel is a flat-bottomed, bucket-shaped form, which may be plain surfaced, paddled with a check or curious linear stamp, or decorated with **incising.** The coarse and flaky paste was tempered either with vegetal fiber, feathers, or coarse sand or with all three.

In particular, slatework was merely roughed out and used unsmoothed. Houses were large and substantial, heated by lamps and fireplaces, the latter being rare in the Arctic. At this site, no drum pieces, engraved bone, sled or boat parts, or evidences of ceremonialism

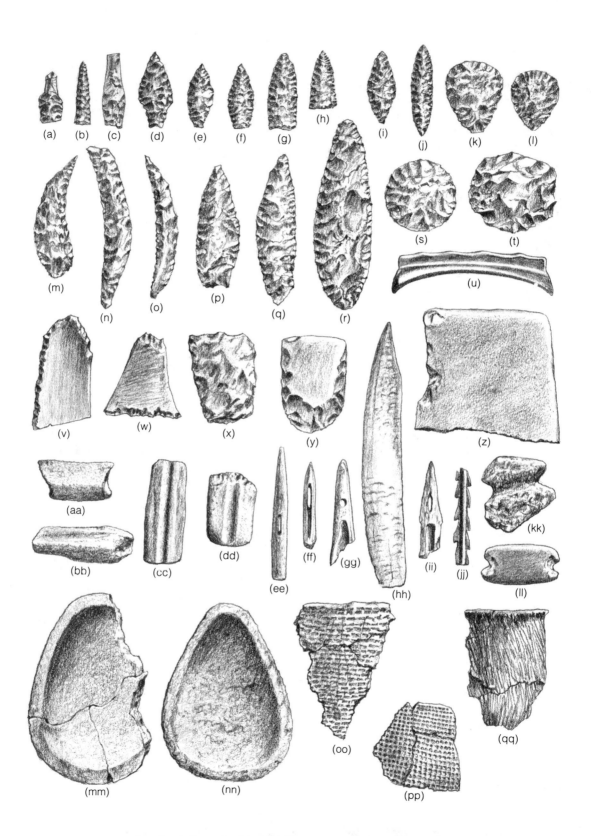

(a)　(b)　(c)　(d)　(e)　(f)　(g)　(h)　(i)　(j)　(k)　(l)

(m)　(n)　(o)　(p)　(q)　(r)

(s)　(t)

(u)

(v)　(w)　(x)　(y)　(z)

(aa)　(bb)　(cc)　(dd)　(ee)　(ff)　(gg)　(hh)　(ii)　(jj)　(kk)　(ll)

(mm)　(nn)　(oo)　(pp)　(qq)

were recovered. This no doubt represents accidents of preservation, but because of these lacks the culture is regarded as distinctive (in its impoverishment) from others. But at the Ipiutak site, viewed by some as a Norton varient, some unusual and downright beautiful artifacts were recovered.

The Ipiutak village is huge—some 600 houses, up to 20 feet square. There is no stratigraphy, the midden is thin, and the artifacts are very uniform, so a relatively short use is postulated for the settlement. The lack of certain hunting tools—float plugs, **wound plugs,** meat- and boathooks, fishhooks and sinkers, rubbed-slate blades—and of other artifacts, including pottery, lamps, **bow drills, ice creepers,** and ivory sled runners, argues for less emphasis on sea hunting at this location. However, other sea weapons—harpoons and fish spears—are present, as well as scores of other familiar artifacts. The site is primarily famed for its delicate and elaborate art forms, such as masks, snow goggles, chains, animal effigies, and ornaments carved from ivory (Figure 4.49).

At one time the classic Eskimo sequences of cultures of the past 2000 to 2500 years carried individual local names. The earliest (about 2500 B.P.) was called the Okvik. It was followed by the Old Bering Sea, Birnirk, and Punuk. Then by 1000 A.D. the modern or Thule form appeared. Because the full sequence is so similar, the classification is here simplified by using the term *Thule* to identify material after the Norton.

The Thule Tradition was, as before, focused on the sea; walrus, seal, and whale were the primary game. The whale provides considerable food and has a dominant position in ceremonial life and religion, but the other two species are the standby staples. The entire tradition shares the shoreside settlement pattern: permanent villages of rectangular subterranean houses with long entrance passages used for storage as well as for trapping cold air. A typical early house at Miyowagh on St. Lawrence Island was 18 by 22 feet with an entryway (including an antechamber) 27 feet long. The entryway sloped downward toward the house so that one crawled up from the passageway into the house through a trapdoor in the floor. The entryway and house were paved with stone; its walls and roof were made of timbers; stones; and whale jaws, scapulae, skulls, and ribs (Figure 4.50). Old Bering Sea period homes were smaller than houses of later periods. Figure 4.51 presents a modern Point Barrow Eskimo house showing the interior arrangement of furnishings and the mode of entrance; the use of space is undoubtedly similar to that of the prehistoric houses.

The artifacts of hunting are numerous and of quite specific use. The basic weapon was the harpoon, an ingenious and complex device. It was made of wood, walrus ivory, bone, and sinew or hide strips so that after the quarry was struck, the shaft and foreshaft came loose, leaving the head and point imbedded in the animal; the prey exhausted itself pulling air-filled bladders and a circular drag fastened to the long line attached to the head of the harpoon. In addition to serving as a drag, the bladder served as a marker buoy so that the hunters could follow the wounded game (Figure 4.52). Hunting was done from both the kayak and the open umiak. Bows and atlatls were both used with light, pronged, **bladder darts**. Other general traits included skin boats,

Figure 4.48 Artifacts of the Norton stage of the Norton Tradition: (a)–(c) drill bits, (d)–(h) projectile points, (i) and (j) sideblades, (k) and (l) bifacial knives, (m)–(o) scrapers, (p)–(r) lance points or knives, (s) and (t) discoidal knives, (u) labret, (v) and (w) polished slate fragments, (x) and (y) adze blades, (z) whetstone, (aa) and (bb) faceted whetstones, (cc) and (dd) sandstone abraders, (ee) antler harpoon foreshaft, (ff) antler arrowhead fragment, (gg) antler harpoon head, (hh) ivory harpoon head or possibly icepick, (ii) antler harpoon head, (jj) leister prong fragment, (kk) and (ll) stone net sinkers, (mm) and (nn) stone lamps, (oo) and (pp) check-stamped potsherds, (qq) linear stamped potsherd. Variable scale.

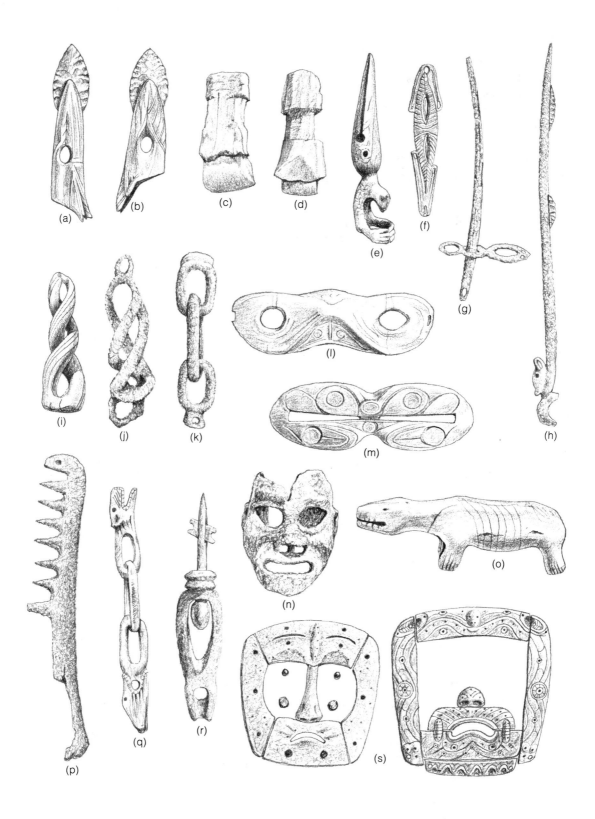

(a)

(b)

(c)

(d)

(e)

(f)

(g)

(h)

(i)

(j)

(k)

(l)

(m)

(n)

(o)

(p)

(q)

(r)

(s)

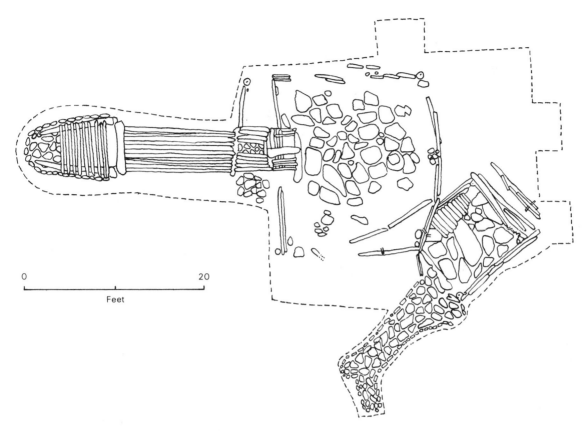

Figure 4.50 Ground plans of houses (corner of larger house superimposed over smaller one) excavated on St. Lawrence Island.

hand sleds (dog-drawn sleds later), tobog-gans of **baleen,** implements of rubbed slate and chipped bone, lamps of both pottery and stone, adzes, mattocks, the crescent-shaped ulu or rocker knife, snow goggles, needle cases, ivory and wooden dolls, and tambour-

Figure 4.49 Artifacts of the Ipiutak variant of the Norton Tradition: (a) and (b) harpoon heads, (c) and (d) bone adze heads with slate blades, (e) ivory openwork carving, (f) ivory ornament, (g) and (h) ivory lance heads or daggers, (i) ivory swivel, (j) ivory openwork carving, (k) ornamental linked ivory object, (l) and (m) ivory snow goggles, (n) human effigy of antler, (o) ivory polar bear effigy, (p) unidentified ivory implement; (q) ornamental linked object, (r) swivel, (s) masklike ivory carvings usually found associated with burials. Variable scale.

ine drums. Toy models of the kayak and umi-ak, as well as broken pieces of both kinds of boats, are recovered (Figure 4.53).

Despite the subsistence emphasis on sea mammals (and the corollary preference for permanent coastal villages), there was an equal, seasonal interest in land animals, par-ticularly the caribou and musk-ox, where the latter were available. The evidence is that there was extensive summer hunting of caribou; aside from hides (which were preferred for clothing) and meat, antler was needed to make numerous tools. Ethnologists and archaeol-ogists agree that the alternative preying upon land and sea creatures has always been a fun-damental part of Eskimo culture, although emphasis on land animals was greater in the

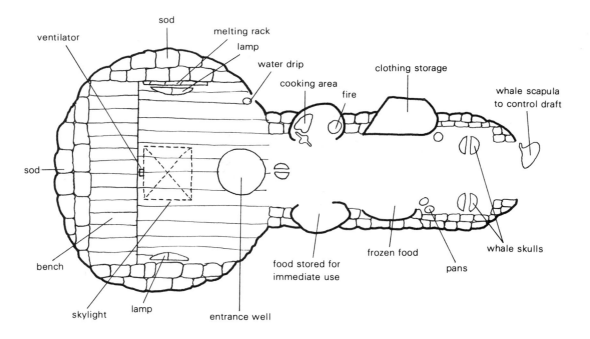

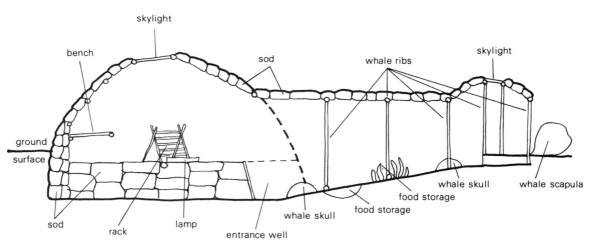

Figure 4.51 Floor plan and cross section of a Point Barrow Maritime Eskimo house.

east and along the northern coast than on the Bering Sea.

One of the Thule type sites is Birnirk itself, near Point Barrow. There is a detailed report of excavations there. It described the Eskimo as "gadget-burdened," and the inventory of tools and other artifacts securely documents the statement. In a village of twelve or thirteen houses seven were partially excavated.

The houses were rectangular, subterranean, wooden structures with domed roofs sodded over and long sunken entryways—all standard features. The raised sleeping platform at the back of the house was also standard. The trash heaps lay on each side of the entrance.

From the houses, the fill over them, and the midden pits came thousands of specimens preserved by the permafrost. These make a

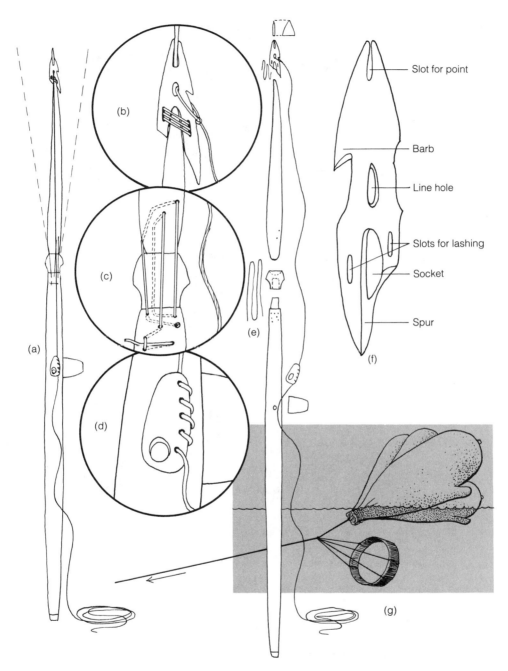

Slot for point

Barb

Line hole

Slots for lashing

Socket

Spur

Figure 4.52 Harpoon assembly: (a) assembled harpoon (dashed lines indicate flexibility of foreshaft); (b) harpoon head; (c) flexible joint showing shaft, shaft head, and foreshaft lashed together; (d) line retainer secured to shaft by knob; (e) component parts of harpoon; (f) idealized harpoon head; (g) sealskin floats and drag attached to end of line. Variable scale.

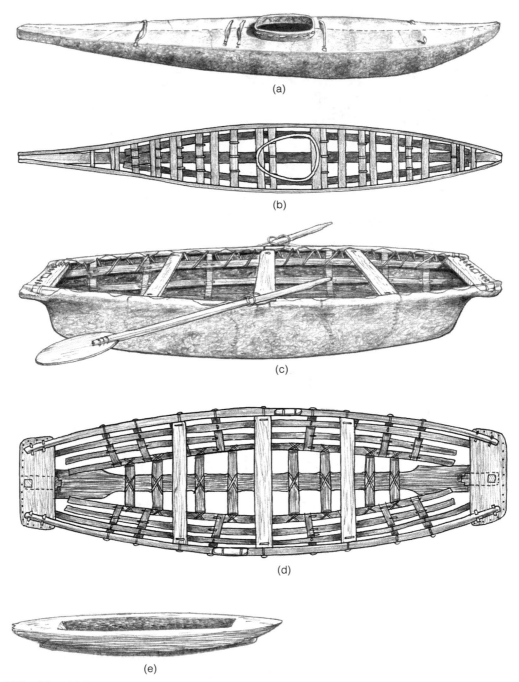

Figure 4.53 (a) and (b) kayak and plan view of framework, (c) and (d) umiak and plan view of framework, (e) toy wooden model of umiak.

long list by class or type alone, and the stylistic variations within the classes are also numerous (Figures 4.54 and 4.55). The following items are described under *hunting equipment:* harpoon heads (nineteen types), harpoon blades, foreshafts, socket pieces, shafts, harpoon finger rests, ice picks, lances, lance points, seal float bars, **mouthpieces** and plugs, wound plugs and pins, ice scoops (two types), **seal scratchers, seal killers,** rattles, dragline handles, atlatl dart shafts, bladder floats, inflation nozzles, bird dart points, bows and arrows, arrow shafts, bone arrow points (sixteen types), chipped flint points, wrist guards, **arrow shaft wrenches,** feather-cutting boards, and bolas (three classes). *Fishing gear* included spears, gill hooks and gorges, and fishhooks. *Transportation* involved toboggans, sleds, kayaks, umiaks, and their many parts. Miscellaneous gear for travel includes snow probe ferrules, snow knives, snow shovels, ice staff rings, and snow goggles.

Materials classed as *men's tools* included men's knives (three types); whetstones; engraving tools; flint flakers; bow drills; fire sets; baleen (whalebone) shovels, mattocks, and picks; adzes and splitting wedges; blubber hooks; and the component parts of all of these. *Women's tools and utensils*—from wooden buckets to needles and needle cases of bone, ornaments, clothing, musical instruments, and children's toys—stretch the list even further.

The early Thule cultures had developed on the northwestern and northern coasts of Alaska. Possibly because it was a highly successful lifeway, it had begun to expand well before 1000 A.D. It extended south part way to Kodiak, but northward it followed the Arctic Ocean along the Arctic Coast all the way to Greenland, where it was established by 1000 A.D.

By way of summary, the Alaska sequence goes broadly thus: The Paleoarctic came first at perhaps 11,000 B.P.; the tools were the prismatic flakes and heavy choppers and knives, similar to Asiatic complexes of that time. By 8000 B.P. the adaptation to the seacoast seems to have been accomplished at Anangula where prismatic blades were still the dominant tool. There is then a hiatus followed at 6000 B.P. by the northern Archaic, which spread from the south to cover much of western Canada and Alaska. In less than two thousand years, the Arctic Small Tool Tradition, which probably focused on land mammals, appeared and spread widely. Out of the Arctic Small Tool Tradition developed the Norton, which had a strong coastal and sea mammal orientation. Then, possibly by 2500 years ago, the Norton evolved into the Thule and final Eskimo cultures still with an overall ocean-hunting emphasis. But in the Aleutian, Kodiak, and Southern Georgia Strait traditions, we noted a much earlier turn to the sea. This is seen in the 6000-year-old Ocean Bay Tradition, which gave rise to the Kodiak Tradition. It established itself, or its influence, southward along the entire coast where the rich waters backed by the wealth of inland game permitted the evolution of the Kodiak and Straits of Georgia traditions into the northwest cultures of wealth and abundance.

An Ethnographic Sketch

To appreciate the annual round of Arctic cultures for the past 3000 years we have only to consult any standard ethnology of a modern tribe. The Eskimo of Point Barrow are used here as an example. Whaling is of dominant importance. The whale, the largest extant mammal, once came in large pods in April and provided a focus for Eskimo life. The whale was not the only food source, but it was the center of social and ceremonial life. Whaling occupied only two months (April and May) of the year, after leads opened in the ice. It required the cooperative effort of all the men of a village. Preparation for the hunt involved ritual purification and the performance of magical rites to ensure success, to say nothing of making new hunting gear and

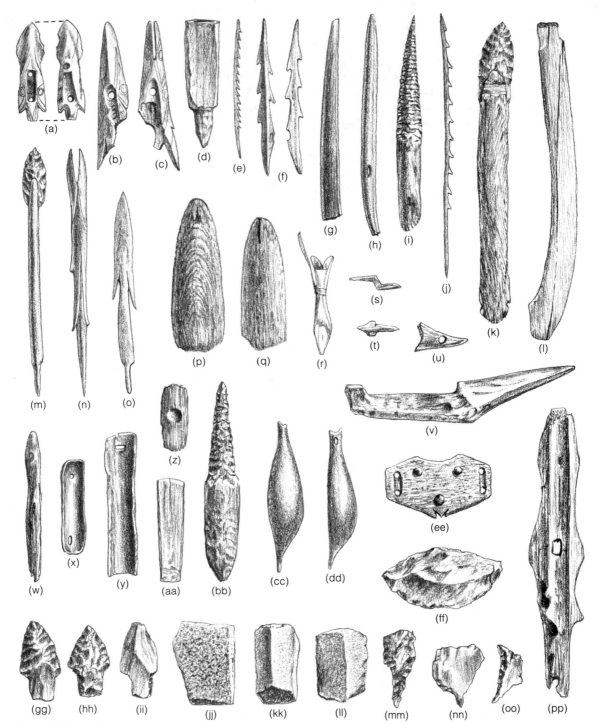

Figure 4.54 Artifacts of the early Thule Tradition from St. Lawrence Island: (a)–(c) ivory harpoon heads, (d) ivory harpoon socket piece, (e) ivory fish spear point, (f) ivory sideprongs for bird darts, (g) ivory harpoon foreshaft fragment, (h) ivory harpoon foreshaft, (i) ivory icepick, (j) ivory fish spear point, (k) hafted knife, (l) wooden adze handle, (m)–(o) arrowheads, (p) and (q) wooden wound plugs, (r) walrus-tusk knife sharpener, (s) and (t) ivory pegs for end of throwing board, (u) ivory finger rest for harpoon shaft, (v) ivory meathook, (w) wooden drill shaft, (x) and (y) ivory fat scrapers, (z) ivory drill mouthpiece, (aa) ivory wedge, (bb) ivory icepick, (cc) and (dd) ivory fishline sinkers, (ee) bone ice creeper, (ff) ulu blade, (gg)–(ii) knife blades, (jj)–(ll) whetstones, (mm) hand drill, (nn) and (oo) gravers, (pp) throwing-board fragment. Variable scale.

Figure 4.55 Artifacts of the Thule Tradition from St. Lawrence Island: (a) ivory vessel, (b) and (c) wooden snow goggles, (d) toy wooden kayak, (e) drum handle and rim fragment, (f) antler spoon, (g) antler ladle, (h) ivory **browband,** (i) ivory comb, (j) bark doll, (k) bone drill point, (l) and (m) ivory awls, (n) baleen ice scoop, (o) bone ladle, (p) wooden pottery paddle, (q) and (r) hafted slate knives, (s) baleen vessel, (t) wooden pail handle, (u) wooden bow drill, (v) and (w) slate ulus with wooden handles, (x) pottery lamp, (y) toy wooden bow, (z) and (aa) ivory sled shoes, (bb) toy wooden sled runner, (cc) and (dd) ivory sled runners, (ee) bone snow shovel. Variable scale.

clothing. The hunt itself was a solemn affair without the laughter, joking, and teasing the Eskimo so enjoy. Pursuit of the prey was a hazardous operation carried out in a fragile, open umiak paddled by six or eight men. The harpooner sat in the bow; success depended on his skill and the strength of his magic songs. The skill of the steersman was equally important. When a whale was sighted, the boat was brought alongside the powerful animal, and the harpooner sank one or more sharp blades wherever he could. The whale would usually sound, dragging the floats attached to the harpoon headlines. When the whale surfaced for air, more harpoons were sunk and more floats thus attached. When the animal was weakened by slight loss of blood and the effort of dragging several floats, the boat was brought close enough for the harpooner to thrust the killing lance time after time into the heart and lung cavity. The kill was the high point of danger, with the animal wallowing in pain and threshing the water with broad flukes. Success required the utmost coordination of the crew's efforts. When dead, the whale was towed to the beach where the huge carcass was cut up and divided with ceremonial thanksgiving among all members of the village. Most of it was stored in pits (into the permafrost zone) for winter. Even one whale was a good catch; four or five per season was enough to ensure a well-fed winter.

By the end of whaling, full summer had come; and villagers dispersed to summer work, food collection, and storage. The summer round of one family—June to October—exemplifies the patterns: After whaling the hunter puts his umiak into one of the streams, loading it with clothing, fishnets, harpoons, and sled. The dogs, straining along the shore, pull the boat upstream for several days until a fishing station is reached. Here the hunter leaves the women and children to catch, dry, and store fish until he returns. After killing some caribou for meat and skins, he goes back to the coast, where he perhaps assists in a walrus hunt and finally goes with other men on a trading trip along the coast. He returns to the fishing camp by September and, with the first snow, loads umiak, gear, and family onto the dogsled and returns to the subterranean winter house. He then makes many trips to the fish camp by dogsled to bring the fish and caribou meat to the village for winter food. As the winter night closes in, there are literally tons of animal food stored, but the hunting continues, along with repairing and making new gear for the hunt. Seals, small land animals, and birds (while available) are sought throughout the winter until the spring, when the annual round begins again with the whale hunt. Such is the life of the Eskimo hunter.

The Eskimo woman has equally arduous tasks and responsibilities. She devotes much time to tanning skins and tailoring the clothing and footgear for the house, tends and teaches her daughters, and sometimes participates in food gathering.

While not emphasized here, the Eskimo have a rich mythology and an important ceremonial life. Stories are told, dances and feasts are common, and there is considerable social exchange during the winter months, but the kinship and other social bonds are loose. Families may move from one village to another to be with friends or to avoid constant contact with a disliked person. The social ties are more likely to relate to cooperative work needs and ceremony than to any village or group alliance.

Men and women both age rapidly under the stresses of arctic life, with its many dangers and demands. Survival requires continuous concern with food and the upkeep of tools, utensils, and other gear. There is no recorded evidence of game or environmental management except in the many ceremonies aimed at placating and increasing the sea mammals through ritual and magic. That is the age-old picture of arctic life.

Canada

In Canada there is a much simpler situation than the one just considered in Alaska and on the Northwest Coast. There are several reasons for this, but probably the main reason is that much of Canada was partially covered with shrinking glacial ice and was simply not habitable for many centuries after the first Alaskan cultures were established. When people began to invade the Canadian area, the expansions were from Alaska and the south. Most of Canada's north shore fronts on the Arctic Ocean or the many islands in it. That climate is always severe, because the Arctic Slope barrenness does not stop at the Alaskan-Yukon Territory boundary but extends across the top of the world into Greenland. But the coastal sea life is abundant.

Another fact to be remembered is that the Canadian landmass is almost divided by the vast Hudson Bay. All but the southern quarter of the land around the bay tends to share the arctic bleakness of the tundra. Until recently caribou and musk-oxen were plentiful on the Arctic Slope, and other game abounded in many places. For our purposes, the zone of transition from the tundra to the evergreen forest (**taiga**) marks the boundary between the Arctic and the Subarctic as far as the environment and the conditions of life are concerned. The tree line is far south of the Arctic Circle over most of Canada (see Figure 4.56).

Perhaps the dominant feature of all Canada is the Keewatin or Laurentian Shield. It is a huge area, some 300 million square miles in extent, that surrounds Hudson Bay. The bay itself was formed by the Keewatin ice mass; the weight of the ice caused a downwarping of the earth's crust where Hudson Bay now lies. The bay is still growing shallower and shrinking in area as the earth slowly rebounds. The Laurentian Shield covers about half of Canada. It is a flat, barren area of lakes, bare rock, peat bogs, and tundra because the

soil and surficial rock layers all the way down to the pre-Cambrian continental core were swept clean by the glacial ice as it pushed out from the center. Today a thin mantle of soil covers most of it.

The taiga surrounds the Shield. Particularly in the transition zone or ecotone where the stands of trees are thin and other vegetation can exist, it supports big game—elk, moose, deer, and bear—and many smaller mammals. The dense taiga supports only a limited biomass, while the tundra, with its once seemingly inexhaustible caribou herds and their predators, is higher in biomass. Therefore the tundra has adequate food resources for humans. Furthermore, interior Canada—east of the Rockies—is bitterly cold because it draws its weather from the Arctic, unimpeded by mountains and untempered by warm seas or north-trending tropical air. For example, west of Hudson Bay, $-30°C$ ($-23°F$) temperatures have persisted for as long as sixty days at a time. The windchill factor is difficult to imagine, if not calculate. The eastern coast and the Gulf of St. Lawrence are perhaps less hostile but still lack any but taiga forests. However, since most of Canada is dotted with lakes connected by streams, there are aquatic resources in most parts of the interior.

The cultural history of the arctic portion of Canada and Greenland is short and familiar. The earliest is the Arctic Small Tool Tradition, variously called pre-Dorset, Independence, or Sarqaq (Figure 4.57a). It appears about 3500 to 2000 B.P., depending on whether western, northern, or eastern (where it is latest) Canada is being discussed. It is the earliest evidence of human use observed there. It is followed by the Dorset (Figure 4.57b), Thule (Figure 4.57c), and Canadian Eskimo traditions. The pre-Dorset, being both land and sea oriented, extends onto the Shield on both sides of Hudson Bay and into Greenland. The artifacts are the same meager ones seen in Alaska, but the flint is not usually as well chipped. It tends to be crude and irregular in

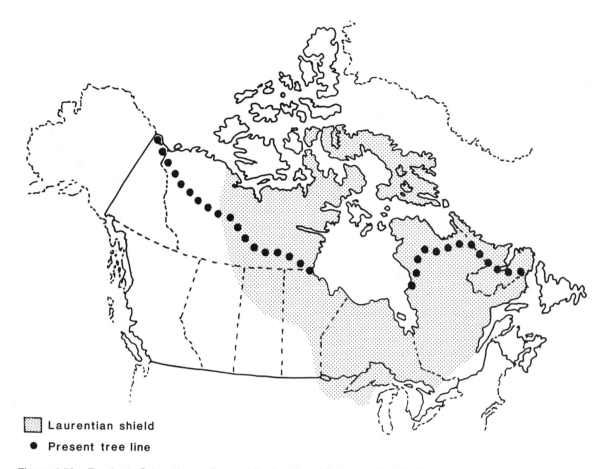

Figure 4.56   The Arctic-Subarctic tree line and the location of the Laurentian Shield.

outline. There are, of course, the flake microblades and burins, several specialized scrapers and blades, and both stemmed and stemless flint points. There are also harpoons and fish spears of bone. No houses have been found, but there are oval, rectangular, and circular outlines made of stone, often with central hearths. These are thought to be the sites of tent dwellings, the stones having been used to hold down the bottom of a tent made of hide. They are not arranged in villages but may be widely scattered for a distance along ridges or beaches. Food scrap is rarely present, but when it is, it includes bones of both musk-oxen and caribou.

This scanty inventory and lack of secure housing leave one curious about how these pioneers survived in the Arctic, particularly during the winters. It is speculated, but with no proof, that they built snow houses. This eminently feasible practice was used as recently as the historic period. In any case the remains are not numerous and the population was thin and widely spread.

By 2800 B.P., the pre-Dorset had evolved into the Dorset, which is more restricted in its distribution, appearing only on the coasts from Greenland down to Newfoundland and around Hudson Bay, which, of course, contains many sea mammals. The Dorset people

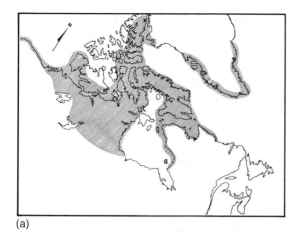

(a)

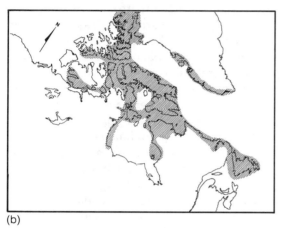

(b)

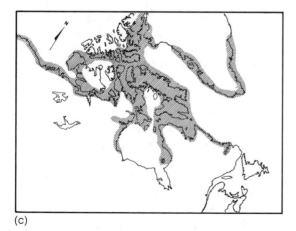

(c)

Figure 4.57   (a) Area probably occupied by the Arctic Small Tool Tradition; (b) area probably occupied by the Dorset culture; (c) area probably occupied by the Thule culture.

lived in small villages in rectangular pit houses with a rim of sod around the pit. The tops are presumed to have been either of snow or skin, perhaps depending on the season. In summer skin tents were probably used. The artifact inventory is enlarged, but its roots in the Arctic Small Tool Tradition can be identified (in fact, some authors apply the Arctic Small Tool Tradition to the Dorset remains).

There were several types of bone harpoon heads and lance points. There were fish spears of polished slate and chipped stone points. The burins and microblade knives are set here, as elsewhere, in the edges of flat, wooden handles. A few examples of these latter have been recovered during excavation. There were new elements in the artifact list as well: stone lamps and stoves, hand-drawn sleds or sledges, and bone ice creepers to be tied beneath the feet. The latter were probably used on the sea ice when hunters were after walrus and seal. There are scattered pieces of evidence for the presence of the kayak. The settlements were often located near strong fisheries, but no fishing gear has been found except the spears, so their summer fishing season is inferential. Toward the end of the Dorset, there were what are called shaman kits. These were miniature harpoon heads; wooden and ivory effigies of men, bears, and birds; and several ivory objects of unknown use. These are interpreted as having magical properties, which the shaman invoked in treating illnesses or before a hunt.

Along the Arctic coast, the Thule culture already described from the Bering Sea area, had arrived in Canada before 1000 A.D. in its spread east to Greenland. The prehistoric Beotuck Indians of eastern Canada were in evidence by this time or a little later.

Most scholars credit the first appearance of the Arctic Small Tool Tradition and Thule to an Alaskan thrust. While both may originally have been Asiatic complexes they did, indeed, reach Canada from Alaska. But the remainder of the Canadian archaeological record points to southern origins. An exception may be the ocean- and bay-oriented Maritime Archaic, which appeared earlier than that food-focus appeared in the Ocean Bay Tradition on the southern coast of Alaska. The maritime emphasis can thus be presumed to have been separate Canadian and Aleutian developments, not necessarily a surprise given the ocean richness.

The Maritime Archaic persisted in Quebec until about 2500 or 3000 B.P., to be followed by the Arctic Small Tool Tradition and Dorset, which have already been reviewed. In the prairie provinces of extreme western Canada (part of Manitoba and Saskatchewan) where the ice-free corridor existed, the earliest remains are those of the Plains PaleoIndian groups. The PaleoIndian fluted point tradition, of course, is represented in extreme southeastern Quebec by 10,000 B.P. at the Debert site and in Maine by the Vail site (described in Chapter Three). Those sites were created by PaleoIndians moving north from New England or from the west around the great southern lobe of ice where the Great Lakes are now. But in the prairie provinces the Plano cultures arrived from the Plains states by perhaps 8000 B.P. After the Plano (by 7,000 B.P.) the Shield Archaic emerged in western Canada. It is found over most of Canada, its distribution essentially coinciding with the Laurentian Shield which, as mentioned earlier, covers half the nation. This tradition persisted until 3500 B.P. or even later. The artifact inventory is again slim, but the complex has been recognized.

Found over most of the Shield, the Shield Archaic constitutes the first evidence of human occupancy in interior Canada. As the thinning ice sheet melted and its edges contracted toward the center, the plants slowly advanced, followed by animals; the slow advance followed years behind the shrinking ice. Once the floral and faunal populations were established, a straggling human population followed. The Shield Archaic population is thought to have been the remnants of a ter-

minal Plano people. At the same time, there was an influx of Archaic bands from the Plains and Midwest, both following the game. The game is supposed to have been largely caribou, the most abundant species of the tundra. The mixed origin, that is, people from both the Plains and midwestern woodlands, is suggested because the scanty toolkit seems to be a blend of Plano, with midwestern and eastern Archaic tool types. The diagnostic artifact, at least in the early Shield Archaic material, is a lanceolate point in two forms called Acasta and Keewatin (Figure 4.58). They are said to be modified Agate Basin points with basalar side notches or heavily ground basal edges.

There is also a variety of less well made stemmed and notched points, end and side scrapers, an occasional burin made on broken projectile points, large ovate knives, and a few heavy choppers. Prismatic flake tools are not reported, but there were denticulated (toothed or notched) saws or scrapers.

The small Shield Archaic sites are widely scattered. Because they are normally found on streams where caribou have crossed for millennia on their annual migrations, it is assumed that caribou were the usual game. The Aberdeen site, west of Hudson Bay in the Keewatin district, is typical. The site lies on the south bank of the Thelon River near where it enters Aberdeen Lake. Located on a steep bluff overlooking the river, it is opposite an island that female and young caribou use as a rest stop in their crossing of the river. As the caribou breasted the steep banks of the river after crossing archaeologists excavating the site came within 20 feet of the herd and could easily have harvested the animals with spears. The calving area today is just west of Aberdeen Lake; it has probably been used for millennia.

The site itself consisted of two shallow, basin-shaped houses and the associated debris of living. The floors had often been carpeted with moss, which in the years since abandonment had been transformed into peat. The debris was thin but yielded a full range

Figure 4.58 Type specimens from the Shield Archaic, chipped from coarse-grained quartzite and found at several interior Barren Grounds sites northwest of Hudson Bay: (a) and (b) Keewatin lanceolate points, (c) and (d) burinated points, (e) biface knife, (f) skin scraper, (g) and (h) snub-nosed end scrapers.

of the flint tools to be expected in a late Shield Archaic site. It dated to about 3000 B.P., making it one of the latest Shield Archaic sites reported.

South of the widely distributed Shield Archaic in Manitoba, Ontario, Quebec, and around the Gulf of St. Lawrence, the early cultures are northern extensions of those already described for New York and New England. Thus the Maritime and Laurentian are found in Quebec; the Old Copper culture and the Laurentian are well represented in Ontario; and the McKean, from the Wyoming high plains, is rather widespread in Manitoba.

Research has established abundant evidence of considerable climatic variation in both the Arctic and Subarctic of Canada. It is presumed that the distribution of archaeological material is to some unknown extent controlled by these fluctuations in overall environment. Harp (1983) has excellent material on the Canadian environment and climatic fluctuations. He specifically ties some of his archaeological interpretations to climatic variation, which is evidently quite securely established. McGhee (1978) is equally concerned with fluctuations in the high arctic climate.

In quick review there are a few points to be reiterated: Caribou seem to have been the major subsistence resource over much of Canada but were supplemented by fish and other mammals. The north and east coasts were populated from the west (with the possible exception of the Maritime Archaic). The remainder of the increments were from cultures to the south. Some believe the Shield Archaic to be a blend of the late PaleoIndian and Archaic technologies, possibly even of actual populations.

The Importance of the Archaic

This has been a long chapter as the Archaic stage has been surveyed across the continent. The treatment of the Northwest Coast and the Arctic sequence of cultures as Archaic may surprise some readers. It is consistent, however, with the goals of this book. Some see the Archaic, indeed all cultures, as being markedly different from each other locally or regionally. Others perceive the similarities of adaptive strategy, procurement technology, and persistence through time as evidence of the Archaic cultures' overall similarity over the continent and through time. That treatment allows the reader to per-

ceive and appreciate the slow cultural evolution from the PaleoIndian, whose limited toolkit and probable use of vegetable resources, developed smoothly into the new Archaic cultures in the face of drastically changed environments and additional resources as the continental climate changed to an essentially modern one. As world climate warmed and the glaciers receded, the vegetation and attendant animal populations followed. This can best be appreciated by reconsulting Figure 2.5, which clearly shows the contrast in the distribution of grasslands or woodlands between 10,000 years B.P. and today and the consequent changes in resources.

None of the above denies the fact of cultural change. The point is merely that the changes are rooted in the many subsistence practices. The basic direction of change seen in American prehistory is toward wider exploitation of the environment. There was an increasingly complex cluster of procurement technologies. The organization of food-collecting strategies was becoming more efficient with time. That efficiency was perhaps forced on the Archaic people by increasing populations. Not all scholars believe that population growth led to more efficient food collection, however. Some argue that the success of the foraging strategy required the maintenance of a population well below the maximum carrying capacity of the land in average or poor times. The survival of a group would depend on there being some basic minimum of subsistence resources. Whatever the stimulus, the record of the Archaic appears to have been one of slowly increasing population accompanied by an increasing efficiency in the use of the available resources.

But as the narrative leaves the Archaic stage, the cultural elements that comprise the Archaic cultural fabric foreshadow many of the practices of the so-called higher cultures that follow. For example, there is ample evidence of a concern for the dead, which leads to the assumption that the conception of the sacred and a belief system invoking the supernatural were becoming more highly structured. It is not just material objects that persist past the Archaic, although many do. It is the cluster of concepts or practices that demonstrate the continuity underlying what seems superficially to be dramatic change. And, of course, the basic foraging—the collecting of wild foods and taking of wild game, aquatic animals, and birds—was never abandoned. Several particular practices stand out and can be easily traced into the cultures that developed after 2500 B.P. One of the most obvious is the concept of reducing hard seeds to palatable form by milling, a processing technique that allowed the development of a series of staple vegetal foods. It must be remembered that the flat milling stone had appeared in the West by 8000 B.P. The stone (and probably wood) mortar and pestle were in the East by 5000 B.P., or earlier. And the mortar or hopper mortar in California was equally early. All three milling techniques continued in use until the final disruption of tribal life. In fact, the trough or flat metate of the Southwest remains in use today. Of course, the millstone is both a material object and part of an idea and a technology.

Perhaps the most pervasive and widespread behavior is that of trade or exchange. From Middle Archaic times exotic objects are found in excavated sites. Copper is an excellent example. Apparently fabricated in the upper Midwest, objects of Lake Superior copper are found around the Great Lakes and in Kentucky Archaic sites by 5000 B.P. Its movement continued into protohistoric times as we shall see. Marine shells in quantity are found deep inland: Pacific cowry and *Dentalium* are found far up the Columbia River; Gulf of Mexico shells occur in Ohio and Kentucky by that time and remained in use in the area until the tribes were dispersed; *Olivella* and *Oliva* shells are common in the western Archaic. Perhaps obsidian is the best example of long-distance exchange. Because each obsidian flow has a distinctive chemical content, the quarry of or-

igin can usually be determined. When this sourcing can be done, it permits the archaeologists to establish precisely how far the obsidian traveled. Since obsidian is not only beautiful but also can be chipped more readily and finely than most stone, it was highly prized and travelled enormous distances. The classic example, of course, is the obsidian found in a few Ohio Hopewell graves that was sourced to one of three famous flows in what is now Yellowstone National Park.

Exotic pieces probably conferred prestige or were indicators of status, but for whatever reason they were valued. The exotics form a large percentage of the goods accompanying burials. The mechanism of the exchange cannot be specified on present knowledge, but one suggestion is that a trade network existed. That idea implies that there were a few individuals who had some kind of tie or bond, perhaps real or fictive kinship, with other traders in neighboring districts, who in turn had more distant ties. Thus desired objects in two quite separated areas could be moved in both directions from one to another in a chain of traders. What was traded for the exotics could have been special foodstuffs, medical plants, or perishable objects like hides, featherwork, or tobacco. No evidence for what was exchanged for the exotics has been detected archaeologically.

Another suggestion is that a separate social class of merchants actually carried objects for trade from the point of production or manufacture along well-developed routes, periodically stopping to exchange their goods for local goods, which they knew to be in demand elsewhere along the route. Following a vaguely circular route, the traders ultimately returned to their base with locally valued exotics from distant provinces where the resources were different from those of their home district. There are many documented historic records of the latter system of merchant travelers.

Another suggestion is that cultural needs may simply have been met by dispatching a task force to the source spot to collect or trade materials or already fabricated objects and return home. That system of acquisition is also well-documented in historical accounts.

Regardless of mechanisms, the distribution of special flints, obsidian, shells, copper, and other minerals like red ocher, mica, galena, and even a few scraps of silver attest to the exchange. Often overlooked are the communications established by the trade activities. Some of the best evidence of the extent and vitality of the communication networks that reached all over aboriginal America lie in the patterns or styles of projectile points during the eastern Archaic. For example, there is the Kirk-LeCroy-Stanly-Morrow Mountain sequence first observed and reported in North Carolina. It is now known to have extended north to New England and as far west as Illinois. Generally, these are all small triangular points with serrated, but not very well chipped edges (probably because of refractory chert). The stems tend to be side-notched. The forms are simple and were probably quite effective in either piercing or cutting. Another example would be the earlier widespread Dalton type that seems to mark the end of the PaleoIndian stage in the East.

An even better example, perhaps, are the fluted points of a generalized Clovis style, which appear plentifully in most states east of the Rockies and scantily all the way to the West Coast. One might argue that the projectile point styles were dispersed by the movement of bands of people colonizing empty territory, and that explanation might have been true during the PaleoIndian times when the population of the continent was thin. But it can hardly explain the later Archaic form types that were successively so popular over both the West and the East. The simpler explanation is to postulate the transmission or diffusion of the idea by means of traders or other travelers who became aware of trends in other places and perhaps even brought samples of different points back to their home districts where the local flint workers copied them. Why

the styles gained popularity over the earlier, very widespread fluted types is puzzling. The above conception of the reason for the distribution of artifact styles is probably the mechanism called stimulus diffusion.

At this moment, diffusion as an explanation is somewhat out of fashion. Instead many students see the evolution of Native American cultures as happening in place. Those who depend on this explanation exclusively ignore such things as the diffusion of maize, ceramics, and stone masonry from Mexico into the American Southwest. That source for those items is an article of archaeological faith. Regardless of the current tendency to see local origins for North American cultures, we shall invoke both (1) long-established local developments, some of which are catalogued above, and (2) diffusion of both objects and ideas. We shall use whichever seems simplest and most economical and avoid as much as possible convoluted explanations that ignore the simpler ones.

There was probably a *lingua franca* in existence for wide-ranging traders. Inevitably ideas and knowledge of new ideas, inventions, products, or technologies would have been learned by the traders and brought back. Just what happened isn't known, but in the Southwest the new grass maize, the technology for raising it, and perhaps some of the uses of the grain were passed from northern Mexico to what is now the Southwest, where no earlier evidence of agriculture exists. In the East, however, all that was needed to create a maize horticulture was the introduction of the maize plant itself because the resident populations understood the nurture of plants and the uses of grain already. They merely incorporated the new grain into their own existing horticultural complex.

It is therefore argued that all the American populations had a continuous flow of knowledge, through trade and travel, of events over large areas of their world. To suppose that each valley or drainage was a cultural isolate is to be blind to the evidence. Indeed in the surveyor's notes of the early nineteenth century there is actual rather than inferred evidence of communication. As these surveyors established the General Land Office system of Ranges, Townships, and Sections, they indicated every Indian trail in their notes and maps and noted old fields and abandoned Indian towns. The fact is, the entire East and Midwest was a vast network of local and major trails. Pioneer roads, such as the one through Cumberland Gap that opened Tennessee and Kentucky to the early pioneers, followed an Indian trail centuries old. The Natchez Trace from Nashville, Tennessee, to Natchez, Mississippi, merely followed a linked, pre-European system of trails, even fording streams at the same well-known shoals where fording was always possible. All the passes in the Rockies and Sierra Nevada where highways run today were used by native populations. From historical records it is known that there was travel for its own sake or for social reasons. Obviously trade and communication are not the same, but they probably reinforced and supplemented each other as they do today.

Another custom that has roots deep in the Archaic is the use of iron oxides: red and yellow ocher for decoration on objects and for bodily adornment. Although they are common minerals, they do not occur everywhere, so a heavy trade in iron oxides must be assumed. Red ocher was used liberally in burials of important persons. Whether the color red was merely sacred, or also conferred prestige on the living, or both is not known. But even before the Maritime Archaic (the L'Anse Amour site in Labrador and the Red Paint graves of Maine by 7000 B.P.), ocher was used at some Early Archaic sites in the South. It was also common in California. In addition to the ocher smeared on objects and graves, small caches of the pure pigment have been found. Ocher was prized by many cultures well into the nineteenth century.

In the next chapters we trace the evolution of the North American high cultures in the high cultures of the East. They are marked by the beginnings of monumental earthworks, more strictly stratified societies, increased trade in exotic goods, elaborate mortuary rituals and probably other ceremonies, and eventually maize agriculture and other traits. Many items from the earlier Archaic combined to produce the cultures encountered by the waves of European immigrants who eventually destroyed all but a few of the Native American tribes.

Chapter 4
BIBLIOGRAPHY

The first cited references are varyingly easy to read. The simpler sources are followed by a second list that contains quite technical, sometimes more difficult material.

Aikens, C. Melvin

1983   The Far West. In *Ancient North Americans*, edited by Jesse D. Jennings, pp. 149–201. W.H. Freeman. New York.

Antevs, Ernst

1948   Climatic changes and pre-white man. In *The Great Basin, with Emphasis on Glacial and Post-glacial Times. Bulletin of the University of Utah 38:20, Biological Series* 10:7, pp. 168–191. Salt Lake City.

Dumond, Don E.

1983   Alaska and the Northwest Coast. In *Ancient North Americans*, edited by Jesse D. Jennings, pp. 69–113. W. H. Freeman. New York.

Funk, Robert E.

1983   The Northeastern United States. In *Ancient North Americans*, edited by Jesse D. Jennings, pp. 303–371. W. H. Freeman. New York.

Harp, Elmer, Jr.

1983   Pioneer Cultures of the Subarctic and the Arctic. In *Ancient North Americans*, edited by Jesse D. Jennings, pp. 115–147. W. H. Freeman. New York.

Kirk, Ruth, and Richard D. Daugherty

1978   *Exploring Washington Archaeology.* University of Washington Press. Seattle.

McGhee, Robert

1978   *Canadian Arctic Prehistory.* National Museums of Canada. Ottawa.

Tuck, James A.

1976   *Newfoundland and Labrador Prehistory.* National Museums of Canada. Ottawa.

1984   *Maritime Provinces Prehistory.* National Museums of Canada. Ottawa.

Wright, J. V.

1972a *Ontario Prehistory: an eleven-thousand-year archaeological outline.* National Museums of Canada. Ottawa.

1972b *Quebec Prehistory.* National Museums of Canada. Ottawa.

More Advanced Material

Phillips, James L., and James A. Brown (editors)

1983   *Archaic Hunters and Gatherers in the American Midwest.* Academic Press. New York.

Smith, Bruce D.

1986   Archaeology of the Southeastern United States, from Dalton to DeSoto (10,500 B.P. to 500 B.P.). In *Advances in World Archaeology*, Vol. 5, edited by Fred Wendorf and Angela E. Close, pp. 1–92. Academic Press. New York.

Transition and Culmination

Continuity and Change in the Eastern United States

Developments in the eastern United States in the period between 3000 B.P. and the permanent presence of Europeans after 1500 A.D. constitute the content of this chapter. That sequence appears to involve more complex behaviors and relationships than either stage reviewed so far. It is more difficult to unravel than either the PaleoIndian or the Archaic, which indeed gave enough trouble.

The Archaic stage in the East is considered ended by about 3000 B.P., less because it had ended or disappeared than because the pace of evolution had quickened. By about that time archaeologists recognize the beginning of a major cultural transition, signalled by new cultural elements. As was true with the PaleoIndian, no distinct time boundary can be set between the Late Archaic and this transition. The Archaic merely fades as many of the behaviors that developed during its long history are elaborately modified. It is an Archaic so enriched as to be something else.

The onset of many changes and considerable cultural complexity are seen in mortuary practices, trade, and horticulture, for example (accompanied, of course, by a continuation of many cultural practices). But in the East new forces can be recognized by the appearance of several markers. These cultural markers include the appearance of pottery, a new class of artifact that seems to have been developed or introduced in the deep Southeast. A second marker is the deliberate construction of mounds for burial of the presumably important dead and other much more elaborate mortuary procedures.

Probably the third marker was the intensification of the nurture of native cultigens, which provided a more stable subsistence base. Without the beginning of food production during the Late Archaic, some scholars insist that the elaborations recorded in this chapter would probably not have occurred. A fourth artifact marker may be the tubular pipe, but it is doubtful that tobacco had been introduced so early. In fact, it doesn't appear (as seeds archaeologically recovered) until about 400 A.D. More probably the many aromatic herbs of the East were being smoked, presumably in curing or other ritual procedures. It should be noted that only the events of the East and Midwest are being reviewed here. The prehistory of the cultures of the American Southwest that followed the Archaic in the West is the product of a set of stimuli entirely different from those identified east of the Rockies. (The Southwest sequence forms the substance of Chapter Six.)

The Woodland Tradition

The cultures of the East have been lumped together under the unsatisfactory term *Woodland*. The label is a relic of earlier scholarship and includes a wide variety of local adaptations that can be subsumed under the following very general description:

- A dominant hunter-gatherer subsistence pattern augmented in some areas with the products of the Eastern Agricultural Complex described in Chapter Four

- Manufacture and use of coarse but durable grit-tempered pottery, usually surfaced roughened

- Burial in cemeteries as in the Archaic, in artificially constructed earthen mounds, and occasionally in low natural eminences

- Dwellings made of wood and bark, in small permanent or semipermanent settlements

- More emphasis on stone lapidary and other art forms

- An enlarged toolkit and improved technology, particularly in ground stone

- An elaboration of burial ritual and trade

Even these traits are not entirely new: The use of cemeteries and perhaps mound burial, cremation, the forager subsistence pattern, use of red ocher as part of the burial mortuary complex, and the use of copper objects, shell, and cut jaws of wolf and bear were all part of the eastern cultural package during Late Archaic times. It is the few new ideas, combined with the elaboration of the older ones that makes the Woodland transition visible and definable. It is therefore believed that after 3000 B.P. the more complex cultures of the East largely evolved from an Archaic base. What is different is merely the elaboration of earlier traits and, of course, the addition of other ideas from various sources.

One of the new ideas, of course, is the concept of pottery. Because the presence of pottery is usually the primary criterion in establishing the designation of an assemblage of artifacts as being Archaic or Early Woodland, and remains even more important in cultural comparisons and classification, it is appropriate here to examine pottery and some of its uses for the archaeologist.

A momentary digression is necessary for definition of the terms used in connection with pottery. *Temper* refers to any substance (sand, grit, crushed shell, plant fibers, or straw) added to pottery clay to inhibit shrinkage and cracking of the clay as it is air-dried before firing, or during the firing process. The kind of temper also effects toughness and shock resistance of the pottery. *Paste* refers to the clay and temper from which the pottery is made.

Pottery is the product of a chemical change that results when a mass of plastic clay is subjected to high heats. It is transmuted from a plastic to what could be called artificial stone, hard and nearly imperishable. Because it survives most natural forces, whole vessels and fragments, called **sherds,** do not deteriorate in the earth. Hence pottery is often recovered during archaeological excavation. Because clay is plastic before firing, pottery can have many forms. In form and decoration the clay can be modelled to fit the cultural needs or preferences of the potter and society. Firing then perpetuates the form and surface treatment. Because cultures change and the ceramics may be (usually are) modified with the change, pottery becomes a time-sensitive indicator of these changes. As time-sensitive artifacts, pots and potsherds are indispensable tools for the archaeologist, often taking on critical roles as chronological markers. They are also used as cultural diagnostics. Thus they contribute toward recognizing both culture change and chronological succession.

But pots are functional artifacts. They are tools created in a variety of specific forms for a variety of more-or-less specific purposes. A ceramic vessel is a container, created for solids or fluids to be stored, transported, or heated. But only a *whole* pot can function. A broken pot is a broken tool. And despite (or because of) its hardness, a ceramic vessel is fragile. It is vulnerable to both thermal (rapid changes in temperature) and impact (hitting or dropping) shock. Any of those stresses will rupture the vessel and destroy its usefulness (although potsherds can be used for other tasks).

The form of the pot and its paste composition, including temper and wall thickness, all influence its resistance to shock or stress. All such mechanical factors must be balanced against its intended use. The number of shapes ceramic objects can take may not be infinite, but it is large. Pots may be large to small, hemispherical, tub-shaped, flat or bowl-shaped, cylindrical, tapered, or squat. They

may have large or small orifices, flat or round bottoms, elongated necks, or any of a number of shape combinations. But the attributes of form, including rim and lip shape and thickness and wall thickness, all relate to the vessel's function and its shock resistance. For example, a storage vessel need have no thermal shock resistance, but a cooking vessel must resist such stress; a carrying pot must be most resistant to impact shock; and in general, the thinner the wall the more effectively it transfers heat from the source to the vessel's contents.

Knowledge of the mechanical results of attribute variation can permit interesting nuances of understanding. In one instance, a study was made of a collection of midwestern Woodland ceramics. Along with changes in vessel shape, a decrease in wall thickness was noted. This change was correlated with an increasing dietary reliance on starchy seeds, a fact already determined archaeologically.

Starchy seeds are far more digestible, to say nothing of more palatable, after long boiling, which suggests that the vessel form and attributes changed in response to a change in dietary emphasis. There are scores, if not hundreds, of studies of the attributes of aboriginal pottery. Each provides a new insight on some technical, stylistic, or functional aspect of pottery, thereby extending its usefulness in interpretation of archaeological data. The discussion above helps explain the emphasis placed on ceramics in succeeding chapters.

Apparently the first North American pottery was being made in Georgia by 4500 B.P. The paste was soft and, tempered with Spanish moss or other fiber, somewhat fragile. A simple thick-walled bowl was the usual shape. There was normally no decoration. Dispersal of the idea to the north and west seems to have begun fairly soon. Sturdier wares, decorated with incised lines and punctations, were found all over the South as far as Louisiana by 3000 B.P. By the same time or earlier it was in New York, in Ontario by 2600 or

2700 B.P., and in the Midwest by 2600 or 2500 B.P. The earliest New York pottery, called Vinette I, did not much resemble the first Savannah fiber-tempered pieces. During the expansion of pottery technology many technical changes took place. They resulted in larger, more durable wares that probably performed new functions. First observed at Orient culture sites, Vinette I vessels had thick walls (1/3 to 1/2 inch). The paste was tempered with coarse grit, usually crushed rock. It is gray, black, or buff, and the pots are uniformly straight sided with a cone-shaped base and a wide mouth with straight or flared rim. The surface was roughened, showing impressions of fabric or cord possibly affixed to a paddle used in smoothing or thinning the wall during manufacture.

As the concept of pottery spread, there were many modifications. The earliest pottery in Wisconsin and Illinois, called Marion Thick, is as thick as 3/4 inch, with coarse granular paste tempered with crushed rock and "decorated" with cord impressions. The cord-roughened exterior is a by-product of manufacture—patting or paddling the vessel with a cord-wrapped paddle to compact the paste. It was probably not decorative in intent. The vessels are tub, barrel, or flowerpot shape with flat, thickened bases. They are usually found with Kramer points, which have lanceolate blades and long, straight, edge-ground stems. The presence together of Marion Thick pottery and Kramer points defines an otherwise Archaic assemblage as being Early Woodland wherever found. However, Marion Thick seems to be the prime cultural diagnostic trait, because it is sometimes found with other kinds of points. As mentioned, it appears about 2600 B.P.

The thick but fragile pottery is generally believed to have been used for boiling crushed hickory nuts and walnuts for oil extraction, the oil being used as a sauce or condiment with less tasty foods. The oil itself could have been stored in either skin bags or other pots. Great variation in details of local adaptation

is evident in the Early Woodland cultures distributed from the East Coast to the foothills of the eastern Rockies. The variation is clear when the archaeological literature of the Midwest is examined. Local and regional specialists have defined dozens of phases with differing artifact assemblages but always with a pottery component; such assemblages are uniformly labelled Early Woodland.

One of the Archaic cultures that can be seen as truly transitional is the Orient of New York. It is represented at several sites, the Stony Brook site on Long Island being one of the better known. This habitation site yielded radiocarbon dates covering a span from about 3000 to 2700 B.P. The subsistence was shellfish centered and plainly Archaic in nature. The many midden pits contain remains of oyster, scallop, quahog, long clam, periwinkle, and whelk. Land animals recovered included the white-tailed deer, turkey, box turtle, woodchuck, coon, gray fox, mink, and rodents. The artifacts indicate the Orient phase to be an outgrowth of the Laurentian or Maritime Archaic. It yields Vinette I pottery as well as steatite vessels.

But a better example of Early Woodland is the Meadowood culture of New York and southern Ontario. The culture reveals clear descent from an Archaic base to the west—probably the Red Ocher of Illinois—in the presence of such things as large, well-shaped lanceolate bifaces called turkey-tail blades; use of red ocher in graves; large caches of mortuary blades; copper awls, beads, and three-quarter grooved axes and celts; tubular pipes (made of pottery in Meadowood); **galena** cubes; and deep pits for storage and for flexed, bundle, and cremated burials (Figure 5.1). Its age, by radiocarbon assays, ranges from 3000 to 2600 B.P. Most of the data come from burial sites, so no good information on village life is available. Such evidence as there is points to the same kind of pattern seen in the Archaic—hunting, gathering, and fishing. Caches of seeds of goosefoot and smartweed, in addition to charred scraps of netting and

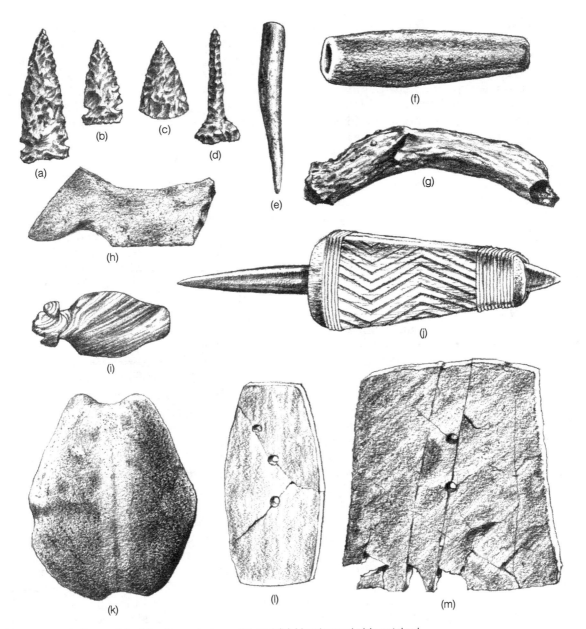

Figure 5.1 Artifacts of the Meadowood phase: (a) and (b) Meadowood side-notched-type projectile points, (c) "cache blade" or projectile point preform, (d) expanded-base drill, (e) deer antler awl, (f) tubular pottery pipe, (g) cut section of deer antler, (h) and (i) birdstones, (j) copper flaking tool in wooden handle (restored), (k) ovate pebble netsinker showing imprint of cord attachment to net, (l) and (m) two-holed stone gorgets. Variable scale.

basketry, support the idea of cultivation and storage of seeds from those plants. The creation of special, if small, cemeteries argues perhaps for a somewhat more sedentary life, but this cannot be proved. The popularity of cremation of the dead has prevented the preservation of skeletal material, so nothing can be said about the physical type of the people. As the artifacts in Figure 5.1 reveal, the Meadowood material would be identified as an Archaic stage collection, were it not for the presence of pottery. As already noted, the widely distributed, crude, surface-textured pottery is important for the definition of stage, but the net effect of ceramics on the basic Archaic lifeway, whether in the North or South, is imperceptible.

The transitional stages of nascent Woodland can be found almost everywhere east of the Rockies, in about the same distribution as the eastern Archaic. And as a generalized "stage," Woodland persisted until historic times over the coastal areas of the Northeast, East, and South. The transitional sites are fairly numerous. Listed as Early Woodland are such assemblages (or sites) as Baumer, Crab Orchard, Black Sand, Red Ocher, and Marion in Illinois; Boone in Missouri; Watts Bar and Candy Creek in Tennessee; Tchefuncte in Louisiana; and Glacial Kame in Michigan. There are many others to be found over the East and Southeast, to say nothing of the wide, but later, representations over the Plains and down into Oklahoma.

Described from several sites in a restricted area in southern Illinois, the Baumer assemblage again documents how little the Archaic is modified in the early steps of the transition. The Baumer site itself lies on a ridge—a prehistoric natural levee of the Ohio River—in the "Black Bottom" in extreme southern Illinois, an area still rich in plants, land mammals, fish, and mollusks. Tests revealed that this complex occurred at many sites in the region, basal in all stratigraphic contexts. At Baumer the settlement covered the ridge, an area some 1500 by 300 feet covered with rich

humus (black earth) to a depth of about eighteen inches. This layer yielded pottery, stone artifacts, and food-bone scrap in quantity. Originating within this layer were many straight-sided and cylindrical or bell-shaped pits, which were sometimes lined with clay and may have been used first for food storage and later for refuse after they had "soured," crumbled, or otherwise become unsuited for storage. Sometimes the pits were used as graves (during cold weather when the ground was frozen?) after the original storage purpose had been served. The outlines of square houses built of vertical wooden posts were found. These structures were about 16 feet square; posts some 6 inches in diameter were set in individual postholes at 2-foot intervals. No internal features such as fireplaces or storage pits were found, and no evidence of roofing techniques was discovered. Artifacts included heavy, stemmed knives or projectile points, a variety of scrapers and disc-shaped cores, the fully grooved ax, the smooth-tapered celt, gorgets of ground stone, and grooved plummets, as shown in Figure 5.2. An unusual artifact type is a large oval object made of chipped stone and much polished by use, which is thought to have been a digging tool—probably a hoe used in gardening or in harvesting roots.

The hoe and the pottery are the non-Archaic elements; the pits, chipped stone, and polished stone ornaments are seen in older cultures. The pottery is described as consistently coarse and crude. The favored tempering material in the thick, dense paste was crushed limestone, which had often been leached out by soil acids to leave a pitted surface. Most of the vessels were typically Woodland. The surface was commonly roughened

Figure 5.2 Artifacts of the Early Woodland: (a) and (c) projectile points, (b) and (d) scrapers, (e) and (f) hoes, (g) and (i) stone pendants, (h) stone gorget, (j) plummet stone, (k) grooved ax, (l) and (m) idealized pottery forms, (n) and (o) cord-marked sherds, (p) typical pit forms in cross section, (q) postmolds of square house plan. Variable scale.

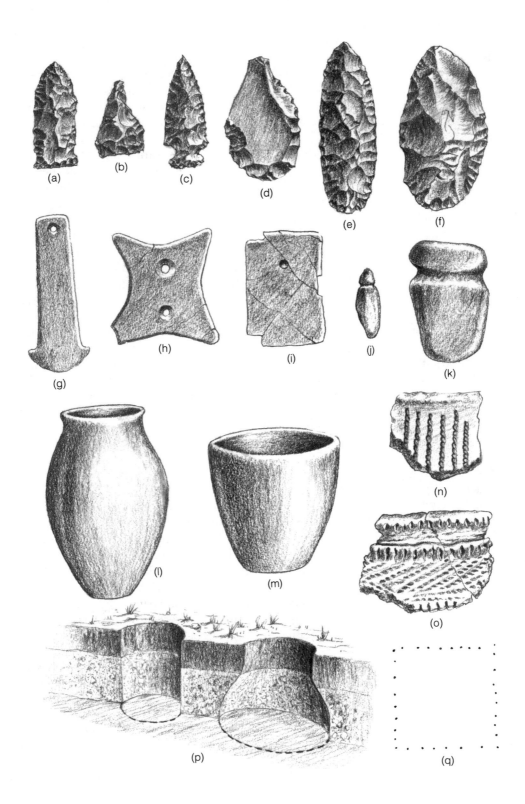

(a)

(b)

(c)

(d)

(e)

(f)

(g)

(h)

(i)

(j)

(k)

(l)

(m)

(n)

(o)

(p)

(q)

by impressing with basketry or matting, or possibly by pressing a cord-wrapped stick against the moist clay. The cord marking mentioned earlier also occurs but less often. The Woodland custom of burying the dead in low, domed, earthen mounds had become well established.

Adena

The Adena is the best known of all the Early Woodland cultures. It was concentrated in a small area, where its history extends from about 2800 B.P. to 100 A.D. It preceded and helped shape the later Middle Woodland Hopewell and related traditions. There were probably 300 or more known Adena sites, many now destroyed. Most of the sites fall within 150 miles of Chillicothe, Ohio, extending into Indiana, Kentucky, West Virginia, and Pennsylvania. Many lie near Lexington, Kentucky. The culture's importance derives from its influence rather than its areal extent.

Many of the sites in the core area are characterized by vast (and unexplained) earthworks. As the name implies, these are high, narrow ridges of earth enclosing large "fields." The enclosures may be circular, square, or pentagonal, or the earthwork may follow the irregular edges of flat-topped spurs or promontories. Apparently only the circular ones are Adenan. Scores of examples were recorded in the mid-nineteenth century, but they have disappeared beneath plow and progress.

Conical or domed burial mounds might occur inside the enclosures. Mound groups without associated earthworks were equally common. Some mound groups were built directly over villages. As in the Archaic, subsistence was based on knowledgeable selection from scores of species. Knowledge of wild foods comes from perishable specimens recovered from the Adena caves and shelters of Kentucky and from rare preserved plant fragments from excavated sites. Several food species were identified from fecal matter in

the caves. The analysis of human fecal matter as an aid in ecological analysis has become routine, but the 1936 study of Newt Kash Shelter vegetal remains was one of the earliest. The feces contained sunflower and goosefoot seed in quantity; both are thought to have been cultivated. There were also bits of bone and feather, a grasshopper leg, and a beetle fragment in the specimens studied.

The full list of species, presumably food sources, from both excavated sites and caves is almost endless. It includes large mammals such as deer, elk, and black bear and smaller ones such as woodchuck, beaver, and porcupine. Turkey, trumpeter swan, and ruffed grouse were common, as were box turtle and catfish. Vegetal foods included several species of nuts and the edible seed grasses. The bounty of the land offered a wide dietary range. The cultivars must have been distinctly secondary food sources. It is only fair to point out that the artifacts from eastern Kentucky caves were not particularly special: The foodstuffs identified could equally well have been from Archaic strata, with a few of the associated artifacts apparently of Adena affiliation.

Other perishables from the cave sites included wooden pestles, perhaps for use in the frequent "hominy holes" (mortars carved into bedrock) in the crushing of nuts and seeds for cookery. Woven sandals of grass and fiber and beds of grass and leaves were recorded.

Work at Salts Cave (Kentucky) has verified the variety of wild plants used by the Adenan peoples, including the probably native bottle gourd and squash. Moreover, the perishable artifacts preserved in the cave—sandals, cloth, cordage, torches, wooden bowls, gourd utensils, and imperishable mining tools—extend the artifact inventory. Salts Cave was evidently important for the crystalline mirabilite and gypsum deposits that were mined extensively from about 3000 B.P. onward. Mirabilite is an effective cathartic, while gypsum was evidently prized as a white pigment. It is entirely possible that both were important in trade, although no evidence can be offered.

In addition to the mines deep in the caves where minerals were dug out by the light of cane torches, the sheltered mouths of the caves (for example, Salts and Mammoth Caves) evidently served as dwelling sites.

More information is available about the mounds and death rituals of the Adena than about other aspects of the culture. Early excavators were perhaps more interested in burial rites than in the mundane matters of foods and handicrafts. The burial mounds are artificial hillocks built laboriously from individual loads of earth scooped from nearby borrow areas. The small loads were of different colors depending on the borrow zones; when the mound fill is sectioned, it presents a mottled patchwork of earth colors. This phenomenon of ''loading'' characterizes most artificial earthen fills.

Mound design varies enormously. Some of the smaller ones were built in one stage to cover the body of a single important person. The corpse might be placed in a simple pit with the mound quickly erected over it after whatever ceremony was involved. In other instances, burial was in large, log-lined pits or simply in a clay-lined basin with only some charred or calcined human bones remaining to attest a crematory rite. Some of the larger Adena mounds, such as the Robbins Mounds site in Boone County, Kentucky, were built in a series of separate incidents. There were a dozen burials, each covered by an extensive blanket of earth; with new increments the mounds grew larger and taller. Aside from a few log tomb burials (Figure 5.3), in which one, two, or three individuals smeared with red ocher or graphite were interred in extended position with grave furniture, cremation was the most common form of burial. Total cremation occurred in clay-lined basins. Partial burning of the body was usually found in conjunction with a log-lined tomb. The preoccupation with death and fire is remindful of the extensive crematory rites of the Orient and other Archaic cultures to the east of the Adena center.

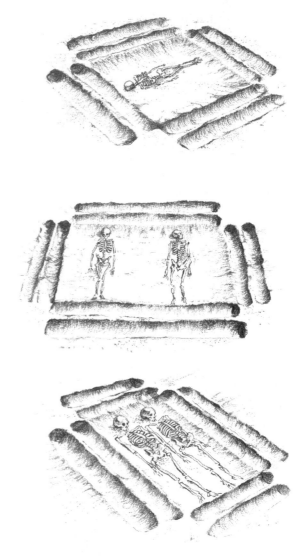

Figure 5.3 Log tomb burials as excavated at the Robbins Mounds.

The round Adena structures, once thought to be houses, are unique in construction. The walls were of paired posts set in the ground to slant outward. The rafters were supported on four sturdy center posts, spaced in a square around the central fire area, and perhaps projected beyond the walls to form eaves. The roof may have been of matting or thatch and the walls of flexible withes or cane woven or wattled around the posts. Most of the restoration in Figure 5.4 is conjectural because the construction details were not preserved. The round Adena structures varied greatly in size—from 20 to 80 feet in diameter. Many were destroyed by fire; the outlines formed by postholes are frequently encountered under the mounds, as if the burning of a house was the first step in construction of a burial mound. It has been suggested that the Adena "houses" were actually mortuary structures called **charnel houses** where bodies were defleshed and stored until the major ceremony: the burning of the house, placement of bodies in the crypts, and the building of the initial mounds. That suggestion makes good sense. In slightly later times charnel houses have been uncovered in many sites: McKeithen and Fort Center in Florida, Irene in Georgia, and Bynum in Mississippi are examples.

Grave goods were not common in the Adena tombs, but the few reported are of interest. There were smooth stone (rarely copper) gorgets or chest ornaments of several shapes: rectangular, lozenge, oval, or reel-shaped. The reel varies in shape but is essentially a rectangular body with four symmetrically flaring arms or prongs (Figure 5.5). The gorgets are

quite well made, often being fashioned of banded slate and other striking stone, polished to a high luster.

One of the distinctive Adena artifacts is the engraved tablet; several examples exist. These are rectangular slabs of stone about 3 by 4 inches and 1/2 inch thick with zoomorphic figures engraved on one or both sides. Birds— probably raptors or water birds—are usually depicted (Figure 5.6), but geometric designs are also found. The cultural function of these tablets is not known; they have been interpreted as stamps for decorating the body or clothing. What is interesting, however, is that the bird and other motifs are also found later throughout the Hopewell culture, normally on pottery and copper plaques or cutout forms.

The use of pottery for grave goods was not an Adena custom, but for ordinary use there was good plain and cord-marked pottery of standard Woodland type, that is, the cone-shaped or round-bottomed jar form. There are also several check-stamped wares bearing specific type names. The **check-stamping** is done by paddling the soft paste with a grooved wooden paddle; the two sets of grooves are at right angles to each other. The clay is flattened by the raised portions of the paddle, while the grooves leave ridges. The carved paddle is presumably a development from the cord-wrapped paddle; at this period check-stamping is very common all over the Southeast. A special pottery type, Montgomery Incised, is decorated with a nested, incised lozenge design.

The Adena textile arts were well developed. Plain plaiting, **twilling,** and several variations on twining have been noted. The textiles have been recovered from open sites, preserved in copper salts when left near, or wrapped around, copper objects.

Other artifact classes are not particularly diagnostic. There are awls of several styles; rather heavy chipped knives, points, and scrapers; flint hoes; nut- or cupstones; river mussel pearls; shell beads; spoons from ter-

26' diameter

Figure 5.4 Postmold plan and cutaway view of restored Adena structure that may have had a mortuary function.

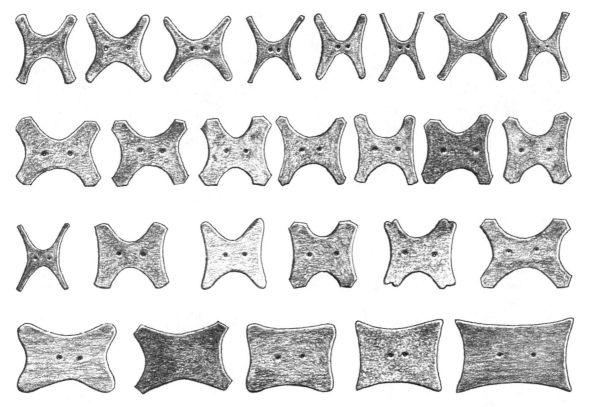

Figure 5.5 Adena and Middle Woodland reel-shaped gorgets. The earliest forms are at lower right, the most recent are top row. Variable scale.

rapin carapaces; cut animal jaws; celts with a circular cross section; and bowls from human crania. A few examples of an unusual artifact have been reported. It's the upper jaw of a wolf, cut so that the incisors and canines are intact on a kind of handle made by carving the palate to a spatulate form. It probably was part of an animal mask; the user would have had his upper incisors removed, putting the spatula in his mouth through the opening thus created (Figure 5.7). Human skulls thus mutilated have also been found, lending some credence to the idea.

Of the many Adena sites investigated, one of the more complex was the Robbins Mounds near Big Bone, in Boone County, Kentucky. In it were fifty-two tombs of four types: (1) an earthen-walled enclosure lined with logs and bark with a log roof; (2) a tomb within a fortuitous cavity made by collapse of the roof of an earlier tomb; (3) a log enclosure on a flat surface, covered by earth fill; and (4) a tomb constructed on a slope, by cutting a level floor into the slope. These tombs occur on all levels of the mound; the latter had been erected through the addition of six to eight stages or increments, each associated with the addition of another tomb.

Hopewell Tradition

With a general background from the Adena culture and a glimpse at one of the famous sites, we now turn our attention to the more extensive Hopewell Tradition. Most of the classic Hopewell sites were dug during the antiquarian era of study. As a result, many data are missing from the classic core area in

Figure 5.6 Engraved Adena tablets. Bird design elements shown at right center. About one-third size.

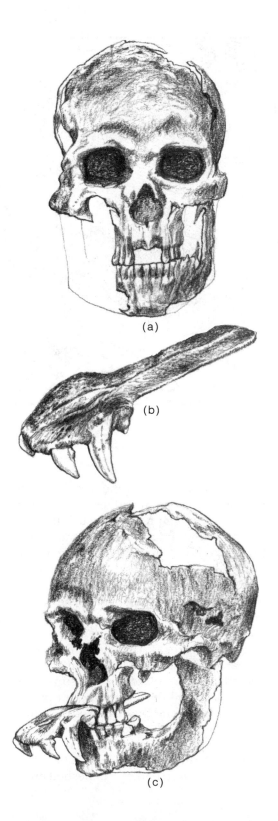

(a)

(b)

(c)

southern Ohio. However, the culture has been the object of continuous study over the Midwest, Northeast, and Southeast, and fuller data are finally available on several, though not all, aspects of the culture. The many expressions of the tradition are widespread.

The Hopewell culture is one of the many called Middle Woodland. It seems to have appeared in Illinois by about 2300 B.P. The southern manifestations lasted until 400 A.D. and later. The Ohio Hopewell probably grew out of the strong local Adena pattern, so the elaborate mortuary complex called Classic Hopewell actually developed in Ohio. That complex of traits and its associated relationships has been called the Hopewell Interaction Sphere, a phrase that takes account of a cluster of **traits,** artifacts, burial customs, and special burial mounds—a mortuary cult or religion rooted in a veneration of the dead— that can be recognized almost everywhere east of the Mississippi River.

But the Interaction Sphere traits seem to lie as an overlay or veneer on scores of locally different Middle Woodland cultures. The complex, although recognizable through artifacts (particularly the mortuary ceramic vessels), tends to weaken proportionally with its distance from the Illinois center labelled Havana, or the Ohio center labelled Scioto. The more distant manifestations include Point Penninsula in New York and Ontario; Marksville in the lower Mississippi Valley and Louisiana; Porter-Miller in Mississippi and South Alabama; South Appalachian in Tennessee, Alabama, and Georgia; and Santa Rose-Swift Creek in Alabama, Georgia, and most of the Florida Gulf Coast. Finally there is Crab Orchard, a probably small area lying between the Havana and the South Appalachian tradition area (see Figures 5.8 and 5.9 for the distribution of these eight traditions).

Figure 5.7 (a) Adena skull with upper incisors missing, (b) spatula-shaped artifact made from wolf jaw, (c) skull with artifact in gap created by missing teeth.

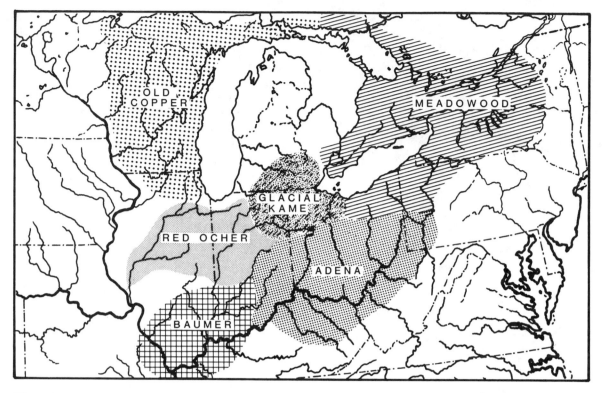

Figure 5.8   Late Archaic and Early Woodland manifestations in the Great Lakes and Ohio Valley regions.

The distribution of artifacts has led some to suppose that the entire Interaction Sphere was economic, built on trade over half the continent. Other data have led some to put greater credence in the original idea of a cult led by powerful priest-chieftains. No satisfying explanation has been offered for the mechanism of dispersal of the religious ideas or artifacts.

A description of the Hopewell Tradition is in order now. The constellation of artifacts, structures, and behaviors that are observed at the Scioto area sites forms the basis of the description. First is the monumental architecture: the burial mounds and earthworks. Most often these are located on elevated landforms alongside or in the broad, fertile river valleys. The mounds are large, conical, or domed earthen tumuli built laboriously by hand, one

basketful of earth at a time. Frequently there are raised walls or low ridges of earth of linear or geometric form nearby or surrounding the mound or mound groups. The mounds were the burial monuments to the many important dead. Again the purpose of the ridged enclosures is not known. Usually they are free of debris or other evidence of use. The dead were buried extended in the flesh inside simple log crypts or tombs (as at Hopewell) that were roofed with other logs, or sometimes they were cremated (in Mound City), as in the Adena. The bodies were placed in pits sunk beneath the surface, laid on the ground, or placed on low platforms, and then a low earthen mound was erected over the spot (Figure 5.11). Sometimes the primary mound was raised over a burned charnel house, a place where the honored dead were perhaps defleshed and oth-

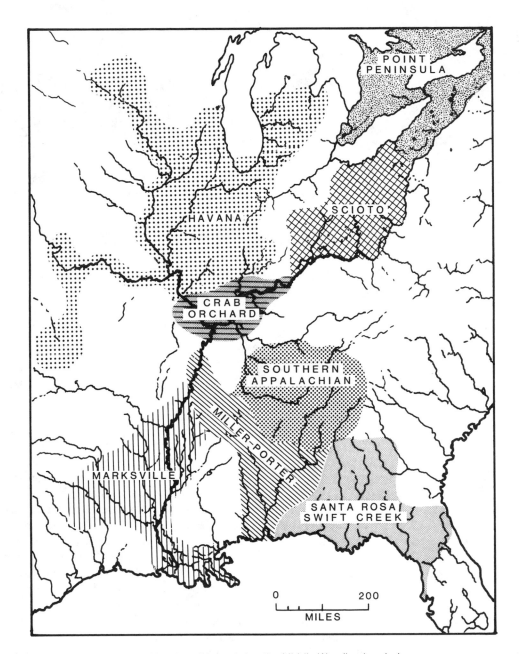

Figure 5.9   Distribution of major regional traditions during the Middle Woodland period.

erwise prepared for burial. Later increments or earthen blankets containing other burials enlarged and raised the mounds.

In the mounds were rich caches of goods, not always with the burials. The cached ob-

jects were created from exotic materials, both local Ohio items and imported ones. Mica (isinglass), in sheets or cutout geometric or animal forms, was a commonly used mineral (Figure 5.12). Copper, recovered in free sheets

Figure 5.10 Sources for some of the exotic items found in Ohio and Illinois Hopewell tombs.

and nuggets from the Lake Superior sources, was used for ear spools, headdresses, masks, bracelets, beads, chest ornaments, celts, and panpipes. *Busycon* (a giant sea snail) shells, from the Gulf of Mexico, were used for cups, while the central whorl was cut out and used for beads. Pearls (from river mussels) were used as beads for anklets and armlets and were sewn on garments. Figurines were carved from stone or modelled with great fidelity from clay (Figure 5.13). There was a special class of mortuary vessels, usually deep bowls with an expanding or globular base. The decoration was very uniform, as described later.

Platform pipes of stone with realistic effigies of birds, animals, and people for bowls were exquisite examples of stone sculpture (Figure 5.14). There were a few huge ceremonial bifaces of obsidian imported from Yellowstone National Park. The Yellowstone

obsidian occurs mostly in the Scioto area. Bear teeth were strung as beads or pendants as were cut wolf and bear jaws. Alligator skulls and teeth, baracuda jaws and shark teeth were also prized. In all, some twenty-two kinds of exotic materials were used to create the grave goods. Of those twenty-two, sixteen were minerals. Only two or three of the minerals were found in Ohio, so the rest had to be imported. (See Figure 5.10.) When placed in the grave with the dead, the objects were often smeared with red ocher. Sometimes the body itself was also covered with ocher.

The presence of skillfully manufactured objects seems to point to an artisan class. The finely wrought objects not only were beautiful, but also may have had extra value because of their cost in effort both to import and to manufacture. Their mere possession would no doubt give the owners prestige, and their innate properties may have included sacred

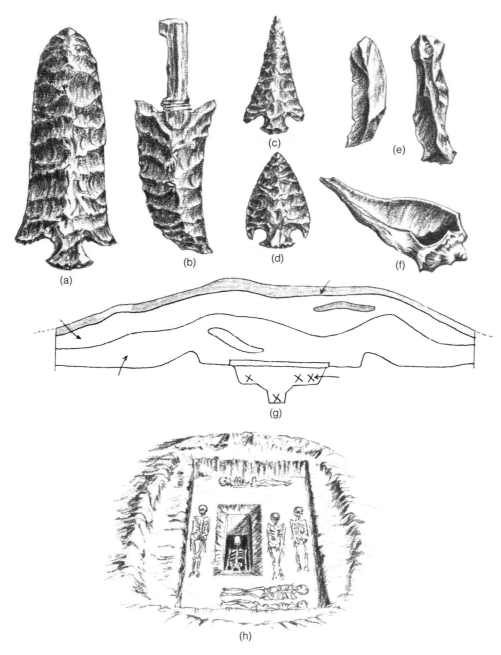

Figure 5.11   Hopewell artifacts and diagram of burial mound: (a) obsidian knife or spearhead, (b) obsidian knife (wooden handle restored), (c) and (d) spearheads, (e) flake knives, (f) conch shell dipper, (g) cross section of WH6 burial mound, (h) view of central tomb in WH6 mound.

Figure 5.12 Hopewell artifacts from Ohio and Illinois: (a)–(h) ornaments of sheet mica—(f) represents bear claws and (g) a bird talon—(i) stone ear ornament; (j)–(p) copper artifacts—(j) represents a fish, probably a sucker; (k) a robe ornament; (l) ear ornaments; (m) bird with pearl eye; (n) ax head; (o) bracelets; (p) probably a serpent's head—(q) pottery vessel. Variable scale.

or symbolic values beyond whatever other values they may have had. The splendor of the Ohio center was never equalled elsewhere, but a few specific Ohio artifact types are found all over the interaction sphere. They are the single and double cymbal ear spools of copper (Figure 5.12l), the *Busycon* shell bowls (Figure 5.11f), copper panpipes, and mica mirrors (?); those are the only items found in graves in *all* of the eight traditions. But

Figure 5.13 Hopewell ceramic figurines from the Knight site in Illinois. Reduced about one-third.

Figure 5.14 Hopewell stone pipe sculptures: (a) hawk or eagle attacking a man, (b) highly polished platform pipe, (c) beaver, (d) hawk or eagle tearing at a small bird, (e) cougar or wildcat, (f) toad, (g) bear, (h) tufted heron with a small fish. Slightly reduced.

some uniformly styled pottery types were common in all areas. The pottery was usually of local manufacture but conformed to a broad pattern of shape and decoration to be described later.

What can be inferred from the above description? Whatever the reason, the central theme, the power of the interaction sphere lay in the mortuary ritual and the trappings that accompanied it. To call the force religious is to claim more than can be proved, but religion is a force that can flow across cultural and linguistic boundaries as an overlay or veneer upon the local cultures. To stretch the point, world history offers such obvious examples as the spread of Islam and Christianity. At any rate, a religious motivation for the Hopewellian cult is not totally unreasonable. Usually (though not always), religion implies a superordinate priesthood, that is, a class of specialists with superior status. Priest-chieftains combining both sacred and secular powers can be postulated. The presence of a priesthood suggests a stratified society, an idea supported by the rich grave offerings for a few of the dead. The huge earthen monuments and a probable artisan class suggest a measure of secular control over the community, perhaps resembling a corvée or labor tax. During Hopewell times, there was probably some intensification of the cultivation of native plants.

Most of the Ohio Hopewell sites were dug is the early twentieth century. The excavations were motivated by expectations of rich booty rather than any intent to reconstruct the prehistoric lifeway. The result, of course, is that from the early work only mortuary data were recovered and some of the sites are now completely gone. In more recent work in Illinois and over the Southeast where there were sites still to be found, more complete recovery is beginning to round out our picture of the full culture. For example, at Clear Lake near Pekin, Illinois, the dominant meat food was deer. Represented in the food scraps were turtle (three species), muskrat, beaver, duck, raccoon, buffalo, elk, turkey, and many rodents. Shellfish—snails and mussels—were well represented, as were catfish, suckers, and bass. From the Apple Creek site (also in Illinois), came caches of pigweed, lambs-quarter, and grape seeds, with hazelnuts, walnuts, and pecans also in evidence. Probably sunflower, goosefoot, and cucurbits were also cultivated.

In the lower Illinois River Valley, continuous study of the settlement pattern (site distributions) and resources convince one that the major cultigens—corn and beans—were not well known to Hopewell farmers. The many wild foods mentioned above for Apple Creek are common and may well have been cultivars. The analysis of the food scrap recovered at the Scoville site, a late Hopewellian settlement (450 A.D.) on the Spoon River in the central Illinois Valley, highlights once again the richness of the river bottom environment and a selective exploitation of these resources. From the four complementary ecozones within a 10-square-mile circle (a 1.8-mile radius from Scoville), the documented presence of wild foods so varied and in such quantity made extensive food cultivation unnecessary. For example, within a half-hour's walk from Scoville there would annually be from 182,000 to 426,000 bushels of acorns, 100 to 840 deer, 10,000 to 20,000 squirrels, and 200 turkeys. Not computed were seeds, fruits, smaller animals, fish, mussels, and migratory birds (six million mallards were estimated to be in the Illinois River valley in 1955). Scoville residents seem to have secured 92 percent of their meat from deer and 4 percent from turkey. Hickory nuts (71 percent) and walnuts (27 percent) were collected, as were seeds from several species, goosefoot and knotweed being dominant. The site was not occupied from early spring to midspring or during mid- to late autumn. These periods of abandonment coincide with the waterfowl migrations; probably the Scoville people left their village to harvest waterfowl on the major flyway along the Illinois River a few miles away twice a year during the migrations.

Several Middle Woodland village sites have been explored. In Illinois the house patterns were oval, and the Ohio houses were also oval or possibly round-cornered rectangular. Presumably they were domed, mat- or bark-covered structures, with no internal supports, very like the wigwams of the remanent Late Woodland tribes of historical times. However, rather large houses, which were probably dwellings, have been found at the Norton site in Michigan and the Seip Mound State Memorial in Ohio. At Norton a house floor had evidently been partly scraped away in preparing the floor for a mass burial and mound. It was a rectangle about 18 by 25 feet; postmolds marked the shape and size. Two other houses from Seip appear to have been essentially square structures with rounded corners and double-sided walls. One was 44 by 48 feet. Another was littered with mica scrap, sherds, and other debris; probably it was occupied by craftsmen specializing in the fashioning of sheet mica ornaments. There was an entry or door at each end. Most of the house structures that have been reported to date have lain under mounds, as at Norton. They are usually ascribed to some funerary practice as mentioned earlier.

In ceramics (involving a most tractable of material that becomes imperishable when fired) a very sensitive record of aesthetic styles and changes is preserved. Regional styles can be segregated by the knowledgeable, but in general Hopewell day-to-day ceramics are merely good-quality Woodland ware, grit-tempered, and roughened with a cord paddle or wrapped stick. The usual form is a flat or conoidal base and the familiar flared mouth. But the 1 or 2 percent of the pottery used in burial ritual is distinctive. The form is about the same, usually a squat vessel or jar with a somewhat constricted neck. The thickened rim is almost always diagonally hatched or cross-hatched. Frequently the body of the jar has four symmetric bulging lobes that are relevant in the careful and sometimes repeated design. Designs begin below the constricted neck and

are worked out in broad, shallow U-shaped grooves made in the clay with a round, pointed implement. The design is emphasized by texturing either the figure or the background with a toothed rocker or roller pressed into the clay in a zigzag pattern. Bird designs are common, along with a variety of geometric and cursive designs. One design is the roseate spoonbill. It is of passing interest that a spoonbill, evidently ceremonially buried with "full honors," was recovered from a log tomb in Gibson Mound 3, Calhoun County, Illinois. The inclusion of a spoonbill in a Hopewellian tomb suggests that the birds held special importance for the Hopewell people. The flamingo was often used as well. Another characteristic design element is a series of nodes formed by pushing a reed or bone tool against the interior to raise a series of spaced bosses or lumps on the exterior near the rim. Beautiful Hopewell figurines were also fashioned from clay. Some of the most elaborate come from the Knight Mound group in Illinois. Details of headdress, clothing, ornament, and even motor habits can be learned from them (Figure 5.13). Note the female sitting posture, the big painted beads on ankles and wrist, and the short skirts. Male ornaments and breechclout are also portrayed.

In the Wabash Valley in eastern Illinois is the Wilson site. Mound Wh6, 90 feet in diameter and 13 feet high, is a typical two-stage site. Construction of the mound was begun by removing the topsoil down to a blue clay subsoil. A tomb 11 by 15 feet was dug into the blue clay; a second, deeper pit, 2 by 5 feet, was dug into the center of the tomb. The spoil dirt was arranged in a low dike encircling the tomb. Seven extended burials were placed in position, logs were laid over the tomb, and the first stage of the mound was built; the second mantle of earth was added soon after.

At the Norton site, in the western sector of the lower peninsula of Michigan, the report from Mound M describes an elaborate multiple burial resembling the Wilson site. At several Norton mounds the practice was to remove the surface soil over a large area and spread a thin floor of clean, light-colored silt on this surface. A low, mounded enclosure was added around the clean floor, leaving a central crater to mark the limits of the tomb. A second blanket of earth covered the tomb and the enclosing fill and extended outward to the full diameter of the final mound, in one case about 100 feet. After some fourteen bodies and large quantities of grave goods were laid in place, the craterlike tomb edges were lined with bark, and the final construction stage was added.

The grave goods were numerous but not particularly flamboyant. There were pottery vessels, many turtle carapace dishes, several *Busycon* shell bowls, awls, projectile points, scraps of mica, mussel shell spoons, numerous lumps of much oxidized pyrite, eagle and falcon jaws, beaver incisors, bone and antler scrap, and some cobble hammers or anvil stones. An interesting note was that many of the crania had perforated left parietal bones. The excavators speculate that these individuals may have been sacrificed as part of the burial ceremony. The pottery particularly shows marked similarity to the Illinois Hopewell variant, leading the assignment of the Norton group to an Illinois expansion, rather than to the nearer Ohio Hopewell climax.

In Louisiana is the Crooks site (representative of the southern Hopewell variant called Marksville). It had a flat, square burial platform erected on the original surface. On this platform 214 burials were made, 168 bodies having already been included in the upper earth fill of the platform itself. A yellow clay dome capped the burial platform and a steeply conical primary mound was constructed. Later the secondary fill was added. In it hundreds of other burials were laid in shallow pits. From the site came many fine Hopewellian mortuary pieces, all of local manufacture (Figures 5.15, 5.16).

The Marksville site in Louisiana is one of the most famous Hopewell sites, lending its name to the entire lower Mississippi Valley complex. Excavations there demonstrated the two-stage construction and familiar mortuary function of the mounds.

The Bynum Mounds site in northeastern Mississippi is clearly Hopewell-derived and is assigned to the Miller-Porter Tradition. The central sunken tomb and the flat, first-stage mound are both represented in the six mounds at the site. There were large, circular post-mold patterns and myriads of unpatterned molds over the village that lay adjacent to the mounds. The circles of posts were large—one was 78 feet in diameter—so there is some doubt about whether they were for houses; they may have been post enclosures for some unknown use.

The Florida Hopewellian derivative is called Santa Rosa. Usually correlated with the Santa Rosa is a Georgia culture called Swift Creek. (Swift Creek pottery occurs at the McGraw and Wilson sites in Illinois.) Santa Rosa shows no big centers or elaborate stage-construction mounds. Burials were, of course, in the mounds but were not so formally interred. It is in the ceramics, with distinctive zoning and **rocker stamping** on somewhat bizarre vessel shapes, and the copper ornaments that the Hopewellian connections are obvious. Figure 5.17 shows the ceramic evidence. The sites themselves are nondescript shell heaps. Subsistence emphasized sea and land mammals and the wild flora characteristic of earlier seacoast dwellers of the Archaic stage there. All the local Hopewell traditions—Marksville, Miller, Santa Rosa—seem to be later than the sites of the core Ohio Valley area.

The Effigy Mound culture of Wisconsin, Illinois, and Iowa is an interesting and anomalous phenomenon, now seen as Late Woodland. The remains attract attention because of the range of animal forms represented by the low effigy mounds. There are sometimes burials at the "vital" points—hips, head, or heart area—of the animals, but there are only the simplest of grave goods. Burials are either flexed or bundle types. At one group, Sny-Magill (now a national monument in Iowa),

Figure 5.15   Hopewell pottery types from the Crooks site: (a)–(d) Marksville Plain, 2½ to 3½ inches high; (e) and (f) Marksville Stamped, both 4 inches high; (g) and (h) Marksville Incised, both 4½ inches high.

Figure 5.16   Typical Hopewell vessel from the Marksville site. Note roulette decorated area outlining design.

two mounds of the group seem to be of earlier Hopewell construction and content. The sites often lie on ridges overlooking a stream valley. The mounds take about a dozen shapes: conical, biconical, oval, linear, panther, bear, bird (goose or raptor), deer, bison (?), turtle, lizard, wolf or fox, and beaver. They are arranged in lines or clusters with no regularity in the forms depicted; the linear and conical ones are mixed with the effigies. The groups may contain dozens of mounds. The Kletzien group had thirty-two; the Nitschke, sixty-two. The complex is a limited local development on a simple Woodland base.

In New York, the Point Peninsula Tradition begins with the Squawkie Hill phase, where cult artifacts are found in mounds. In fact the typical rocker stamping is very extensive in the Northeast, being found well beyond the other Hopewellian diagnostics. After about 250 A.D. the Hopewell Tradition traits disappear there. It is about that time that the

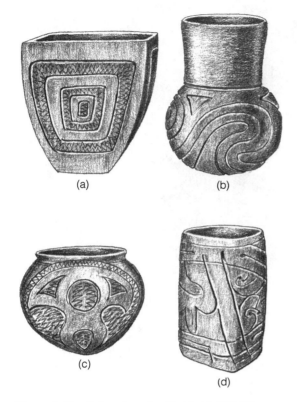

(a)   (b)

(c)

(d)

Figure 5.17 Pottery from the Florida Gulf Coast: (a) and (c) Alligator Bayou Stamped, 15 and 5 inches high; (b) and (d) Basin Bayou Incised, 6½ and 6 inches high.

cultures of the Midwest and East developed stronger regional differences, with many local sequences replacing the more uniform culture characteristic of Hopewell dominance. Even so, as in the widespread dentate pottery decoration, vestiges of Hopewell ancestry can be noted. In New York, for example, the development of late Point Peninsula into Owasco and even historic Iroquois can be tied through a few ceramic traits to Hopewell.

Late Woodland

The Owasco culture of New York, accepted as being ancestral to the Iroquois, is dated at 1000 to 1300 A.D. Several sites have been studied, and it is certain that

the subsistence of this late Woodland culture was diversified, with gardening being of some importance. Beans and corn have actually been recovered during excavation but not cucurbits. Nonetheless, hunting, fishing, and gathering continued to be important, as was true even into historic times among the Iroquois. The sites yield charred specimens of many fruits, seeds, and nuts: apple, cherry, plum, hickory nuts, hazelnuts, acorns, and others. Farming tools included elk-scapula hoes, as well as two types of flint hoe. Food storage pits are common in some sites.

Settlements were sometimes located on water courses or near tidal areas, but in late Owasco times the settlements were not on waterways. Several houses made of flexible saplings set in the ground and brought together to a rounded roof comprised the stockaded villages. The covering was probably big sheets of elm bark. At the Maxon-Derby and Bates sites, at least, the long communal house is present. In fact longhouses are characteristic of the Owasco. The material culture shows no great changes from earlier times except perhaps in the pipes, which are characteristically well made, usually of clay. The shape was similar to modern briars, except that the decorated bowl was usually set at an obtuse angle to the stem rather than at the more familiar right angle. The pottery was usually of the familiar Woodland shape, with more elaborate rim treatment (Figure 5.18).

Later than the Owasco culture there are sites that are clearly Iroquois. The Getman site, dated at about 1400 A.D., is typical. Small and surrounded by a stockade, it contained five or six longhouses—one 114 feet long by 22 feet wide—with slightly rounded ends. The stockade that enclosed the 1-acre village was of posts arranged in a continuous double row with a 4- to 5-foot space between the rows. There was a single entrance. Withes or bark strips were interwoven with posts to form a tight wattle. The houses, built of poles and covered with slabs of elm bark, were communal dwellings. Each family had its sleeping

Figure 5.18 Artifacts of the late Prehistoric St. Lawrence Iroquois, from the Roebuck site, Ontario (Late Woodland stage): (a) rim sherd of Durfee Underlined type; (b) rim sherd of Onondaga Triangular type; (c) sherd of Corn Ear type; (d) rim sherd of Black Necked type; (e) rim sherd of Swarthout Dentate type; (f) crescent pipe bowl; (g) ringed, elongated conical pipe bowl; (h) and (i) perforated deer phalangeal cones (tinklers); (j) fragment of a human-skull gorget; (k) steatite bead; (l) bone projectile point; (m) bone awl; (n) barbed bone harpoon. Slightly reduced.

benches along the walls with the family hearth in a central aisle that ran the length of the building (Figure 5.19). The hearths were merely shallow basins in the floor.

In New York larger, later villages identified as Mohawk have been investigated. But some of the most extensive data on the earliest Iroquois remains comes from Ontario, Canada, between Lakes Huron, Erie, and Ontario. In that area by 1000 A.D. (contemporary with, and similar to, the Owasco), there were two groups: the Glen Meyer and Pickering. The Pickering seems to have evolved from the Point Peninsula culture, whose influences from Hopewellian have been mentioned. Apparently the Glen Meyer was absorbed or displaced by the Pickering, so that by 1300 A.D. a uniform, recognizably Iroquois culture had developed and spread into New York.

Warfare seems to have been common at that time, as the villages are palisaded and located on hills or steep stream banks where defense was easier. The communal longhouse existed by then, albeit smaller than the later Iroquois structure. Thus the essential elements of the Iroquois pattern—corn agriculture, villages palisaded in defensible positions on streams, an artistic treatment of tobacco pipes, bone-bundle burials, dogs sometimes used as food, and ceramics clearly ancestral to historic Iroquois pottery—were present by 1300 A.D.

One of the best examples of that basic Iroquois culture comes from the Draper site 22 miles north of Toronto, Ontario. It was completely explored in 1974 and 1978, just ahead of total destruction by an expansion of Toronto International Airport. As is the case with most emergency operations, the excavation was hurried, requiring ingenious and innovative uses of power machinery and the volunteer and paid labors of many people. It is the only excavation of an entire Iroquois village accomplished to date.

Dating to about 1400 to 1450 A.D., the Draper site is on the bank of Duffin Creek, which has at least fifteen other villages in its watershed system. Draper was a stockaded village that contained 35 longhouses (the largest was huge—25 feet wide and 225 feet in length), covering an area of 8.5 acres (Figure 5.20). An estimated 1000 people lived there. Across a ravine to the south was a smaller hamlet of seven longhouses, not stockaded. Because Draper was completely excavated, it was possible to discover a history of growth and expansion and possibly a general population increase. Expansion occurred four times. Each time more houses were built and the stockade enlarged.

Building of longhouses required a large outlay of labor. Scores, if not hundreds, of the proper size posts were cut and assembled, and many large slabs of elm bark were peeled and brought to the site. Then the posts were set in individual holes to create the timber framework, and finally the bark was tied to the frame. With only stone tools, the work would go slowly. Each house must have represented thousands of work-hours. Some restored longhouses have been built to a series of specifications derived from archaeological and ethnological data. These striking examples can be seen at the Lawson site and the Museum of Indian Archaeology, near London, Ontario, and at the Crawford Lake Preserve a few miles from London (Figure 5.21). They are impressive testimony to Iroquois industry. (William Finlayson, Director of the Museum of Indian Archaeology, provided an estimate of the time required to build the restored longhouses at the Lawson site: twenty people for two to four weeks or 1600 to 3200 labor hours using eight-hour days.) The artifacts from Draper indicate the expected use of ceramics and stone pipes (Figure 5.22), pottery of Late Woodland type, and a few bone tools.

The Ontario tribes that evolved from the Pickering base were the St. Lawrence Huron, Petun, Neutral, and Erie. They were not part of the Iroquois Nation centered in New York, although they shared language and material culture with them.

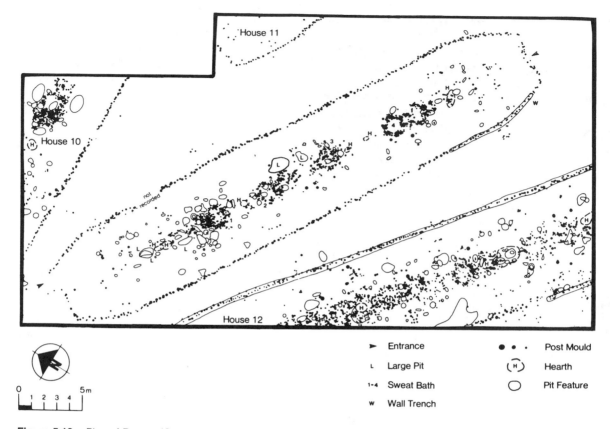

Figure 5.19   Plan of Draper (Ontario) site house 21 and portions of houses 10, 11, and 12.

While there are other Iroquois sites in both Ontario and New York, it seems appropriate to describe briefly the Iroquois lifeway, partly because the tribes figured prominently in American history of the Colonial period. This account is based on historic ethnographic accounts of the New York tribes—Mohawk, Oneida, Onondaga, Cayuga, and Seneca—that made up the Five Nations or Confederacy.

An Ethnographic Sketch

The Iroquois of both Canada and the United States are thought of as probably the most advanced, politically and culturally, of the northeastern Woodland tribes, possessing a remarkable representative form of tribal government. The basis of the tribal and

confederacy control was the matrilineal kinship system. The maternal lineage was the effective social unit on all levels. The longhouse, shared by a household of families of maternal kindred, was dominated by a female acknowledged to be the head of the household line. Husbands of women in the household lived with their wives in the longhouse but had no rights in the house or in governing. Their children, however, were of the wives' lineage and belonged "to the house." The males' allegiance was to the lineage and household of their mothers. There were, however, male chiefs who represented households and villages in tribal affairs.

In day-to-day matters there was a strict division of labor, and this probably merely continued an earlier pattern. Men hunted and

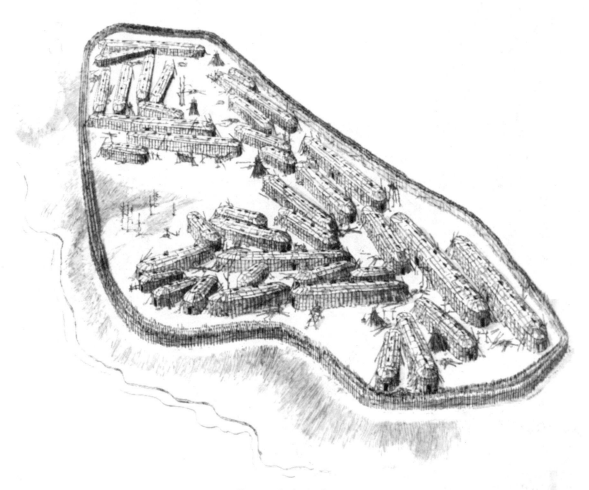

Figure 5.20   Artist's restoration of Draper site village at its largest.

fished; made weapons and such items as canoes, paddles, snowshoes, bark barrels for food storage, and other wooden objects; built houses; assisted in clearing farm lands; and participated in the harvest. Of course, they were also warriors. Women did the gardening and cooking; cared for children; gathered roots, berries, fruits, and nuts; made pottery; wove cloth; tailored clothing; and aided the men in some aspects of hunting.

In the woodlands hunting was done by stalking or trapping. Deer were stalked by a lone hunter, who moved slowly behind cover (through a thicket or from one bush to another) until he was close enough to be certain he could mortally wound the animal. Often the stalking was done with a decoy; a deer head with antlers covered the shoulders or was held in the hand of the bowman as he crept toward the quarry. With the decoy the hunter imitated the movements of a browsing deer until he was close enough for the kill. There were many kinds of traps. The deadfall was a heavy log that fell and crushed carnivores and bears as they dislodged it in taking a bait or tripping over a trigger string. Bent sapling snares with a looped cord, set in animal trails, were common and could even trap deer and bear. Small loop snares pegged to the ground in runways were used for lesser animals.

Figure 5.21   Restored palisade and longhouse at Lawson (Ontario) site.

The list of wild foods taken is far longer than that recorded for the Owasco because the gathering was observed, rather than inferred from archaeological remains. Vegetables and fruits were dried; fish and venison were dried and smoked. Surplus meat was stored in pits lined with leather. Dried squash and pumpkin were stored in bark-lined pits. Maize was kept in bark barrels. With this wealth of food the Iroquois cooked a wide variety of tasty dishes; many, such as corn bread, hominy, and succotash, are still common American foods. Maple syrup and sugar were important condiments. The Iroquois had a well-developed religion and much ritual, and a comparable development can be assumed for the earlier cultures.

Through this brief excursion into the recorded lifeway of a historic tribe, one can look beyond the remains of an archaeological complex and glimpse the daily or even annual rounds of the people as they may have been.

As the northern Hopewell climax passed and the Woodland cultures settled into a peripheral and tranquil status the cultural initiative shifted from the Midwest to the middle reaches of the Mississippi Valley. Here Hopewell has been presented as having grown out of Adena, with the Adena origins in turn embedded in the Archaic cultures. But there remains the problem of Hopewell's added flamboyance and rapid spread. And still unsettled is the argument about whether the raptor, snake, death hand-eye, and other motifs in art or the copper ear spools of cymbal type were indigenous or derived from Mexico in the centuries before Christ. The burial mound and the two-stage Hopewellian con-

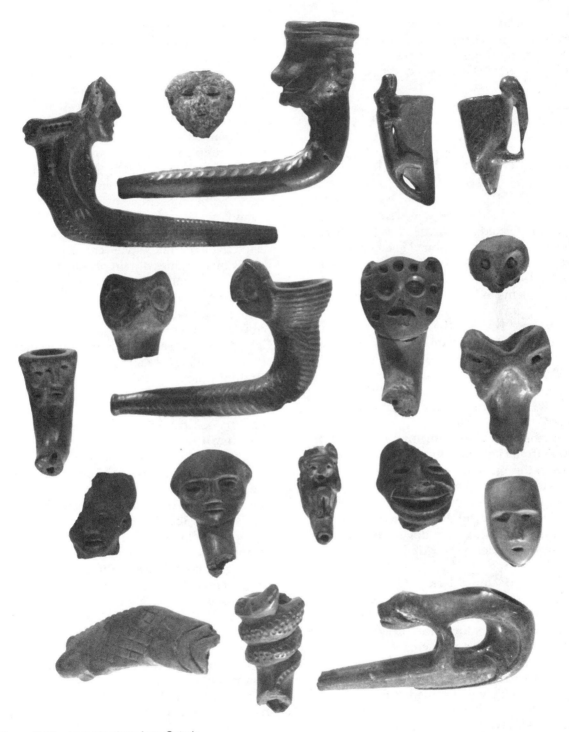

Figure 5.22 Iroquois pipes from Ontario.

struction, at least, can be viewed as indigenous to the northern area. Whether any Mexican traits helped shape the Hopewell cultures remains an open question.

The Mississippian Tradition

After the decline of the Hopewellian related cultures, the local (Late) Woodland groups continued in much the same way over most of North America. Foraging continued, while the use of domesticated plants seems to have increased. Starchy seed plants, such as maygrass, goosefoot, and knotweed, became the major crops. Moreover, large caches of these seeds in storage pits have been recovered, so there is positive evidence of collecting and storage of surpluses. Storage is known as well from some Middle Woodland (Hopewellian) sites excavated in recent years.

Farther downriver for example, the transition from Hopewellian to something else begins in the Yazoo Basin of Mississippi, where the Hopewell changed somewhat to become the local Issaquena culture. At Troyville, Louisiana, another local Hopewell-influenced complex seems to have developed. Both are regarded as terminal Marksville by most scholars.

The distinctive Marksville Tradition was followed by several less memorable cultures. They lack the flamboyance of the earlier Marksville, yet differences in ceramics and other practices and an increase in population appear to be documented. The Baytown (once called Deasonville) was perhaps the strongest, most widely distributed of these cultures and is found over much of the lower valley. But by 800 A.D. (possibly earlier) Coles Creek replaced the Baytown over most of the area. The most distinctive trait of the Coles Creek

manifestation was the construction of mounds, not conical or domed but carefully shaped, truncated pyramid structures from 6 to 10 meters in height. Buildings of wood and probably thatch were erected on the flat summits. These are regarded as having been temples or shrines. The concept of such mounds is usually explained as a direct diffusion out of Mexico—a simpler process than inventing the concept locally, especially since such substructures had existed there for some 2000 years. Sometimes there were two or more mounds set around a plaza, another Mexican practice. Associated with the mounds was a distinctive ceramic style characterized by deeply incised lines drawn parallel to the rim. The incising tool was held at a steep angle below the rim so the edges of the incised grooves seem to overlap or overhang those below. Subject to many variations through time, the Coles Creek incised ware is readily recognizable over a wide area for perhaps two or three hundred years.

But while the evolution of the lower valley cultures proceeded, a comparable phenomenon was occurring in the Midsouth, a broad area from the Mississippi River to the Appalachians south of the Mason-Dixon Line. A new culture called the Mississippian Tradition seems to have evolved across that broad front and is recognizable by about 800 A.D. over some of the area. No location of origin is pinpointed; none needs to be selected. We do not know at what spot any aboriginal culture began, nor will we. Cultures evolve; they are not created spontaneously.

The tradition is called Mississippian because it was first recognized in that valley and reached its ultimate complexity there. The largest North American site lies just south of the confluence of the Illinois, Missouri, and Mississippi Rivers. It is called Cahokia and is situated a few miles east of St. Louis, Missouri, in a broad alluvial plain called the American Bottom. The site takes its name from the dominant mound group of the entire complex, the Cahokia group. The group is centrally located in the bottom, which forms a shallow crescent 35 miles long and 10 or 11 miles wide at its widest point. It was first observed in 1811 and reported in 1818. Its worldwide fame and cultural importance was recognized when it was designated a World Heritage site, the only American location to be so designated. One reason for its fame is Monks Mound (Figure 5.23), an earthen flat-topped pyramid 100 feet high, covering 16 acres! Its height and area result from the addition of thirteen enlargements to the original tumulus. Low platforms were also added to the front of the truncated pyramid. The site has been extensively studied almost since discovery, but most work has been in the last 50 years. That research has revealed that the location was in continuous aboriginal use for at least 5000 years, since the beginning of Late Archaic times. The many mound groups themselves date varyingly from 800 to 1450 A.D., when the population dwindled and finally disappeared. More detailed treatment of Cahokia appears later in the chapter.

According to some students, the transition from simpler cultures to the Mississippian came when maize was first added to the already established horticultural technology possessed by the Archaic and Woodland cultures. A stronger overall stimulus may have been the cultural adaptation to a very special and productive ecosystem to be found in the wide valleys of meander streams. The American Bottom provides a classic example of the setting. The term *meander stream* simply refers to the fact that a strong river with a heavy, silt-laden flow and slow current because of a very slight gradient, continuously shifts its bed back and forth across the valley (Figure 5.24). The path of a meandering stream is a sinuous series of loops. Sometimes the continuous erosion of the banks cuts through the narrow neck of land between two loops; this changes the course of the river by bypassing the loop. The bypassed loop is called an ox-bow lake. Such lakes support catfish, drum, and other stillwater fish. Of course, these slow,

meandering streams are agrading, slowly filling their broad valleys. As is well-known, there are annual floods on all North American rivers following the winter snow melt. On such streams as the Ohio, Mississippi, and Missouri Rivers, the floods once covered the entire valley with many feet of water. Each flood carries millions of tons of silt, a load of sediment that is dropped as the stream velocity decreases. The velocity decreases as soon as the floodwaters breach the banks and the water spreads laterally and more slowly onto the flat valley. The sand and other heavy silt particles are dropped as soon as the water flow decelerates, so a ridge called a levee is created along both banks. The ridges contain the larger particles being transported. The fine particles are dropped only toward the edges of the valley where the floodwaters are essentially still. The dozens of natural levees that appear as ridges lining the banks of abandoned channels across the valley of the meandering stream provide rich, light agricultural soils as well as house and hamlet sites.

In addition to the levees, which comprise a relatively small percentage of the whole valley area, there are marshes and numerous oxbow lakes in the low areas between levees. The varying soil and moisture situations of the floodplain support a profuse biota of both terrestrial and aquatic species. Rich as the valley systems are in their own right, they also provide large energy resources that originated elsewhere. For example, the fish in the lakes are partially restocked annually during the floods, the river fish being trapped in the low areas when the floodwaters recede. But more important, the valleys, which are north-south oriented, constitute the major flyways for tens of millions of migratory waterfowl each spring and autumn as they follow their age-old annual migration rounds, resting on the lakes and marshes. It is estimated that 50 percent or more of all protein harvested by the Mississippian people in some areas came from fish and waterfowl. The remainder came from the bear, deer, turkey, and lesser animals

Figure 5.23 Monks Mound at Cahokia (East St. Louis, Illinois) with human figure on first level for scale.

in the dense forests and thickets of the bottomlands, which also provided edible fruits and berries. Deer and other game, as well as various nuts, were taken in abundance from the wooded uplands beyond the bluffs that border the valley. The supplies of fish and waterfowl provided what has been called an "externally powered" rich protein biomass that was subject to regular and heavy harvest with no danger of species depletion.

It is clear that a cluster of quite specific environmental or ecological attributes constitute the setting for the adaptation made by the Mississippian Tradition. It is also exactly the situation where the earliest and eventually largest sites are found. The largest sites are on the Mississippi and major tributaries from St. Louis southward, up the Ohio for a distance, and on the river systems of the Black Warrior in Alabama, and the Etowah and Ocmulgee rivers in Georgia. The Tennessee River is also lined with similar but smaller sites. Such a dispersal pattern implies deliberate search for optimal locations and their colonization. Of all these rivers the Mississippi provides the richest setting for this adaptation, the success of which is so evident in its distribution. When settlement pushed the later Mississippi populations into less resource-rich valleys, the usual high density of population could not be sustained. Thus the sites up the creeks and small rivers are usually smaller.

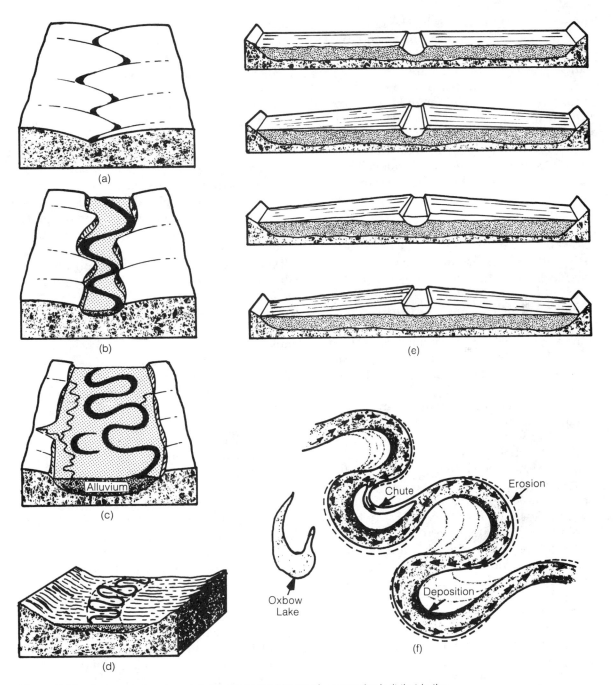

Figure 5.24 A meandering river: (a)–(c) shows the history of a meander belt that is the full width of the valley that encloses a meandering river, as in (d). (e) in greatly exaggerated scale, shows the construction over time of a natural levee. The levee remains when the river changes course. (f) shows the presence of the chute that will eventually "steal" the main current and leave the meander belt without stream flow thus making another oxbow lake.

(a)

(b)

(c)

Alluvium

(d)

(e)

(f)

Chute

Erosion

Deposition

Oxbow
Lake

There are also typical sites on the northwest coast of Florida, in Illinois, Iowa, and Wisconsin, where similar, but not identical, resources are available in quantity.

Although the farmsteads were in the bottoms, the big towns with mounds and plazas were often on the bluffs alongside the streams, although some major ones are also found on high ground out in the bottomlands themselves. As mentioned earlier, Cahokia lies on high ground in a north-central situation near an oxbow lake in the American Bottom near St. Louis.

As can be imagined, the details of the Tennessee or Wisconsin occurrences of the Mississippian, as well as some of the southern ones, differ from the core area where the tradition is believed to have taken form. The existence of such regional variants can only be noted. There is no space to describe each of them. Suffice it to say that the variants tend to be delimited by the distribution of distinctive ceramic systems that dominate the subregions.

The only reasonable way to avoid the swamp of detail required by a consideration of the local variations is to construct a composite account of the constellation of material, architecture, and subsistence traits and of the inferred accompanying social behavior at the zenith of Mississippian climax at 1400 to 1450 A.D. This description can be considered a blend of midwestern and southern manifestations of the culture. It must be kept in mind, too, that the extraordinary success of the Mississippian lifeway resulted from the adaptation to the special river valley–upland econiches and the intensive food production made possible by the cultigens: corn, beans, squash, sunflower, and gourd. Possibly some of the more prolific cultivars (maygrass, knotweed, and goosefoot) exploited during Archaic and Woodland times were still used, but their lower yields would have caused them soon to be dropped from the list of cultivated plants. The mix of agricultural and natural products constantly being harvested and a series of

storage techniques would ensure subsistence support for a relatively dense population. More intense agricultural practices would, of course, permit an increase in population through time.

A digression about maize and its effect on the culture history of eastern North America is in order here. Maize, Indian maize, or Indian corn, usually simply called corn, is an indigenous New World plant. Along with a number of other foods, such as chocolate, capsicum peppers, pineapple, avocado, tomato, white and sweet potatoes, and the common bean, maize became varyingly popular when introduced into the Old World. Among all these, however, maize is the most adaptable and has achieved the greatest worldwide distribution, even though it is of tropical or subtropical origin. It was originally, and is today, regarded botanically as a grass. What mutations it went through to achieve its modern form and what species of grass was its ultimate ancestor are still debated by botanists and plant geneticists. The mystery of maize remains in spite of four centuries of concern, study, and speculation. Origins may or may not be settled by biologists, but that is not the prime question facing archaeologists. Their concern is with corn's place in prehistory.

Evidently corn had achieved its familiar form when it reached the eastern United States. By then the plant had a few broad leaves, feathery, pollen-covered tassels, and a few ears studded with (usually) eight rows of tightly packed kernels protected by overlapping layers of husks, all on a sturdy stalk. That basic form was achieved in northern Mexico well before 2000 B.P. Its mutations, evolution, and phenotypic changes had in fact begun by 7000 B.P. in the Valley of Mexico where teosinte, the strongest candidate for the progenitor role, still grows.

Corn is perhaps the most adaptable of all cultivated plants. It now grows from sea level to the high Andes; its distribution extends from Canada in North America as far south as Chile in South America. Its distribution around the rest of the world is comparable. The only constraints maize appears to face are a short growing season and inadequate moisture at planting time and again at about two-thirds of its growth toward maturity. It must have hot growing weather. A few aboriginal strains could mature in 90 to 100 days, although most modern farmers consider 110 to 120 days to be the minimum corn season. After decades of work by geneticists, there are now sweet corn strains that mature in as little as forty to fifty days and flour corns that mature in one hundred days or less. The aboriginal strains undoubtedly matured more slowly. Where weather permits (in the tropics), two crops a year are often grown.

The importance of corn to the original Americans has been overemphasized in the past. The reason for this is that before the discovery of the plants of the Eastern Agricultural Complex, scholars, had reasoned that the sophisticated Adena and Hopewell cultures could not have developed without a maize agriculture base. The mistake came naturally by projecting back deep into time the quite evident dependence of historic Native Americans on corn, beans, and squash.

Corn was evidently introduced into the Southwest no sooner than about 2700 B.P. After the terminal Archaic population there began cultivating it, using Mexican techniques, the plant spread rapidly from southern Arizona to Colorado, Utah, and northern New Mexico well before 1 A.D. It was also found in the Rio Grande Valley. Thereafter it was part of the subsistence mix for all the agricultural groups of the Southwest. Even the late-arriving Apache groups, including the Navajo, slowly adopted limited corn agriculture. But corn was not common in the East until after 800 A.D. or later.

Although a maize grain from the Icehouse Bottom site was assayed by TAMS at 175 A.D. ± 110, no other reliably dated specimen is that old. In fact most Midwest students today view the early Mississippi cultures of about 900 or 1000 A.D. as the first intensive cultivators of corn in the East where it was possibly introduced through the Plains from the Southwest.

The basis for the present position that corn became important in the eastern diet so recently rests on solid, if inferential, evidence. Like some other tropical plants, corn takes up and fixes more ^{13}C than most plants in the temperate zone. Bones preserve the $^{12}C{:}^{13}C$ ratio, so animals eating temperate zone plants show less ^{13}C than animals living on tropical plants such as maize. It is assumed that a human population with more ^{13}C in its bones shows evidence of a heavy maize component in its diet. When skeletal remains from sites dating from 4000 B.P. to 1000 A.D. were assayed, the ^{13}C content of Archaic Old Copper and Early Woodland burials showed very low ^{13}C, while human bone from Aztalan and Cahokia showed a significantly higher range of ^{13}C than the earlier, presumably non-maize-growing populations. Interestingly, the low-status burials at Aztalan had more ^{13}C than high-status ones. The situation was reversed in the Cahokia burials tested, the elite having had the heavier maize diet. Other tests, from Archaic and Mature Mississippian sites in Arkansas and Missouri, gave identical results, showing maize to have become important in the Mississippian sites there only after 1000 A.D. Bones from early Arkansas and Missouri sites show no ^{13}C difference from the preceding Middle Woodland period.

Squash, by now an important item of diet, was noted in the Late Archaic as early as 5000 B.P., but its status as a cultigen at that time is dubious. Beans, however, do not appear until after A.D. 1000 and examples are few. Thus the dietary base observed in the first historic contacts had been fully established only about 500 years, contrary to earlier beliefs. The rise of the Mississippi culture; the strength of the villages along the rivers of the Plains; and the potency of the Iroquois, Illinois, and Creek tribal confederacies are usually credited to maize. However, maize is by no means the perfect food. It lacks necessary protein, enzymes, and vitamins. It must be combined with beans, squash, and some animal protein to provide its part of a balanced diet.

The discussion of maize as a staple food requires review in the context of the much larger concept of food production. It is interesting to note that worldwide, coincident with an increasing dependence on any cereal, the overall health and quality of life of a population deteriorates in many ways. As mentioned in Chapter One, many diseases and nutritional deficiencies or stresses leave evidence of their occurrence in the bones of the body. Thus it is possible for a paleopathologist to detect in the skeleton many of the unhealthful conditions individuals have experienced during their lives. Thanks to research with archaeological populations recovered from locations in the Americas, Europe, and the Near East, it has been possible for scholars to arrive at some general observations that are contrary to one's expectations. Most of the paleopathologies observed in both historic and prehistoric skeletal populations are related to nutritional stress. Foods lacking in minerals, basic fats, proteins, and amino acids and, more commonly, insufficient food over varyingly long periods of time leave their marks.

Diseases that cause bone lesions, as well as others that leave no skeletal evidence, are more likely to attack during periods of nutritional stress. Even more conducive to infectious diseases are the unsanitary conditions attending sedentism, a living pattern that usually accompanies the practice of horticulture. When prehistoric people lived together in permanent or semipermanent housing in clustered situations, the incidence of tuberculosis increased markedly, in some Midwest farming populations, for example, over the Woodland incidence of the disease.

Some of the common stresses leave distinctive signs such as enamel hypoplasia (uneven or incomplete deposition of tooth enamel). Caries can result from inadequate protective veneer of enamel, but more im-

portant, they are encouraged by the preponderance of carbohydrates in the soft mushy foods made from cereal grains. None of the worldwide cereals used as permanent items of diet provide balanced nutrition.

Equally easy to identify are Harris lines. These occur in the long bones of children when normal growth is temporarily halted. Thus Harris lines record successive periods of illness or food shortage, followed by normal health or food intake. The bones preserve these events in a permanent record of childhood stresses. The cranium can show both surficial cortical loss and porosity as well as abnormal thickening, a condition caused by chronic anemia. Long bones also reveal cortical loss as a result of continued stress. Of course, reduction of stature (stunting) occurs if the population is chronically stressed by inadequate diet. There is, oddly enough, a decrease in the frequency of arthritis among farmers. While it is still common it is less frequent than among hunter-gatherers. Presumably there are fewer incidents of extreme physical stress on farmers than on hunter-gatherers.

A surprising finding was that intensive agriculturalists had a shorter average life expectancy than the earlier hunter-gatherers. Overall then, the quality and length of life declined as farming supplemented the earlier foraging subsistence pattern. As has been noted, however, no prehistoric American population or culture ever abandoned the collection of wild faunal and floral foods. If the use of wild foods had not persisted, the record of American health might have been even more dismal. In any event, it seems clear that greater reliance on grain carbohydrates in the diet leads to nutritional imbalance, disease, and stress as described above.

We return now to a description of the Mississippian culture. Most Mississippian sites and mounds (if any) are small, so the sheer size of the few well-known Mississippian sites is overwhelming. These sites are characterized by clusters of mounds, some of which are truncated pyramids, arranged around a plaza (Figure 5.25). There may be conical mounds adjacent, but they are arranged in no apparent pattern. Even today after centuries of erosion many sites reveal an encircling embankment; outside the palisade of posts atop the earthen embankment the borrow pit stood open as a moat. Villages were not always nearby or inside the palisade. Normally they were scattered through the farmlands in the valleys. These huge sites can be thought of as religious, administrative, or even economic centers such as are presaged in the Hopewellian sites and are common in Mexico and Central America. These centers were sup-

ported by a large, dependent population that provided both food and thousands of hours of corvée labor for powerful priest-ruler and artisan classes.

The temple mounds are larger and far more pretentious than the Hopewell burial mounds ever were. These pyramidal earthworks reached enormous size as one increment after another was added to quite sizable nuclei. As many as six or eight or more construction phases have been identified in some of the mounds. The flat tops of the mounds supported presumably religious structures built of wood, mud, and thatch, usually in rectangular form. The mounds were enlarged by

Figure 5.25 The Anna Mound group near Natchez, Mississippi. It is situated on a projecting loess bluff on the east bank of the Mississippi River. The shape of the area prevented the building of the usual four-square plaza.

the periodic destruction (sometimes by burning) of the shrines or temples and addition of another layer or shell of earth over the entire pyramid to create a larger, higher structure on the same spot in the same pattern. Thus the larger mounds resemble a Chinese egg, with each pyramid enveloping an earlier, smaller one. While primarily built to support a structure, the mounds often contained burials of important dead accompanied by rich grave furnishings.

The largest known mound, called Monks Mound, is at Cahokia in the American Bottom. The major mound at Etowah is over 60 feet high and 330 by 380 feet at the base. Even at lesser sites the dominant mound is commonly 40 to 50 feet high. The figure one computes for cubic feet of earth (22,000,000 for Cahokia, 4,300,000 for Etowah—every ounce carried on human backs), is awesome when transformed into work-hours. Access to the steep-sided mounds was by means of almost equally steep ramps into which log steps were sometimes laid. These ramps can still be seen on some of the late sites. Several important sites or portions of them have been preserved as national or state monuments—the Macon group, Etowah, Moundville, Angel, and part of the Cahokia group for example—and their testimony to lost glories is indeed eloquent.

Although none of the Mississippian sites has been completely excavated and analyzed in detail, partially because of their great size and the costs of archaeological work, many have been sampled. Thousands of ceramic pieces have been taken from the large cemeteries adjacent to the villages and from the burials of important dead interred through temple floors on the flat summits of the pyramids. Furthermore, each site is littered with broken pottery; tons of sherds have been collected and studied and have aided in interpretation. Regional and local chronologies alike are built on pottery differences and likenesses. Restricted as we are to the ceramics, however, there are other data of considerable strength, including what early European ex

plorers saw and recorded of the culture. Thus we are sometimes able to infuse the dead evidence with life from ethnographic analogs.

Much is known of the subsistence and technology. Maize agriculture was everywhere the base with squash and beans and some now-wild species also cultivated or collected. Deer were usually the major source of meat, as well as of hide and bone for raw material. This is to say nothing of the bear, elk, and wide spectrum of smaller animals, preyed upon since the earliest Archaic stage, that continued to be important food sources. Freshwater shellfish and fish, especially the drum, were another steady source of protein. Because the sites lie open in an area of much vegetation and heavy rainfall, perishable materials have usually not survived the centuries of alternate wetting and drying unless they have been accidentally charred. So, although adequate evidence for basketry, matting, bark cloth, and skin utensils exists, most artifacts are of bone, shell, antler, stone, and fired clay, with some of copper and other minerals. The gardening was done with large hoes of chipped flint weighing several pounds. The shoulder blades of large mammals also made good hoes, as did large bivalve shells. Cutting tools were of fire-hardened cane and chipped stone, as were the hunting tools and weapons. The bow was the standard weapon; the arrows were tipped with small, triangular, notched, chipped points or with bone or antler points. Fish were commonly taken on hooks of copper or bone, very probably on long setlines. A variety of chipped stone tools include knives (with wooden handles), scrapers of many types, drills, and other forms. Shell was used for beads of several types and for cups, hoes, bowls, and dippers; after being heated and crushed, fresh or burned shell was also widely used as pottery temper, a marked advance in ceramic technology. Physical and chemical tests have shown that shell, especially if burned, increases a pottery vessel's resistance to cracking, shattering, and thermal shock. Ground stone specimens include pipes, celts, axes, adzes, and some mill-stones, although most milling was done with wooden mortars and pestles. Bone awls, needles, chisels, pins, and arrow wrenches were made in a bewildering variety of forms.

While the above items are relatively standard and resemble to some degree similar items from earlier Woodland cultures, most diagnostic materials are ceramic. Clay is completely responsive to the modeler's touch and can reveal either rigid tradition or the passing whim of the artisan. Mississippian pottery is the most varied in form and decoration and the most sensitive reflector of changing style, or other influence, of any in America north of Mexico. The skilled potters turned out two general classes of pottery. Perhaps 95 percent was utilitarian. Its surface was almost always plain, although in some areas brushing, fabric imprinting, or even cord marking was practiced. The utilitarian wares were unpainted red, brown, or gray, the color being merely a function of firing temperatures and the chemical content of the clay itself. Shell-tempering was also the dominant practice, but other aplastics are noted. One described type (here accepted as typical) is Neeleys Ferry Plain jars, with globular body, recurved rim, and a vague shoulder as the most common shape. This vessel shape (Figure 5.26) is the "standard Mississippi jar." Bowls and bottles are also standard and widespread.

There are many secondary features in some classes of the pottery. Loop and strap handles occur (twinned or arcaded). Flat rim lugs (which were handles), zoomorphic rim ornaments, and appliqued fillets to form conventional animal or human effigies are among the common adornments (Figure 5.27). The treatment of the plain clay surface is remarkably varied as well. Incising (sometimes engraving), **trailing,** punctation, or encrusting with clay fillets are among the techniques. Hatching and cross-hatching; graceful, cursive, trailed designs; fluting; and zonal whorls and spirals are among the decorative motifs executed on the plastic surface. Some analysts

see many of the designs as well as the techniques themselves as easily traced back through the transitional stages such as Troyville and Issaquena to Hopewell originals, although the vessel forms differ from the Woodland models.

The ceramics found as grave furniture tend to include more decorated ware (as described above); the use of paint and **negative painting** is more common, and more effigy jars and bottles are found. As Figure 5.28 demonstrates, many of these pieces are extraordinary examples of ceramic art, whether judged on technological or aesthetic grounds. Generally the lower Ohio Valley and the Tennessee-Cumberland valleys provide the most exquisite sculptured effigy bottles, although many specimens are found in the central Mississippi Valley as well. Wherever salt licks are found, the aboriginals manufactured salt in flat pans of very coarse, thick ware. These were often deeply marked with netlike fabric. Along with the work of the compulsive potters of the Southwest (being done at about the same time), the thousands of extant Mississippian vessels comprise a rich array of Native American art. Mississippian decorative techniques had little influence on the pottery of the extreme Southeast in coastal South Carolina and most of Georgia. There the simple paddle stamping that began in an Archaic context persisted until the advent of the Europeans.

The potters were only one of the artisan groups. Shellworkers engraved and carved *Busycon* shell with the columella removed for ornaments and pendants, and used the columella to make knobbed hairpins; tubular, disc-shaped, and globular beads; and other ornaments as well. Other skilled craftsmen made bracelets, beads, headdresses, and a few hairpins from the copper produced locally in Tennessee and northern Georgia, and decorated thin sheets of hammered copper with a repoussé technique. Copper was also used to cover, or "jacket," wooden ornaments.

Turning from artifacts to other technology, there are reliable data on architecture. From

0   6 in.

Figure 5.26   Neeleys Ferry Plain jars from Mississippi.

many reports we know that the Mississippian houses, as well as the temples (shrines), council chambers, and chiefs' houses were soundly built of poles, often with sturdy, vertical, wattled (woven) walls and probably gabled roofs with rafters and thatch. Often the wattled timber elements (flexible canes or withes threaded between, or tied to, posts up to 6 inches in diameter) were plastered with mud inside and out to make a thick, impervious wall (but one that required frequent repair). Posts were sometimes set in narrow trenches up to 18 inches deep or in deep individual postholes. Although almost every house shape—square, rectangular, rectangular with rounded corners, oval, and circular— has been found and reported in the literature, most houses seem to have been square or rectangular.

Inside the dwellings there was a more-or-less centrally located fireplace or hearth. This was a shallow pit or basin with a raised, modeled ring of clay baked to bricklike hardness through repeated firings. Often the floor was of specially selected clay, "puddled," (thoroughly wetted and packed down) so that it was exceedingly hard and durable. In Tennessee some structures, called ceremonial lodges, had raised platforms called altars built along the wall opposite the entrance. Temples or chiefs' houses atop the mounds show about the same interior features, but we know from sixteenth and seventeenth century accounts that these special structures had effigy and other adornments on their roofs. All in all, the recent literature is of good quality, and the student wishing to specialize in studying the Southeast will find it a stimulating, if still

Figure 5.27 Mississippian bowls and bottles: (a) Neeleys Ferry Plain Bowl; (b) and (c) Bell Plain bowls; (d) Old Town Red bowl; (e) and (f) Neeleys Ferry Plain bird effigy bowls; (g) Bell Plain effigy bowl; (h) and (i) Bell Plain human effigy bowls; (j), (k), and (m) Neeleys Ferry Plain bottles; (l) Neeleys Ferry or Bell Plain bottle with perforated base.

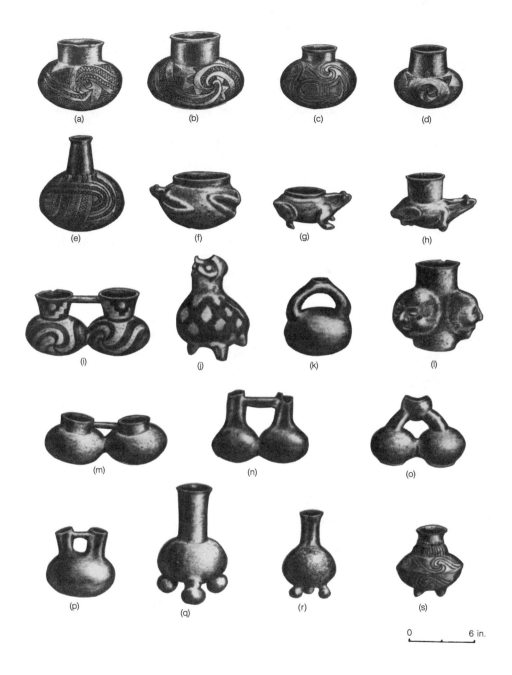

Figure 5.28   Mississippian pottery: (a)–(e) variants of Walls Engraved bottles, (f)–(h) Bell Plain frog effigy vessels, (i) Nodena Red and White double bottle, (j) Nodena Red and White hooded owl effigy bottle, (k) Bell Plain or Neeleys Ferry stirrup-necked bottle, (l) Bell Plain human-effigy bottle, (m) and (n) Bell Plain double bottles, (o) Bell Plain modified stirrup-necked bottle, (p) Neeleys Ferry Plain double bottle, (q) and (r) Bell Plain tripod bottles, (s) tripod bottle.

incompletely understood, sequence of cultures. The Mississippian is merely the overwhelming end product of a long process of interaction and interinfluence between the cultures.

A bit more should, perhaps, be said about settlement patterns in view of the recent great interest in that phase of the tradition. Among other things analysis of settlement patterning has shown that it both exemplifies and reinforces the social system. The use of space is seen as particularly revealing. The Cahokia and Moundville sites can serve as examples.

The sequence of cultures in the American Bottom, where Monks Mound sits, and the bluffs overlooking the valley from the east extends from 5000 B.P. to about 1500 A.D. There must be earlier evidence long lost in the deep sediments; certainly the resources of the area would have attracted inhabitants from PaleoIndian times onward. Knowledge of the Cahokia chronology has been accumulating over the years; it is based largely on ceramics. In 1975 the construction of Interstate Highway I 255 (originally I 270) led to a massive and well-designed salvage excavation and mitigation program. The new highway was routed along the foot of the bluffs, and there were many borrow pit areas on the edge of the low ground as well. Scores of sites were in danger within the 21-mile right-of-way; others lay in the borrow areas outside the corridor. Of these sites 101 were excavated, many completely. The corridor intercepted sites that could be identified with all the major known or suspected phases in the area. The data permitted the refinement of the broad Mississippian sequence established in the 1970s. It also identified several earlier Archaic and Woodland manifestations. When the I 255 research began, the Mississippian sequence consisted of four phases. By 1984 eleven phases (some tentative) were described for the same span of years—800 to 1450 A.D. Of course, many of the distinguishing characteristics from phase to phase are ceramic, but differences

in settlement pattern and architecture are also present. Before 800 A.D., however, the sequence runs back to at least 5000 B.P. The sequence now established is as follows:

Date	Local Phase	Cultural Tradition
1600–2000 A.D.	Colonial and American	Historic
1400–1600	Vulcan	Oneota
1250–1400	Sand Prairie	Mississip-
1150–1250	Moorehead	pian
1050–1150	Stirling	
1000–1050	Lohman	
950–1000	Edelhardt-Lindemann	
900–950	Merrell-George	
800–900	Reeves Loyd-Range/ Dohack	Emerging Mississippian
600–800	Patrick	Late
475–600	Mund	Wood-
300–475	Rosewood	land
1–300	Hill Lake	Middle
2150 B.P.–1 A.D.	Cement Hollow	Wood- land
2300–2150 B.P.	Columbia	Early
2600–2300	Marion/ Florence	Wood- land
3000–2600	Prairie Lake	Late
3900–3000	Labras Lake	Archaic
4300–3900	Titterington	
5000+–4300	Falling Springs	

Most of the sites were small, especially in the early phases, but during Middle and Late Woodland times, there were hamlets with twenty or more houses or other structures. The Late Archaic villages were found in the floodplain and on the uplands, with the Middle Woodland only on the plain. Late Woodland sites were in the lowland. In fact, Late Woodland artifacts were found under the Monks and Powells mounds on the valley floor. There is neither space nor need to attempt a summary of the I 255 findings. That has already filled one volume (Bareis and Porter 1984). The intent of this passage has been to demonstrate the richness and complexity of the prehistoric episodes in the American Bottom.

We turn now to a description of the Cahokia site itself. Cahokia is only one of the sites located in the American Bottom. Before extensive destruction incident to metropolitan development and intensive agricultural use, there were over 100 platform and conical mounds clustered on the high ground around Monks Mound.

Monks Mound dominated from its north end a vast plaza of some 200 acres enclosed in a bastioned palisade or stockade of large posts. Along each side of the plaza were twelve or more platform and conical mounds with a single platform at the south end of the plaza. Outside the Monks Mound enclosure to the north, south, east, and west were dozens of other mounds dominating smaller plazas. But there were four other large, but lesser mound groups clustered around smaller plazas (Figure 5.29). One was where St. Louis now stands; another was immediately across the river. Both were on the bluffs overlooking the Mississippi. To the south end of the American Bottom, near the mouth of the Meramac River stood the Pulcher site; to the north, opposite the Missouri's confluence with the Mississippi, stood the fourth, called the Mitchell Group. Each of these mound groups covered more than 125 acres. Near the Cahokia and Mitchell groups were four locations marked

by only one low mound. Everywhere over the entire bottom and on the valley bluffs to the east were scores of hamlets and farmsteads, which are believed to have supported the centers with foodstuffs and services.

The distribution of the big sites, their locations on water courses, and their very size lead some scholars to postulate that they were religious and administrative centers, peopled primarily by a powerful upper class that controlled trade and, possibly, population distribution and, of course, possessed absolute political and religious power. Cahokia was said to be the center of this system; Mitchell, Pulcher, and the St. Louis sites were perhaps the seats of district administrations. The St. Louis and Mitchell sites especially could have controlled the rivers, the avenues of commerce and communication.

There is no doubt that there was an elite Mississippian social class. This is attested by the rich mortuary offerings and the (presumed) elaborate ceremonies with which the burials were made. Burials occurred on the tops of the pyramid mounds, a mortuary ritual that can be identified wherever the mound groups are found. The uniformity of occurrence has led to the interpretation that there were elite lineages and that their high status was ascribed by virtue of birth, because even children were sometimes accorded elaborate burial ceremony and grave goods. However, near or in the towns were large cemeteries, where lower-class citizens were buried. Here, too, there is an occasional richly accompanied burial, but the objects are of a different nature, such as the tools or creations of a craftsman. Such persons are believed to have achieved a relatively high status through merit rather than birth.

Given the concept of the stratified chiefdom social system, the interpretation of the function of the large mound groups as control centers for political, religious, or economic reasons, or all of them, seems quite reasonable at first glance. But none of the big sites was built in a day; there seems always to have

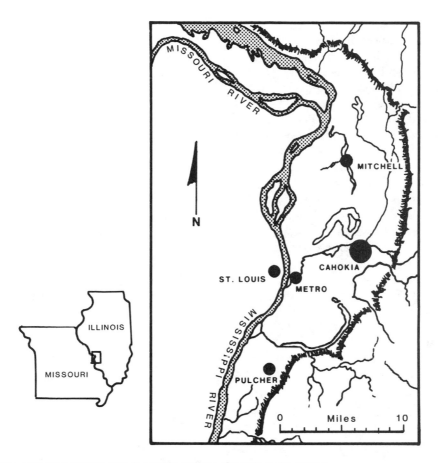

Figure 5.29   The American Bottom showing major centers. Cahokia is the largest.

been a modest beginning, a period of building and expansion, and finally a period of shrinking, decline, and final abandonment. (Monks Mound construction extended over 300 years from 900 to 1200 A.D.) Moreover, the major mound groups are of different ages. The Pulcher site seems to have been abandoned by 1050 A.D., whereas the first construction at Mitchell is thought to have occurred 100 years later at 1150 A.D. Monks Mound itself was begun at 900 A.D. It is evident that there were marked changes in population density over the American Bottom through time. It appears that the outlying centers were serially occupied and were never at full strength at the same time.

Several studies show that population density, from Cahokia southward, was greatest during the Stirling phase, and diminished steadily thereafter. Cahokia was probably occupied during both the Emergent and Mature Mississippian sequence; it was also the largest group. Perhaps it was dominant, perhaps it exercised some measure of control over the entire bottom and was indeed at the top of the community hierarchy. But the concept of a hierarchy of sites remains in the realm of theory, requiring further testing.

Another vital Mississippi community that lasted from 1200 to 1500 A.D. was at Moundville, on the Black Warrior River floodplain not far from Tuscaloosa, Alabama. The ecological situation there is entirely comparable to the conditions along the Mississippi River except that it is smaller in scale. The Moundville cultural central place is a series of platform mounds around a 100-acre plaza bounded on three sides by a stockade and on the fourth by the bank of the Black Warrior River. The dominant mound is almost 60 feet high; the plaza was ringed with buildings of varying sizes and functions (Figure 5.30). Some of the smaller platforms held richly accompanied burials. Along the edges of the plaza was a vast cemetery from which over 3000 burials were recovered. From these burial data came the firmest evidence of the stratified nature of the Mississippian society (similar studies have been made at Etowah and other southern sites). Moundville is central to a series of sites situated along a 20-mile stretch of the Black Warrior River valley. There are seventeen mounds or mound groups (with a solitary one 15 miles farther downstream), Moundville itself being the largest.

Moundville's highest status citizens were buried with elaborate artifacts, including large copper celts and specimens of the exquisite black-filmed, incised and engraved pottery so common at this site. They were interred in pyramidal, platform, and domed mounds. In and near the platform mounds were burials of less-exhalted status but still rich in grave offerings.

The purpose of the palisades that are almost always found at large sites after about 1200 A.D. is not altogether clear. They are often interpreted as defenses against rival centers,

Figure 5.30 Aerial view, looking northwest, of Moundville (Alabama) group. The large mound with the building on it (center of photograph) is almost sixty feet high.

or even marauding non-Mississippian peoples, because they sometimes surround the entire town. They more likely should be seen as barriers between the elite and the bulk of the population, the lower classes who lived in the scattered hamlets of the hinterland. At any rate, the palisades appear to have been maintained and often rebuilt. Similar palisades are reported for some of the very late prehistoric tribes of the Missouri River. Of course, the Plains culture adopted many of the Mississippian concepts quite early as they were transmitted up the Missouri from the American Bottom metropolis at Cahokia.

In addition to a history of Mississippian initial stages, expansion, and final decline, many of the famous Mississippian centers show continuous use by much earlier cultures. An excellent and well-reported example is the Lake George site near Holly Bluff, Mississippi (Figure 5.31). On a broad, natural levee, it is a cluster of mounds in a plaza arrangement (the tallest 55 feet high) in a 55-acre enclosure on the bank of Lake George, an old meander of the Yazoo River. The rectangular embankment (once supporting a palisade of logs), encircles the site on the three sides away from the lake. Along the lakeshore, which forms the north side of the enclosure, were perhaps a dozen other mounds or terraces.

The excavation program revealed a 3000-year sequence at the Lake George site. The earliest Mississippi Valley culture represented was the Poverty Point, which has already been described. Then came scattered finds of Tchefuncte/Tchula (Early Woodland) and Marksville (Middle Woodland) materials. Next was the Baytown/Deasonville and construction of two small platform mounds west of the main mound. The first phase of the large platform mound was erected during the ensuing Coles Creek occupation. Most of the pyramidal mounds were built during Early Mississippian times, here called Plaquemine. In the final phases of the Mississippian occupation, there was only a renewal of the dominant

mound, construction of the stockade, and ultimate abandonment by 1500 A.D. or earlier.

The Southern Cult or Southern Ceremonial Complex

At about 1200 A.D., when the Mississippian cultures were approaching the height of their strength, a complex of exotic artifacts appeared. The distribution of these objects is pan-Mississippian. They are found at major sites from central Illinois to eastern Oklahoma and from Georgia to the tip of Florida. The widest variety of objects, however, came from a few widely scattered southern sites. Etowah in Georgia, Spiro in Oklahoma, Moundville in Alabama, and some sites on the Tennessee River seem to have yielded the best known and largest collections.

The objects are an exquisite expression of artistry combined with skilled craftsmanship. The artifacts were created in every medium: wood, shell, clay, stone, and hammered copper. The art is concerned with depicting animals, humans, mythical creatures, tools, and weapons, using dozens of themes and scores of motifs. The artifacts are not utilitarian but ornamental and are undoubtedly rich in conventional and symbolic meaning. As a subject for study they have attracted attention for a century. Much speculation has attended that study; the complex of artifacts is said to have been a death cult because of the skull, hand-eye, and other motifs. But what function the artifacts served is not yet completely known. (Our ignorance of the function of these art pieces is in strong contrast to that of the Northwest Coast (Chapter Four), where rich ethnographic data provide knowledge of the symbolic value of that art.) Some scholars interpret them as being merely prestige items. Others see them as symbols of powerful ancestor personages and thus imbued with strong supernatural power, perhaps similar to the Polynesian concept of *mana*, which car-

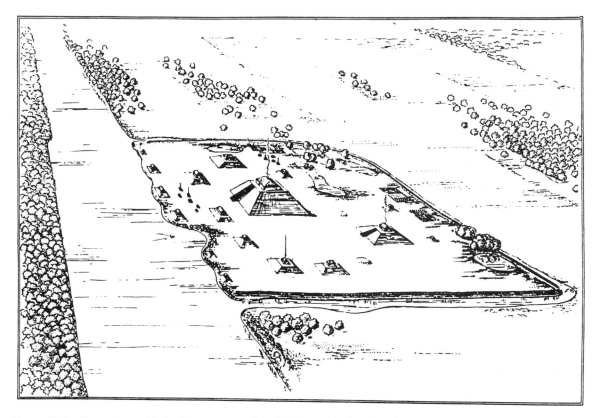

Figure 5.31   Reconstructed Lake George group (as of 1200 A.D.) in the "delta" near Holly Bluff, Mississippi. The dominant pyramid is 55 feet high.

ries the twin connotations of sacredness and danger.

Since the cult objects are recovered from, or near, high-status mound burials, the pieces are presumed to be part of the paraphernalia of rank or priestly status and most probably used in rituals. Some of the themes may point to human sacrifices.

The artifacts are quite varied in form, but the same themes recur. Copper was used in headdresses; to jacket wooden earplugs; and for plaques with cult designs in raised relief, celts, and indeterminate shapes (Figure 5.32). The designs were engraved on Gulf shell cups,

bowls, gorgets, and pins. Elaborate sculptured human and animal forms were depicted on heavy stone pipes (Figure 5.33). Monolithic stone axes replicating the form of a celt set in a wooden handle are found. Beautifully detailed and highly polished, those objects must have been highly prized; they are rarely found. Round stone plaques or paint palettes are fairly common. Some of the frequently used motifs are the hawk, eagle, and ivory-billed or pileated woodpecker. Animals include the raccoon, spider, rattlesnake, and mythical *piasa* (depicted as a sinuous dragon shape with legs). Human parts used are the hand, the eye, the weeping eye, the hand-eye (with the eye in the palm of the hand), severed or trophy heads and skulls, and leg bones. Other motifs are the arrow, the bilobed arrow, and the forked staff. Among the favored themes is the winged warrior or bird-man, paired or single; entwined snakes; snake-men; central spider; and central severed bird head. Large, eccentrically shaped blades of skillfully chipped flint are standard cult items. The representations of human sacrifice in pipe sculpture, the daggers in the hands of some of the bird-man warriors or priests, severed heads, and many of the other symbols strongly suggest warfare or rituals of human sacrifice. Some of these artifacts and motifs are not new. Some seem to be a legacy from the Hopewell and even the Adena. On the other hand, the depiction of human sacrifice is interpreted by some as evidence of strong Mexican cultism, even perhaps of an increment of high-ranking individuals into the South. Others defend it as a climax phenomenon, developed autonomously **in situ** from the ceremonialism already evident throughout the East for some 2000 years. Some specialists in Southeast prehistory even deny cult or any coherent cluster of behavior surrounding the special objects. Instead they assert that the value of the cult artifacts is intrinsic. They hold that the wide dispersal of the objects, well beyond the Mississippian sphere of influence indicates that the rare exotics were created exclusively for trade.

The Moundville and Etowah are equally renowned locations where these objects have been found. Details of the Etowah site and some of its special pieces are presented in Figure 5.34. Other "cult" objects are pictured in Figures 5.35–5.37. Note the similarities between Spiro and Etowah axes and **mace**like artifacts.

Even during its decline or decay in the face of European pressures (and donated diseases such as measles, tuberculosis, and the common cold), the bloody strength of Mississippian ritual could still be seen in the burial

ceremony for the Natchez warrior Tattooed Serpent. The ceremony was reported in 1725 with unnerving realism by the Dutch author DuPratz, who was living in the French colony near the present town of Natchez, Mississippi (see below).

Although by no means a complete discussion, the above paragraphs and figures can convey an idea of a generalized Mississippian. At the height of its strength, a Mississippian center would have been exciting to visit. The tall mounds towering above the flat river valley, with thatched temples adding several feet of height to the pyramids, would have been visible above the palisade for many miles as one approached along well-worn trails past extensive fields. Carved effigies of birds and other creatures perched on the rounded temple roofs or ridge poles would have given added color, while from each temple drifted the smoke of an eternal fire. At sunup the priests, in rich regalia and ornaments of copper, shell, and feathers, would offer prayers and greetings to the sun, calling his blessing on the land.

On festival or ritual days the plaza would be the scene of fiercely fought ball games akin to lacrosse or complicated dances done to the rhythm of drums and rattles and the music of many singers. Like the priests, the dancers would be colorfully dressed in rich costumes and ornaments. The Creek Busk or Green Corn festival of thanksgiving, held on the dance ground even into the twentieth century, probably preserves a faded vestige of the Mississippian splendor. Some of the rituals would have involved purification and long-drawn-out ceremonies of human sacrifice to one or another god, while the people from all supporting villages crowded the plaza to watch the dancers and priests go in procession up the steep stairways to the summit of the mound, where the sacrificial climax was reached.

At other times, the scene at the plaza would involve the death and burial of a priest-ruler. These rituals also involved many days of

Figure 5.32 Artifacts from the Spiro and Etowah mounds: (a) embossed sheet-copper eagle, 11½ inches high; (b) embossed sheet-copper human head; (c) copper-covered ear spools; (d) embossed sheet-copper feather; (e) embossed sheet-copper snake; (f) shell gorget of hand symbol, 3⅜ inches high; (g) embossed sheet-copper design; (h) shell gorget of world symbol with woodpeckers; (i) shell design of the piasa, 8 inches in diameter; (j) shell design of two snake dancers, 12⅜ inches long; (k) embossed sheet-copper design of dancer wearing eagle paraphernalia, 20 inches long; (l) sheet-copper symbol.

Figure 5.33 Artifacts from Spiro Mound: (a) shell-inlaid mask of red cedar, 11 ⅜ inches high; (b) monolithic stone ax, 5 ½ inches long; (c) hafted copper ax, 13 inches long (pileated woodpecker effigy, shell-inlaid eye); (d) turtle effigy rattle of red cedar, 6 ⅞ inches long; (e) front and side views of human sacrifice clay effigy pipe, 9 ¾ inches high; (f) chipped stone **mace,** 20 inches long; (g) polished stone mace, 13 ¾ inches long; (h) polished stone **spuds,** longest 23 inches; (i) human effigy of red cedar, 11 ¼ inches high; (j) composite animal-bird stone effigy pipe, 2 inches long at base; (k) stone effigy pipe, 9 ⅞ inches high (woman with mortar and ear of corn).

Figure 5.34 Etowah (Georgia) and associated artifacts: (a) reconstruction of site with human figure at foot of ramp for scale; (b) monolithic stone ax; (c) problematical flint forms; (d) copper ax head with wooden handle fragment. Artifacts are variable scale.

Figure 5.35 Feline figure, Key Marco, Florida. Southern Cult object, six inches in height.

Figure 5.36 Engraved or incised beaker from Moundville, Alabama. The Key Marco cat and the Moundville beaker are two of the more striking Southern Cult objects and are often illustrated.

Figure 5.37 Repoussé breastplate of hammered native copper found in Union County, Illinois. Southern Cult object.

prescribed processions, feasts, and sacrifice. As already noted, DuPratz saw and reported a Natchez chieftain's burial ceremony in 1725. That mourning ceremony for Tattooed Serpent, Brother of the Sun (or Chief), lasted for several days and involved all the Natchez villages. As part of the burial ceremony, the dead man's two wives and his "speaker," doctor, head servant, pipe bearer, and sister were ritually strangled. Several old women who, for one reason or another, had offered their lives were also strangled. The two wives were buried with Tattooed Serpent in the temple, his speaker and one of the women were buried in front of the temple, and the others were carried to their respective village temples for burial. His sister, also buried with him, was reported by DuPratz to have been reluctant to participate in the ceremony. As was customary, Tattooed Serpent's house was burned. The burial of personages within and near houses and the subsequent destruction of those houses by fire are well attested archaeologically. Had the Natchez culture not been weakened to near extinction, the next event might well have been the enlargement of the mound and the building of a new structure.

At intervals there would have been a company of impressed laborers in the plaza engaged in repairing or remodeling the mounds, the palisade, the plaza, and the priests' dwellings. On rare occasions there would perhaps have been a market where traders bartered with the farmers for local goods in exchange for imported goods. Outside the ceremonial center there would have been extensive fields and many scattered settlements of a few houses each. The women would have tended fields of maize, while the men hunted, conducted raids, or manufactured tools, weapons, utensils, and ornaments. The women probably made the pottery, wove mats and cloth, made moccasins and clothing from deer hides they had tanned, and tended their homes and children in a life of never-ending toil. Except for the frequent ceremonies, festivals, and market days, the daily round of

labor for both sexes would have been continuous and arduous and of much the same pattern as reported by the ethnographers.

The Plains

Eastern influences on the Plains began during the Archaic stage, but by about the time of Christ, the Woodland Tradition had diffused into the quite different world of the Great Plains. The Plains environment has been variously described as "hell on earth" or "not fit for humans." Theodore Roosevelt noted that it was "hard on women and horses." As opposed to the Woodland environment, it is described as a land of low relief, few trees, and little rainfall—of sun, wind, and grass.

Clearly the Plains can be defined in many different ways. Descriptions of it usually reflect the writers' interest, which can be geography, physiography, climate, vegetation, ecology, or something else. Because of the great area of the Plains—nearly 1 million square miles—and its extent—from the Rockies to the Missouri River—it is expectably variable in many aspects. The upper half is dominated by the Missouri River, which with its tributaries drains half, or a little more, of the vast area. The Plains extends from deep within the Canadian Prairie provinces almost to Mexico. Figure 5.38 shows the area as it is usually defined. As one traverses the land from east to west, there is no relief; just level lands stretching out ahead, covered (originally) with endless miles of waving grass. Although the land is level, monotonous, and windswept, it is not hostile because the prairie is broken by hundreds of east-flowing perennial streams. At the brink of the deeply incised streams the grass gives way to trees, shrubbery, and small meadows where vegetable food, small game, arable land, and wood for fuel abound. The dual environments—the

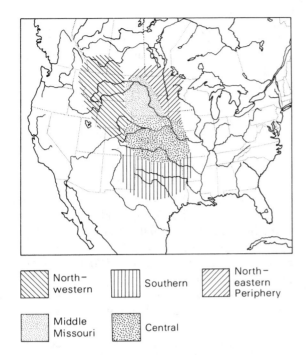

North-western

Southern

North-eastern Periphery

Middle Missouri

Central

Figure 5.38 Plains region.

prairies with their big game and the narrow fingers of streamside woodland—provide faunal and vegetal resources of great variety.

From about 1 A.D. the cultures show a Woodland origin. After about 900 to 1000 A.D., they are tinged with Mississippian influences. However, the Woodland origins are never obscured.

The earliest Plains Woodland appears to have been the Hopewellian settlement near Kansas City. According to the radiocarbon findings this village is no older than the Christian era. It is derived from the Havana Hopewell and lacks the gaudy goods of the classic Ohio version. Farther west, in the Central Plains area, three nearly contemporary Woodland complexes have been segregated. The oldest is the Valley, followed by the Keith and Loseke Creek complexes. They span a period from 1 to perhaps 700 A.D. None is spectacular, but all seem to have been lightly touched by Hopewell influence. Taking the Valley material as typical of the early Plains manifes-

tation of the Woodland, we find the sites to be located on lower terraces beside minor streams. They appear to have been semipermanent, perhaps seasonal camps. They are small, with shallow deposits and a limited inventory of artifacts. Gardening is by no means proved, but a few corn kernels were found at the type site in Nebraska. Most foods appear to have been wild plants; game animals taken included bison, beaver, deer, badger, and various rodents. Handicrafts were simple. Bone was used for awls, **fleshers,** or scrapers (for removing flesh from hides) and for beads. Chipping of flint was carelessly done; the usual form was a large, triangular, knife blade or projectile point. Ovoid scrapers with a steep bit were also common; probably these were set in a bone or wooden handle. Occasionally a grooved ax occurs.

Pottery, while distinctive, is more durable than beautiful (Figure 5.39). The shape was the familiar Woodland elongated body with a conoidal base and the faint shoulder bulging slightly low on the vessel from a large but constricted mouth. The paste contained sand, grit, or crushed calcite temper, and the vessels were formed by paddling the exterior against the hand used inside as an anvil. The exterior was roughened by the use of a cord-wrapped paddle. Similar pottery is distributed quite widely over the Central Plains.

By about 800 to 900 A.D. the Woodland Plains farmers received a strong thrust of Mississippian ideas from the Early Mississippi developments at Cahokia. At least the strong infusion of architectural style, ceramics, and cultigens resembles that pattern.

The Plains are usually divided into five natural areas for archaeological purposes. These are the Northwestern, Central, and Southern Plains, the Middle Missouri, and the Northeastern Periphery (Figure 5.40). From all these there are good areal sequences, many named cultures, and some reliable chronologies from radiocarbon dating. Although the Southern, Central, and Northeastern Periphery areas had been studied before the 1930s, the Middle

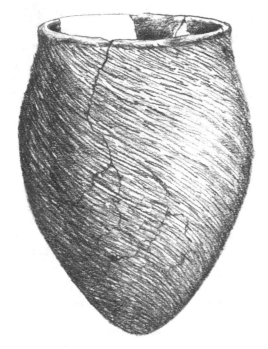

Figure 5.39   Typical example of Central Plains Woodland pottery.

hold several bushels. Some were as large as 5 to 6 feet in diameter and equally deep.

The most distinctive aspect of the Plains culture is the houses. All over the Plains the first houses were rectangular with a short, narrow entryway. A simple central fire basin was surrounded by four posts set at the corners of an imaginary square; smaller vertical posts formed the low walls. Both central and wall posts supported plates for sloping rafters laid from the walls to the central framework. The wall and roof covering was of branches or grass covered by dirt or sod. The houses were built in shallow basins and were often scattered in loose, unstructured villages located on stream terraces. By 1500 A.D., some of the house shapes changed to round. The four-post central roof support system and an entryway were retained however. In profile the round lodge was a dome, with the rafters sloping upward from wall posts to the center.

The Middle Missouri area lies along the Missouri River from Yankton, South Dakota, to Bismarck, North Dakota. It was observed and reported during the excavation of several large sites during the massive Missouri River Basin emergency archaeological program that began in 1946 ahead of the construction of many reservoirs. During excavations at now-inundated sites in the Oahe Reservoir, a local sequence of cultures extending from 1000 A.D. up to historic times was discovered. The sequence began with the Over phase at 1000 A.D., rapidly succeeded by the Monroe, Anderson, and T. Riggs phases. By about 1300 to 1400 A.D., a series of contemporaneous but differing phases evolved up and down the Missouri River. They are the Middle Mandan, Huff, Arzberger, LaRoche, and Bennett. Following these were the Mandan and Arikara of historic times. The earlier phases (Over through T. Riggs) showed compact villages of

Missouri has been understood only since emergency archaeology began in 1945. (See Wedel's excellent summary (1961) cited in the bibliography at the end of this chapter.)

In order to grow corn and beans in the harsh Plains environment, the Plains villagers seem to have developed special strains. Their maize was a tough, hardy, dent variety that could mature in the short growing season. The cold-resistant, quick-maturing corn that was developed from the original, tropical maize is the key to Middle Missouri culture. Special resistant strains of beans were also developed; the famous Great Northern bean is a historic Mandan variety. Plains gardening was done in the fertile and easily worked silts of the stream valleys not on the windswept prairies. The primary tool was the bison scapula, which makes an ideal hoe when lashed to a handle made from a strong, forked stick. After harvesting the crops were stored in deep, bell-shaped caches, or storage pits, that would

Figure 5.40   Chart of approximate time relationships of selected archaeological sites and complexes in the Plains areas.

Date				Northwestern Plains	Central Plains	Southern Plains	Middle Missouri	Northeastern Periphery		Age
	Hunters (W.Pl.)	Plains Village Pattern (E.Pl.)	NEO-BOREAL	Blackfeet Crow	Dakota, Pawnee Cheyenne, Omaha etc.	Comanche Kiowa	Arikara Mandan	Assiniboin Yankton Santee	Selkirk (Cree)	
1850—			NEO-PACIFIC I II	Shoshone			Disorganized Coalescent			—100
1800—						Apache	Post-Contact Coalescent			
1700—			SUB-ATLANTIC SCANDIC	Pictograph Cave IV Hagen	Dismal River	Spanish Fort Deer Cr.	Extended Coalescent		Manitoba	
1600—				Vore B.J. Mummy Cave 38	Lower Loup Great Bend		Initial Coalescent			
1500—				Pictograph Cave III	Oneota					—500
1250—	Bison				Upper Republican Smoky Hill Nebraska	Panhandle Washita R.	Initial Extended Middle Missouri	Dakota Mounds		
1000—				Avonlea Mummy Cave 36		Custer F.		Mill Creek	Avonlea Besant	—1000
500—			SUB-ATLANTIC	Wedding of Waters II Spring Cr. Cave O.W.B.J. 25	Loseke Cr. Keith Focus Valley Focus K.C. Hopewell	Pruitt Chalk Hollow Upper			Pelican Lake	—1500
AD / BC	Pedestrian				Plains Woodland		Plains Woodland		Laurel	—2000
500—				Pictograph Cave I		Chalk Hollow Lower				—2500
1000—			SUB-BOREAL	Wyoming Basin Foragers	Signal Butte I	Burnt Rock Middens	Missouri River Terrace Sites		White shell F. Larter F.	—3000
1500—				Oxbow- McKean Mummy Cave 30	Munkers Cr. LoDaiska C			Hanna Duncan McKean		—3500
										—4000
2500—				Late Oxbow	LoDaiska D	Bison bison	Preceramic	Oxbow		—5000
3500—	ALTITHERMAL		ATLANTIC	Early Oxbow Mummy Cave 21	Helmer Ranch	Gore Pit				—6000
4500—					Logan Creek B				Agate Basin Angostura	—7000
5500—			BOREAL	Lusk Mummy Cave 16 Frederick Cody Mummy Cave 4 Alberta Hell Gap Agate Basin Midland Folsom Goshen Colby Site	Logan Cr. Simonsen Bison occidentalis	Plano Cultures Packard				—8000
6500—	Early Big-Game Hunters									—9000
7500—										
8500—					Folsom Dent	Bonfire Folsom Domebo Blackwater No. 1	?	?		—10,000
										—11,000
10,000—			PRE-BOREAL		CLOVIS		?	?		—12,000
11,000—										—13,000
12,000—					Columbian Mammoth					—14,000
13,000—										—15,000
14,000—										—16,000
15,000—										—17,000

Vertical side labels (Northwestern Plains): LATE PREHISTORIC, MIDDLE PREHISTORIC, EMP II, Early Middle Prehistoric I, EARLY PREHISTORIC

Vertical labels (Southern Plains): Bison Presence III, Bison Absence II, Bison Presence II, Bison Absence I, Bison Presence I

rectangular houses arranged linearly in what could be called streets. After T. Riggs times, the round house was preferred by some groups such as the Mandan.

The Monroe phase was characterized by distinctive rectangular houses with vertical wall posts in a straight line, three center supports (for gabled roofs, as sometimes in the Mississippian), and a fireplace toward the narrow entry ramp. The entry ramp sloped down to meet the sunken floor of the lodge. A striking fact about the Monroe villages was their compactness, in contrast to the randomness of earlier settlements. The houses were located uniformly with the long axis oriented southwest-northeast and with the entryway toward the southwest. Artifacts of bone included scapula knives, bison-rib scraper handles, bison-shoulder-blade hoes, and horn scoops or spoons. Chipped stone was represented by small, side-notched projectile points, a vaguely lunate knife, and end scrapers. The grooved maul and grooved arrowshaft smoother of sandstone were apparently in use too. The major difference from a Woodland artifact assemblage was in the pottery. Although still cord roughened, it was of better quality, more abundant, and different in form from the earlier Woodland ceramics. The basic shape is the globular jar, wide-mouthed with an everted rim (S-shaped in cross section) and a well-defined neck above rounded shoulders. There may be strap handles as well. Incised lines occur on the rims, but the rest of the body is cord paddled.

Several of the later villages (Huff, Philip Ranch, and Arzberger sites) are enclosed by extensive earthworks that have regularly spaced bastions. As in the palisaded Mississippian sites, heavy logs were set into the earthen ridges.

One of America's most remarkable prehistoric villages was built by the ancestors of the historic Mandan tribe of Lewis and Clark fame. It is the Huff site, only some 20 miles south of Bismarck, North Dakota. Tree ring dates and radiocarbon assays agree in bracketing the occupancy from about 1400 to 1600 A.D. A probable date of 1450 to 1550 A.D. can be assigned.

Preserved as a state park, the Huff village is situated on the right (west) bank of the Missouri River, a location that spells its doom. Unless the river changes its course, it will continue to undercut the bluff where the site lies. Each spring until recently huge slabs of earth splashed into the floodwaters, carrying parts of earth lodges or other prehistoric data to destruction. Now a protective revetment along the bluff will reduce the effects of annual floods.

The village is large (Figure 5.41). House lodges even now number more than one hundred; the erosion of the Missouri has destroyed an unknown number. The dominant house type was a rectangular structure built of vertical posts or poles with an entryway opening to the west. Houses were large, averaging 30 by 33 feet. The roof was supported by central posts or pillars arranged down the midline of the house. The covering for the houses is not definitely known, but they are believed to have been roofed with sod. The vertical walls were of **wattle and daub.** A most impressive component of the village was the encircling fortification, an earthen embankment behind which small posts set about 12 inches apart formed a palisade. Ten projecting bastions were equally spaced along its sides and at the two western corners.

The data show that in having horticulture, combined with gathering of wild foods and a heavy reliance on bison, the Huff villagers followed a balanced subsistence pattern established a millennium earlier. This pattern persisted among the eastern Plains villages until the bison were exterminated in the 1870s. Artifacts of bone, stone, wood, shell, and clay were varied and specialized, as required to implement the three bases of the subsistence pattern.

In the eastern part of the cultural plains and the lands east of the Missouri River in Iowa and Missouri, the Nebraska and later

Figure 5.41 Huff Village site.

Oneota cultures bespeak a late Mississippian thrust that well-nigh obscured the Plains influences. The Oneota culture is characterized by shell-tempered pottery with many secondary features and a more varied inventory of artifacts than was true of Plains cultures farther west.

In the Southern Plains a blending of Plains and Southwestern cultures called Antelope Creek has been described in great detail. In Kansas and southern Nebraska a series of local cultures have been discovered and described. Among these the Lower Loup in Nebraska is identified as descended from the Upper Republican phase and as the archaeological remains of the prehistoric ancestors of the historic Pawnee tribe. The Oneota are regarded as the remains of the Chiwere-speaking Sioux.

Figure 5.40 shows the several local cultures over the five areas established for the Plains region. The contemporaneity of the cultures and their span—from perhaps 700 A.D. to the nineteenth century and continuous white contact—are also brought out. In spite of a now huge backlog of supporting data, there are still problems to be solved in the Plains concerning the relationship and direction of interareal influence.

For the Plains village tribes, as elsewhere, the archaeological story does not reveal the complete lives of the people. The earth lodges in the sometimes large villages imply a fully sedentary mode of living, but there are historic records of several Plains village groups, (Pawnee, Arikara, Hidatsa, and Mandan) who regularly went on long bison hunts of several weeks' duration.

An Ethnographic Sketch

The Mandan villages on the Missouri River in North Dakota were observed and often described by a series of explorers. The best known of those who recorded the Mandan customs were Lewis and Clark, who observed them during their historic journey into the American Northwest. The villages were rather large, with several dozen closely spaced earth lodges clustered in no particular order around a central open area, where ceremonies and games were held. Located on terraces above the Missouri River, the villages were protected by high post palisades with a deep ditch just outside. The houses were quite large, ranging from 40 to 80 feet in diameter. Several nuclear families occupied each lodge; the families were members of the same extended family of a matrilineal kin group. The villages were almost deserted during the summer hunt and again during the winter, when temporary quarters were taken up in protected woodland areas in the valley, where game and firewood were more plentiful.

The lodges were round and built of timber, with an earth and sod covering in the familiar Plains pattern (Figure 5.42). The size of the structures necessitated four large center posts as the major supports; rafters radiated outward from the crossbeams of the center posts to plates on the shorter posts set at the edge of the circular floor. Willows and grass or thatch were spread on the rafters to support the earth covering. The roof was open in the square area formed by the central crossbeams on the center posts. This opening was the only source of light and was also the smoke hole. In bad weather, a shield—sometimes one of the round buffalo-hide **bull-boats** used for crossing the river—was placed over the smoke hole. There was a short, covered entryway also made of timber and earth. The arrangement of facilities inside the lodge was evidently more-or-less standard. The fire was within the square formed by the central supports. There were curtained bunklike beds around the back or side walls. On the right of the fire area or behind the fire opposite the entrance was a family shrine or altar where ceremonial objects were kept. At other locations would be a sweat bath, a stall and food for a favorite horse, a food-storage area, and extra clothing. Buffalo-robe seats were ar-

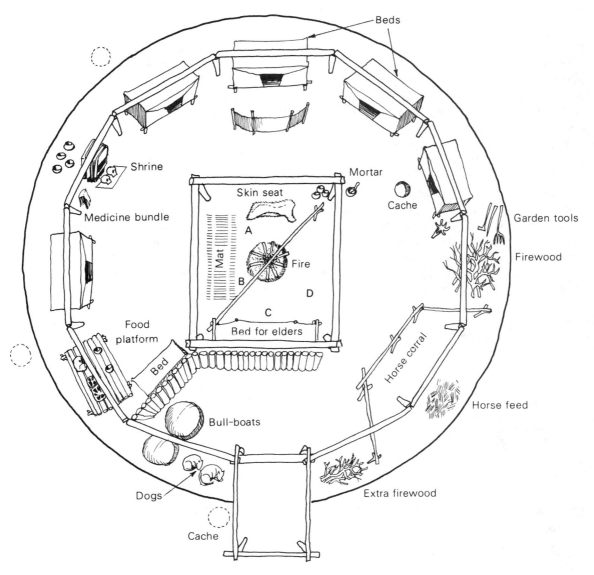

Figure 5.42 Diagram of a twelve-post Hidatsa earth lodge: (a) and (b) places of honor for guests, (c) grandfather's place to make arrows, (d) cook's place. The cooking kettle was suspended from diagonal pole over the fireplace.

ranged around the fire. In the floor were deep, jug-shaped storage pits for corn and other food. Outside the lodges were innumerable scaffolds or racks for drying both vegetable and meat products.

Although the lodges were roomy and comfortable, they would not have fitted modern

conceptions of creature comfort or sanitation. One of these villages was described by an early visitor as "filthy," with "villainous smells everywhere assailing" him. He complained of the swarming dogs and children and described the village as a hogpen. This description can be supported on archaeological grounds because thick midden or garbage dumps are scattered all through the village. Often one can associate a midden area with a specific lodge. The towns would have been malodorous quagmires after a rainstorm, with only slightly less stench in dry seasons.

The Mandan artifact list, of course, reflects both hunting and horticulture, the latter involving the sunflower as well as the familiar maize. Tobacco, important in ritual and ceremony, was grown by the men; the rest of the gardening was done by the women and children on small plots in the loose, rich soils of the Missouri River valley floor. The gardening tools included a wooden digging stick, a bison-scapula hoe, and elk-antler and willow-branch rakes. Corn and beans were planted together, with sunflowers around the edges of the field. Squash was grown in separate patches. Agriculture was surrounded with ritual and ceremony to provide supernatural aid

in production. In addition to gardening, the women tanned skins, made clothing of all sorts, made pottery of good quality, gathered wood, did much of the work of house building and maintenance, cared for children, prepared food, and did other chores. The men hunted, fought if need be, performed many important ceremonies, and competed in games and contests. When necessary, they assisted the women in the heavier labor or harvest and construction.

The Mandan had a rich ceremonial life centered on the vision quest and a number of "medicine" bundles that gave various kinds of "power." Some bundles were quite specific in their effect on crop fertility or weather; others had to do with curing disease. Self-torture was an important element in the religion and was a dominant theme in some of the ceremonies.

Chapter 5
BIBLIOGRAPHY

Bareis, Charles J., and James W. Porter (editors)

1984 *American Bottom Archaeology.* University of Illinois Press. Urbana and Chicago.

This volume is devoted entirely to the I 255 research. It contains chapter-long summaries of each of the cultural traditions represented in the American Bottom as well as analyses of botanical and faunal finds and several useful appendices.

Brose, David S., James A. Brown, and David W. Penny (editors)

1985 *Ancient Art of the American Woodland Indians.* Harry N. Abrams in association with the Detroit Institute of Arts. New York.

This beautiful volume not only contains the finest photographs of Adena, Hopewell, and Mississippian artifacts anywhere assembled, but also contains thoughtful analyses of the culture and art systems.

Brose describes the Adena, Hopewell, and Late Woodland, creating a coherent picture of their interrelatedness and cultural continuity most effectively. Reading his chapter allows for a fuller understanding of the Interaction Sphere than does this chapter. Brown devotes much space to interpreting the southern cult artifacts as being concerned with fertility and ancestor figures rather than with death or mortuary ritual. This book is highly recommended.

Brose, David S., and N'omi Greber (editors)

1979 *Hopewell Archaeology, the Chillicothe Conference.* Kent State University Press. Kent, Ohio.

From this book several chapters are recommended: Miller Hopewell of the Tombigbee Drainage, by Ned J. Jenkins; The Marksville Connection, by Alan Toth; Hopewell and the Southern Heartland, by John A. Walthal; Charnel Houses and Mortuary Crypts: Disposal of the Dead in the Middle Woodland Period, by James A. Brown; and Gathering and Gardening: Trends and Consequences of Hopewell Subsistence Strategies, by Richard I. Ford.

Finlayson, William D.

1985 *The 1975 and 1978 Rescue Excavation at the Draper Site: introduction and settlement pattern.* National Museum of Man, Mercury Series, Archaeological Survey of Canada Paper No. 130, pp. 1–586.

This volume opens with a discussion of the research design and excavation procedures followed during a massive salvage/rescue excavation program. The remainder deals with settlement patterns and details of house structures, with a final report of the artifacts, subsistence, and burial practices. Highly technical in nature, this report reveals thoughtful and innovative excavation and recording procedures with a high recovery of data.

Griffin, James B.

1983 The Midlands. In *Ancient North Americans,* edited by Jesse D. Jennings, pp. 243–301. W. H. Freeman. New York.

Lehmer, Donald J.

1971 *Introduction to Middle Missouri Archaeology.* National Park Service, Anthropological Papers, No. 1. U.S. Department of the Interior. Washington, D.C.

This is a well-illustrated book in which Lehmer outlines the Middle Missouri Tradition in great detail.

Muller, Jon

1983 The Southeast. In *Ancient North Americans,* edited by Jesse D. Jennings, pp. 373–419. W. H. Freeman. New York.

Phillips, Philip, and James A. Brown

1978 *Pre-Columbian Shell Engravings from the Craig Mound at Spiro, Oklahoma, pt. 1.* Peabody Museum of Archaeology and Ethnology, Harvard University. Cambridge, MA.

1983 *Pre-Columbian Shell Engravings from the Craig Mound at Spiro, Oklahoma, pt. 2.* Peabody Museum of Archaeology and Ethnology, Harvard University. Cambridge, MA.

This enormous work contains the finest extant analysis of any known collection of Southern Cult objects. Confined to shell specimens, the two volumes contain exhaustive descriptions and comparisons, several hundred illustrations, and thoughtful passages on style, theme, and motif.

Smith, Bruce D.

1986 The Archaeology of the Southeastern United States, from Dalton to DeSoto (10,500 B.P. to 500 B.P.). In *Advances in World Archaeology,* Vol. 5, edited by Fred Wendorf, and Angela E. Close, pp. 1–92. Academic Press. New York.

Smith, Bruce D. (editor)

1978 *Mississippian Settlement Patterns.* Academic Press. New York

This is a very useful volume. Several articles are especially relevant to this chapter.

Wedel, Waldo R.

1961   *Prehistoric Man on the Great Plains.* University of Oklahoma Press. Norman.

1983   The Prehistoric Plains. In *Ancient North Americans*, edited by Jesse D. Jennings, pp. 203–241. W. H. Freeman. New York.

Williams, Stephen, and Jeffrey P. Brain

1983   *Excavations at the Lake George Site, Yazoo County, Mississippi, 1958–1960.* Papers of the Peabody Museum of Archaeology and Ethnology, Vol. 74. Harvard University Press. Cambridge, MA.

The Southwest

Readers are familiar with the Southwest because it is much photographed and chronicled, and many have personally experienced its grandeur, its mist-softened mountains, its shimmering heat, and its lavender sunset charm. Within the lure of the Southwest are included the enclaved Pueblo Indian tribes along the Rio Grande and on the high mesas of the desert, peoples whose timeless cultures seem so admirably suited to a harsh, but not necessarily hostile, environment. Those who treasure the colorful tribes as almost part of the natural landscape offer unwitting tribute to these ingenious folk who have so long successfully exploited an unwatered waste. This respect is justified by the record this chapter will summarize.

Travelers to the Southwest know the famous prehistoric ruins of Mesa Verde National Park and many national monuments such as Chaco Canyon, Casa Grande, and Bandelier. In these, and at many an unprotected site, the multistoried buildings offer thrilling testimony to a numerous people of long ago. These were people, moreover, who had mastered many skills of survival, whose technology was complex, and whose products were strong and beautiful to all eyes. Interesting, too, is the fact that these ancient southwesterners worked out their destiny separately and a little later than the groups east of the Mississippi River. The prime source of inspiration and stimulus was Mexico to the south. Thence came the ideas of pottery, the cultivated crops, possibly some religious ideas, and other practices. However, the staunch conservatives of the Southwest were little interested in the concept of priest-rulers.

By continental standards the Southwest culture area is quite small. Described loosely as extending north-south "from Durango, Colorado, to Durango, Mexico, and from Las Vegas, New Mexico to Las Vegas, Nevada" on the east-west axis, most of its area of actual dominance falls within the states of New Mexico and Arizona with some of northern Mexico and southern Colorado and southern Utah added (Figure 6.1). Within this restricted zone there developed one of the three aboriginal culture climaxes of North America, and for many people it carries the most interest of any.

The Southwest tribes, both prehistoric and modern, were gardeners from slightly before the beginning of the Christian era. They were thrifty, skillful exploiters of land and available water; the crops were corn, beans, squash, and cotton. Other food plants now regarded as weeds, such as amaranth, sunflower, Rocky Mountain beeweed, and wild potatoes and tomatoes, were cultivated (or at least encouraged) and were equally important to the aboriginal gardening economy. What is often forgotten is that the southwestern farmer depended upon hundreds of wild species as heavily as upon the cultigens. The cultigens

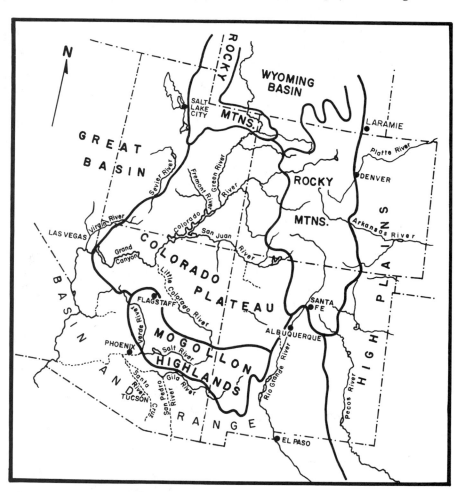

Figure 6.1   Southwestern geographic region.

made possible a denser population, it's true, and were probably of crucial importance to subsistence. Nonetheless, the success of the southwestern cultures was the result of a complex year-round exploitation of all available species, just as in the rest of the continent.

This western symbiosis of human groups and biota is the familiar but often forgotten legacy from the Archaic cultures, overlooked because of the emphasis given to the very fact of food production and the cultural effects of the possession of a gardening complex. That symbiosis is exemplified in the aboriginal ecology of the Glen Canyon area in southeastern Utah. There over 300 wild species of plants were collected in the yearly round. It is clear that horticulture can not be thought of as having been the sole source of food. At the same time, the very existence of extensive gardening in the American Southwest is a minor miracle. No large part of the region is truly suitable for dry-farming operations, even with the most modern techniques. But modern agricultural practices are so different from the aboriginal ones that there is no validity in the comparison.

One can ask: How did a food-producing culture operate where agriculture is not possible? Here the answer is found in the ethnographic analogs—the practices observed among modern tribes—and in the archaeological data. The success of the southwestern farmer rested on a series of realistic techniques for the exploitation of limited water. These techniques, some still in use today, probably included floodwater irrigation of several types, sand dune or subsurface irrigation, and seep springs watering colluvial soils. To the above must be added actual water impoundment and distribution, in essentially the modern manner, in the Salt and Gila Valleys of southern Arizona (by the Hohokam) and to slight extent in the Pueblo areas of New Mexico, Utah, and Arizona. In mountainous areas the use of loose-stone check dams across the minor drainages effectively slowed down rainwater runoff, thus providing additional watered areas and simultaneously trapping soil behind the dams to form what can be called terraces. These little terraces, called *trinchera* plots, though often only a few feet in area, would add precious garden space where a few plants could be grown. Thus in some areas most of the gardening took place in a myriad of small, scattered plots where soil and water could be brought together.

Planting techniques were also special. The seed corn was planted early, ten or twelve kernels to a spot, in deep holes where groundwater ensured germination and the deep soil blanket afforded protection from the late frosts in the northern provinces. These plantings, called hills, were widely, even irregularly, spaced over the plot, so that the limited water was not divided among too many plants. Because of the lack of water, the stalks did not grow more than 3 or 4 feet high, and the hill of perhaps a dozen plants resembled a bush. The outer leaves took the brunt of the dry, hot winds of summer, protecting the inner plants that produced the several ears of corn harvested from each hill.

The scientific record of Southwest prehistory is found in hundreds of monographs and thousands of articles. The detailed literature is well-nigh inexhaustible. The region has perhaps the longest history of intensive study of any area north of Mexico, and many important contributions to archaeological theory and study have come from this long period of scholarly concern. As was true of the Southeast, much attention has been paid to the ceramic arts. As a result of long study and the many ruins and living tribes accessible to visitors, the prehistoric cultures of the Southwest are not complete mysteries but are widely known and understood. Because of the popular familiarity with the region, this chapter will be somewhat curtailed and perhaps even faintly unorthodox in places; the aim is again to present the outline of knowledge instead of the details a regional specialist perceives.

As is obvious, the key to understanding the Southwest lies in water and its use in gardening. For some, this makes it easier to see the whole Southwest as one cultural tradition showing areal variation in some aspects of culture. This unitary view can be defended and at one level of discussion is useful and valid, particularly in a long-range consideration of the local prehistory. Normally, however, three contemporary major traditions or cultures are recognized and are treated as separate, even though their intertwined origins are understood. This three-tradition division will be followed here. The major divisions are the Mogollon or Western Pueblo, the descendant and more widespread Anasazi Pueblo of the northern Southwest, and the Hohokam group, which was confined to the Salt and Gila Rivers and their major tributaries in Arizona. In northern Arizona between Flagstaff and the Grand Canyon quite local cultures—Cohonino, Sinagua, and Cerbat—have also been described. Short-lived, they will not be dealt with further here.

Each tradition evolved in different directions, partly because of different environmental conditions (Figure 6.2). These environmental forces are most obvious in the terrain itself. In the Mogollon province, where the transition from the Archaic stage to horticulture may have occurred first, we find some of the most rugged country in the Southwest. In the core area along the New Mexico-Arizona border are steep mountains and narrow valleys with little arable land. The Mogollon also extends into central Arizona in what is called the Mogollon Rim or Highlands; the area is actually the south edge of the Colorado Plateau. Facing the desert and up to 7000 feet above sea level, it receives generous rainfall and supports a wide variety of species. Few extensive villages ever developed here because of the mountainous terrain and narrow valleys. The difficulties of large-scale gardening were offset by the rich wild biotic offerings in the relatively well-watered mountains, and there

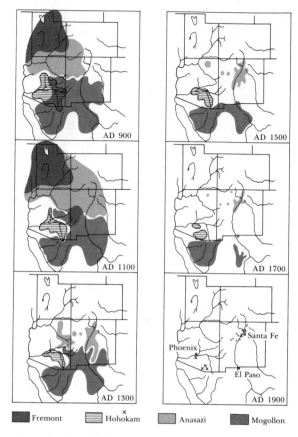

Figure 6.2   Approximate distribution of principal late cultures, 900–1900 A.D.

seems to have been a greater reliance on wild species than in the other traditions. The year-round climate was milder and showed a less-extreme temperature range than either the Hohokam or the Anasazi heartlands.

The Anasazi flourished to the north in the Colorado Plateau, an area characterized by high mesas and many deep canyons, some with swift, clear streams in often narrow valleys. Many streams, however, are dry except after storms or during spring runoff. Because many of the strata are sandstone, there are numerous springs even in the dry canyons. Temperatures range from below zero to the high nineties, and unseasonable frosts are frequent. There are many areas of naked rock, and soils are thin. Horticulture was practical only in the valleys where alluvial soils had accumulated or on the mesas in aeolian deposits, as at Mesa Verde. The tablelands, being well watered, now support forests of pine. Below 7000 feet, the forests are largely piñon and juniper. Game tends to be plentiful even today. At lower elevations shrub and grasslands are dominant. Gardening appears to have been on a dry-farming basis in the higher, better-watered locations and on a combined dry-farming and irrigation basis at lower elevations.

The Hohokam were generally restricted to the deserts of the southern Basin and Range province along the lower Salt and middle Gila rivers (and a few of their tributaries) and used these waters for large-scale irrigation. The modern city of Phoenix, Arizona, is built upon the ruins of many Hohokam settlements and the complex system of irrigation ditches that made life possible. The major canals of the Hohokam system underwent constant repair and modification. The biotic resources in these valleys were undoubtedly much restricted, as they are today. The summer heat is intense. Faunal resources are scarce, but many edible plant species occur, including fruits of several cacti and beans from tree legumes such as acacia and mesquite. Rainfall is low except to the east, and of the three traditions the Hohokam were probably the most dependent on their fields for food.

As described above, the southwestern cultures represent a complex subsistence pattern of balanced gardening and gathering in a land where farming is difficult, if not impossible. The environmental settings of the three traditions range from Colorado's green mesas to the sere wastes of Arizona's deserts. All depended on the careful use of limited water. There has long been general consensus that all three traditions evolved from the local Archaic cultures after stimulus from an unspecified Mexican source.

The Hohokam

At one time it was thought that the Hohokam represented an introduction *en bloc* from Mexico by 2500 B.P. of such key traits as canal irrigation; figurines; sculptured stone; pottery making; formalized house construction; cremation; the troughed metate; carved shell; **turquoise** mosaics; copper bells; and the macaw as a pet, object of worship, or source of colored feathers. Because of these well-developed traits and practices (and complete lack of any antecedent local manifestations), scholars once credited a group of colonists from the south with having selected the Hohokam area for the transplanting of a viable and ready-made pattern of life.

That view is no longer held. Today the date for the earliest Hohokam phase, the Vahki, is put at 300 A.D. or later, while the full-blown culture with ball courts, canal irrigation, platform mounds, and painted pottery fall after 800 A.D. So the current consensus is that the Mexican traits were diffused to the Hohokam over a period of time. For example, the copper bells were not there until after 1000 A.D.; the slate palettes not until perhaps 900 A.D.

The Hohokam first concentrated in the Salt and Gila river valleys. The two streams head in the well-watered Mogollon highlands in New Mexico but their middle reaches pass through some of the driest deserts of North America. Here gardeners could not survive without irrigation; the irrigation works of the Hohokam are the most sophisticated to be found north of Mexico. Extensive modern agricultural practices have destroyed most of the evidence, but two (observed before 1900) near Phoenix were over 10 miles long, swinging out from the river intake to bring water to fields quite distant from the river. When sectioned, these canals proved to be wide channels, U- or V-shaped, and sometimes lined with clay. One is 12 feet deep by 18 feet across. Although the most extensive canal systems are estimated to date from after 800 A.D., less-elaborate networks of canals may have existed earlier. It is believed that the entire idea was imported from Mexico.

The most famous Hohokam site is Snaketown, although numerous other sites have been excavated and reported. Even so the earliest period, the Pioneer, is not yet very well understood. Students divide the culture into four major periods; in each are one or more finer divisions called phases. These periods cannot be convincingly correlated with the Mogollon and Anasazi sequence. The oldest period is called the Pioneer (Vahki, Estrella, Sweetwater, and Snaketown phases); the Colonial (Gila Butte and Santa Cruz) came next, then the Sedentary (Sacaton), followed by the final or Classic Period (Soho and Civano) (see Figure 6.3).

The Pioneer period is dated from about 500 to 800 A.D. While the ceramics included a red ware, as in earlier Mogollon, they were largely of unslipped buff ware and made by paddle-and-anvil technique instead of by the coil-and-scrape method of the Mogollon. In the earliest or Vahki phase, the houses were large and rectangular with four central support posts (Figure 6.4). A few of these resembled the Mogollon houses in that they were true pit houses; this means the wall posts or leaners were set on the ground surface, so that the pit edge was inside the house and constituted a part of the wall. After the Vahki phase, however, all the houses came to be set in shallower pits and were less pit houses than houses *in* a pit, because the vertical wall poles were set inside the excavation pit edges instead of on the ground surface outside the pit. The pole framework of the house was covered with smaller branches and grass, and mud was applied as the final element. The sloping roofs may have been thatched, but the flat ones were mud-plastered. Annual repair of roofs and walls would have been necessary. The village layout tended to be loose and scattered, as in Mogollon, until Classic times.

Distinctiveness in ceramics also begins in the Pioneer period. The basic ware is the buff ware mentioned earlier, with simple bowls and wide-mouthed **ollas** being the dominant forms. The surfaces were undecorated. Painted decoration, red on gray or red on buff, soon appeared and remained the dominant Hohokam decorative motif. Thereafter, unique pottery forms also appeared, the most common being a hemispherical jar with small mouth, swelling outward toward the base, with the greatest diameter being only an inch or two above the flat base. Out of the flat bowl shape a shallow plate evolved, and some tripod and tetrapod legs on shallow bowls appeared in Colonial times. The major shapes are presented in Figure 6.5, which also shows one of the favored decorative styles: the endless repetition of zoomorphic designs, both realistic and stylized.

The common stone tools for cutting, digging, and other tasks are about the same as found elsewhere among the gardeners of the region and may show some relationship to earlier Archaic forms. The metate, if not basin-shaped, is troughed, it tends to be thick and shovel shaped. The usual inventory of chipped stone and bone tools persist as elsewhere. Few perishable artifacts were recovered from the open sites, so data about basketry, textiles, wood, or skin objects are rare or derived from charred and otherwise preserved fragments. The three-quarter-grooved ax is a common and distinctive form, as are graceful, thick-walled bowls carved from stone.

The most distinctive aspect of the Hohokam, however, is found in other than workaday artifacts. It was once argued that this was a Mexican colonial territory because of the irrigation, the pottery tradition, and the distinctive artifacts. Opposed to the notion of an actual Mexican population, equally strong opinion prefers to interpret the Hohokam as an indigenous development receiving strong and frequent stimuli from Mexico. The Mexican items include decorated, flat, stone paint

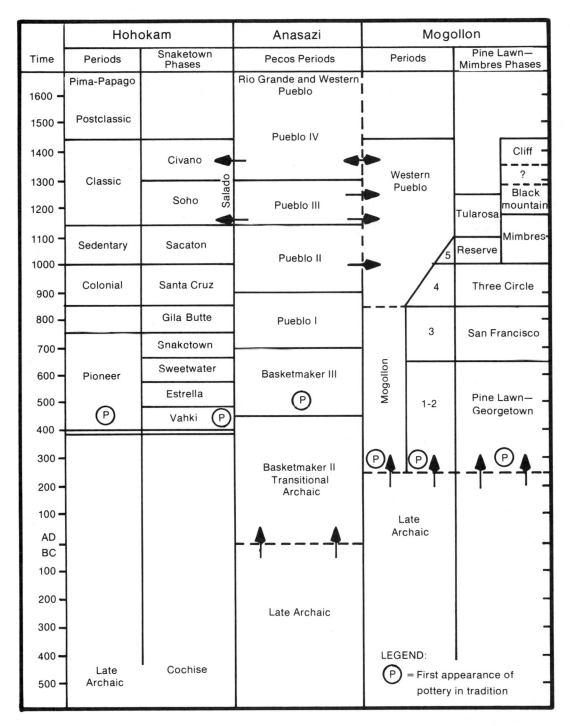

Figure 6.3 Correlation of Hohokam, Mogollon, and Anasazi cultural sequences.

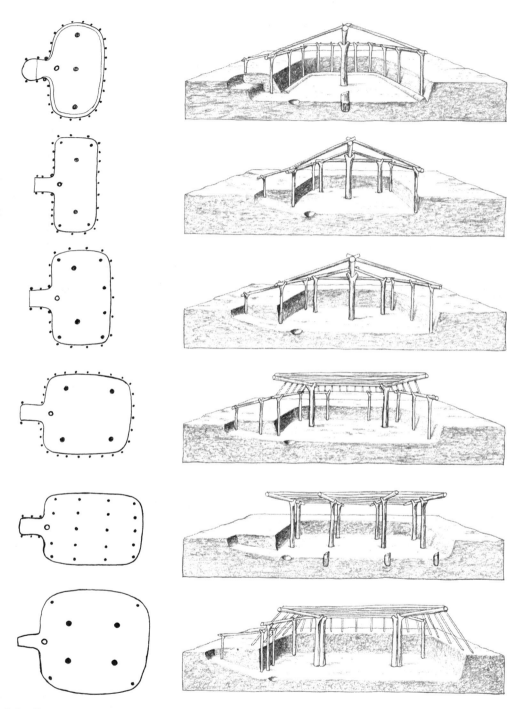

Figure 6.4 Floor plans and cross sections (postulated roof constructions) of Hohokam houses at Snaketown, arranged from early (bottom) to late (top).

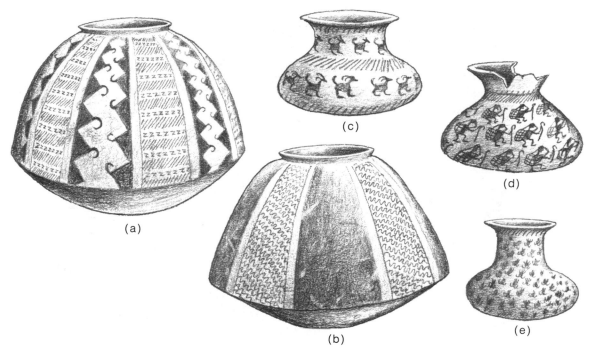

Figure 6.5   Examples of Hohokam decorated pottery: (a) and (b) Sacaton Red-on-buff, (c)–(e) Santa Cruz Red-on-buff. Much reduced.

palettes with pigment stains still visible; stone effigy bowls (sometimes in the Chac Mool style with a basin in the abdomen of a reclining figure); exquisite rings, bracelets, and pendants of acid-etched shell; inlaid mosaic mirrors of pyrites on a round slate backing; copper bells; beads of stone (turquoise, steatite); and other items (Figure 6.6). Life forms were the dominant decorative themes. Lizards, frogs, turtles, bears, and various birds are commonly depicted. There was also a figurine cult, exemplified by realistic, if crudely modeled, baked-clay female statuettes, with the facial features executed in a vaguely Mexican manner. However, in view of the early popularity of the figurine in Anasazi and Fremont cultures to the north, the Mexican origin of this trait may be challenged. The bells, of course, are of great interest, being among the few objects of smelted and cast metal found north of Mexico. They are made by the Mexican **lost wax** casting technique and are presumed to be actual imports.

Even more convincing evidence are the stepped pyramids and the ball courts. The outstanding examples of the Hohokam ball court are found at Snaketown (Sedentary period) and in the Painted Rocks Reservoir area (Sacaton phase), although about 200 are known over all the Southwest. The ball court is an oval depression with arcing earthen embankments on each side. At the Gatlin site the puddled **caliche** playing floor was about 100 feet long and 35 feet wide. After a period of disuse, the floor had been replaced once, and the sloping floor edges had been repaired or remodeled several times. The game is presumed to have resembled the Central American ball game; center and end markers of stone or even small basins modeled in the floors are found. Two rubber balls have even been found, but not in association with courts.

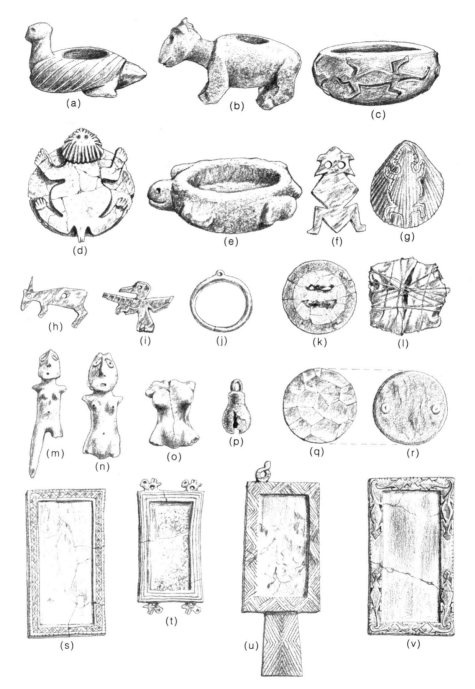

Figure 6.6 Nonutilitarian Hohokam artifacts: (a)–(e) zoomorphic stone bowls and censers, (f)–(j) zoomorphic shell ornaments, (k) pyrite mirror, (l) pyrite mirror in wrapping, (q) face of same mirror, (r) reverse side; (m)–(o) clay anthropomorphic figurines, (p) copper bell, (s)–(v) stone palettes. Variable scale.

At the Gatlin site there was also a platform mound or truncated pyramid that had been rebuilt and enlarged several times. Although made of mud and surfaced with caliche plaster, the structure can be likened to nothing but the stone-faced platforms of Mexico, which were substructures for temples as in the Southeast. At the Gatlin site and many others, crematory basins where calcined human bones are found attest the universal local practice of cremation instead of burial. After about 1000 A.D., of course, Hohokam traits are observed at distant points. Examples include the ball court at the famous Wupatki site north of Flagstaff, Arizona, and the small villages near Montezuma's Well in the Verde Valley and on the Aqua Fria near Dewey, all in Arizona. After 1200 A.D., too, Anasazi or Western Pueblo traits are blended into the Hohokam fabric in what is called the Salado culture. The huge multistoried structures at Casa Grande (and the now-destroyed Los Muertos) show this same blending, as do the ceramics.

While details of this culture seem to be known and its affiliations much discussed, very few sites have been thoroughly studied. It has been said that detailed knowledge of the full range of Hohokam content and variants is lagging forty years behind the rest of the Southwest. Its ultimate fate is not yet fully known. Most specialists see the modern Pima-Papago as the remanent Hohokam but that continuity has not been fully demonstrated through focused research.

The Mogollon

First defined in 1936 the Mogollon tradition possibly developed out of the Chiricahua and San Pedro Archaic. It seems to have acquired maize before 1 A.D., but pottery came considerably later at about 300 A.D. Once erroneously believed to have had maize by 4000 B.P. and ceramics by 2300 B.P., the Mogollon time span has been reduced by later research to less than half of those figures.

Usually the Mogollon is divided into four or five periods. The Pine Lawn-Georgetown begins about 300 A.D. and lasts until about 650 A.D., to be followed by San Francisco, Three Circle, and Reserve, which ends at 1100 A.D. With the end of the Reserve phase, the simplicity of the Mogollon is lost and heavy increments of Anasazi concepts—aboveground masonry dwellings, black-on-white pottery, some religious ideas, and increasing village size—essentially change the Mogollon into what is today called the Western Pueblo Tradition.

From Tularosa Cave, already described in Chapter Four, was recovered a rich record of about 800 years of the Mogollon sequence and the rich Archaic that underlay it. Occupancy of the cave continued until about 1100 A.D. In addition to spanning most of the Mogollon history in the Reserve district, the cave yielded a rich inventory of stone, ceramic, and perishable artifacts; these data also allowed the listing of many more specific Mogollon traits than had been possible before. Although there is a detailed listing of material and nonmaterial culture traits, it is necessary to report here only the classes of materials recovered. Wickerwork sandals are earliest, this having been the dominant technique in Pine Lawn times; plaited ones were dominant by the Reserve period. Ornaments included bracelets of shell; tubular bone beads; and pendants of wood, shell, stone, and bone. String aprons and both fur and feather robes were present. Milling tools included several metate styles and mortars, with varied handstone types. Snares, digging sticks, bows and arrows, many chipped flint forms, and netting were among the food-getting artifacts. Aside from cultigens and wild game, foods included **yucca,** cactus, walnuts, acorns, grass, and sunflower seeds, but amaranth was not mentioned. Textiles abounded. There were cradles; carrying nets; **tumpline** straps; twilled, twined, and coiled baskets; twilled and twined matting;

cotton cloth; the netting mentioned earlier; and blankets. Antler and bone tools included awls, notched ribs (musical rasps?), fleshers, punches, hammers, flakers, and wrenches. Wood was used for tool handles; scoops; trowels; awls; ladles; lapboards; spatulas; weaving tools, including spindles and whorls; flutes (reed); dice; and many other articles, including the painted plaques or *tablitas* used in headdresses (?) or in ritual. Tubular pipes of stone and clay were replaced by reed cigarettes. Figurines were common in both human and animal forms. Pottery was increasingly abundant; the earliest was a brown ware of good quality called Alma Plain, which continued to be manufactured for 800

years. Companion types are Alma Roughened and Alma Red. The above list of portable artifacts is, of course, not complete, but testifies to a heavy Archaic carryover in the tool and utensil inventory.

In all phases save the late Reserve, the Mogollon dwelling was the semisubterranean house or pit house, but no uniformity in design can be detected in the early phases. Eighteen architectural patterns have been identified. Suffice it to say that the houses were usually built in shallow pits with a narrow passageway or ramp descending from the ground level. Many were round; but D-shaped, kidney-shaped, and rectangular ones also occur. Figure 6.7 shows three phases of

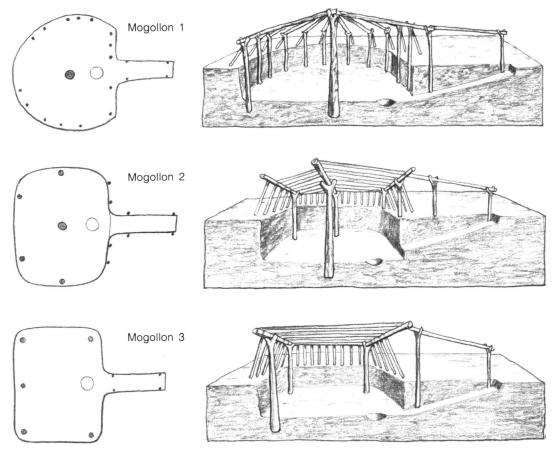

Figure 6.7 Floor plans and cross sections (postulated roof constructions) of Mogollon houses at the Harris village site.

house form and construction from the Harris village. Built of wood, the houses may have been covered with mats or reeds or plastered with mud. In Mogollon 1 times the houses varied greatly in size, had rough, uneven floors pocked with holes and pits, and were generally crudely executed. In later times, the pit houses were more uniform in size and more rectangular in shape, a form that persisted until after 1100 A.D. At this time, Anasazi stone masonry was introduced, and the pit house almost disappeared. At the same time (at the close of the Reserve phase), the Mogollon abandoned the northern sector, spreading west and east. The Zuni are largely descended from the Mogollon.

The Mogollon villages were often occupied over very long periods; at the Harris site housestyles changed over three phases in a well-defined stratigraphy (Figure 6.8). While continuous use cannot be proved, it is deemed likely on ceramic evidence. To be noted is the loose and unstructured village arrangement characteristic of the Mogollon settlements in all phases until the introduction of masonry. The elevated location of the Harris site is also typical. The occasional large houses found at Mogollon villages during all the phases are regarded as having been ceremonial structures larger than, but resembling, the dwellings. Whether they were communal meeting places is difficult to determine; certainly they bear little formal resemblance to the famous kivas of the Anasazi, other than being built in deep pits.

Perhaps the most famous Mogollon settlement is that at Point of Pines in Arizona. Lying just west of the Arizona-New Mexico line on the San Carlos Apache Reservation, the general region contains over 200 sites. The sites span thousands of years of aboriginal use, from the Archaic of the Cienega Creek site to almost modern times. The area was systematically studied for more than a decade by members of a permanent field school where dozens of professional archaeologists began their training. The school was operated by The University of Arizona.

One of the Point of Pines sites is Crooked Ridge Village. The site, about 6000 feet above sea level, was settled by 100 A.D. and was continuously occupied until 900 A.D. The low, broad ridge is aligned almost north-south; the village lay on the gently sloping eastern side. Culinary water, always a problem, was obtained from walk-in wells along the stream to the east. These walk-in wells were essentially small, deep reservoirs that collected subsurface water flowing above an impervious blue clay toward the intermittent streams of the area. (Somewhat similar wells were identified at the Cienega Creek site; hence in that area the walk-in well goes back to the Archaic stage of at least 4000 B.P.)

At Crooked Ridge there were over twenty pit houses of varied shapes and sizes and two ceremonial structures. There were several cases of pit house superposition. This evidence, as well as ceramic and other data, demonstrates a long occupancy for the village. The houses were true pit houses, resembling the sequence from the more easterly Mogollon. The quadrilateral house with a simple entry ramp was most common (fifteen examples), with four others showing vestibule entryways and three having an annex on the south side. The floors were pocked with pits (for storage?) and were otherwise irregular. Most houses had four major supports; replacement of posts during use sometimes resulted in more than four at the time of recovery. Without discussing the entirely typical artifacts (and some exotic goods from nearby areas), the site as a unit can be noted as having contributed significantly to the understanding of Mogollon architecture. Only one-fourth of the site was dug, with about seventy-five structures yet to be examined.

Published description has tended to emphasize the Mogollon pit house and the many northern Fremont and Pueblo or Anasazi traits derived from the Mogollon as early as 400 A.D. By 900 A.D. Anasazi traits were spreading back to the south. Foremost were the concept of stone masonry and the manufacture of black-

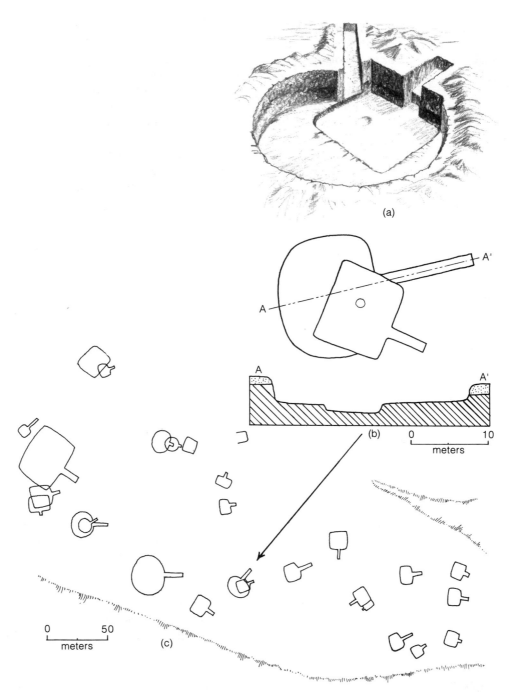

(a)

A'

A

(b)

0   10
    meters

(c)

0   50
    meters

Figure 6.8   The Harris site (New Mexico): (a) view of excavated superimposed pit houses, (b) plan and cross section of (a), (c) map of village and location of (a).

on-white pottery. Thus, by about 1100 A.D., a superficial areal uniformity, mentioned by several authors, can be recognized as the Anasazi and Mogollon come to share more and more traits (Figure 6.9).

The Mogollon culture as such continued over a wide area, including the Jornada Branch in eastern New Mexico and western Texas until about 1400 A.D., when a noticeable contraction can be charted. Sites of interest in the period later than 900 A.D. and on into the fifteenth century include Table Rock and Hooper Ranch (1200 to 1375 A.D.) among many others in eastern Arizona on the headwaters of the Little Colorado.

Anasazi influences were conspicuous in the southern part of the Mogollon region in the Mimbres area. The large, compact villages of stone masonry, adobe houses, and distinctive black-on-white pottery have long been famous. The Swarts Ruin and the Mattocks Ruin are two well-known sites. The much-prized

pottery is characterized by graceful insect, animal, and human life forms and many bawdy scenes from folktales and mythology, featuring such characters as the humpbacked flute player. Despite the Anasazi element in ceramics and architecture, the Mogollones of the Mimbres area retained in all else a simplicity and backwoods quality at variance with the more flamboyant technology of the Hohokam and Anasazi.

The Anasazi

By far the most extensive Southwestern culture was the Anasazi, which developed from the stimulus from the more southerly Mogollon. The Anasazi that are best known and often regarded as typical are those of the famous Mesa Verde and Four Corners

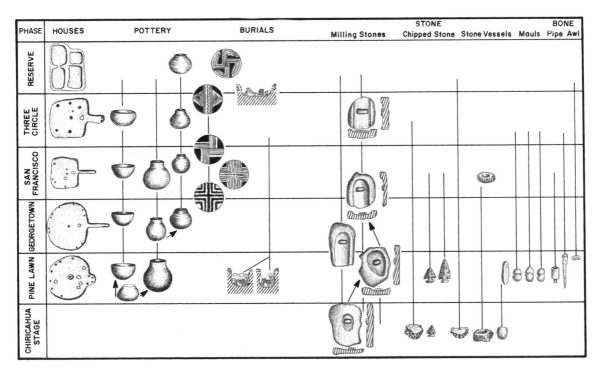

Figure 6.9 Synopsis of Mogollon cultural development.

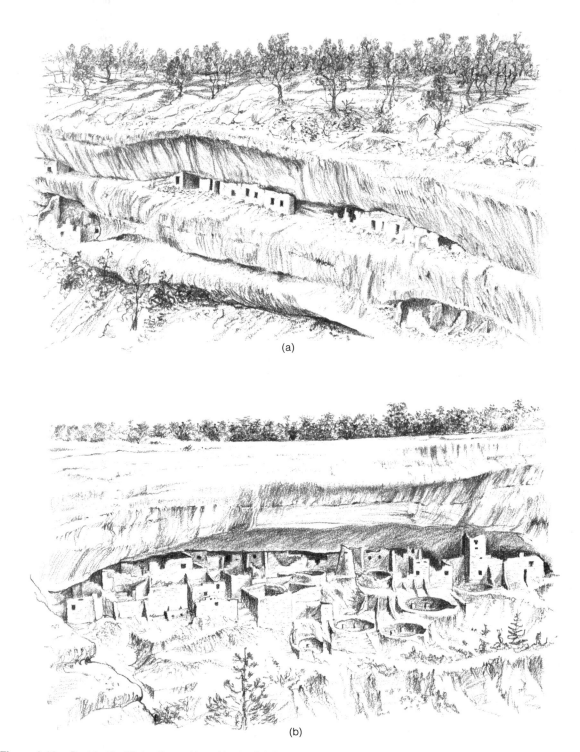

(a)

(b)

Figure 6.10 Pueblo III cliff dwellings, Mesa Verde: (a) Double House, (b) Cliff Palace.

areas. Although they are on the northern frontier, the Mesa Verdeans are *the* Anasazi for most laymen and many students. Their fabled cliff houses have stirred the imaginations of hundreds of thousands since their discovery in the nineteenth century (Figure 6.10). It must be remembered, however, that those grandeurs grew out of the Archaic cultures in response to the spread of Mogollon traits—red-brown pottery, pit houses, and the cultigens so important in the American climax stages—and that the few cliff houses are merely a very special end product evolving from simple beginnings, not the whole story.

The Anasazi territory is broken today into the San Juan area, Chaco and de Chelly canyons, the Kayenta, and, some would say, the Fremont. (The Fremont is found only in Utah, southern Idaho, and eastern Nevada (Figure 6.11), and the appropriateness of including it with the Anasazi will be touched on later.) The Anasazi have been described in some detail by many authors who all drew on an enormous literature in summarizing the available evidence according to their individual interests and biases.

Intensive study of the Southwest was begun in the Four Corners area primarily because of the Wetherills, a clan of rancher-explorer-collectors who brought the wonders of Mesa Verde to the attention of the world about 1890. They noted the sequence from early nonpottery deposits into the later ceramic-using, stone architecture sites. Richard Wetherill actually applied the term *Basketmaker* to the prepottery levels.

As a result of several decades of study, Alfred Kidder (1924) was able to write a comprehensive introduction to the Southwest. He summarized some of the discrete data of the Anasazi. Furthermore, he pinpointed the several subareas (for example, the Hohokam), where knowledge was insufficient for systematic appraisal. Thus, his brilliant book became a guide to study. By writing the volume Kidder came to realize that a better ordering of the Anasazi regional data was possible. Ac-

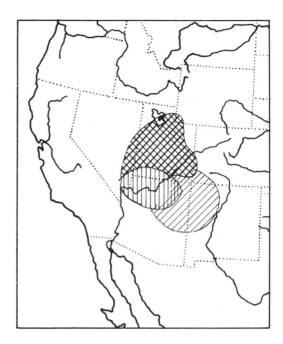

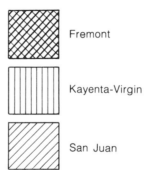

Fremont

Kayenta-Virgin

San Juan

Figure 6.11   Distribution of Fremont, San Juan, and Kayenta-Virgin.

cordingly, in 1927 he called a conference of southwestern specialists at Pecos, New Mexico (where he was then excavating). The conference devised a basic classification that is still used by students today. The classification was intended to be tentative and flexible, but all too soon it became rigid and was applied as a yardstick to all the Southwest well beyond limits of its applicability. The classification was the first one developed in North America following intensive fieldwork. It was based on sequential cultural development, but it has come to be used as if it were entirely chronological. Prehistoric time was broken into eight segments, and these "periods" were separated on the basis of traits present or absent in the findings. The periods are listed below. The dates shown here were established long after the 1927 conference and are still occasionally adjusted in some regions.

Latest:	Pueblo V	1700 A.D. to the present (the Rio Grande and Eastern Pueblo)
	Pueblo IV	1300–1700 A.D.
	Pueblo III	1100–1300 A.D.
	Pueblo II	900–1100 A.D.
	Pueblo I	750–900 A.D. (where it exists)
	Basketmaker III	450–700 A.D.
	Basketmaker II	1–500 A.D.
Earliest:	Basketmaker I	Before 1 A.D. (no longer used)

Basketmaker I was hypothesized in 1927 as a logical necessity since knowledge then ended with Basketmaker II. The widespread terminal western Archaic culture has long since been accepted as filling the gap, forming the base with the requisite traits upon which pottery, horticulture, and so on were grafted. Hence the Basketmaker I label is long since obsolete. The other units in the scheme, however, are still in use. Indeed, their accuracy has been generally accepted. The significance of the periods has shifted from content to chronology, probably because there is so much variation in the detailed trait associations from one district to another.

Initial Basketmaker II is now dated at about the time of Christ, persisting until about 500 A.D. Its identifying traits are familiar, being those cited for the Archaic culture (Chapter Four) and remindful of the material from Tularosa Cave. The sites are most often to be found in caves, alcoves, or overhangs. In such situations, the perishable artifacts are preserved, as are the bodies of the dead. The practice of skull deformation which later proved popular, had not yet appeared.

The difference between Basketmaker II and the preceding Archaic is not in the basic inventory of objects—such as woven sandals, basketry, cloth of several types, wooden scoops or trowels, clubs and assorted bone and chipped stone tools, string aprons, cordage of all kinds, fur blankets and skins, atlatls, darts, **gaming pieces** or dice, bone whistles, crude figurines—but in the addition of new traits. These are horticulture (corn and squash) and a unique style of architecture. The corn is of a different strain from the earliest Mogollon variety.

The dwelling architecture of the Four Corners Basketmaker II is unique. The dwellings were rounded, shallow basins, some 12 to 18 feet in diameter, with walls made of horizontal logs laid in mud mortar. Evidently the walls slanted upward toward a domed top; entry was through a side door. These structures have been reported at the Talus Village site, where a sizable village was uncovered, and at a few other locations in the same drainage area near Durango, Colorado. The houses were built on shelves or terraces constructed by cutting a level floor into the sloping rubble against the cliffs. The resulting area was, therefore, level with the surface at one edge and sunk 2 or 3 feet below the sloping surface on the side toward the cliff. The houses cannot be thought of as pit houses; the log "masonry" was built on the leveled area, so the structures must be thought of as surface dwellings. There were no fireplaces as such; "heating" pits, full of firecracked and mottled stones, which must have been heated outdoors, are the rule. These pits are lined with mud plaster or are merely unmodified basins with no secondary features. No fires were kept, or at least there was no reddening of the clay, which is characteristic of true fireplaces. There were cists and storage pits dug into the irregular floors. And there were many carefully made storage rooms and burial cists outside the houses; some were of clay, and others were carefully lined and floored with flagstones. The Durango log-and-mortar technique has not been noted elsewhere, so that form was atypical; the more usual form is the pit house. The Durango villages were occupied for some 200 years (from 50 to 260 A.D.), and the houses were rebuilt, or new ones were built over old ones, several times.

Not too far from Durango, at Navajo Reservoir near Farmington, New Mexico, are surface masonry structures made from cobbles set in mud mortar, which have been identified as Basketmaker II houses of the Los Pinos phase (1 to 400 A.D.). Horizontal logs around the edges of the oval floor area resemble the Durango finds. Moreover, the Los Pinos phase sites yielded a small amount of polished Mogollon wares of the time. This is the earliest pottery reported from the Four Corners area. Maize was also discovered at these New Mexico sites, although it occurs earlier in late Archaic sites farther north in Colorado and Utah.

The Basketmaker III house type is much better known and is represented by numerous excavated examples. One can generalize that both Basketmaker III and Pueblo I pit houses tended toward the rectangular and were actually semisubterranean, the roof being erected over a room carved as deep as 3 or 4 feet into the earth. Certain special features were normally present, such as a tunnel entrance leading from an antechamber to the main room, a southeast orientation, four post roof supports, and benches around the walls. Later, the antechamber gave way to the ventilator, and the posts were replaced by roof-supporting pilasters set on the bench. Finally, the kiva, the subterranean ceremonial structure, which was not used for habitation, evidently evolved from the pit house as surface masonry structures came to serve as dwellings by 700 A.D. in the San Juan Anasazi area. But to the west—in the Kayenta and more westerly districts—the pit house remained a popular architectural form until the end of the thirteenth century.

The basic Anasazi settlement pattern developed during Basketmaker III. This is a village orientation along a southeast-northwest axis; the storage rooms were the "back" of the settlement, with the pit houses to the southeast and the midden area and burial ground southeast of the dwellings. When the clustered above-ground houses first developed, they were to the northwest, with the pit houses, or kivas, and the refuse toward the southeast. Figure 6.12 is a cross section of a late Basketmaker III pit house at Mesa Verde showing many of the same features as the kiva (Figure 6.13). The classic kiva or ceremonial center is restricted to the San Juan Anasazi, but rectangular structures believed to have had the same function are found in the Kayenta and other western districts as well as among the Mogollon. Pit house architectural details have come to be understood as important in establishing district relationships over the Southwest. Of course, the concept of the semisubterranean dwelling is at least 4000 to 6000 years old in the Northwest (see Chapter Four). Those houses are, however, by no means as elaborate as the Basketmaker III dwellings.

But the Southwest is noted more for above-ground dwellings than for pit houses. After 900 A.D., except in the Fremont and Kayenta regions, the tendency toward settlements of contiguous rooms or, more accurately, clusters of contiguous rooms, became the rule.

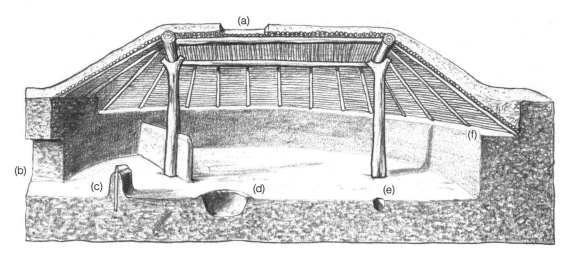

Figure 6.12 Postulated reconstruction (cross section) of a late Basketmaker III pit house: (a) hatchway and smokehole, (b) tunnel entrance to antechamber, (c) **deflector,** (d) fire pit, (e) **sipapu,** (f) bench.

The clustering of dwellings and storage rooms with a kiva to the south or southeast has been interpreted as evidence of a pattern of clan or subclan or even family residence. Even though the town or village may have consisted of many houses, the clustered groupings almost certainly preserved family or lineage integrity. This interpretation is largely drawn from ethnographic analogy.

The richness of the Anasazi begins to be seen in Basketmaker III times in the beautiful sandals woven of finespun string dyed in several colors; decorated, loose-coiled basketry; twined and netted bags; elaborate atlatls and curved throwing sticks; and fired gray pottery. Designs were sometimes painted on the bowl interiors, but most of the pottery is plain. The brown or red-brown wares of the Basketmaker II were displaced by gray. The dominant Anasazi ceramic style continued to be white or gray, with decoration done in black. The subsistence base was broadened by the addition of beans by the end of Basketmaker II, and the domestication of turkeys may have occurred this early.

The differences between Basketmaker III and Pueblo I are negligible, being largely a matter of ceramics. (The latter "period" is actually restricted to a small area in the Anasazi heartland and has little validity elsewhere.) In addition to the fine ware of plain gray, black-on-white, and black-on-red and the introduction of a **slip** and **corrugated** neck bands on culinary pottery, there is a complex of bizarre vessel shapes. These include trilobed vessels with constricted necks, duck and gourd effigy pots, stirrup-spouted vessels, and other forms not found elsewhere in the Southwest. Other additions to the Pueblo I trait list include cotton cloth, **jacal** (wattle and daub) construction, and the practice of cranial deformation—a steeply angled flattening of the occipital area—resulting probably from the use of a rigid cradleboard. Both the cotton and the cranial flattening (of a milder sort) appear earlier in Mogollon.

It was during Pueblo II (after about 900 A.D.), however, that the distinctive flavor of the Anasazi, as well as its greatest areal extent, developed. The pit house dropped from favor in the Mesa Verde area and the typical architecture became the block or arc of contiguous rooms with a frontal kiva.

There was an expansion during Pueblo II time. The spread of Anasazi influence can perhaps be credited particularly to a somewhat favorable rainfall pattern and possibly to new strains of cultigens. But credit must

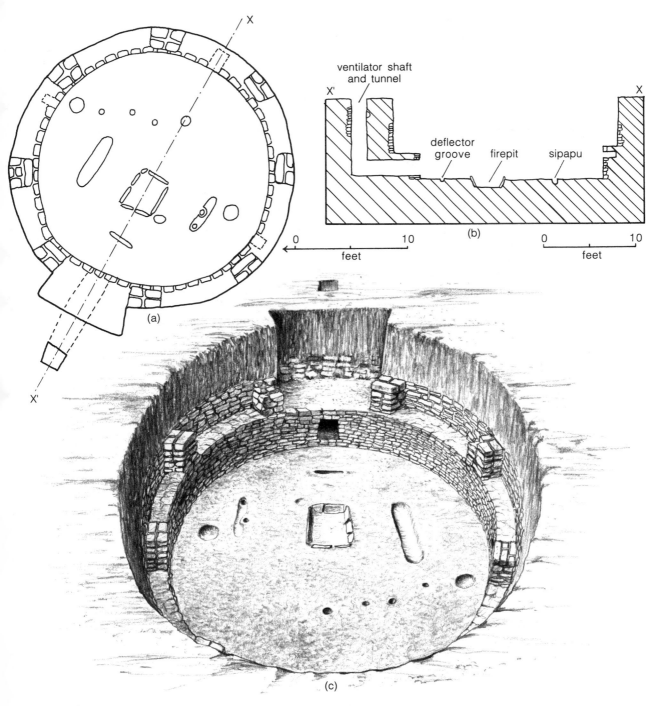

Figure 6.13 Pueblo II kiva at Mesa Verde National Park: (a) plan view, (b) cross section, (c) view of excavated kiva.

also go to the Anasazi family or lineage farmstead pattern of life. Small ruins occur by the hundreds wherever there was water to put on the fertile soil; thus the population spread as family after family "hived off" to make new homesteads, and the culture spread into marginal areas far beyond the favored areas where resources could support heavy aboriginal use.

In Pueblo II ceramics there is an increased use of coarse, wavy corrugations over the full surface of cooking vessels (Figure 6.14). The use of painted decoration increased on most vessels except on the cooking wares. The open-ended metate, increased use of cotton, coiled basketry, and bow and arrow are all found with some stylistic and decorative changes; but the form and overall inventory of Anasazi tools and implements changed remarkably little through time (Figure 6.15). The major stylistic changes are found in the pottery. The appearance, period of popularity, and disappearance of distinctive pottery styles or types have been extensively studied and are well charted. Ceramics have provided the clues to regional boundaries and evidence of interregional communication, and they also form the backbone of the chronological system. The undecorated wares enjoyed long lifespans and are not very useful in either cultural period or chronological ascriptions, although corrugation techniques have some chronological usefulness.

Aside from the widest distribution ever achieved by Pueblo people, the Pueblo II era is notable for the occurrence of some distinctive local social systems that were apparently quite complex. These have been called "systems of regional integration." The best known and by far the best studied of these distinctive regional subcultures is called the Chaco Phenomenon. It developed in the San Juan basin in northwestern New Mexico and impinged to some extent into extreme southwestern Colorado. The Phenomenon, centered in Chaco Canyon was short-lived, lasting about 200 years, from 900 A.D., or a little later, until just after 1100 A.D.

Chaco Canyon itself had been occupied from Basketmaker II times onward. By 900 A.D., the alluvial valley of the canyon supported a number of the small towns typical of Pueblo II. Characterized by an aggregation of twelve to twenty contiguous rooms, the hamlets were apparently built singly to no particular plan. They were simple mud masonry architecture and had a small kiva in the room block, so they were in no way architecturally distinctive. Called the Hosta Butte style, they occur up and down both sides of the Chaco stream called Chaco Wash with more located on the south side than on the north side of the wash. The Hosta Butte settlements stand in extreme contrast to the unique Bonito-style towns located in a 10-mile stretch on the north bank of the wash.

The Bonito-style towns are large, preplanned structures, averaging more than 200 rooms each, that were built as a continuous construction project rather than in the intermittent accretional manner typical of most Pueblo architecture. Some of the buildings were as much as four stories in height. The masonry was not the irregular stone and mud, like the Hosta Butte style. It was instead an elaborate core-veneer construction involving a sturdy mud-stone masonry core and an external facing of thin, tightly fitted, small tabular stones usually accented with linear bands of larger, thicker stones (Figure 6.16). The handsome veneer so painstakingly created was then lost to view under a coat of **adobe** plaster!

The town plan was to some degree standardized: three straight walls in an open, rectangular or squat U shape with the fourth side enclosed in a sweeping arc created by a wall or, more often, by a curving shallow room block of single rooms set end to end. Additionally, there were three early, much smaller rectangular towns in the Bonito style at the west end of the cluster of nine. In the large

Figure 6.14 Pueblo II and III artifacts: (a) wickerwork sandal of yucca leaves, (b) bone scrapers, (c) wooden comb, (d) stone pipe, (e) ring basket of twilled yucca leaves, (f) bifurcated basket, (g) spindles with whorls and a distaff of spun yarn, (h) black-on-white bowl, (i) black-on-white ladle, (j) digging stick with sheep-horn blade (restored), (k) black-on-orange bowl, (l) partially corrugated utility vessel. Variable scale.

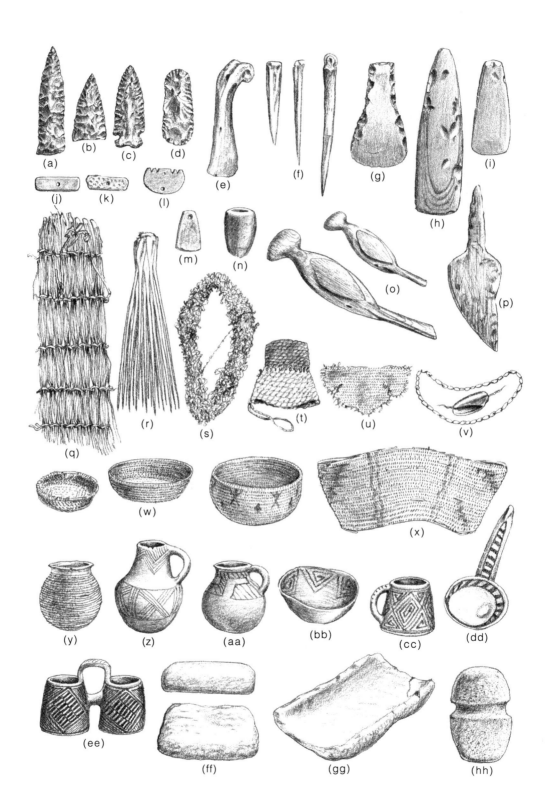

(a) (b) (c) (d) (e) (f) (g) (h) (i)
(j) (k) (l) (m) (n) (o) (p)
(q) (r) (s) (t) (u) (v)
(w) (x)
(y) (z) (aa) (bb) (cc) (dd)
(ee) (ff) (gg) (hh)

◀ **Figure 6.15** Pueblo III artifacts: (a)–(c) points, (d) stone scraper, (e) bone scraper, (f) bone awls, (g)–(i) polished stone celts or hoes; (j) and (k) bone gaming pieces, (l) stone gaming piece, (m) stone ornament, (n) stone pipe, (o) carved wooden birds, (p) wooden utensil, (q) fragment of woven mat, (r) yucca bundle used as hair brush (?), (s) skein of cotton string, (t) woven bag of dog and human hair, (u) twilled cotton fabric, (v) bone scraper, (w) baskets, (x) fragment of carrying basket, (y) corrugated pot, (z) black-on-red jar, (aa) black-on-white pot, (bb) black-on-white bowl, (cc) Mesa Verde black-on-white mug, (dd) Mesa Verde black-on-white ladle, (ee) black-on-white twin mug, (ff) manos, (gg) metate, (hh) full-grooved stone ax. Variable scale.

Figure 6.16 Decorative veneer patterns in Bonitan masonry.

enclosed plaza created by the arcing wall there was a free-standing great kiva. Sometimes there were two great kivas, while many smaller ones were incorporated into the room blocks. Occasionally the second kiva was called a tower, which simply means a kiva with at least two stories.

The great kivas, as much as 50 feet in diameter, were sometimes 10 feet deep and roofed with a horizontal domed cribbing of logs. There was a raised square fireplace flanked by two large masonry vaults, that is, pits lined with masonry (Figure 6.17). The walls and the encircling bench were also of thick stone masonry. Four huge posts or stone pillars for central support of the high, cribbed roof were arranged in a square a few feet in from the peripheral bench. On the wall above the bench were a series of rectangular niches which were usually empty when found. A few had caches of special artifacts inside, however, and were plastered over. The great kivas were entered by a stairway. The crib roofs of the kivas required more than an estimated 300 heavy logs. Usually these logs were pine, fir, or spruce that came from many miles away in the mountains to the northeast and west. In a desert setting such as Chaco Canyon, the ritual or symbolic value of the large kivas must have been enormous to warrant the effort expended in obtaining timber. The cost in labor and transport time would already have been high for the excavation and masonry lining of the kiva pit.

Chaco is characterized by a series of quite distinctive artifacts. These include macaw skeletons and feathers, religious and ritual artifacts, copper bells, cylindrical vases of a distinctive ceramic ware, as well as some turquoise and other stone inlay on jewelry (Figure 6.18).

But impressive as the nine large towns that were built and abandoned in 200 years may be, there was clearly a Chaco network or power sphere that exercised some form of social, economic, religious, or ritual control over

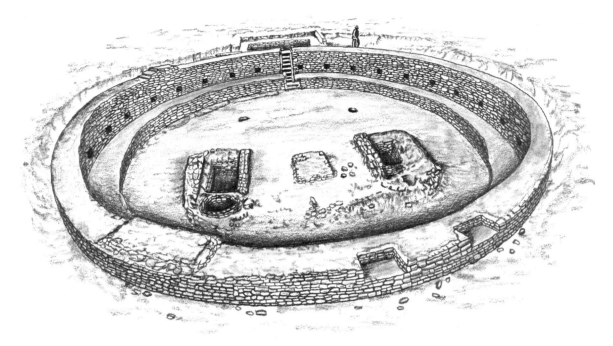

Figure 6.17 Great Kiva at Chetro Ketl. The standard great kiva features include the wall niches and encircling bench; central, square, raised firebox; paired rectangular masonry ''vaults''; and stair entryway. The antechamber beyond the stairs is also a common great kiva feature.

the eastern half of the San Juan Basin. There were outlier towns up to 80 kilometers from Chaco Wash where large structures of Bonito-style construction and great kivas and communication centers were established. The settlements clustered near each outlier were, of course, the simple stone and mud masonry in the casual, accretional room blocks seen in the Hosta Butte style villages.

Most surprising was the system of roadways connecting the central towns with the outliers (Figure 6.19). These are like nothing else. They are not haphazard fortuitous linkages of existing footpaths between settlements. Instead, they are broad roadways laid out in straight lines for many miles without regard for terrain. When the road alignment met a ledge or cliff, there would be hand and toe stairs, evenly cut stone steps, or ramps of earth faced with stone that led the traffic over, never around, the obstacle. More than 400 kilometers of road have so far been observed

and mapped to the north, south, southeast, and southwest of the Chaco Canyon center; the roads run directly to many of the outliers. The roads are an incredible 9 meters wide and can still be found because they were either excavated below the surface, marked by masonry or lines of stone, or, in some cases, merely cleared of vegetation and loose stones.

Figure 6.18 Selected artifacts from Pueblo Bonito: (a)–(c) shell ornaments; (d) **jet** ornament, 2.5 inches long; (e) and (f) bone dice, 1 inch long; (g) jet ring (bird has turquoise inset wings); (h) copper bells; (i) turquoise bird effigy, 2 inches high; (j) ceramic bear effigy; (k) turquoise pendants, 1 inch long; (l) turquoise bead; (m) turquoise necklace; (n) bone scrapers with jet and turquoise inlay, 6.5 and 5 inches long; (o) wooden snake effigy; (p) bone awls, 4.5 to 7 ¾ inches long; (q) bone needle, 2 ¾ inches long; (r) flint knife, 7 ¼ inches long; (s) projectile points; (t) fragment of ceremonial staff; (u) black-on-white bowl, 2 ¾ inches high, 7 inches in diameter; (v) stone pipe, 3.5 inches long; (w) pottery pipe, 3.5 inches long; (x) Old Bonitan pot, 13.5 inches high; (y) bifurcated basket, 15.5 inches high, 12 inches wide.

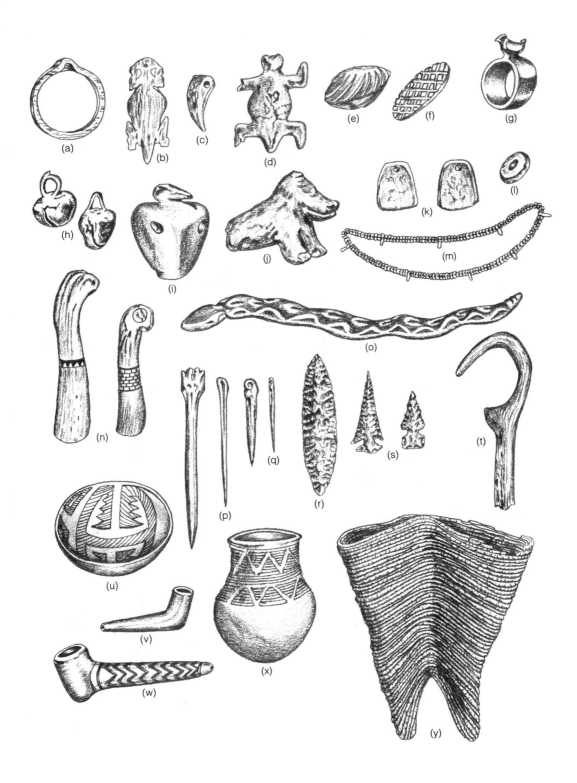

(a)

(b)

(c)

(d)

(e)

(f)

(g)

(h)

(i)

(j)

(k)

(l)

(m)

(n)

(o)

(p)

(q)

(r)

(s)

(t)

(u)

(v)

(w)

(x)

(y)

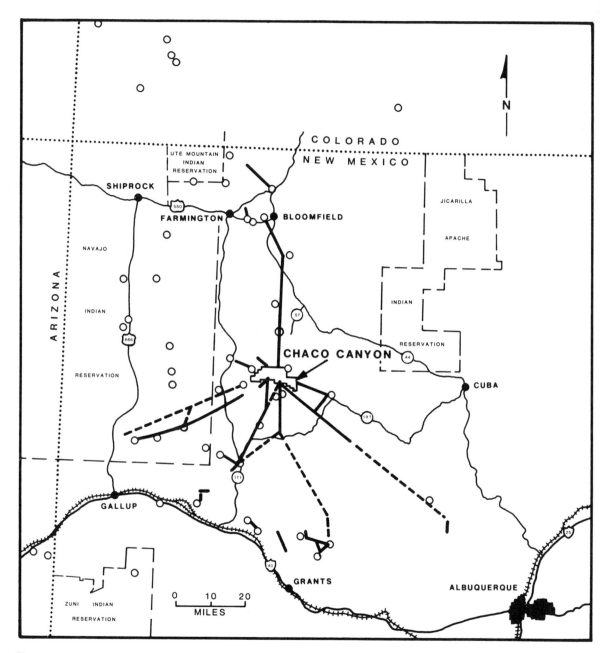

Figure 6.19 Chacoan road system and outliers. Chacoan outliers are indicated by open circles. The road segments shown as solid lines have been documented by ground surveys; the broken lines were taken from aerial photographs.

They seem unduly elaborate for mere foot travel from one place to another, but no other function than connecting roadways has been suggested.

There seems also to have been a signal system between the centers and the outliers. The so-called signal stations are arc-shaped, semicircular stone structures on high points providing line-of-sight vision from one to another of the Bonito towns in the system. (A night test of visual contact was conducted with red flares; watchers in each tower could see the flares in the stations to each side, thus demonstrating the feasibility of signaling with lights. The test, of course, suggests rather than proves what the Bonitans had in mind.)

There are other details and ramifications comprising the Chaco Phenomenon as currently hypothesized. The reasons for origins of the phenomenon and its suggestion of control remain obscure but not for lack of proposed explanations. An older school of thought tends to view the exotic Mexican artifacts as having arrived *en bloc*. Such traits as copper bells, macaws, inlaid shell, core veneer architecture, the great kivas and tower kivas, and cylindrical jars, are interpreted as imports. These traits, along with the evidence of central authority such as the building of huge towns to a standard plan, are not seen elsewhere. The influence of small bands of priests or traders (pochteca) who brought attractive new objects and ideas from the more complex and sophisticated Mexican cultures is often cited. Whether persuasion, force, or religious awe of the glamorous strangers provided the leverage toward acceptance is never clear. The idea of extensive trade, especially in turquoise, with the south has also been invoked, and there is good evidence for it. Turquoise occurs in Toltec sites in quantity. The few copper bells or macaws also suggest a systematic northward trade traffic in those commodities, but not a very extensive one. Whatever the explanation, the complex of roads, architecture, and exotic objects still appears anomalous in the Pueblo setting. It has

been proposed that the roads facilitated the transporting of the thousands of huge logs used as roof beams in the houses and kivas.

A second, later school sees the entire Chaco development as the complex end product of indigenous factors and influences to be analyzed and understood as a regional event and system. One popular theory is that by 700 A.D., cultigens were becoming a more significant part of the diet and the settlement of Chaco Canyon where arable land was plentiful increased to the point that by 900 A.D. all the prime horticultural lands in the wash or the valley were in use. But further population expansion, either through local increase or continued immigration, led to the exploitation of marginal lands away from the rich valley. The notoriously fickle southwestern summer rainfall and the violent, localized thunderstorms that fall capriciously over the San Juan Basin jeopardize farming somewhat. The crops in one district might prosper while nearby ones failed for lack of moisture.

Such a situation, it is theorized, led to the creation of a network of exchange in which towns or districts with good crops shared with their less-fortunate neighbors. The theory calls for central storage and redistribution centers and some specialized control to make the system work. The big towns are given the role of central storage and distribution. Presumably they also housed the managing priests or chieftains or whoever was responsible for distribution and storage. The ultimate expansion and creation of outliers until 1100 A.D. is seen as the evolution and growth of the network of pooled resources that had begun in Chaco Canyon two centuries earlier. Variations on the trade and pooling network have also been proposed. None are any more precise or convincing than the first or the Mexican diffusion model. About all that can be safely said is that the monumental Bonito structures of the canyon, the outliers, and the roads; the inferred social control system; and the underlying rationale still await a unifying, convincing explanation.

The central or pooling system itself seems to have collapsed by about 1125 A.D. and was gradually erased as an Anasazi population from the Mesa Verde district took over the canyon. Two of the northern outliers (probably locations actually colonized by Chacoans), the Salmon and Aztec sites (New Mexico) show the same patterned construction of a major town followed by decline and replacement by a Pueblo III Mesa Verde population.

At the same time, however, other things were going on that deserve mention. Interestingly, there is good evidence of Hohokam dominance over a far larger area than the San Juan Basin at the same time as the Chaco Phenomenon. Between 900 and 1100 or 1125 A.D. Hohokam expansion stretched from well south of Tucson to north of Flagstaff (i.e., Wupatki Ruin). Whereas a trade system is postulated but not proved for Chaco, there was a wide dispersal of artifacts and many architectural traits up the Verde River onto the Mogollon highlands, well past Flagstaff toward the Grand Canyon, and as far west as Gila Bend. Macaws, copper bells, onyx ornaments, and ball courts reached beyond Flagstaff. In the Verde Valley there were large Hohokam settlements with both platform mounds and ball courts. There were also many smaller support villages. Many artifacts in the Hohokam style and materials, including large numbers of finished shell bracelets, have been found in the Verde Valley.

Some scholars suggest that the ball courts and mounds served a ritual or religious function and that the outlying peoples shared a belief system with the Hohokam. The scholars who hold this view reason that the socioreligious system was spread and perhaps made palatable through trade activity. That is, the exotic trade objects were symbols of, and embedded in, the religious system. There is evidence that the towns in the western extension of the Hohokam down the Gila River were critical to the heavy shell presence in all Hohokam ceremonies. Towns near the source

of the shells in the Gulf of Lower California quite clearly acquired the unworked shell, and their artisans created the bracelets and etched and carved shells that are unique to the culture. From the lower Gila towns, the finished products moved over the entire Hohokam dominion. In fact, it seems that the evidence for the Hohokam as operators of a regional trade and colonizing system seems far stronger than that adduced for the Chaco. Certainly the trade is documented, but again, *planned* towns like the Chacoan ones do not exist in the Hohokam area.

A little later, perhaps from 1050 or 1100 A.D., half a dozen very large towns grew up by accretion in the southern or Mimbres region of the Mogollon area. The Mimbres is largely known for the distinctive black-on-white bowls already mentioned. Natural, mythological, and occasionally lewd designs in black on a stark white background characterize these well-proportioned bowls, and they possess genuine artistic merit. Though prized today by collectors (whose greed to own them has led to the almost total destruction of all Mimbres sites), there was apparently no particular call for them aboriginally; at least very few are found outside the small Mimbres district. With masonry of crude boulder and mud construction and little external trade, there is no real evidence for the regional dominance some scholars ascribe to the Mimbres.

At Mesa Verde in the northern part of the Southwest, where the huge cliff palaces represent *the* Pueblo for most Americans, there is not the slightest evidence for a control system or extensive trade. The many kivas and the elaborate paraphernalia suggest a deep concern for religion, ritual, and ceremony. Unlike the big Chaco towns, the cliff towns, though impressive in their storied niches, are merely casual, accretional structures built to no perceived plan.

Even so, it must be remembered that the Four Corners Pueblo III seems to have expanded south as far as Chaco Canyon, where it replaced the Chaco Phenomenon as well as at the Aztec and Salmon sites. Just west of the Mesa Verde, there are several large towns, the Yellowjacket Ruin being the best known. The ceramic complex in the Yellowjacket district duplicates the Mesa Verde one. The district was fertile, well watered, and heavily populated. There are more rooms in the Yellowjacket ruin alone than in all the cliff castles combined. Therefore, it has been suggested that the Mesa Verde cliff structures comprised a religious center that by 1250 A.D. or earlier dominated a larger territory than Chaco ever had. The Mesa Verde sacred center can possibly be described as controlling, without the administrative structure postulated for Chaco, an equally large domain through religious rather than economic means. In any case, the Mesa Verde area should be regarded as a regional specialization as distinctive as Chaco. The suggestion that the Mesa cliff houses are the source of religious dominance, supported by the large towns (and their satellites), deserves further study and exposition.

It is in Pueblo III that the large settlements and multistory "communal" dwellings appear at Mesa Verde, Canyon de Chelly, and two smaller sites, Betatakin and Keet Seel in Navajo National Monument in the Kayenta area. At this time the spread of masonry southward and an intrusion of some Hohokam influences (such as ball courts) northward as far as Flagstaff, Arizona, led to the final "leveling" off of all the Southwest traditions. This leveling off or uniformity, which began by 1000 or 1100 A.D., is real enough but does not obscure the comparable reality of certain minor districts—Patayan, Salado, Sinagua—where regional specialists have perceived local blendings of a distinctive nature.

Because of the impact the large Pueblo III settlements have always had on laymen, the reports of their excellence are often more enthusiastic than accurate. However glowingly it may be described, Anasazi and other southwestern masonry (other than that at Chaco) was neither very sophisticated nor particularly good. The mortar was mud (adobe) and the building stones were whatever lay at hand. Although masonry was often **coursed** and the stones were sometimes shaped, the structures usually reveal little planning or foresight, and no special engineering principles (such as the arch or cantilever span) were achieved. The unit of construction was a single, four-sided cell or boxlike room. Its walls were stones laid in mud mortar. Mud sometimes makes up 30 or 40 percent of the volume. The room width was controlled by the length of available timbers strong enough to support a roof of mud placed on a platform of sticks and bark or grass athwart the major beams. Given this cellular module (and walls of sufficient thickness), one could raise a structure to two, three, four, or five stories in height and extend it horizontally indefinitely merely by adding more single cells or units. Most ruins testify to accretional growth, room by room, as each new room abutted and shared one or more walls with an earlier room or rooms. Even the symmetrical and smoothly terraced Pueblo Bonito shows several periods of accretion or remodeling by later users after the original building was finished. In effect these were like all other aboriginal dwellings, handmade from locally available materials by the user (or his spouse) to a pattern but to no rigid detailed specifications. Where stone was lacking, jacal was used, or coursed adobe alone. No great effort was made to create artistic textured effects, except in the Chaco area. Usually the walls, including the textured, decorative veneered ones at Chaco, were covered with mud plaster so that the masonry was not visible. One has the impression that the niceties of stone masonry were generally ignored. To point out the simplicity of the architecture is not to deprecate it; the structures' appropriateness for the environment, sturdiness, and formal charm still impress all beholders.

In crafts, Pueblo III can be thought of as an age of specialization. The quality of the already good pottery improved, and the famous

Mesa Verde mug was added to the list of vessel forms. Polychrome painting and black paint on yellow and orange base colors extended the color range. Decorations were elaborate and meticulously executed. In each district, distinctive styles developed, and the different ceramic types are readily identifiable. There was much trade in pottery during this time, perhaps indicating widespread popularity of different styles. Culinary vessels became increasingly elaborate with fine, often patterned coiling over all the exterior. While pottery became more exuberant, the textiles tended to be undecorated, albeit well made, except for cotton cloth, where complex, lace-like, loom-made designs became the mode.

The collections from Pueblo III sites are enormous. The artifacts range from cobbles used as hammerstones to exquisite ornaments of turquoise and turquoise mosaics. Tools of bone, stone, wood, and antler occur by thousands. Textiles—mats, bags, baskets, sandals, nets, cordage, aprons, robes, and blankets—demonstrate great skill and artistry. Personal ornaments such as pendants, bracelets, or beads, as well as religious objects, are found by the hundreds.

The closing years of Pueblo III were marked by the extreme contraction of Anasazi territory; all of Utah and much of Arizona and Colorado seem to have been abandoned. Some Kayentans seem to have migrated to east-central Arizona, while the Anasazi shrank almost to the limits of the Rio Grande Valley. Although the extent of the cultural areas shown in Figure 6.2 is based largely on ceramic data, these data are sufficient to convey the shockingly sudden decline of all southwestern cultures. Just why this sudden contraction should have occurred is not known. Reasons suggested include a long drought, the pressure of "enemy peoples," or a change in precipitation pattern from winter to summer rain, with a disastrous attendant flooding-and-gullying cycle that made horticulture difficult. All these theories lack proof, although there is evidence of frequent summer floods on a scale

that would ensure repeated crop failures in some areas. For even part-time gardeners, successive crop losses would ensure privation and the death of the very young and aged as rations grew shorter.

As for enemy peoples, there is evidence for attack and slaughter of members of a settlement at some locations, but most ruins reveal little violence at the time of abandonment, with many valuable items being left intact. Of course, foot travelers cannot carry many household furnishings on a long trek, so the discarding of pottery vessels, tools, and clothing when a starving, weakened family abandoned its home forever would not be surprising. Even so, there could have been alien pressure without warfare as the Shoshonean-speaking tribes of the Great Basin spilled over into Utah, Colorado, and Arizona. This is known to have occurred 600 to 800 years ago, a time coincident with the southward movement of the Anasazi. In the face of double demand the attrition of the natural resources could have begun with the Shoshonean entry. There could also have been additional pressure, such as crop raids and miscellaneous thievery by the newly arrived Great Basin foragers. Similar pressure may well have been felt in the Hohokam and Sinagua areas as the Yuman-speaking tribes pressed eastward from California at about this same time. If enemy pressure is conceived thus, instead of as warfare, present data make this speculation defensible.

No single explanation of the Anasazi decline is especially convincing, and a full explanation is still lacking although many have been offered. While the San Juan Anasazi were in full climax in Pueblo III, the provincial areas were by no means as impressive.

The story of Pueblo IV is one of territorial contraction and consequent increase in population in restricted areas. As Figure 6.2 reveals, by 1500 A.D., Pueblo settlements were found only in the Upper Rio Grande Valley, the Acoma and Zuni districts, and the Hopi villages. Two outstanding advances in ceramic technology were the use of metallic glazes, in both the Zuni district and in the Rio Grande Valley, and the development of the Hopi Sikyatki Polychrome, featuring graceful, realistic designs in lieu of the early geometric motifs. Some of the finest pottery north of Mexico was produced at this time. The ancient settlement pattern—storage-dwelling-midden axis—gave way to the enclosed or central-plaza village plan.

Pueblo V is primarily a story of European contact and the stresses of acculturation with the Spanish, with the Native Americans in continuous, varyingly intense cooperation or conflict. The Pueblo tribes became even more conservative, retaining their languages, religion, and other traditions in the face of economic, military, and religious pressures. Resistance in 1680 took the form of outright revolt, and the Southwest was free of Spaniards, including priests, until 1692. In the sphere of material culture the tribes were more receptive. European plants, domestic animals, iron tools and weapons, and some architectural features were accepted from the conquerors. But in all other things the Pueblo preserved their old ways remarkably intact, although the shrinkage of territory and the decrease in population continued under Spanish and, later, American rule.

The Navajo

The decreases in territory and population during late Pueblo IV and V can now be more certainly credited in part to alien pressures. Sometime before 1500 A.D. the nonagricultural Athabaskan tribes came into the Southwest from Canada and the Plains. These emigrants are known today as the several Apache bands and the numerous Navajo. By 1500 A.D. the land was largely empty of permanent settlements, and the Navajo and Apache began to spread into the empty spaces.

They also put heavy raiding pressures on the usually peaceful Pueblo. The newcomers not only took food and women but also borrowed many traits, such as horticulture, weaving, and elements of religion. In fact, the most impressive trait of the Navajo tribe is its adaptability. The Navajo religion, material culture (including weaving and metalworking), pastoral life of sheep rearing, and settlement patterns are a blend of their original culture with elements from all the peoples they have touched. As pastoralists moving in a seasonal rhythm, the Navajo achieved a sort of symbiosis, albeit sometimes uneasy, with the sedentary Pueblo, with each group exploiting somewhat different ecological niches.

Some of the fuller archaeological reports of excavation of Navajo sites comes from work in the San Juan Basin. There the sites are consistently located on the edge of the first or second terrace or bench above the river floodplain. The time span is from 1550 to perhaps 1775 A.D. The remains are divided into three phases: the Dinetah (1550 to 1696 A.D.), the Gobernador (1696 to 1775 A.D.), and the Refugee Pueblo. (The late, fairly heavy Pueblo presence came as the Pueblo fled northward from the Spanish reprisals following the Pueblo Revolt of the 1680s.)

The typical Navajo site shows evidence of one or more hogans and limited debris. The normal living pattern is, and presumably was, a cluster of two or three hogans sheltering an extended family. The clusters are widely scattered; only in modern times have "The People" developed the loose settlements of a dozen or so hogans strung out a few hundred feet apart along a wash. The hogan traditionally had a tripod frame of forked posts with sticks and branches forming the walls of the tipi-shaped dwelling. An entryway opened to the east (Figure 6.20). The hogan contained a basin-shaped or even flat fireplace in an oval, saucer-shaped floor and few other internal features. Outdoor firepits, a shade or ramada, and metate rests accompany the hogans. This style is often called the summer hogan.

Figure 6.20   Typical Navajo hogan.

Another, more durable design was a circular structure of stone. Cribbed logs, resulting in a hexagonal or octagonal shape, have commonly been used in recent years. The one or more small hogans near each settlement are sweat lodges. Artifacts are scant and rarely diagnostic, except for pottery, which in many attributes resembles Woodland pottery in shape, surface texturing, coarse temper, and general crudity (Figure 6.21). The pottery offers some support for the idea that the Athabaskans reached the Southwest by way of the Plains.

Although much more attention has been paid to Navajo prehistory since about 1970, there appear to be few differences in the architecture and settlement patterns outlined above and the findings in other parts of the Navajo area. One hopes that a synthesis of Navajo archaeology based on research over the full reservation will one day be written.

The Fremont

Unique to the plateaus and high valleys of Utah is the Fremont culture. Derived from the Desert Archaic of the Eastern Great Basin, it received stimulus from the same early Mogollon thrust in the centuries prior to 400 A.D. to which the Anasazi Tradition is linked. The Fremont was described in 1931

Figure 6.21   Navajo utility vessel (restored). Approximately 12 inches high.

from its "core" area, east of the San Rafael Swell in Utah. The culture clearly shows its initial Pueblo influences, but there seems to have been a heavier emphasis on hunting and gathering, a legacy from the Archaic. Dismissed as "peripheral Anasazi" until the 1960s, research on Fremont content has now progressed to the recognition of five subareas; forty radiocarbon dates demonstrate a time span from about 450 to 1300 A.D. The northern Utah sites are the oldest and least resemble the Anasazi. For example, the houses were shallow basins, with tipilike roofs composed of long poles that met over the center of the basin where a firepit was constructed. These resemble the lodges of the Plateau much more than the Anasazi pit houses. The southern sites are more recent and show distinct ceramic contact with the Kayenta-Virgin Anasazi Tradition; hence it is speculated that the early traits of ceramics and horticulture, if not pit houses, were introduced straight out of the Mogollon by about 400 A.D. The development of Fremont went on in relative isolation until after 1000 A.D.

The San Rafael subarea has perhaps the richest artifact assemblage. It is particularly known for its elaborate figurine (see Figure 6.22) and pictograph styles.

In summary, the Fremont material is earliest (500 A.D.) in the north, with the radiocarbon dates of the Parowan and San Rafael variant sites falling after 900 A.D. The southern sites show evidence of more direct and more intimate contact with the Anasazi, particularly in ceramic design (Figure 6.23). While the Fremont may have evolved in Utah from local Archaic variants, its genesis must be credited to southwestern (specifically Mogollon) influences. The dominantly brown-to-gray pottery of good quality, the southern pit house, and the horticultural pattern can have no other origin. What is remarkable is the lack of heavier and more continuous exchange with the Mesa Verde Anasazi just to the southeast.

Research in the Southwest

This chapter has attempted to document one of the miracles of Native American achievements: the establishment of a sedentary, horticultural lifeway in the southwestern deserts and plateaus. The admiration their ruins excite should be extended equally to the people who created them.

The chapter can be closed appropriately with a brief examination of the course of archaeological thought and research in the American Southwest. Although the splendid remains and artifactual riches of the Midwest and Southeast attracted scholarly attention earlier, many important theories and procedures were developed in the Southwest. This short sketch is included because Southwest research influenced all subsequent American archaeological study.

The period of exploration and the first glimmerings of scholarly interest came as early as the 1880s and 1890s. Since those early scholars the Southwest has been more systematically studied than any other part of the United States; Mexico, of course, was being exploited archaeologically earlier than that. The continuing intense interest that the Southwest has engendered has been explained in various ways, but certainly one of the major factors leading to discovery, especially in the Mesa Verde area, was the quantity and quality of the artifacts that began to appear. They were coveted by major eastern United States, European, and many university museums. Thus the collecting (or looting) expeditions for some twenty years after about 1890 had a single goal: the acquisition of aesthetically pleasing aboriginal objects. Chronology, culture history, provenience control, stratigraphy, or insights into early environments were not yet matters of concern.

On the heels of the collectors, and usually with more intellectual or scientific goals, a few universities and museums began explorations and limited excavation programs. The Chaco ruins had been described by a Mexican military observer as early as 1823; the Mexican author had also described Pueblo Pintado. However, the first English account comes in 1844 from Josiah Gregg, a Santa Fe trader who had been in New Mexico for a number of years. He described Pueblo Bonito. In 1849 Lieutenant J. H. Simpson of the U.S. Army Topographical Engineers visited the Chaco system and noted eleven of the twelve large towns. He applied names to eight of them, the names being local ones supplied by his guide.

The discovery of the Mesa Verde cliff towns is usually credited to the Wetherills sometime in the 1880s. They guided the Swedish scholar Nordenskiold to them. He made large collections and returned with them to Stockholm, where they are today. His excavations and "robbery" of the artifacts so incensed western scholars—particularly E. L. Hewitt of the University of New Mexico—that they lobbied the

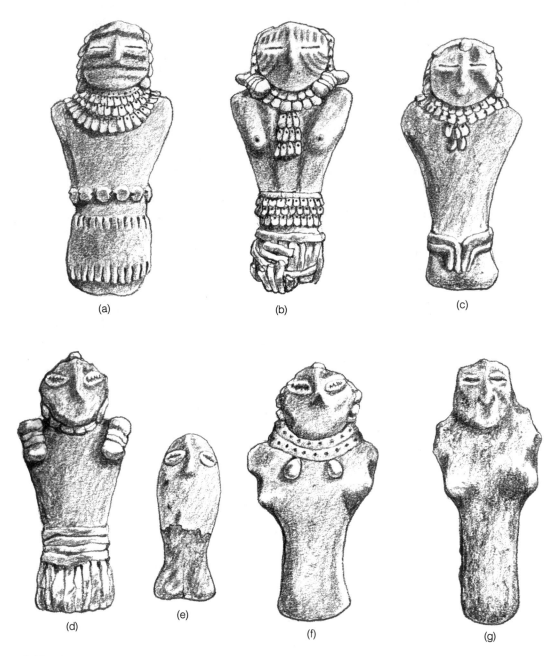

Figure 6.22 Fremont clay figurines: (a)–(c) Pillings Cave, Utah; (d)–(g) University of Utah collection. (a), (b), and (d) one-half size; (c), (e)–(g) two-thirds size.

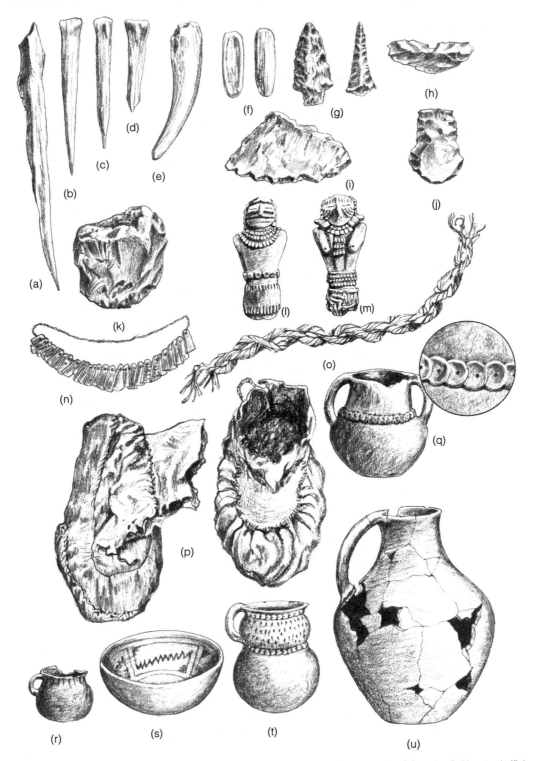

Figure 6.23 Artifacts of the Fremont culture: (a) bone splinter awl, (b)–(d) bone awls, (e) antler flaking tool, (f) bone gaming pieces, (g) projectile points, (h) shaft scraper, (i) and (j) scrapers, (k) rough hammerstone, (l) and (m) clay figurines, (n) bone necklace, (o) bark rope, (p) leather moccasins, (q) pot and enlarged view of applique treatment, (r) small pot, (s) black-on-white bowl, (t) pot with applique at rim and restricted waist, (u) plain grayware vessel. Variable scale.

passage of the United States Antiquities Act in 1906. Thus the antiquities act can be credited to the archaeologists of the Southwest.

Among several other pioneer scholars of the nineteenth century were Adolph Bandelier and Walter Hough. Those two, along with Hewitt, are noteworthy for their occasional interest in chronology and their attempts to identify or establish successive cultural sequences in the limited data they had collected through excavation and survey. Given the century of interest and exploration in the Southwest, the many new concepts, procedures, theories, and innovative approaches to data that have been applied or developed there are no great wonder.

Many methodological innovations, useful to all archaeologists gathering and manipulating data, were developed in the Southwest. Of critical importance was N. C. Nelson's application of the principle of stratigraphy to trash mound excavation in 1914 in the Galisteo Basin of New Mexico. Of course, it must be pointed out that the idea of stratigraphy was known and was being applied in Mexico, Peru, and California considerably before Nelson used it in the Southwest. A. V. Kidder, perhaps the most famous of all Southwest researchers, immediately adopted the procedures at Pecos and in northeastern Arizona. The basketry, ceramic, and architectural sequences developed by Nelson and Kidder and other later excavators led eventually and directly to the Pecos Classification, which we have used in this chapter.

At the same time two ethnologists, Alfred Kroeber and Leslie Spier, established seriation as a useful technique for establishing a valid chronological sequence of ceramic types from surface collections from many sites. The technique provided a synthetic stratigraphy without excavation; of course the sequence provided only relative time. The first culture sequence for any American archaeological region was published by Kidder in 1924. This was followed in 1929 by the first reliable classification and chronology of the culture of any

North American culture sequence. Interestingly, the first estimate of the time span of the Pecos Classification, Basketmaker I through Pueblo V, allowed some 4000 years for the full sequence. In 1929, with the aid of beams from Pueblo Bonito at Chaco, and at Showlow, astronomer A. E. Douglass assembled the tree ring calendar now so important as an absolute dating technique. Douglass and his students had already established two long tree ring calendars. One was based on living trees or those of known cutting date; the other "dangled" because its record did not overlap with the one anchored by the living trees. The famous beam at Pueblo Bonito bridged the gap, thus creating a calendar back to about 700 A.D. Douglass's calendar not only provided true dates but also cut the estimated age of the Basketmaker-Pueblo sequence to about a 2000-year total.

PaleoIndian studies at several Southwest sites extended the time of Southwest occupancy back 10,000 or 11,000 years and tended to focus attention on the long gap between the PaleoIndian and the high cultures. This gap was slowly erased as more and more sites of Archaic affiliation were discovered. The Terminal Archaic, of course, fit the description of the hypothesized Basketmaker I phase of the Pecos Classification so that the Basketmaker I label dropped from use.

Analytical study and classification of the plentiful ceramic remains into types found widely (because of trade) over the Southwest provided another device for making fine distinctions between archaeological districts. In combination with tree ring data and earlier seriation studies, ceramic typology created a passably accurate means of assigning dates to individual sites and culture units.

Another strong contribution to archaeological interpretation was the effort to discover and define a relationship of culture history to the environment, a concern that was predominant in the 1940s and 1950s. One result was the further emphasis on general ecology and settlement patterning that we note today. Such programs were first confined to the Southwest. By the late 1960s, many students were interested in developing and testing hypotheses about social organization, cultural change, and the details of adaptation to specific environments. Most such questions were first asked in the Southwest and tested in excavation programs there. Close-grained studies of subsistence, paleodemography, settlement patterns, systems of trade or exchange, and sampling procedures in survey, are among the many pioneered in the Southwest. That advanced research has stimulated similar research in areas far from the Southwest. One can repeat: Southwest archaeology, valuable in its own right, has influenced all American archaeology through the years.

Chapter 6
BIBLIOGRAPHY

Cordell, Linda S.

1984   *The Southwest*. Academic Press. New York.

This book is a very careful analysis of much of the new thought about the entire Southwest. Cordell devotes a lot of attention to the initial stages of maize agriculture in the Southwest and has thoughtful discussions of the Chaco phenomenon and other special interest areas in the Southwest. Although written for specialists, the serious student can enjoy this book.

Haury, Emil

1976   *The Hohokam: Desert Farmers and Craftsmen: Excavations at Snaketown, 1964–65*. University of Arizona Press. Tucson.

This book, written primarily for specialists, describes the painstaking excavation of the famous Snaketown site, and its contents form the basis for the Hohokam section in this text. The difference is that the time span for the Hohokam culture, as well as some of the others used in this chapter, is somewhat shorter than Haury has allowed.

Kidder, Alfred V.

1924   *An Introduction to the Study of Southwestern Archaeology, With a Preliminary Account of the Excavations at Pecos*. New Haven, (published for the Department of Archaeology, Phillips Academy). Andover.

This is the first synthesis of Southwestern prehistory. While outmoded in some ways, it is still a fascinating account, with some of Kidder's speculations being remarkably accurate.

Lipe, William D.

1983   The Southwest. In *Ancient North Americans*, edited by Jesse D. Jennings, pp. 421–494. W. H. Freeman. New York.

Lipe's chapter is somewhat longer than the same chapter in this book. It is very systematic and thorough and is highly recommended.

Lister, Robert H., and Florence C. Lister

1981   *Chaco Canyon*. University of New Mexico Press. Albuquerque.

This book written for a popular audience contains many fine illustrations and a good description of the development of research and thought with respect to Chaco. Dr. Lister once directed the Chaco Research Center, which developed the Chaco Phenomenon concept.

Cultural Resource Management and Historical Archaeology

This last chapter explores two of the most important emphases in American archaeology. While neither is new, both have burgeoned to become dominant forces today. And they are related activities. Cultural Resource Management (hereafter CRM) is concerned with cultural and social values, not merely with prehistoric archaeological materials. Therefore many CRM programs deal directly with places and events that are linked with the nation's history and possess corresponding values for American citizens. We begin with a review of CRM and continue with an account of the work being done in historical archaeology, a special interest of increasing numbers of young archaeologists.

Cultural Resource Management

CRM, the major activity in American archaeology today, appeared in the early 1970s. Although touched on in Chapter One, it deserves a fuller treatment here. Both resources and management require definition. The cultural resources to be managed, as defined by Fowler (1982), are

> Physical features, both natural and manmade, associated with human activity. These would include sites, structures, and objects possessing significance in history, architecture, archaeology, or human (cultural) development . . . cultural properties are unique and nonrenewable resources.

Resource management is the attempt to plan, organize, direct, control, and evaluate the preservation of important aspects of our cultural heritage for the public good. The definitions obviously include many locations and structures not archaeological in nature, but almost all the early efforts at management involved archaeological remains. This conception later broadened, as will be noted.

The CRM concept did not emerge spontaneously; it was a culmination of many conservation forces and some government actions reaching back into the nineteenth century. It is important to note that from the very beginning, legislation covering conservation and preservation always included either "human knowledge" or "the public good." It is clear, therefore, that the rationale for CRM is neither new nor unique to that legislation.

A rudimentary conservation ethic has been revealed in the actions of the United States Government since before 1850. The emphasis laid on archaeological and ethnological research by the Smithsonian Institution from its inception is a strong example. This interest led to the establishment of the Bureau of American Ethnology, which eventually undertook a sweeping study of the prehistoric mounds of the Midwest and Southeast. The next step was taken when Congress passed the Antiquities Act in 1906; then in 1916 it established the National Park Service (NPS). From the outset the NPS has had as one of its objectives the preservation, in perpetuity, of the wonders of the nation. Evidences of prehistoric inhabitants were included; Mesa Verde was one of the first preserves created after the passage of the Antiquities Act. Concern with archaeological locations increased from the 1930s onward as government agencies varyingly supported the massive recovery of archaeological data in the Tennessee, Missouri, and lesser river valleys during the construction of huge dams that flooded thousands of square miles of floodplain where 10,000 years of prehistory were concentrated. The result of the salvage programs was a manyfold increase in knowledge of American prehistory.

A second force for conservation was what can be called the awakening of nationalistic pride in the American past, and a desire to preserve inspirational places and buildings that mark landmark events in national history. This long concern led to the Historic American Building Survey Act in 1935; the National Park Service (NPS) was designated to evaluate and establish national historic sites. This action thrust the NPS into an even more active cultural management role. The National Trust for Historic Preservation, a quasi-governmental agency, had been established by 1949, and the preservation of national historical places was brought to full flower with the 1966 establishment of the National Register of Historic Places, which required the identification and listing of archaeological and historical locations, including buildings.

In 1969 the National Environmental Policy Act became the third force that, joined with the preservation and nationalism forces, heralded the emergence of the CRM concept and activity. The immediate impetus lay in Executive Order 11593, signed in 1971. This order mandated that federal agencies administer, maintain, and preserve cultural resources in a spirit of trusteeship for the future. This order put government fully into CRM. The initial reaction of most federal land-administering agencies to their new role can be charitably described as languid at best and downright hostile at worst.

Archaeological sites are fragile, finite in number, and disappearing because of construction (dams, roads, airports, and subdivisions), vandalism, and natural forces. Government's tacit acknowledgement of its responsibility to mitigate the loss of knowledge (because of site destruction) became evident in the era of dam construction in the 1930s, but especially after the mid-1940s. Thanks to the environmental legislation, federal interest in archaeological resources is even greater today. Any construction on public land must be preceded by an Environmental Impact Study (EIS), which is undertaken to determine what cultural or natural values will be jeopardized and whether the deleterious effects of the several impacts will outweigh the advantages of the construction proposed. An archaeological resource survey would be part of the EIS. If the archaeological study shows, for example, that building a major pipeline, highway, or transmission line will destroy archaeological sites, the task of the cultural resource manager is to convince the builders to relocate the facility to avoid disturbing the resource—in this case, an archaeological site. If relocation costs exceed the cost of excavation, then as a last resort, the endangered data are salvaged for study. But in the CRM ethic avoiding the site is preferred because it preserves the resource.

Many managers are employed by federal agencies, from national offices down to local districts, where they are expected to interpret and enforce regulations. Moreover, they must master departmental procedures and learn the jargon of their employer. At the same time they must educate their new and often indifferent agency colleagues to the importance and values of archaeology. They continuously make management decisions that they must then persuade the administrators to enforce. Thus most of them are working in situations and against odds for which standard archaeological training leaves them ill-prepared. Fortunately most of them believe in the importance of conservation and its values. It has been said that CRM is more than archaeology, and it should be, but it isn't research.

It is at that juncture—between research and management—that differences between government-inspired and academic archaeology are manifest and compounded. In general, though not always, the academic archaeologist is concerned with increasing the fund of knowledge about prehistory. That increase is arrived at by "pure" research, usually rooted in a series of questions or problems. But the agencies for whom the archaeologist works often have a massive disinterest in research or scientific knowledge. Federal land-administering agencies have been forced to make vast site inventories as they attempt to carry out the injunctions of Executive Order 11593; they must find their resources before they can preserve them. Similarly, construction companies who pay for environmental impact statements simply want compliance clearance so they can proceed with their work. Neither agency administrators nor the company engineers necessarily care about archaeological research or even prehistory per se. They are equally indifferent to such things as significance and values.

For a few years the situation was chaotic. There were not enough university-connected archaeologists to cope with the flood of immediate, usually emergency, demands for surveys of routes and areas. Pressures were heavy on the university researchers, some of whom even denied any responsibility for such "applied" archaeology as the "service" work implied. They refused to assist, saying quite correctly that the mere search for sites was not the path to knowledge. Moreover, few if any universities had a permanent archaeological staff available for extended field studies on a year-round basis. Those scientists were doing their own research, teaching, and guiding graduate students.

What happened next was predictable. Companies, accustomed to business procedures, began asking for bids when universities could not accommodate their needs. Private companies claiming archaeological skills appeared overnight and began receiving contract awards; the lowest bidder received the contract. Neither the qualifications of the archaeologists, the quality of their reports, nor any other professional concern was considered; only the dollar figure was germane. The builders only wanted the work done so that compliance could be certified. Neither research design nor scientific goals were required. Knowledge was not served by hundreds of such studies; it was a mindless numbers and "clearance to proceed" game. Academics held that without research goals and associated tests of theory the money spent on the surveys was wasted. It was at this point—about 1975—that the problem of management became acute.

The picture has greatly brightened. Companies and agencies proved to be educable and began insisting on higher personnel qualifications and better performance from their contractors. Several universities established archaeological contract offices and staffed them with able personnel. And the academic view began to prevail. Proposals for salvage or mitigation projects are now being designed so that research goals and the study of findings are incorporated in the design, and the costs of study are part of the bid offered.

An outstanding example (and one of the earliest) of a research approach to contract archaeology is provided by Schiffer and House (1975). Their report is far too long for an effective summary here because it explains in great detail how they transformed a reluctant pro forma request from the Corps of Army Engineers into a scientific venture. The request was for an assessment of the archaeological resources (and their significance) in the Cache River valley in eastern Arkansas. The funds available were far from adequate, and the time allowed was too short for the task. The study area was the Cache River basin, where the Corps planned an extensive canalization project on about 140 miles of the river's major tributaries. The object of the project, of course, was to improve and increase agriculture in the basin. In all, 2018 square miles were involved, although the direct impact (construction) area was smaller. The time constraints imposed by the Corps, and the unreasonable request for "a comprehensive inventory" of the direct impact area (the wide strips of land on each side of the channel), forced the investigators to develop a design

that could fulfill the goals of the project, be scientifically valid and defensible, and, conceivably, arrive at accurate estimates of the resources and their broad significance as well.

The first step decided on was a 12.5 percent sample in search zones selected randomly in the basin; 546 sites were already known, but the chronological range of the cultural sequence of the area was but sketchily understood. To enhance the mere inventory estimate that the random sampling could provide, the research goals were aimed at (1) learning what locations would be destroyed by construction of levees and channel changes; (2) determining the indirect impacts on the archaeological sites through intensive land clearing and consequent agricultural use; (3) assessing the distribution of sites and speculating about what paleoenvironmental conditions led to the observed settlement patterns; (4) attempting to classify flint tools as to actual function; (5) discovering the settlement pattern of the Dalton complex, which is the earliest extensive archaeological horizon in the basin; (6) discovering the sources of lithic raw materials and their differential use; and, of course, (7) confirming the presumed culture history of the area. Moreover, the survey itself was scheduled for scrutiny to answer such questions as: What sampling procedures are most efficient? Is it necessary to know all the sites in order to arrive at valid assays of significance? Will every survey serve all future data requirements? How will such physical factors as plowed fields or timberlands affect the discovery of sites, and thus skew the survey findings about site density? As these and other goals were pursued, many important serendipitous discoveries emerged and were varyingly followed up. For example, the beginnings of a palynological column were established; and a 400-year dendrochronology of the basin was derived from bald cypress.

The lengthy report by many volunteer authors documents the success of the design; the goals were met. An added dimension was a design for a continuing multidiscipline research program to mitigate the destructive effects of the canalization project. Despite its frequent and tedious explanations of theoretical issues and some freewheeling speculations, the report records a successful combination of the sponsor's goals and the interests of the scientific community. Moreover, the effort must have extended the intellectual horizons of the Corps of Engineers if one can judge by their acceptance of the Schiffer-House report and its recommendations. As of 1981 none of the proposed construction had been undertaken; so the multidiscipline program has never been implemented, most likely because of the complexity and cost of the suggested program of salvaging the endangered data.

Perhaps the most important aspect of the Cache River basin study was the extent to which it was a CRM effort. In every way it illuminates the twin goals of preservation and management of resources. First there was the sample inventory. Then followed the several listed research goals and the derivative findings that contributed to an understanding at several levels of significance and provided new data. Finally the detailed plans offered for further study emphasized methods of mitigation of harmful impacts, such as rerouting the canals, selective dumping of spoil dirt from dredging, and so on. There were even suggestions about the circumstances and conditions under which archaeological material in jeopardy could be ignored.

Altogether different was the problem faced by Elston (1979) in Nevada. Highway US 395 was being built from Stead, near Reno, to Hallelujah Junction a few miles across the Nevada-California line. In April 1974 the highway departments of California and Nevada requested that the right-of-way be surveyed for archaeological resources. Elston treated the task as a research opportunity, not merely survey and mitigation as required. He created a design that aimed to answer five questions by applying a series of specific strategies to the field and laboratory research. Twenty-one sites were jeopardized by the 16-mile-long highway project, which happened to provide a sort of sampling transect across five topographic features and their differing vegetation zones. Elston first consulted ethnographic sources to construct a settlement model that would enable him to predict where certain types of sites (hunting stands, base camps, winter villages, etc.) should be found. Site discovery was followed by excavation (mitigation) of several locations, one being an extensively occupied village. Artifact analysis was aimed at determining what activities were carried on at each site: the full domestic round or some special purpose. Functional analysis of the stone tools was done as part of the recognition of an activity. The five research goals served by the project were (1) to build and apply an ethnographic model of land use and resources as a guide to settlement; (2) to decide how precisely the sites related to topography and resources; (3) to determine the range of activities represented at each site; (4) to investigate the relationships between culture change and environmental fluctuations; and (5) to develop a cultural chronology for this small area that was comparable to those for other Nevada regions. All the goals were met to Elston's satisfaction.

In the Nevada case, the task was very specific: The roadway could not be rerouted to avoid sites, and the only reasonable preservation of data was through excavation. The data are reported in detail, so that they, as well as the design, are permanently on record. Elston concludes that the mitigation was adequate in preserving the data.

The two quite different examples given above have been followed by others of equal merit, and there appears to be an increase in well-designed environmental studies. The two research-oriented EIS contract projects above were done by scholars from universities or museums. Such projects are increasing in frequency.

Finally the American archaeological profession reacted positively to many of the problems created by the huge demand for archaeological service. The Society for American Archaeology appointed a task force to recommend remedies for the particular problem of unqualified personnel. The task force established a code of ethics for contract archaeologists, the minimum qualifications for performing archaeological research, the facilities necessary for an institution doing resource study and research, and a list of specialties within archaeology. In 1976 the task force incorporated the Society of Professional Archaeologists (SOPA), thereby setting up minimum standards against which the quality of personnel could be measured. Many federal agencies began to specify that their contractors should be members of SOPA or should demonstrate equivalent qualifications. As of 1986 the society had some 1100 members. Although its influence has been beneficial in many ways, its power as an accrediting agency is slight. It can police only its own members; it has no professionwide powers.

It is clear that despite early chaos and many distractions CRM has begun to assume stature as a professional subfield. It is an increasingly complex activity requiring a variety of skills beyond competence in field and laboratory archaeological research. Knudson (1986) suggests that for many decades most archaeology will be supported by funds generated in implementing the National Environmental Protection Act's goals. Management will be conducted in the context of multiple public objectives, the rationale for that management being ". . . that the long-term conservation of . . . our cultural past is good for the human community." It is thus evident that CRM is no longer an archaeological "trend" but the dominant force in American archaeology, the source of most funds, and the vehicle through which most archaeological research will be effected for many years.

Historical Archaeology

A specialty of new importance is historical archaeology, although excavation of historic sites is far from new. The name provides a clue, but definitions are less than precise. Historical archaeology includes, but is not restricted to, what is called "historic site archaeology," which normally applies to historical places identified with specific segments of history. Fontana (in Schuyler 1978) defines *historic site archaeology* as being ". . . carried out in sites which contain material evidence of non-Indian culture or concerning which there is contemporary non-Indian documentary record." Such studies as examination of historic battlefields of the Revolutionary or Civil wars, or at frontier forts or settlements, from Roanoke to the Missouri Valley to Fort Vancouver in Washington, are examples. But other interests of the historical archaeologists would include colonial archaeology, underwater exploration, and urban and industrial archaeology. The present strength of the subdiscipline is attributable to the preservation movement and legislation of the 1930s and 1940s. Perhaps the best known and most elaborate historical archaeological project ever undertaken (other than Pompeii) is the town of Williamsburg, Virginia, where excavations (inept in the beginning) laid the groundwork for authentic restorations that are now visited by millions who savor the spirit of the life of early European settlers on the East Coast.

The work done by the historic archaeologists has been denigrated by prehistorians. Guided by various documents, including maps and plans, the archaeologist on a historic site has been seen as merely the handmaiden of history. Using archaeological techniques to confirm or challenge existing records, to discover phenomena not preserved in the record, and to recover artifacts of the time has been perceived as the historical archaeolo-

334 CULTURAL RESOURCE MANAGEMENT AND HISTORICAL ARCHAEOLOGY

gist's only role. Few invoked the limited archaeological theory currently available, and an overall research strategy was rarely devised. The problems in historical archaeology are usually set by the significance of the site and the factors leading to its excavation long before the archaeologist is involved. Archaeology has, therefore, been seen as a series of techniques that supplement the historian's effort to recreate the lifeway of some specific time or stage in the past. Despite that generally held view, some archaeologists insist that historical archaeology can and should contribute to archaeological theory. South (1977) is one who claims that the perception of lawlike regularities in human behavior can result from routine historical projects. He offers his own work in the Southeast as an example. Deetz (1978) sees the value of some historical archaeology as shedding light on the manner in which aboriginal populations responded to European contact and control, that is, the acculturation process.

I regard historical archaeology as a perfectly proper and normal use of archaeological techniques in that the long-range goal, that is, the reconstruction of a past lifeway, is no different from the prehistorian's goal. And historical archaeologists often do a better job because the European artifacts can be closely bracketed in time, their place of manufacture is often known, and even the person or firm making the objects is sometimes a matter of record. Such things as clay pipes, metal buttons, ceramics, bottles of all kinds, ornaments (beads), and tools—knives, or shears, and the like—all provide the precise chronological controls prehistoric archaeologists rarely have.

The best way to appreciate the work of the historical specialists is to review a sample of the projects. Many projects are sponsored by the United States National Park Service, because it is the custodian of many national historical sites and famous battlefields. One such is the extensive study of Jamestown reported by Cotter (1958). Excavations went on for sev-

eral years. Over 130 "structures," a term that includes churches, houses, walkways, an ice house, a brick causeway or bridge, brick and pottery kilns, glass furnaces, and blacksmiths' or armorers' forges, were discovered under the surface and fully exposed. Artifacts ranged from horseshoes to broadswords, wine bottles, and clay pipes, exactly as the history of the town would predict.

The specimens were readily datable, allowing the excavators to establish the time of the earliest settlement at 1607 A.D., a settlement long ago lost as the James River continuously cut away its banks. Excavators charted the slow expansion of the town after bricks were locally made and used in construction as early as 1640 A.D. The abandonment of the location as the seat of government of Virginia Colony when Williamsburg was founded to be the capital could be detected in the record. Except for bricks and stoneware pottery, all tools and utensils, such as hardware, nails, tobacco pipes, decorated tiles, china, and weapons were imported from Europe. A local attempt at making glass failed twice, although the local pottery was of good quality.

The archaeologists found evidence—in the quantity and range of tools—of the period 1640 to 1660 when Jamestown was the center of the beginning of the Virginia tobacco industry. The tools common during that period were those used by carpenters and coopers for making casks for tobacco. When the growers moved out to larger tracts and established the scattered plantation pattern, such tools were no longer used in Jamestown but were used on the plantations. Altogether the archaeological program collected data fully confirming, and in many ways correcting, the recorded history of the ill-starred town. Even the well-filled cemeteries spoke eloquently of hard times, disease, and starvation.

The founding of the "Cittie of Ralegh" on Roanoke Island in 1585 was even earlier than Jamestown. The first colonists returned to England discouraged. A second try at establishing a town was made in 1587. Here the vanished Virginia Dare was born. The colonists were left on their own, and the colony had disappeared when a ship returned to the site of the settlement. No clue to the fate of the second colony has ever been discovered. The problem set for Harrington (1962) was to discover the outlines of the original earth and wood fort as a guide to restoration, and to locate where the houses of the settlement had stood. He was successful in the first objective but found no trace of habitation except a charcoal-making pit. Interestingly, evidence of earlier aboriginal settlement was found at both Jamestown and Fort Roanoke.

Far more appealing to students of recent American history are Caywood's excavations at Fort Vancouver (1955). The fort was established by the Hudson Bay Company in 1824 as a trading post and supply depot. A better location led to the erection of a new fort in 1828. It was closed in 1860 after serving as a fur trade center and eventually as the hub of business, agricultural, and social activities for the entire Northwest during the expansion years.

By 1947, when excavation began, the fort had entirely disappeared under later construction, including an airport runway. Caywood's task was to locate the fort, outline its extent, and locate and identify the many structural features known to have been inside it. Evidently he found all the buildings except a church and a carpenter shop. Those found included storehouses; an office; several shops, such as the blacksmith and harness-making shops; pit latrines; wells; and root cellars. Artifacts of the fur trade were common from the beginning; later came the tools of all the artisans required for a self-sufficient establishment engaged in fishing, lumbering, farming, dairying, and overseas shipping.

The site was a treasure trove of frontier artifacts; abandoned wells as well as latrine pits were standard places to discard broken or unwanted objects and provided many material objects. There were over 95,000 pieces of iron scrap, for example. From standard iron

shapes (bars, rods, and plates) shipped from England the fort's smiths made tools, traps, cutlery, ploughs, nails, and so on. The study provided fascinating and intimate views of the fort's distinguished history, adding to the already rich historical data available.

Yet another historical project is that reported in Deetz's (1978) summary of the excavation of La Purisima Mission in Lompoc, California. Although the history of the excavation goes back fifty years, our interest is in the interpretation Deetz made of the discrepancy between the artifacts found in the women's barracks and the men's dormitory. The tools used by women in domestic tasks were of the kind and quantities that might be found in any aboriginal village. From the male quarters, however, Deetz recovered only a few male activity tools and little else. He suggests that the females were doing the same work they had always pursued, but the men were (probably traumatically) learning completely new roles required to operate the mission, including herding, farming, perhaps wine culture, and many unfamiliar crafts with unfamiliar tools. Thus, through the mere distribution of artifacts, Deetz adds to our understanding of one of the processes of acculturation employed by the priestly emissaries of Spain. Overall the study documents the advantages of combining ethnohistory, documents, and archaeological research not only in support of preservation and interpretive goals but also in deriving anthropological conclusions.

Returning to South (1977), in a summary of his reporting of data from the Carolinas, he criticizes historical archaeologists for reconstructing lifeways but ignoring culture process. His work reveals the importance of patterning to interpretation. By *patterning* South means the repetitive occurrence of artifacts or behaviors over a broad geographical area. He says cultural regularities can be deduced from patterns. In fact, he says that the archaeologist's "first responsibility is pattern recognition." Quantification—the actual count of objects—is prerequisite to discernment of patterns.

In dealing with patterning South uses archaeological data from the investigation of the site of Brunswick Town, North Carolina. There he discovered and defined the Brunswick Pattern. The pattern is: "In British-American sites of the eighteenth century a concentrated refuse deposit will be found at the points of entrance and exit in dwellings, shops, and military fortifications." As Murray (1980) noted, sedentary folk tend to collect debris and deposit it at some customary spot: In this case the occupants threw their trash out either the front or back door. This is secondary deposit behavior. The pattern has proved accurate and has through prediction benefitted research at other sites of the same historical era.

On a greater level of detail South then identified what he calls a Carolina Artifact Pattern using data from dwellings, shops, and military installations at several locations. The pattern, of course, has to do with distribution and frequency of several classes of common artifacts, such as nails, furniture hardware, glass and ceramic sherds, clay pipes, and other items. The pattern was remarkably uniform, because the immigrants were all products of British culture valuing and using the same objects in the same ways. What this means is that the ratio of kitchen objects, architectural items, clothing and clothing manufacturing pieces, personal items (watch keys, fobs, and mirror fragments), and other classes were remarkably similar to each other in the five sites South investigated.

Of course in certain sites there were extreme contrasts in some items. At Fort Moultrie the amount of firearm-related debris was predictably higher, but the ratios of the other classes were congruent with other sites. South predicted that a fort at Signal Hill, Newfoundland, would conform in its midden ratios to the Carolina pattern, and this proved to be true.

Perhaps not in the mainstream of American archaeology but of interest to many is the perennial question of Viking (or Norse) discovery of America some centuries before Columbus reached the Caribbean in 1492. There have been dozens of claims of Viking buildings and other structures (such as Benedict Arnold's tower in Massachusetts) having been positively identified. Many stones with spurious Runic inscriptions have also been "discovered." The interest stems from the ancient Norse sagas, which make it clear that Viking explorers did reach America. Where they landed is not clear, but most scholars think the saga references were to the New England coast.

Until recently, the objects and rune stones of New England have proved dubious or false. Now, however, thanks to archaeological work in the 1960s (reported in 1977), we can speak confidently of a short-lived Norse village on the north Newfoundland coast near L'anse aux Meadows (Meadow Bay). A small bay to the west, called Epaves Bay, catches much flotsam, including driftwood from Labrador and Belle Isle. The settlement there contained nine houses, the first three evidently having been built at the same time. There were also remains of four boathouses, a charcoal oven, many cooking pits, and a smithy. All the structures had sod walls and sod roofs supported by (drift?) wood frames. Artifacts were scanty, the thinness of the few middens led to the conclusion that occupancy was very short. Bog iron was smelted somewhere nearby because there was much slag scrap in the smithy as well as a stone anvil, much ash, and charcoal. The lack of artifacts and the short occupancy, combined with the ephemeral traces of the sod walls, made this site difficult to dig and even harder to interpret. But by comparing the Epaves Bay finds with early Norse settlements in Norway, Iceland, and Greenland, the Norse origin for the settlement was well established. The artifacts included fully oxidized iron nails, a ring-headed pin, a rivet, a fragment of bronze, and many fragments of iron and iron ore. Food-bone scrap was rare, but seal and whalebone were common, with one piece of bone identified as pig or sheep.

The date of the site may be as late as 1000 A.D., that being the "preferred" date indicated by the archaeology. But the radiocarbon dates, based on charcoal, are no doubt skewed by the heavy use of old driftwood by the first settlers. They yielded a combined average age of 920 A.D., a date regarded as too early by the excavator. Epaves Bay could be the actual spot of Leif Ericson's famous landfall and brief sojourn as described in the Vinland Sagas. At least the fact of a brief, early visit by Norsemen, and the exact location of one settlement, is archaeologically established.

More space than expected has been devoted to this section, and some other studies such as one made at St. Augustine, Florida, where a complex sequence of occupation was sorted out, have not been summarized. The extra emphasis results from a conviction that the work of this group is becoming more important in the heritage movement, most of them are enriching our appreciation and awareness of the formative years of American history, and there is good evidence that higher theoretical and interpretive goals have been set in recent years. It is through the emphasis on method and theory that historical archaeology can contribute to general archaeology and erase the stigma of the appellation "mere technologists." I hasten to repeat my view that their contributions strike me as fully justifiable as they correct, modify, and amplify the stereotypes of history and the contents of historic places.

Ending this book with a survey of CRM (and some aspects of historical archaeology) was done deliberately. The shift from the evolution of Native American cultures to the evolution of a profession is calculated to help the beginning student recognize that archaeology is practiced not in seclusion but in a world of change. So in the evolving archaeological profession, thanks in part to CRM, students will perhaps encounter slightly different values for scholarship and science than those held by their professors. Some changes in those values are already evident. I see the changes as neither good nor bad; one either accepts or rejects them. The change continues.

There are of course many other changes than those associated with CRM. Perhaps the most exciting is the preference today's students have for more-difficult and finer-focused studies of the mechanisms and causes of human behavior. Such things as edgewear on flint tools or pottery function as it affects the paste, temper, form, and fabrication yield new and astonishingly informative data. These and many other research avenues testify to a strong and viable discipline.

With this final sentence I welcome those students who become professional archaeologists to a dynamic and vital field of study—understanding human behavior through archaeological materials—one that is intellectually stimulating and therefore endlessly rewarding.

Chapter 7
Bibliography

Caywood, Lewis R.

1955   *Final Report Fort Vancouver Excavations.* U.S. Department of the Interior, National Park Service, Region Four. San Francisco.

Cotter, John L.

1958   *Archaeological Excavations at Jamestown, Virginia.* U.S. Department of the Interior, National Park Service, Archaeological Research Series No. 4. Washington, DC.

Deetz, James F.

1978   Archaeological Investigations at La Purisima Mission. In *Historical Archaeology: a guide to substantive and theoretical contributions,* edited by Robert L. Schuyler, pp. 160–190. Baywood. Farmingdale, NJ.

Elston, Robert G.

1979   The Archaeology of U.S. 395 Right-of-Way Corridor Between Stead, Nevada, and Hallelujah Junction, California. (Report submitted to the California Department of Transportation and the Nevada Department of Transportation; on file, Special Collections, Getchell Library, University of Nevada, Reno.)

Fowler, Don D.

1982   Cultural Resources Management. In *Advances in Archaeological Method and Theory,* Vol. 5, edited by Michael B. Schiffer, pp. 1–50. Academic Press. New York.

Harrington, Jean C.

1962   *Search for the Cittie of Ralegh: archaeological excavations at Fort Raleigh National Historic Site, North Carolina.* U.S. Department of the Interior, National Park Service, Archaeological Research Series, No. 6, National Park Service, pp. 1–63. Washington, D.C.

Ingstad, Anne Stine

1977   *The Discovery of a Norse Settlement in America: excavations at L'anse anx Meadows, Newfoundland 1961–68.* Universitetsforlaget, Irvington-on-Hudson, New York. Distributed by Columbia University Press. New York.

Knudsen, Ruthann

1986   Contemporary Cultural Resource Management. In *American Archaeology Past and Future: a celebration of the Society for American Archaeology, 1935–1985,* edited by David Meltzer, Don D. Fowler, and Jeremy A. Sabloff, pp. 395–413. Published for the SAA by the Smithsonian Institution Press. Washington, DC.

Schiffer, Michael B., and John H. House

1975   *The Cache River Archaeological Project.* Arkansas Archaeological Survey, Research Series, No. 8. Fayette.

Schuyler, Robert L. (editor)

1978   *Historical Archaeology: a guide to substantive and theoretical contributions.* Baywood. Farmingdale, NJ.

South, Stanley

1977   *Method and Theory in Historical Archaeology.* Academic Press. New York.

Glossary

Adobe Mud used as mortar in aboriginal masonry. More recently, an unfired, sun-dried brick made from clay mixed with vegetal fibers and used in the Southwest and Mexico as a building material.

Adze A stone tool with a thinned, convex cutting edge that is hafted at right angles to a handle (compare **Ax**). Used mainly for woodworking, rarely as a weapon.

Alluvium Sand, gravel, or soil deposited by running water as it loses velocity on floodplains of streams or in valley floors.

Alveolar Prognathism Projection of the facial bones in the region of the teeth.

Antler Flaker An implement made from an antler tip or tine and used in **pressure flaking** stone.

Arrow Wrench A device for straightening arrow shafts. Made of stone, bone, ivory, or antler, it was fashioned either with a small, pierced hole or with a circular hook through which the shaft could be pulled.

Artifact Any object or location shaped or modified for human use.

Asphaltum A black-to-brown mineral pitch used as an adhesive for hafting purposes and for applying decorations on objects.

Atlatl A short board or stick, 20 to 24 inches long, fitted with a handle on one end and a groove or peg at the other, used in throwing a dart or lance. Widely used in the New World.

Awl Sharply pointed tool of bone, antler, metal, or wood used in sewing. It was used to make holes for thread, string, or sinew, as well as natural or spun fiber, in making garments of leather or fiber. The awl was also extensively used in making coiled basketry, the coils being sewn to each other with flexible fibers.

Ax A stone implement with a sharp cutting edge to be used for chopping or crushing chores. It is usually grooved for hafting to a handle; "fully grooved" means the groove encircles the ax and "three-quarters-grooved" means the groove runs around three sides. An ax is hafted with the cutting edge in line with the handle (compare **Adze**). An ungrooved ax is often called a **celt;** an ax that was to be held in the hand is often called a fist or hand ax.

Baleen The horny substance found in the mouths of certain whales (especially the right whale) that serves as a strainer to collect and retain food. It grows from the whale's upper jaw in fringelike plates from 2 to 12 feet long and is used as a raw material for utilitarian and ornamental objects.

Bannerstone A polished stone artifact (usually perforated) having a variety of forms (winged, boat-, bird-, or animal-shaped, etc.), probably used as an atlatl weight but possibly having a ceremonial function as well.

Basalt A form of igneous rock that is compact and dark gray to black. Used for many **ground stone** implements.

Beamer A long bone roughened lengthwise by cutting or scoring. Used for cleaning and softening the flesh side of animal hides.

Beringia The land bridge that existed between Siberia and Alaska during the Ice Age.

Biotite A type of **mica,** generally black or dark green, used primarily for ornaments or for decorative purposes.

Bladder Dart A dart, used in hunting seals, with a bladder float attached to serve as a drag and a marker buoy.

Blade A long, narrow **flake** with parallel sides, sometimes called a lamellar flake. Blades are usually struck from a prepared **core.** Small specimens are called **microblades.**

Blank An unfinished stone tool partially worked to the shape and size of the intended implement. Blanks may have been stockpiled for later completion.

Bodkin A long pin or awl made of bone or copper used for making holes in fabric. Also, a blunted needle with a large eye.

Bolas A hunting weapon consisting of two or more grooved stone balls tied on separate thongs to a longer line. It was thrown at the legs of animals and at birds in flight, entangling them and preventing their escape.

Bone Tube A short section of hollow bone believed to have been used by **shamans** in curing ceremonies to suck out the causes of illness or pain.

Boreal The northern and mountainous areas of North America, Central America, and Greenland where the mean temperature of the hottest season does not exceed 21.6°C (64.4°F) and characterized by coniferous forests.

Bow Drill A drilling device operated by twisting the string of a bow around the drill stick and moving the bow back and forth rapidly. Used in perforating bone, stone, ivory, and so on and in making fire.

B.P. Before present; same meaning as *years ago*.

Browband An Eskimo ornament to be worn across the forehead.

Bull-boat A tub-shaped boat made from a whole buffalo skin stretched tightly over a light willow frame. Used by the Plains Indians.

Burial, Bundle Reburial of defleshed and disarticulated bones tied or wrapped together in a bundle.

Burial, Extended   A form of burial in which the body rests in a supine or prone position with legs extended and arms at the side.

Burial, Flexed   A form of burial in which the arms and/or legs are bent up against the body; fetal position.

Burin   A **flake** or **blade** stone tool with a small, angled chisel edge or a sharp, beaked point. Used for sculpturing and engraving purposes.

Calcite   Calcium carbonate that has crystallized. Used (crushed) as temper for ceramics.

Calcium Carbonate   The substance of limestone. Often found in caves, where it can seal cultural deposits and protect them from disturbances.

Caliche   A crust of **calcium carbonate** that forms within or on top of soils in arid and semiarid regions.

Catlinite   A red, naturally hardened clay found in the Upper Missouri region and used for making tobacco pipes. Also called pipestone.

Celt   An ungrooved **ax** used mainly for woodworking. It is often shaped somewhat like a **chisel** but has a broader blade.

Chalcedony   A variety of quartz with a waxlike luster used for **chipped stone** implements.

Charmstone   Any stone object believed by the owner or wearer to bring good fortune, ward off danger, and so on.

Charnel House   A structure for receiving the dead. A structure where the dead are prepared for burial.

Check-stamping   A design of small, impressed squares used in decorating pottery vessels and produced by a paddling or stamping technique.

Chert   An impure **flint,** usually brown or gray-black, used for **chipped stone** implements.

Chipped Stone   Stone artifacts manufactured by **percussion** or **pressure flaking** techniques. Chipped stone implements are predominantly used as projectiles and as cutting or skinning tools.

Chisel   A **celt**like implement with a narrow blade chipped to a thin edge. Used mainly for woodworking.

Chopper   An **ax**like implement that is chipped/sharpened only on one edge.

Coiling   Both a pottery and a basketry manufacturing technique. In pottery long rolls of clay are added one on top of another in a circular fashion starting at the bottom of the pot and continuing to the desired height. The inner and outer surfaces are then smoothed. In basketry a spirally coiled foundation of warp strands is sewn together in horizontal rows, the weft strands looping over the warp strands in an overcast stitch.

Columbia Plateau   The area between the Cascade and Rocky Mountains in the western United States, comprising southern and western Idaho and eastern Oregon and Washington and containing the drainage systems of the Snake and Columbia rivers.

Cooking Ball   See **Stone Boiling.**

Core   A stone from which flakes have been removed to make implements. A prepared core is one that has been purposefully worked so that the shape of **flakes** or **blades** can be more effectively controlled.

Corrugated   A type of coiled pottery found in the Southwest in which the outer surface, instead of being smoothed, is finished by letting the edges of the clay coils overlap to create a scalloped effect. This type of pottery was used primarily as utility ware.

Coursed   An architectural technique in which stones or bricks are arranged in continuous horizontal layers.

Cupstone   See **Nutstone.**

Debitage   Waste flakes, scraps, and irregular pieces of stone created during the chipping of stone implements.

Deflector   A floor structure of uncertain function found in early southwestern pit houses and (later) kivas. It was always constructed between the firepit and the tunnel or ventilator shaft and probably served as a draft control for the fire.

Dibble Agriculture   A primitive form of planting crops by using a pointed stick (dibble) to make holes in the ground into which seeds are dropped.

Dolichocephaly   Long- or narrow-headedness. Since most early human skulls are dolichocephalic, it was once believed to be an earlier form than the **brachycephalic** or the **mesocephalic.**

Drill   The stone bit attached to the end of a drill stick, which is rotated rapidly, as in the **bow drill,** to perforate dense materials. This term also refers to any device used for drilling purposes or for making fire, in which case a drill stick without a bit is used (see **Fire Drill**).

Ear Spool   A spool-shaped ornament to be worn in the earlobe.

Fire Drill   A device for making fire, consisting of a drill stick which is twirled rapidly in a small pit in a piece of wood (the **hearth**). The friction creates heated sawdust which eventually begins to glow and will ignite a piece of tinder of shredded dry grass or other vegetal fibers.

Flake   The thin, flattened piece removed from a stone by **pressure-** or **percussion-flaking** techniques. Flake tools are usually **retouched.**

Flesher   A blunted stone or bone tool used to scrape off flesh and fat from the inner surface of a hide.

Flint   A catchall word applied to a wide variety of tough, glassy stones that are readily

shaped by chipping (both by **percussion** and **pressure**) into tools used for cutting and drilling.

Galena   A lead ore, bluish-gray with a metallic luster. Crystals and lumps were used for ornaments and for trading purposes.

Gaming Piece   An artifact believed to have been used in any aboriginal game of chance and skill.

Genotype   The genetic composition shared by a group of individuals (compare with **Phenotype**).

Glottochronology   The chronologic study of languages by comparing their basic vocabularies in order to discover relationships and common origins between languages.

Gorge   A small, double-pointed implement that is attached to a line and used to catch small animals and fish. It is usually baited with meat or fat; when taken, it imbeds itself crosswise in the throat or stomach of the game.

Gorget   An ornament usually worn over the chest and perforated for attaching to clothing or suspending on a cord.

Gouge   A **chisel** with a scoop-shaped cutting edge to be used in woodworking, for removing bone marrow, and so on.

Graver   A small trimming or cutting tool with a sharp point or edge used for woodworking.

Great Basin   The area of internal drainage in the western United States comprising Nevada, eastern California, southeastern Oregon, southern Idaho, and western Utah.

Great Plains   Generally the area lying east of the Rocky Mountains and west of the Mississippi-Missouri Valley, usually characterized as a treeless, semiarid, flat grassland.

Ground Stone   Stone artifacts manufactured by pecking and abrading techniques. Usually included in this category are grinding and pounding implements such as the **mano, me-**

tate, **mortar,** and **pestle,** as well as pipes and statuary pieces.

Hammerstone   A rounded stone used as a hammer, sometimes grooved (see **Ax**) for hafting to a handle. Usually ungrooved, however, it has a variety of forms ranging from a crudely shaped sphere to a finely ground ovoid with a use-battered end.

Handstone   See **Mano.**

Hearth   See **Fire Drill.**

Hematite   See **Ocher.**

High Plains   The outwash belt along the eastern base of the Rocky Mountains, creating broad, flat uplands that extend from the southern boundary of South Dakota almost to the Rio Grande.

Ice Creeper   A roughened or spiked piece of ivory or bone attached to the bottom of the Eskimo's footgear to facilitate movement while hunting on the ice. A crampon.

Incising   A method of decorating pottery vessels by cutting the design in the wet clay surface with a sharp implement.

In Situ   A Latin phrase meaning "in place." Archaeologically, it refers to an **artifact** or object found in its original, undisturbed position. Items found *in situ* provide an opportunity for establishing firm stratigraphic or other associations for dating purposes.

Jacal   See **Wattle and Daub.**

Jasper   An opaque, uncrystalline variety of quartz, found in many bright colors, used for ornaments and **chipped stone** implements.

Jet   A velvet-black stone (a hydrocarbon) that takes a high polish. Used for decorative purposes and for jewelry.

Kayak   The arctic canoe, which has an enclosed cockpit and is covered and decked, usually with sealskin (hair removed).

Killed   A term used to describe the ceremonial (?) mutilation or breakage of an object being placed with a body at time of burial.

Labret   An ornamental plug to be worn in the lower lip.

Lacustrine   Of or pertaining to a lake or an inland sea (for example, the deposits, the flora, and the fauna).

Lamellar   See **Blade.**

Lanceolate   Leaf-shaped, being tapered at one or both ends. In archaeological usage the term usually refers to long, slender chipped stone points or knives pointed at one or both ends.

Lapstone   See **Milling Stone.**

Leister   A fish spear with at least three barbed prongs.

Llano Estacado (Staked Plains)   A vast plateau in western Texas and eastern New Mexico of approximately 20,000 square miles and bounded on three sides by nearly vertical escarpments from 500 to 1000 feet high. The location of several early sites, including Blackwater Draw, Plainview, and Scharbauer (Midland).

Loess   An unstratified deposit of windblown sand or clay, yellow or buff, which occurs on the flanks of glacial maxima.

Lost Wax   A casting process in which a clay model is coated with wax and then covered with clay. When the mold is heated, the wax melts, leaving a hollow space between the core and the outer mold. The casting material is poured into the space and after it has hardened, the clay mold is removed.

Mace   A club with side projections at one end. Could have been used as an offensive weapon, but may have had only ceremonial use.

Mano   The upper stone used on a **metate** to grind corn and other grains. Handstone is another term used for the upper millstone.

Maul A stone implement with blunted or rounded edges to be used as a hammer for heavy work such as driving wedges or breaking stone or for lighter work such as pounding seeds or pecking and flaking operations. It may be grooved (see **Ax**) for hafting to a handle.

Mesocephalic Referring to a head of medium breadth (compare **Dolichocephalic**).

Metate The lower **milling stone,** usually made of semiporous stone, used for grinding grains, nuts, and occasionally pigments. The upper part of the mill is the **mano.**

Mica Any of a group of crystalline silicates characterized by perfect cleavage so that they separate into paper-thin sheets. Used primarily for ornaments or for decorative purposes.

Microblade See **Blade.**

Midden The accumulation of refuse near a habitation site or dwelling.

Milling Stone A general term for all types of stones used as the lower part of a grinding mill. It may be flat, or slightly or deeply hollowed out.

Mortar A heavy, deeply basined stone or wooden bowl used with a **pestle** to pulverize various materials and foodstuffs.

Mouthpiece, Seal Float A perforated wooden or ivory plug to be lashed into small openings cut in the skin of a harpooned seal. Air was blown through the perforation to inflate small areas between the blubber and muscles. The mouthpiece was then stoppered, and the captured air kept the seal bouyant while being towed. (See also **Wound Plug.**)

Muller See **Pestle.**

Negative Painting A method of painting designs on pottery by covering the background elements of the design with wax and then painting the rest of the design with the de-sired colors. During the firing process, the wax melts, leaving the lighter color of the clay outlining the design.

Nutstone A flat slab or boulder with small depressions to hold nuts for cracking.

Obsidian Volcanic glass, which, because it can be worked to an extremely sharp edge and point, is highly prized for **chipped stone** implements. Because of its reflective qualities when in thin flat sections, also used for mirrors in Mesoamerica.

Ocher An iron oxide ranging in color from yellow to brown, used as a pigment. Red ocher (hematite) is very often used for ceremonial purposes.

Olivella A genus of marine univalves, found on the North American Pacific Coast and in the Gulf of Mexico, whose shell was widely used as money and for making necklaces.

Olla A Spanish term used in the Southwest for the widemouthed water jar.

Palynologist One who studies past vegetation and climates through microscopic analyses of pollen recovered from soils or sediments.

Percussion Flaking The technique of shaping stone or heavy bone, using sharp hard strokes with another stone or cylinder of wood or bone. If a finer-finished tool was desired, the surface and edges were further worked by **pressure flaking.**

Permafrost Permanently frozen subsoil, found in the **tundra** areas of the arctic region.

Pestle A club-shaped or conical implement used to pulverize various materials in a **mortar.** Also called a muller.

Phenotype A physical or outward expression of the interaction of the **genotype** with the environment. For example, variation in skin pigmentation.

Pièces d'esquille Somewhat vague term that applies to the wedge-shaped flakes that result when a cobble resting on a flat stone (called the anvil) is forcibly struck from above by another cobble (**hammerstone**). What are called "bipolar" flakes are then removed at the point of impact of the hammerstone and at the point of contact with the anvil. The wedge-shaped flakes are said to have been used for splitting wood or bone.

Pipestone   See **Catlinite.**

Plane   A stone artifact with a flat base, a humped back, and a sharp edge, which may have been used for woodworking but is probably a **core** from which thin flakes have been struck.

Playa   In an arid region a shallow basin or dry lake bed in which water from rain or run-off collects and stays until it evaporates.

Plummet Stone   A top-shaped weight used in various ways: In spinning as a whorl weight, in fishing as a net sinker, in construction as a plumb bob, and so forth.

Pluvial   Of or pertaining to rain. Also refers to the wetter periods during a major, extended dry period.

Pressure Flaking   The technique of removing **flakes** from a stone by pressing a blunt-pointed implement of antler or bone against the edge being worked. This method permits greater control over the size and direction of the flakes removed than does **percussion flaking.**

Provenience   The location of an **artifact** or object described in terms of map grids, stratified levels, and/or depth from ground surface. It provides for control of artifacts and associations once the items have been removed from the context of the site.

Pulper   A conical, blunt-ended stone implement whose use has not been definitely determined. It could be a reject or a worn-out tool. (See also **Plane.**)

Quartzite   A compact, metamorphic granular rock composed of quartz, used for **chipped stone** implements.

Quid   A piece of vegetal matter (yucca, tule, corn husk, etc.) that was chewed to extract the juice and nutriments and then spat out. Chewing was probably also a technique for separating and softening vegetal fiber prior to spinning or weaving.

Retouch   Secondary flaking of a stone implement to remove surface irregularities and to refine or modify the cutting edge; usually done by **pressure flaking.**

Rocker Stamping   A design of connecting zigzag lines used in decorating pottery vessels and produced by rocking a small disc attached to a handle back and forth on the wet clay surface.

Rubbing Stone   A small, smoothed stone, often found stained with red pigment, perhaps used for smoothing pottery.

Scraper   A stone implement used to remove fat from the underside of a skin, to smooth wood, to scrape leather, and so on. Different types are described in terms of the shape and/or position of the cutting edge: side scraper, end scraper, snubnosed scraper, thumbnail scraper, scoop scraper, and so on.

Seal Killer   A round stone, often attached to a leather thong or encased in a rawhide net, used to club seals to death once they were harpooned.

Seal Scratcher   A long, pronged implement used to decoy seals at their breathing holes in the ice. Often, seal claws were attached to the prongs to better imitate the sound that might be made by another seal.

Setline   A long, heavy fishing line to which a series of short lines with baited hooks are attached at intervals.

Shaft Wrench   See **Arrow Wrench.**

Shaman   A medicine man or any individual who used his or her supernatural powers to cure ailments or interpret strange phenomena. These powers were also used to inflict harm or cause disaster.

Sherd   A broken piece of pottery vessel, the most durable of archaeologic specimens other than stone.

Sipapu   The Pueblo Indian name for a small, circular pit in the floors of the early pit houses and the later kivas. The tribesmen believed that their original ancestors came up into the world through the sipapu.

Slate   A dense, fine-grained rock used for sculptured pieces, as well as for sharply edged tools.

Slip   A thin, surface coat of very fine, un-tempered clay in liquid form, which is applied to the surface of pottery prior to firing.

Soapstone   See **Steatite**.

Spokeshave   A **scraper** with a rounded notch in the edge used for such chores as scraping arrow shafts.

Spud   A shovel-shaped stone implement probably used for digging purposes but which eventually may have had only ceremonial use.

Steatite   A variety of talc, grayish-green or brown, used for pots and other items. Also called soapstone.

Stone Boiling   A method of cooking by dropping hot stones or clay balls into a basket or container filled with liquid or the substance to be cooked.

Taiga   The swampy, coniferous forest area that begins south of the **tundra**.

Throwing Board   Another term for the **atlatl** or spear thrower.

Tinkler   A small, conical or cylindrical or-nament probably worn in clusters as a fringe on a garment or garter.

Trailing   A variant technique of **incising** a design on pottery vessels by making broad, U-shaped lines in the wet clay surface.

Trait   A diagnostic **artifact** or other charac-teristic element of a culture.

Tule   A bulrush or reed found in the South-west, California, and Mexico. Used for mak-ing such things as mats, sandals, and decoys. It was also chewed (see **Quid**).

Tumpline   A cord or strap placed across the forehead or the chest to support burdens car-ried on the back.

Tundra   The treeless plain within the Arctic Circle that is marshy in summer and frozen in winter. The subsoil is permanently frozen, but the surface soil supports mosses and lichens.

Turquoise   A blue to greenish-gray, copper and aluminum phosphate stone highly val-ued for jewelry and other decorative purposes in the Southwest.

Twilling   A weaving technique in which the weft strands are taken over one or two warp strands and then under two or more. Each row is subsequently offset one warp strand, and the visual effect achieved is that of a series of steps or stairs.

Twining   A weaving technique using par-allel warp strands between which two weft strands are threaded in and out, one weft going over the warp as the other is going un-der. The wefts are twisted together in half turns between each warp, making a strong, smooth weave.

Twist Drill   A chipped stone drill bit with a beveled, pointed end similar to the modern metal-cutting drill.

Ulu   The Eskimo rocker knife, which has a semicircular blade usually fitted into a slotted wooden handle.

Umiak   A flat-bottomed, open, arctic boat that has a wooden frame covered with a wal-rus hide. It is not as maneuverable as the **kayak**.

Varve   A regular, annual layer of silt and clay formed in lakes fed by melting glacier water. Since each varve in the laminated bed is the result of one summer's melting and represents one year, the number of years required for deposition can be determined by counting the varves.

Wattle and Daub   A construction technique in which a frame of poles and interwoven twigs is plastered with mud. Also called jacal.

Wicker   A type of weaving in which the flexible, slender weft strands are passed over and under the more rigid and thicker warp strands. The most elementary of the weaving techniques.

Winnowing Basket   A shallow, tray-shaped basket in which dry foodstuffs were tossed so the wind could carry away the chaff or unwanted portion. It was also used to separate fine and coarse particles of clay.

Wooden Cylinder   A straight, peeled stick with the ends cut off at right angles and carefully smoothed. Has been variously described as a noseplug, gaming stick, or toggle.

Wound Plug   A tapered plug to be inserted in the wound of a harpooned seal to stop the flow of blood.

Yucca   A member of the lily family, with long, sharply pointed, fibrous leaves, found in arid and semiarid regions. The fleshy leaves were chewed (see **Quid**); the fibers were used for various purposes; and the sap from the roots, which sudses when mixed with water, was used for soap and shampoo.

Illustration Credits: J. V. Wright for the photograph of Iroquois pipes, National Museums of Canada, Negative K 71-3, from Ontario Prehistory: an eleven-thousand-year archaeological outline, by J. V. Wright, Archaeological Survey of Canada, National Museum of Man, Ottawa (Figure 5.21). Dr. Wright also offered advice and other help.

Stephen Williams for the artist's reconstruction of the Lake George site (Mississippi) at about 1200 A.D. (Figure 5.31), courtesy of the Lower Mississippi Survey of the Peabody Museum, Harvard University, Cambridge.

William Finlayson for the photograph of a reconstructed Iroquois longhouse at the Lawson site in London, Ontario (Figure 5.18), for Ivan Kocsis' reconstruction of the Draper Village site (Toronto International Airport) at approximately 1450 A.D. (Figure 5.19) and a plan of longhouse 27 at the Draper site (Figure 5.20), all by courtesy of the Museum of Indian Archaeology, London, Ontario.

George Quimby, Patrick Kirch, and Victoria Wyatt for photographs of a Tlingit bentwood box (from the Museum collections, photograph 5929-A, by William Eng) (Figure 4.41) and a Tlingit plank and pole house (photo from Viola Garfield collection, negative L-3652) (Figure 4.42), all by courtesy of the Thomas Burke Memorial Washington State Museum, Seattle.

Jefferson Chapman for the photograph of Early Archaic projectile points from Tennessee (Figure 4.1) and for permission to use the Hixon shell gorget on the cover, by courtesy of Frank H. McClung Museum, University of Tennessee, Knoxville.

Dirk Bakker and Kay Young for providing photographs (by Dirk Bakker) of the seated feline figure from Key Marco, Florida (Figure 5.35), the engraved beaker from Moundville, Alabama (Figure 5.36), and the Hixon shell gorget (cover), courtesy of the Detroit Institute of Arts.

Bruce Smith: For the photograph of copper plate from Union County, Illinois (Figure 5.37), and permission to use the photo (see above) of a feline figure from Key Marco (Figure 5.35) in the Smithsonian Institution Collection (by courtesy of the Smithsonian Institution, Washington, DC).

Paula Cardwell for permission to use Figures 2, 3, and 4 from *The Handbook of North American Indians, Great Basin,* Volume 11 (Figures 4.14, 4.15). Courtesy of the Smithsonian Institution, Washington, DC.

Vincas P. Steponaitis for permission to use his personal photograph of the Moundville group (Figure 5.30) taken in January 1979.

Douglas E. Jones for permission to use the photograph (see above) of the engraved beaker from the Moundville site (Figure 5.36), by courtesy of the Alabama State Museum of Natural History.

Richard Dougherty and Ruth Kirk for the photograph of the carved dorsal fin of a killer whale from the Ozette Village site (Figure 4.35).

Duncan Metcalfe for photographs of clay figurines, wicker figurines, painted and etched stones, and a fawn's head medicine bundle (Figures 4.24, 4.25), by courtesy of the University of Utah Archaeological Center.

George Frison for photographs of Clovis, Eden, Scottsbluff, and Colby points (Figures 3.4, 3.7, 3.8, 3.14, 3.23), by courtesy of the Department of Anthropology, University of Wyoming, Laramie.

Jerry Lyons, of W. H. Freeman and Company for permission to use numerous line drawings previously used in *Native North Americans* edited by Jesse D. Jennings, 1983.

INDEX

Note: Page numbers in *italics* indicate illustrations.